Women and Politics in Iran

Veiling, Unveiling, and Reveiling

Why were urban women veiled in the early 1900s, unveiled from 1936 to 1979, and reveiled after the 1979 Revolution? This question forms the basis of Hamideh Sedghi's original and unprecedented contribution to politics and Middle Eastern studies. Using primary materials gathered from field research, interviews, and oral history collections and secondary sources in Persian and English, Sedghi offers new knowledge on women's agency in relation to state power. In this rigorous analysis of gender politics from the last years of the Qajar dynasty to the Pahlavi period and the current Islamic regime, she places contention over women at the center of the political struggle between secular and religious forces and compellingly demonstrates that control over women's identities, sexuality, and labor has been central to the consolidation of state power, both domestically and internationally. In contrast to Orientalist scholars who view Middle Eastern women as victims, and in opposition to Western policy makers who claim that aggressive incursions into the region will help liberate women, Sedghi links politics and culture with economics to present an integrated analysis of the private and public lives of different classes of women and their modes of resistance to state power. For Sedghi, politics matters to gender, and gender matters to politics.

Hamideh Sedghi is a Visiting Scholar at Harvard University's Center for Middle Eastern Studies and a former Visiting Scholar at Columbia University. A professor of political science, her previous teaching venues include Villanova University, University of Richmond, Hobart and William Smith Colleges, and Vassar College. She is the first Iranian female in the United States who wrote on women in Iran from a social science perspective. Author of numerous publications, Sedghi is the recipient of many awards and honors, including the 2005 Christian Bay Award for the Best Paper presented at the American Political Science Association Meeting.

Women and Politics in Iran

Veiling, Unveiling, and Reveiling

HAMIDEH SEDGHI

CAMBRIDGE UNIVERSITY PRESS
Cambridge, New York, Melbourne, Madrid, Cape Town, Singapore, São Paulo, Delhi

Cambridge University Press
32 Avenue of the Americas, New York, NY 10013-2473, USA

www.cambridge.org
Information on this title: www.cambridge.org/9780521835817

First published 2007
Reprinted 2008 (twice)

Printed in the United States of America

A catalog record for this publication is available from the British Library.

Library of Congress Cataloging in Publication Data

Sedghi, Hamideh.
Women and politics in Iran : veiling, unveiling, and reveiling / Hamideh Sedghi.
p. cm.
Includes bibliographical references and index.
ISBN-13: 978-0-521-83581-7 (hardback)
1. Women – Iran – Social conditions. 2. Women – Legal status, laws, etc.
(Islamic law) – Iran. 3. Women's rights – Iran. 4. Feminism – Iran.
5. Sex role – Iran. I. Title.
HQ1735.2.S433 2007
305.0955– dc22 2006020653

ISBN 978-0-521-83581-7 hardback

To the beloved memory of

Baba,

Hossein Sedghi

(1300/1921–1354/1975),

and Maman,

Afsar Shishehchi

(1307/1928–1375/1996)

Contents

Acknowledgments

Over the past two and a half decades when there was hardly material in Persian or English on the subject matter, I began to research and write on women in Iran, which eventually led to the birth of this book. During this time, I have been extremely fortunate to have had the intellectual and emotional support of many friends, colleagues, and relatives in both Iran and the United States. I am deeply grateful for their encouragement, comments, critiques, and constructive suggestions, and their great sense of humor.

I would like to thank Ahmad Ashraf, Amrita Basu, the late Christian Bay, Hester Eisenstein, Eric Foner, Lynn Garafola, Amy Hackett, Mary Hegland, Joan Hoffman, Fatemeh Moghadam, the late Dankwart A. Rustow, Anne Sassoon, Jonathan Scott, Madeleine Tress, and Victor Wallace. I am indebted to them for their intellectual rigor, reading chapters or sections or the entire manuscript at its different stages, and offering probing questions, critiques, and editorial advice. I also appreciate the support and interesting remarks that Richard Bulliet, Mark Kesselman, Robert Lieberman, Robert Y. Shapiro, and Jack Snyder provided while I was a Visiting Scholar at Columbia University's Department of Political Science. As a new Visiting Scholar at Harvard University's Center for Middle Eastern Studies, I am grateful to Roy Mottahedeh, Steven Caton, Susan Kahn, and Sara Roy for their support and valuable interaction.

My Women and Development group in New York – some permanent and others temporary members – the late Phyllis Andors, Lourdes Beneria, Günseli Berik, Nilüfer Çağatay, Nadine Felton, Helen Safa, Gita Sen, Jayne Warner, and Nancy Weigersma, offered tremendous energy and appreciation of gender. Our monthly meetings over a decade provided not only intellectual nourishment on reading about women and development issues, but an opportunity to read, discuss, and critique each other's work, including earlier versions of some of the chapters of this book.

Colleagues and friends in Middle Eastern women's studies, Iranian women's studies, women and gender studies, and Iranian studies contributed important insights on a range of issues related to the book. My gratitude goes to Nancy Breen, Francine D'Amico, Jennifer Leigh Disney, Erika Friedl, Amany Jamal, Jo Freeman, Mehrangiz Kar, the late Parvin Paidar, and Ruth Ross.

I owe a special word of thanks to Irving Leonard Markovitz, who, as a superlative human being, the reader of my dissertation, and a mentor and subsequently a friend and colleague, offered his consistent help and support throughout my academic career. I am also grateful to my editor at Cambridge, Lewis Bateman, who remained patient and positive, and members of the production and editorial staff for their tremendous assistance.

My biggest debt is to my cherished friend, Marion Kaplan. She read the book, cover to cover, and offered enormous intellectual and moral support. She generously made herself available to read and reread my drafts and made valuable comments. Her tactful and continuous reminder, "how is the book coming along?," gave me encouragement to move forward with this long journey and the never-ending process of completing this book. I would like to express to her my heart-felt gratitude.

Thanks also goes to the American Political Science Association's Caucus for New Political Science for offering me the Christian Bay Award for the 2005 Best Paper, which was based on the last two chapters of the book. The Gender and Globalization Summer Institute that Sachuta Mazundar organized at Duke University provided valuable feedback on various arguments.

Over the years, my students and their willingness to explore new territory contributed much to the energy that went into the making of this book. I thank the participants in my Women and Development, Gender and Politics in the Middle East, and other related courses. My hardworking graduate teaching/research assistant, Nilay Saiya, helped me overcome the technical challenges and last-minute details of producing a book. I could always rely on him to meticulously review material, convert it from Nota Bene to Microsoft Word, and help with its nuances. Thanks also to Goran Peic for converting my bibliography, and to Rachel Schaller for technical assistance.

Many Iranians inside the country contributed to the making of this book. For various reasons I cannot mention all their names. Nevertheless, I acknowledge here my greatest appreciation, particularly to Nooshin Ahmadi Khorasani, Shahla Sherkat, and A'zam Taleghani, as well as editorial members of various feminist publications and many other organizations and institutions.

Last but not least, I want to thank my immediate and extended family for their love and sustained support. My sister, Haideh Sedghi, offered continued affection and moral sustenance. She sent me books, manuscripts, and pamphlets from Iran prior to and immediately after the Revolution and kept me updated with her intelligent conversations and news. My brother, Mohammad Ali (Mamal) Sedghi, presented a great gift when he hand copied an entire pamphlet because I could not do so in Iran. My uncle, Abbas Sedghi, introduced me to his colleagues and librarians at the University of Tehran, and his spouse, Fatemeh Erfan, lent her books and shared her experiences as a former Deputy Mayor of Tehran. My late grandmothers and especially my late aunt, Keshvar Shisheh'ie, divulged the stories of their upbringing and lives.

More than anyone else, my late mother, Afsar Shishehchi, continued to remind me of her and her relatives' experiences in a male-dominated society. But the spirit behind this book is that of my father, who from the earliest days encouraged the intellectual commitments of "the dear light of my eyes," as he referred to me. Unfortunately, neither survived to see this book.

Transliteration and References

The transliteration of Persian and Arabic words widely used in Persian generally follows the system suggested by the *International Journal of Middle Eastern Studies*. For reasons of simplicity, I have eliminated diacritical signs with the exception of those standing for Persian glottal stops represented by hamze and 'ein. For these exceptions, as well as for a more precise transliteration of Persian diphthongs, I have consulted L. P. Elwell-Sutton and have relied on my own knowledge of Persian.[1] Translations and transliterations of Iranian titles, words, names, and concepts are given in parentheses (e.g., *zan*, meaning woman) in the text, notes, and bibliography. Familiar variant names follow the spellings as used by the individuals in question (e.g., Mohammad Reza Shah). In the case of dual languages, I have followed their respective method of transliteration (e.g., *Keyhan*). Persian and Arabic words commonly used in English are spelled as they sound in Persian (e.g., *Qoran*), except when they appear differently in citations (e.g., *Qur'an*). The Glossary highlights my transliteration of the Persian pronunciation of both Persian and Arabic words. Nevertheless, when references are general, the English term, like "clergy," is used for convenience.

Because of space consideration, not all titles are transliterated. But important titles to the reader are transliterated.

The footnotes are constructed differently. In order to save space, I merged several references in the same paragraph. An identifying word or phrase is used to refer to the exact sentence I used in the text. If the identifying word or phrase is based on a specific citation, it is in quotes;

[1] Elwell-Sutton, L.P., entire.

otherwise, it is not. In addition, titles of books/articles are not generally included in the notes, especially that they appear in the Selected Bibliography. When more than one publication is used by the same author, a portion of the title of her/his work appears in the notes as well. Finally, when I refer to the entire article or a book, I refrain from including any specific page numbers. In contrast, page numbers are included when I refer to a specific citation and/or idea. The Selected Bibliography includes full citations of sources.

Introduction

Born at the turn of the twentieth-century in Tehran and confined to the private world of the family, my veiled grandmother took lessons in her native Persian language from a tutor at her parents' home. More mobile, my mother welcomed the opportunity to attend school, to and from which she was always escorted. In 1936 when she was almost nine years old, she later recalled, a local gendarme stopped her, admonishing her to abandon the *chador* in favor of complete unveiling. My own experiences have been vastly different but in some ways similar. I received a superior education, but until the last two years of high school, I was always accompanied. I wore a knee-length school uniform with my hair uncovered, except in mosques or in neighborhoods with major *Shi'i* shrines, where I had to wear the *chador*. Hardly changing my appearance when I left my American university for Iran during the 1979 Revolution, I carried a shawl in my bag to ward off unpleasant encounters. Home after twelve years of exile, I was wearing a black, loose and long tunic to conduct interviews at the University of Tehran when I was approached by a contentious Islamic revolutionary guard who had determined that I was improperly veiled: "Sister, pull your scarf over your forehead to hide your hair completely," he commanded. Hearing similar remarks in 1997 and 2002 but to a lesser degree in 2005, I concluded: history repeats itself, though with twists and not always following the same scripts.

These family stories represent cataclysmic experiences in Iranian history and women's lives during the twentieth and twenty-first centuries. The first Iranian woman in the United States who wrote on women in Iran from a social science perspective, I am still seeking to delve into new territory.[1] For me, these memories raise a key question. Why were urban Iranian women veiled at the turn of the century, unveiled from 1936 to 1979, and reveiled after the Revolution of 1979? Clearly the veil possessed significance greater than merely a cover to cloak the appearance of a Muslim woman, or – as Frantz Fanon argued – to protect her from the eyes of infidels or colonizers. Conversely, the importance of unveiling transcends its association with secularism, Westernism, and modernism. Reveiling, too, means far more than the resurgence of "Islamic fundamentalism" or a return of cultural authenticity and Islamic revivalism. This book will show the connection among politics, religion, and gender.[2]

Significant metaphorically and literally, veiling, unveiling, and reveiling illuminate the contest for political power in the course of Iran's development. During and immediately after the Constitutional Revolution (1905–11), concerns regarding veiling and women's subordinate social and political position fostered challenges to the established power structure and the religious establishment. Later, state-sponsored unveiling contributed to the Westernization posture of the Pahlavi dynasty (1925–79) and its apparent victory over the clergy. The state-mandated reveiling embodied the Islamic identity of the succeeding polity (1979–), accompanied by the restoration of juridical and de facto gender segregation. From the early twentieth-century to the present, therefore, various forms of veiling draw attention to the continuing quest for political power between the state and religion especially over women's sexuality and their labor. Gender remains a core concern of politics. Gender analysis illuminates politics and power struggle: who gets, what, how, when, and why.

Veiling, unveiling, and reveiling also deserve special attention because of their extraordinary significance for the history of women's agency, their responses to the state and clergy, and their attempts to carve out their own place in society and the marketplace. During the course of the twentieth and twenty-first centuries, Iranian women displayed varied political positions. Class background, philosophical persuasion, and political alliance often divided women. Yet some women transcended their differences and joined in common causes defying and subverting culture, politics, and institutions. At the turn of the last century, reacting to patriarchal dominatory tendencies and national and political crises, a handful of women from wealthy households joined open or secret societies, while others

[1] First Iranian woman, Sedghi, "Women in Iran," 219–228; Sedghi and Ashraf, "The Condition," 201–214; Sedghi, "A Critique"; and Sedghi, "An Assessment," 37–41.

[2] Fanon, *A Dying*, 67; and also see Sedghi, "Third World," 88–105.

attempted to awaken women through schools and journals (Chapters 1 and 2).

Women's agency became more evident under the Pahlavis, when women engaged in the beginnings of unprecedented challenges to state and society. A handful of different women's organizations, composed primarily of well-to-do women, attempted to articulate their interests in the 1930s. But "state feminism," or the state's active interference in women's activities preempted all women's organizations. Many awaited the collapse of the autocratic state. During the 1940s independent and organized women gained some autonomy (Chapter 2). They engendered a new group of pioneering and educated women who claimed a unique place in the 1960s and 1970s among future feminists. These decades were crucial because they witnessed a sharp split among women whose interests overlapped occasionally. Active in legislative and political reforms on behalf of women, some "Queen Bees" or "conformist" women who were relatively prosperous members of the society, represented the state's interests and contributed to its national and international legitimacy. On the opposite side were anti-establishment or "nonconformist" women who were less privileged and represented left, secular, and Islamic perspectives. They were critical of the state and its political and economic reforms (Chapter 5).

The quest for gender equality and women's rights in the newly formed Islamic Republic of Iran (IRI) amplifies yet another dimension of women's political behavior, their class background, and varied responses to inequality and discriminatory practices. Both "proponent" women or supporters and "opponent" women who dare to defy the state remain divided on reveiling and the implementation of inequitable political, legal, social, and economic policies. They also present different approaches to gender relations, women's role in the household and society, and women's involvement in politics and feminism. But their interconnected interests on diverse issues including, patriarchy, political power, and women's political participation allow them to engage in temporary and shifting alliances. Women continue to maintain a dynamic presence in the Islamic state (Chapters 6 and 8). The persistent and multiple forms of expression and activity of women suggest that gender is important for political analysis, especially regarding the contest between state and clergy over women in the history of modern Iran.

This book explores Iran's transformation from a gender perspective. It analyzes relations among the state, clergy, and cultural forces and the private and public lives of women of different classes, their work, and their political persuasions and behavior in three distinct yet connected periods of the twentieth and twenty-first centuries: the last years of the Qajar dynasty, or the reign of "veiling"; the Pahlavi dynasty, which made Iran "the Japan of the Middle East" economically and promoted secularization, Westernization, and later Americanization and "unveiling," which culminated in the revolution; and finally, the Islamic state, which restored clerical power and imposed "reveiling." This comparative historical approach highlights development processes and gender politics in one country over a period of time.

Setting the basis for interconnecting gender and politics, this book considers broad and specific themes: how and to what extent unveiling and reveiling measures represented not only the power struggle between the state and clergy over women's sexuality but regime change, how and whether Iran's participation in the global economy elicited shifts in its domestic gender division of labor and women's work, and finally, how political and economic policies solicited active responses from women. These themes raise one basic question: what is the meaning of women's sexuality that its control or decontrol assumes importance for the state and its development strategies? I argue that the state intervenes in women's lives for the purpose of its internal and external policy objectives. Domestically, whether weak or strong, secular or religious, Westernizing or Islamizing, the state manipulates women's sexuality and their labor in order to legitimize its political and cultural position and to consolidate its powers. Internationally, the state uses women and their portrayal as Westernized or Islamized, unveiled or veiled, in order to depict a distinct political identity and message abroad. Women become an instrument of national and foreign policies.

Although the state's ability to modify and reshape gender relations and women's lives is real, its actions, I argue, are limited by the persistence of women's resistance. As active and reactive agents of social change, women respond to and defy state actions. Women pose challenges to the system, constraining and modifying the state's behavior – sometimes successfully, sometimes not. Women's responses vary historically, not only by their class background, ideological dispositions, and religious outlook, but by the degree of their political and feminist awareness and how they can articulate their interests and issues of their concerns. This study explores the private and public lives of women of different classes, women's work (inside and outside of the household and as self-employed laborers), and women's feminist and political conduct in different socioeconomic and political periods (Chapters 1, 2, 5, 6, and 8). It is my firm belief that women's lives are linked with politics and in order to understand women's experiences, we must consider women and gender as an integral part of the political and economic system that they share and experience. Thus, gender can be seen through a state lens both in its domestic and international environments, and conversely, the state can be analyzed through its gender policies and women's experiences.

Urban women are my focus because of their participation in political proclivities and feminist yearnings and also due to the distinct and complex demographic differences in Iran. Where relevant, I refer to rural women, but refrain from investigating changes in the position of rural, tribal, ethnic, or religious minority women. Urban Iran is more homogeneous in culture and language (for example, in large cities the majority of people speak Persian while some smaller towns communicate in Turkish and Azari, and a few rural hinterlands converse in Arabic, Luri, or Kurdish). Urban Iran is also similar in the polarization of class structure, the impact of modernization and labor force participation, Westernization and Islamization processes, and feminist awakening and women's initiatives especially since the Revolution of 1979.

This is a case study of state, gender, and religious relations in Iran. Case studies illuminate areas and subject matters that have been hitherto inadequately examined or not explored at all. They also shed light on comparative analysis when they consider an important aspect of one country's development over a specific time span. Moreover, data-gathering operations, such as the one undertaken here, enable the researcher to test previous propositions developed in other area studies, and/or refine more general theories, or build new ones.[3] This study of Iran demonstrates its historical transformation along with changes in women's lives, their work, and women's proclivities over the past century. It identifies similarities and differences in three politically and economically distinct phases of the same society. More significantly, it offers an understanding of gender-state-religion relations in the Pahlavi era, which has not yet been examined systematically, and suggests viewing it as an explanation for the birth of the system that followed.

This interdisciplinary endeavor cuts across several academic disciplines, including political science, economics, history, religion, anthropology, and sociology, and it is linked to women's studies, developmental and Middle Eastern studies. Within the context of currently significant works in women's and gender studies, developmental studies, and Middle

[3] Propositions, Johnson, 32–38.

Eastern and Iranian studies, I explore women's experiences and activities and draw on gender as a category of analysis in the study of politics and economy and the contention over women's sexuality. Rather than offering a comprehensive review, this introduction focuses on specific areas where feminist work and gender analysis provide new insights on Iran as a developing Middle Eastern society with its unique history and gender dynamics.

Broadly speaking, I draw on and build on literature in several fields. I embark on gender studies that incorporate state studies and illuminate the importance of sexuality, family legislation, and political mobilization of women for the state and state-building. Since the 1979 Iranian Revolution, Islam and Islamic movements have been the central category of analysis within which debates on women and gender have been generally placed. Religion and religious ideologies have been singled out to explain the subordination of women in "Islamic" states. Yet such constructs fail to address the historically specific and varied forms of subordination in different states, particularly those undergoing rapid transformation. I examine religion and culture, but within broader historical and political contexts in which specific cultural forms or religious interpretations are articulated and sanctioned by the state. And as mentioned earlier, I analyze the state in terms of its contest with the religious establishment.[4]

Gender studies consider four basic types of gender-state relations. Some focus on the state's interference in family legislation and reproductive policies that aim at restricting or expanding women's rights and control over their sexuality.[5] A few examine the state's interaction with women in public policy processes and women's roles in policy making.[6] Others investigate women's political mobilization, with implications for gender relations and gender construction.[7] Another body of literature probes how economic policies affect women's and men's work differently.[8] Still growing in number, other works delve into the interaction among gender, Islam, and state projects and women.[9] My analysis highlights state's interaction

[4] Religious ideologies, Minces.

[5] Sexuality, Pateman; and Hoodfar, "Devices and Desires," 11–17, and her "Bargaining With," 30–40.

[6] Public Policy, Nelson and Chowdhury, eds.; and policy, Basu.

[7] Mobilization, Molyneux, 280–302; and Jayawardena.

[8] Economic Policy, Beneria and Sen, "Accumulation," 279–98; and UNDP, *Human Development Report 1995*.

[9] Interaction, Joseph, 3–7; Islam, see Introduction in Kandiyoti, ed., *Women, Islam*; Ahmed; Papaneck; and Haddad and Esposito, eds.

with women of different classes, their work, and political and feminist activities; with men as clergy, secular leaders, and household members; and with political and economic forces.[10]

Drawing theoretical attention to the *political* dynamics of the state, I explore the state in terms of its political struggles and the state's use of gender for mobilization, consolidation, and legitimation purposes both for domestic and foreign policy reasons. Depending on the specificity of the historical period, I refer to the state as an organization that attempts to exercise political domination and hegemony.[11] Beyond reification, the state is a site of contestation, therefore, its nature, activities, institutions, and structures respond to forces of change. In Iran, the twentieth and twenty-first centuries bear the significance of gender politics to the state. Until recently, most studies of the Iranian state paid little attention, if any, to gender. Rather, scholars referred to various states as "weak," "modernizing," "reformist," "petrolic and rentier," "dependent capitalist," "statist," "bourgeois," "populist," "theocratic," "repressive," "fundamentalist," and "Islamic," among many modifiers.[12] None of these characterizations recognized the importance of gender to policy making or to the functioning of the state, nor did they acknowledge the use of gender in political conflicts and competition over power. Introducing a new approach, I view the state in terms of its relations to gender.

In each era of veiling, unveiling, and reveiling, the state comprises a distinct political economy and class structure, political ideology, and unique forms of patriarchy and gender relations that generates its own political contentions to which women respond in different ways. I present four arguments. First, the state is gendered and its policies are often discriminatory. For example, Iranian men were enfranchised in 1906, women only in 1963. Second, the state uses gender as a source of legitimacy in order to consolidate its power. Cases in point are the coercive policies that resulted in unveiling under the Pahlavis and reveiling under the Islamic Republic of Iran. A third, related observation is that the desire to control women's sexuality alludes to power struggles among men rooted in their own sense of masculinity and their related policy choices. For

[10] Activities, Farhi, "Sexuality"; Abu-Lughod; and Sedghi, "The State."

[11] The state has historically embodied its own patterns of conflict and cooperation, and in response to various sources, at times it has been flexible – see, Skocpol, *States*.

[12] Modernizing, Banani; M. Milani; Amir Arjomand; Katouzian; and Abrahamian, *Iran*. Rentier, Skocpol, *States*; bourgeois, Ashraf, "Historical Obstacles"; populist, transitional, and exceptional state, F. Sanat-Carr, "Khomeynism"; and fundamentalist, Abrahamian, *Khomeinism*.

example, Reza Shah Pahlavi used unveiling to emasculate the clergy and to promote modernization and Westernization, as did his son, the Shah. Once in power in 1979, the clergy regained what it had lost: control over women's sexuality and labor that continued to define "the Islamic" posture and identity of the regime. Fourth, gender matters to the global image of the state. The Pahlavis needed Westernized women to promote a secular and modern representation abroad, even as the Islamic Republic required authentic, devout, and "Islamic" women. Thus, state studies are important to gender studies.

In addition to gender and state studies, gender and development works provide valuable insights on women's work (inside and outside the household), the gendered division of labor and employment policies nationally, and within the context of global changes.[13] It is of paramount importance to consider the dialectical relationship between political and economic forces, and how they relate to the gender division of labor in the market and women's reproductive activities. It is also useful to consider the interaction between domestic economy and the larger global market in order to ascertain external economic influences, if any, on internal dynamics. In Iran, economic change reverberated in policy. Iran's integration into the global market under the Pahlavis led to the introduction of modernization projects and Westernization, and welcomed some unveiled women, their educational endeavors, and labor force participation.[14] Conversely, the Islamic regimes' initial antagonism to these processes along with its restricted gender policies restrained women from the public space, thereby, discouraging their work outside the home and encouraging their household tasks and reproduction activities. In contrast, its subsequent economic liberalization and slow participation in the global market created an opening for women, perhaps inadvertently, to advance their quests for women's rights. Thus, the historical and cultural context of development is crucial to identifying the specific circumstances of politics and economics, as well as their interactions with women's work.

Gender and development studies illuminate the impact of modernization on women's work. In a pioneering and influential work, Ester Boserup analyzed the impact of internal development or "modernization" on women's work in Latin America, Africa, and Asia. She introduced the thesis that modernization has an adverse effect on female as compared to male labor by marginalizing or excluding women from the more

[13] Women's work, Boris and Prugl, eds.; and Turpin and Lorentzen, eds.

[14] Modernization, Ch. 3 of this book.

modern sectors of the economy. Boserup attributed women's subordination to a modernization process in which "men are quicker than women to change over from traditional to modern types of occupations." The main consequence of economic development for the urban economy is the "polarization and hierarchization of men's and women's work roles," with men being preferred for "skilled and supervisory" jobs and women the "unskilled and subservient." In distinguishing between women and men in her analysis, Boserup challenged neoclassical economics. But she ignored feminist doubts regarding the neutrality of modernization. She also paid scant attention to the reasons for women's exclusion or marginalization in the labor force, the gendered division of labor in the market and the household, and the impact of sexuality on rewards in the labor market and the family.[15]

Lourdes Beneria meticulously investigated broader gender and development categories. In trying to account for issues surrounding women's work, for example, the impact of structural adjustment on poverty, the gender division of labor, and women's position in production and reproduction, Beneria argued that the core of "women's economic activities is provided by their special role in the reproduction of the labor force." Women's subordination and its various forms in different societies stem from their reproductive activities and are conditioned by "the nature of the productive process and the requirements of a given process of growth and accumulation." She also perceived an intimate link between production processes and women's work at home. As a result of the control exercised over women's reproductive activities, "the focal point of women's work becomes the household" and "the household becomes the very root of patriarchy" and male domination. Thus, the gender division of labor in the market reproduces gender hierarchies and women's work and reproductive activities in the household. Building upon the literature of gender and development, I relate political struggles over women's sexuality to the understanding of women's work in Iran.[16]

Salient aspects of Iran's development included changes in the gender division of labor, women's work, and the modification of traditional mores. Women's work and women's role in reproduction shifted by the transformation of a predominantly agricultural economy in the early twentieth-century to a rapidly developing market economy in the late

[15] "Occupations," "polarization," "skilled," and "unskilled," Boserup, 140.

[16] "Reproduction," "accumulation," "focal," and "patriarchy," Beneria, "Reproduction," 203, 207, 205, 209, and 222; and Beneria and Feldman, eds.

1960s and 1970s and then to the shrinking economy under the IRI that affected women's work and their role in reproduction. At the turn of the century, a "Qoranic division of labor" and a subsistence economy allowed the household to be the focal point of a patriarchal system that held women's sexuality and labor in check. Under the Pahlavis, significant alterations occurred in the economy and polity, and women emerged as important contributors to the economy and society. With the slower economy during its first decade of the IRI, labor force participation of women exhibited a downturn and many women returned to the home and household production. During and after its second decade, the Islamic regime witnessed a greater entry of women to educational institutions and the labor market.[17]

The Pahlavi era illustrates the dynamics of rapid modernization in developing countries. It witnessed an unprecedented growth of capital accumulation by the late 1960s and early 1970s and a relatively high labor force participation of women. In comparison with African and Latin American patterns, Iranian women's absorption in production and their position in the gender division of labor was unique: most employed women were concentrated in the service rather than other sectors of the economy; and the typical pattern of wage work was reversed, as labor force participation was highest among married women between the ages of 20 and 29 years. Household consumption rose with increases in the standard of living, yet domestic work remained primarily the women's domain and locus of reproductive activities, and many men continued to be little kings in their walled homes.[18]

So volatile has been women's experiences in the labor market that they had to adjust continuously to unparalleled situations. Under the Shah, these experiences were contradictory. On the one hand, women confronted the old and new forms of subordination: as wage earners by capital, as women by men, and as women by women in positions of power. On the other hand, women's departure from home and their participation in the educational system and the labor market helped many of them achieve personal and professional self-esteem, becoming active pioneers. By contrast, under the IRI, women's work increasingly intermeshed with the control of their sexuality. With the 1979 Revolution and the establishment of the new state, the integration of politics and religion adversely

[17] "Qoranic division," Sedghi, "Women and Class," Chs. 1 and 2.

[18] 1970s, Iran's women's labor force participation in the region was highest after Israel and Turkey, respectively – see Ch. 3 of this book.

affected women's work as economic decline and concern with women's sexuality drove many out of the market. As women's work in the market decreased, their work in the household increased. By early 2000, more women accounted for the larger share of the labor market and more than 60 percent of university graduates. More women also joined the growing informal market, including the growing rank of prostitutes.[19]

Iran's development model of rapid growth and rapid decline offers insights for understanding women's work. At the turn of the century, women's confinement to the household corresponded to the stagnant and traditional economy. In the 1960s and 1970s, women's increasing participation in the gendered labor force paralleled a rapid growth of the service and industrial sectors. By contrast, in the 1980s and 1990s, lower female employment complemented the shrinking economy and policies that had deliberately discouraged women's public visibility and encouraged their role as mothers and housewives. Thus, women's work in and outside the household and the gender division of labor itself changed according to the nature of the economy: the greater the growth of the economy, the higher the labor force participation of women; and conversely, the slower economic growth, the lower women's participation. These shifts need consideration of development strategies, the level of state interference, and most importantly, those policies that address women's sexuality.

Besides state and development studies, Middle Eastern gender studies are germane to this study.[20] The insights of critics of oriental studies, sexuality and veiling, and post-colonial approaches are also relevant insofar as they relate to culture and resistance in Iran.[21] But specific attention will be given to Nadia Youssef's classic study that sheds light on the relations between women's work, the family, and religion in the Middle East and Latin America. Youssef observed that economic development scarcely promoted women's work in the market because of essentially non-economic forces such as culture, the role of the family, and women's seclusion. These factors explain women's lesser participation in Middle Eastern countries with Islamic religion than in Latin America, where women have not been

[19] Work, Poya; and Chs. 3 and 7 of this book.

[20] Middle Eastern Gender Studies include: Paidar; Kawar; Ahmed; Lazrek; Tucker; and Keddie and Beck, eds.; and others that have been used in this book.

[21] Culture and resistance, Opie; Marbo; Kandiyoti, "Identity"; Hatem; Abu-lughod; Friedl; and Butler and Scott. eds. Because of the shortage of space, I refrain from reviewing the critics of orientalism and the post-colonial literature. In time, I hope to complement these works in my future studies.

secluded and have been more mobile. The link between development, religion, and culture is illuminating, yet Iran's case suggests viewing economic and cultural forces within the context of state activities that are subject to women's responses. Despite the dominance of Islam and gender segregation at the turn of the century, Iranian women participated in politics and economy as many continue to do under the IRI; and aside from variations in different statistical compilation, the overall rate of women's labor force participation remained higher under the Pahlavis. Thus, the role of religion is relevant, but only to a degree.[22]

Other themes in Middle Eastern women's studies concern sexuality and gender and veiling, both of which intersect frequently. Fatima Mernissi noted that the sexual power attributed to women has caused Islamic states to contain and control their sexuality through such social institutions as the veil, the family, the marriage system, and the legal system. Leila Ahmed saw the "Islamist position" on women as "reactive in nature" because it "traps the issue of women with the struggle over culture – just as the initiating colonial discourse had done."[23] Feminist scholars agree that sexuality and the sexual control of women as well as veiling practices have been historically important to the ideology and behavior of Islamic societies. But they caution against Western orientalism and the misinterpretation of Middle Eastern Muslim women with the attempt to undermine them and their struggles. However, disagreements have arisen among women who defend, reject, or believe in Islamic reforms.[24] In Iran, despite variations in state policies, women's sexuality and veiling practices have often been central to conflicts between religious and secular forces. Both manipulate gender issues and sexuality, though they do so for different reasons and to different degrees.

An important theme related to the study of sexuality in Middle Eastern women with implications for Iran concerns the political mobilization of women. Women's exploitation by the state for political support seems especially prominent in postrevolutionary periods when a new regime needs a mobilized population to give it an appearance of legitimacy.[25] Some Middle Eastern and North African studies have explored the

[22] Work, Youssef; F. Moghadam, "Commoditization"; and Sedghi, "The Sexual."

[23] Sexual, Mernissi, *Beyond*; "traps," Ahmed, 237; Gole; Yamani; and Manju.

[24] Orientalism, Sayigh, 22; Hammami and Martin, 1–7; Ahmed; and Hajibashi; defend, Haddad and Esposito, eds.; Saadawi; Hussain and Radwan; and reject, Ghoussoub, 3–13 and her "A Reply." For Iranian women's studies see the following section and Chs. 1, 5 and 8 of this book.

[25] Mobilized, Andors; Massell; and Charrad.

activities and recruitment of women by nationalist and anticolonial forces.[26] But little rigorous analysis exists on how various policies regarding sexuality have been implemented through political mobilization of women in modern Iran. Women's mobilization has been a significant aspect of state-building in Iran, and women's activism is of paramount significance. The Shah's state assigned the task to the state-sponsored Women's Organization of Iran (WOI), presided over by Ashraf Pahlavi, the monarch's twin sister. Visible domestically and internationally, the mostly elite members of the Pahlavi's WOI (or "conformist" women) pressed for gender policies and legislative reforms while promoting the state's interests. But they were challenged by progressive (or "nonconformist") women. The former or the "Queen Bees" included elite women, high level WOI women, and a few women in the state apparatus such as those in the National Iranian Radio and Television (NIRT). The latter comprised "secular left" women, "secular independent" women, and women of the religious opposition.

In contrast, the Islamic Republic mobilized poor and working-class women, initially. Observable on urban streets, the "gender police" or morality police enforced modesty and gender segregation policies. With state consolidation of power, the state opened its doors to Islamic elite or what I consider "proponent" women, composed of a few "devouts" and "trespassers." Diverse in their disposition and interpretation of Islam and Islamic women's movements, they support the state and the unity of state and religion. But more recently, with their growing skepticism of the state, many trespassers are crossing their boundaries and joining hands with their adversaries or "opponent" women. With their secular tendencies, these women pose a challenge not only to proponents but to the religious and state establishments. Included in this category are the "revolutionaries," "rebels," and "reformers" from various age groups, class background, and professional expertise. Thus, acting from religious or secular predispositions or both, mobilized and active women may cooperate politically or contest state policies in order to articulate their known interests. Because of ideological and philosophical differences among women, as well as the nature of their relations to the state, I reject the notion of Islamic feminism.[27] Created in the West as a terminology, Islamic feminism is foreign to the politically active and feminists

[26] Nationalist and anti-colonial, Jayawardena; Yuval-Davis and Anthias, eds.; Peteet; and Sedghi, "Third World Women."

[27] Women, Chs. 5 and 8 of this book.

in Iran. They refuse to refer to themselves as Islamic feminists, although occasionally they make references to feminism, a lexicon that is becoming increasingly popular among both secular and religious women but unused by many women. In addition, as a concept, Islamic feminism has no explanatory power because it lumps together a variety of women into one generic term and fails to distinguish the specific interests, ideological dispositions, and activities of diverse women. Varied in their pursuits, active and/or feminist women may have their interests overlapped periodically.

Iranian women's studies, still in an embryonic stage, are growing. It is not overstating to suggest that they contribute more insights on women in the Islamic Republic of Iran than on the Pahlavis. Despite women's centrality analytically and politically, Iranian studies generally ignored them until recently. English-language literature on modern Iran contributes valuable information on history, politics, economy, culture, and religion but, except for occasional references, women's roles continue to lie outside the scope of most of these studies. Even political science and comparative politics studies that have used Iran as a case study of political development, modernization, dependency, revolution, and theocracy shed little light on the importance of gender for politics, political mobilization, and social movements. Because my inquiry concerns women's experiences and their interactions with state and religion, Iranian studies have provided only a background for my work. Fortunately, sociological, anthropological, historical, and economics literature on Iranian women has partially corrected this neglect.[28]

Prerevolutionary materials on Iranian women exist in English and Persian. Those few that are written in English include a range of historical, statistical, autobiographical, and cultural works as well as memoir and travelers' accounts. Some of these studies are informative, although they lack theoretical perspectives and verifiable documents, and some evince an ethnocentric bias against women and Iranians. Because of the shortage of sources, I relied heavily on Persian materials, which are considerable. These include historical overviews, biographies, political works, and speeches on the status of women made by male and female members of the Pahlavi dynasty; legislative studies pertaining to women in the family; criminal and labor codes during the Shah's era; statistical accounts of women's employment and attitudinal surveys on the employed

[28] Iranian studies, Sedghi, "An Assessment"; and comparative politics studies, Bakhash; Moaddel; and M. Milani.

female population; religious studies, primarily by clergymen; and works by female Iranian activists abroad. Many of these studies are descriptive and incoherent, and most of them are difficult to use because they provide contradictory and inadequate information. Although a large number of these sources disappeared during the 1979 Revolution, I had collected them on field trips during 1973, 1974, 1975, and 1977: they are the best or at least some of them are the only ones available. Such materials have been especially useful for understanding the Pahlavi period, which has not been rigorously studied from a gender perspective by other scholars.[29]

Postrevolutionary scholarship on women is more abundant. They include a variety of works in Persian and English. Persian sources range from statistics on population movements, employment, and education to legal studies, prison memoirs, works by religious authorities on women, and a variety of newspapers, journals, novels, and cultural studies.[30] In English, research addresses the role of ideology and its impact on women, the politics of the veil, women's movements and struggles, women and religious law, the role of sexuality in the subordination of women, the politics of the left and its position on women in Iran, women's work, and immigrant women. Further queries highlight biographies and autobiographies, statistical studies, memoirs, novels, and literary criticism. Most recently, memoirs of the first generation of Iranian American women reveal new stories.[31]

[29] Prerevolutionary, Sedghi, "An Assessment"; ethnocentric, Rice; Persian studies include Manoochehrian, Bamdad, F. Farrokhzad, Sheikholeslami, Plan and Budget Organization's *Degarguniha-ye*, Mazlooman, Motahhari, Rastkar, National Radio and Television's *Bayegani-ye Karmandan*, Dehghani, Ettehadieh and Sa'dunian, eds., other sources in this book and Sedghi, "Women and Class," 1–52.

[30] Persian sources include, Mahmudi; Bagherian, "Eshteqalat va Bikari-ye"; Plan and Budget Organization of Iran, *Gozaresh-e Eqtesadi-ye Sal-e 1368*; Parsiour, *Khaterat-e Zendan*; Central Bank of the Islamic Republic of Iran, *Economic Report and Balance Sheet 1371*; Bank Markazi Jomhuri Islamiy-e Iran, *Annual Review 1373*; Ebadi; Kar; and various issues of *Zanan*, *Zan-e Ruz*, *Payam-e Hajar*, *Zan*, *Huquq-e Zanan*, *Payam-e Zan*, *Negah-e Zanan*, *Pesaran va Dokhtaran* and *Huguq va Ejtema'* among others, and *Nimeyeh Digar* published in the United States.

[31] English works include, Royanian; P. A. Pahlavi, *Faces*; Ferdows; Yeganeh and Keddie; Hegland; Targhi-Tavakoli; Ramazani; Bauer; Shahidian, "The Iranian Left"; Afary, *Iranian Constitutional*; F. Moghadam, "Commoditization"; Touhidi; V. Moghadam; and Hoodfar. Books include, Azari, ed.; Tabari and Yeganeh, eds.; Nashat, ed.; Sanasarian; F. Milani, *Veils*; Amanat, ed., *Taj Al-Saltana*; Esfandiari; Najmabadi, *The Story*; Afshar, *Islam and Feminism*; Moghissi; Mir-Hoseini; Friedl; Shahidian; and Poya. Recent memoirs of Iranian-American women include, Bahrampour; Karim and Khorrami, eds., among others.

Since the 1979 Revolution, more English language books on Iranian women from a social science perspective are being published in the United States and Europe. There are also numerous collections composed of valuable scholarly chapters and many interesting journal articles. In the 1990s, sociologist Haideh Moghissi enriched her study of women, the left, and populism by her own personal experiences, which made her critical of the left forces during the first few years of the revolution. The late sociologist Parvin Paidar provided a comprehensive study of women's position in Iran's political processes. She considered the role of gender in nation building, modernity, and revolutionary discourses, and saw changes in women's lives through shifts in constitutionalism, nationalism, modernization, and *Shi'i* discourses. A meticulous survey, Paidar's work is primarily descriptive and less systematic when it addresses the Pahlavis. Thus, an authoritative historical account is still missing.

Mention must be made of other important works. Shahla Haeri drew on 15 interviews conducted in the summer of 1978 and then in 1981 to examine the *Shi'i* temporary marriage and the relationship of *Shi'i* Islam to sexuality in postrevolutionary Iran. Significantly, Erika Friedl's work on Deh Koh women – based on two decades of field research – skillfully used their own words and perceptions to tell the story of the women of a small Iranian village. In addition, Ziba Mir-Hosseini interviewed *Shi'i* clerics in Qom in order to explore various notions of gender in Islamic jurisprudence. Maryam Poya explored women and work; Hammed Shahidian critically studied patriarchy, sexuality, feminism, and culture; and Afsaneh Najmabadi explored gender and national memory and gender and sexuality in the nineteenth-century. Most of these studies concentrate on women and the revolution.[32]

In contrast, this book emphasizes the entire twentieth and twenty-first centuries. I locate contention over women and their sexuality at the center of politics and power struggle between secular and religious forces (and more recently between different religious factions). Conceptualizing women as active agents, whether supporting or opposing the Shah or the Islamic regime, my focus is urban women of varied classes. In addition, I present new primary material based on oral history collections, field research, and interviews gathered over the years 1973 to 1979 and then in 1991, 1997, 2002, and 2005. Some of my interviews were pre-arranged and formal where I made appointments in advance and met female and male officials with prepared questions. At times, my interviewees referred

[32] English language books include Moghissi; Paidar; Haeri; Friedl; Mir-Hosseini; Poya; Shahidian; Mayer; and Najmabadi, among others.

me to other sources that were more qualified to answer questions and/or would preface their remarks by offering the publications of their organizations. Significantly though, I took advantage of my linguistic knowledge and cultural understanding and conducted on-the-spot-interviews in various places that I visited: ministries, banks, statistics offices, libraries, government or non-government organizations, informal meetings and gatherings, bookstores, universities in different towns, bazaars, or even taxis, buslines, newspaper stands, and hair salons. I was privileged by the opportunity to conduct both formal and on-the-spot interviews and research.

This book concentrates on fifty-four years of the Pahlavi dynasty, especially the two volatile decades before its disintegration. The longest chapters are exactly on this period, in particular those that address thirty-eight years of the Shah's rule and Iran's Americanization, a period that I recall vividly as a student in Tehran. The entire Pahlavi era is significant because of the length of the period, its rapid and unique development, Westernization, modernization, and unveiling. But this period has not been adequately studied from a gender perspective and through women's eyes. The profile and place of "conformist" and "nonconformist" women in politics and gender politics, and in relation to Iran's development under the Pahlavis, is being critically introduced for the first time. In addition, the coverage of the "proponent" and "opponent" women in the Islamic Republic of Iran, presents for the first time, a comprehensive view of women's resistance.

In sum, as an interdisciplinary effort, this book bridges the gap between political science, developmental studies, and Iranian women's studies – a field of scholarship hitherto neglected especially by many scholars of Iran. Within the context of Iranian studies, it offers systematic presentation and analysis of primary materials thus far untapped by scholars; it attempts to transcend the descriptive orientation of most Iranian studies; and most importantly, it insists on the significance of gender and women's studies as integral to politics, more specifically to Iranian studies.

Organizationally, this historical and theoretical understanding of the meaning of women's sexuality for the contenders of political power and women's responses includes three parts. Part I, which encompasses Chapter 1, analyzes the period of veiling during the last days of the Qajar dynasty. It views veiling by looking at women's lives in the patriarchal household, in the work environments that were differentiated by their social class, and in terms of the impact of cultural values and religious mores as perceived by Islamic law. Within the context of domestic upheavals and especially the Constitutional Revolution, as well as international politics, it delves into women's political activism, highlighting the beginnings of gender advocacy in a predominantly agricultural and underdeveloped economy.

Part II focuses on the last dynasty, the Pahlavis (1925–79). The Kingdom of the Peacock throne was the period of unveiling, culminating in the 1979 Revolution. Chapter 2 begins with Reza Shah's attempts at secularization, modernization, and Westernization (1925–41), including his power struggles with the divided religious establishment. Autocracy meant the defeat of women's independent activities and the creation of a new feminism under state auspices. It is with the king's abdication (1941) and the emergence of the "weak state" in the 1940s and early 1950s that educated and professional women asserted their newly gained autonomy. They formed progressive women's organizations and placed demands on the patriarchal structures to promote their civil and women's rights. But the 1953 CIA overthrow (with the help of Ashraf Pahlavi, the Shah's twin sister) of Dr. Mohammad Mosaddegh's government, the subsequent American political and economic support, and Iran's rapid integration into the global market began to affect profoundly the lives of Iranians.

Chapter 3 focuses on the ensuing structural changes in the economy that altered the gender division of labor and women's work inside and outside the home. With increasing integration of unveiled women into the workforce and educational institutions, this chapter analyzes the gender division of labor and explores women's position by major economic sectors, their class background, marital status, and age. It sets the basis for the link between the economy and state gender policies in this period of unveiling, which are examined in the next two chapters. Highlighting public gender policies, Chapter 4 demonstrates the interconnectedness between the economy and the state, and especially the state's manipulation of gender for the purpose of consolidation of its power. It assesses the state's intervention in women's affairs as a focal point of the dynamics of political power, political struggles, and developmental policies. The analysis extends to the effects of legal changes on gender relations and contradictions in legal theory and its application. It also illuminates the gendered state and political reforms in family legislation, labor laws as well as penal codes, and in particular, those injunctions dealing with adultery, rape, and prostitution.

Focusing on women's agency, Chapter 5 is a comprehensive investigation of women's actions and reactions during the reign of the second Pahlavi monarch, a topic long overdue for the critical inquirer. It draws resource material from my fieldtrips, including several studies that I conducted as an analyst at the Plan and Budget Organization of Iran and the National Iranian Radio and Television, and numerous visits to different organizations and interviews, formal and on-the-spot. In addition, it incorporates my reflections and experiences as a student in Iran and subsequently at the University of California in Berkeley in the late 1960s. The main findings allude to deep divisions among women on the nature of the state and class structure. There also existed some areas of overlaps in the way women experienced gender inequalities and patriarchal relations. The sharpest divide occurred among the conformist women – whom I call the "Queen Bees" or establishment women – and nonconformist women. Primarily from elite backgrounds, the conformist women included the powerful Ashraf Pahlavi and the three official wives of the Shah, high officers of the Women's Organizations of Iran, and influential women in the media or the National Iranian Radio and Television.[33] Allied with the state, these women promoted its interests and helped establish its international legitimacy. Some also participated in legislative reforms on behalf of women. Nonconformist women came from more diverse backgrounds. They comprised women of the secular left who held a variety of political ideologies, independent secular women, and finally women of the religious opposition. They criticized the state in their writings and poetry, joined the left and religious movements, and became involved in clandestine operations. Alienated from the state, silenced or tortured, many went into exile. Just as they were divided ideologically, nonconformist women carried heterogeneous views on gender and gender relations. Some former nonconformist women have currently allied themselves with the new state, bolstering its legitimacy.[34]

Part III extends the study to the Revolution of 1979 and creation of the Islamic Republic of Iran, coercive reveiling, and women's responses. The revolutionary era is significant as it sharply reduced the power of the state and thereby created an atmosphere for the increasing politicization of women – a situation similar to the 1940s and early 1950s when the state was weak and women's activities potent. Chapter 6 returns to the theme of a power struggle over women's sexuality and labor. It focuses on twenty-eight years of the Islamic regime, suggesting that just as the secularizing state of the Pahlavis tried to undermine clerical power by

[33] Conformist women, see Ch. 5 of this book and especially, Pahlavi, *A Mirror* and Farman Farmaian (with Dona Munker).

[34] Nonconformist women, see Sedghi, "[Feminist Movements] in the Pahlavi Period."

depriving them from regulating women's sexuality and their social and economic status, the clergy expanded its power by redefining the position of women as the centerpiece of its Islamization program. Reveiling, the creation of the "gender police," and gender segregated policies, laws, edicts, and sermons bolstered the state's posture, while alienating many women. But the state's success can be called into question. Women are responding and claiming their rights. In so doing, they keep the state on guard, and are slowly inscribing a crack in the system: a threat to one of the most important pillars of the Islamic state, its control over women.

Within the context of the Islamic Republic's integration into the global economy and the impact of the Iran-Iraq War (1980–88), Chapter 7 explores the intersection between women's work and gender policies. It traces the importance of sexuality and gender segregation in the labor force as evidenced by the return of many women to the household, wifehood and motherhood during the first ten years of the state. But the "zigzag" nature of the economy and political squabbling introduced shifts in the gender division of labor and women's work during the regime's second decade. With less restricted gender policies under the reformist government, gender police became more invisible. Modifying unveiling practices, more women entered the public space and the formal and informal sectors of the economy. The early 2000s witnessed not only an increasing growth in the labor market but a tremendous rise in women's educational progress and their subversive activities, unmatched with other Muslim countries. This chapter paves the way for the study of women's resistance.

Finally Chapter 8 elucidates reveiling and its counterpart, the politics of resistance. Divided politically and philosophically, women are active agents of social change. Women's activities intersect with their class, ideology, and religious identity. As women's awareness and their discontent increases, their religious identity undergoes some shifts. More secular and middle-class, many opponent women, including "revolutionaries," "rebels," and "reformers" are redefining veiling practices daily. Incrementally challenging gender policies, they are slowly reshaping the parameters of the system itself. In contrast, proponent women, elite and middle-class women, or "devouts" and "trespassers" strive to promote women's Islamic rights within the confines of Islamic law. Despite variations among these women, in particular on reveiling practices and the nature of the system, many have overlapping interests, for example, in their critique of patriarchal tendencies and undemocratic politics. During the 2005 presidential race, a few trespassers began to identify themselves with opponent women, echoing similar interests. Still, proponent women continue to provide the state with legitimacy, upholding its "Islamicized" image and identity abroad. While opponent women vie for power and assertion on a daily basis, they venture to defy and subvert the system. Thus, gender remains central to politics and politics vital to women's experiences.[35]

Does history repeat itself? Veiling led to unveiling. Unveiling gave rise to reveiling. Feminism at the turn of the century cultivated new seeds of active women. New ideas are developing and women's awareness and their diverse interests and concerns are growing. The future of active women and feminism is uncertain, although discontent is increasing among many women. Rejected as a presidential candidate in the May 1997 elections by the all-male members of the Guardian Council, A'zam Taleqani, the editor of *Payam-e Hajar* (Hajar's Message) and a daughter of late Ayatollah Taleqani firmly asserted: "I won't be silent. And if I remain silent, the women won't be silent." Shirin Ebadi received her 2003 Nobel Laureate in peace unveiled. She acknowledged that it is not easy to be a woman in Iran, but argued for a gender-neutral reading and interpretation of Islamic law, human rights, and gender equality. The newly elected president Mahmood Ahmadinejad appears to be not gender friendly. But it seems that as the ebb and flow of change in the state, religion, and gender relations move forward, the paradigm of reveiling and resistance enters the new millennium too. Still the most striking continuity across the past hundred years of Iranian history and politics has been the growth of women's agency, its strength and potency.[36]

[35] Variations among these women, Ch. 8 of this book.

[36] "I won't be silent," A. Taleqani; as reported by Lydens, A report from Iran broadcasted from the National Public Radio in New York City on May 21, 1997. (Taleqani is the founder of *Jame'-ye Zanan-e Enqelab-e Eslami* – (Women's Society of the Islamic Revolution.) In that capacity, she acts as an NGO and participates in international women's conferences. She referred to some of these activities in a conversation in New York City, March 1997 and repeated similar concerns in Tehran, September 1997 – and Ebadi, "Bound."

PART I

WOMEN IN EARLY TWENTIETH-CENTURY IRAN

1

The Qajar Dynasty, Patriarchal Households, and Women

"Behind the closed doors at home, prohibited from everything in life, education, training and social life, women are regarded as mindless, like infants; they are confined to the burdens of household work and child-bearing and are considered the slaves and servants of their husbands," wrote Bibi Khanum Astarabadi (1852–1920), an outspoken and prominent Qajar woman. This was not a tradition in Europe, she noted: "This is our Islamic custom." Similarly, in describing women's absence in public, Seyyed Jamalzadeh, a noted novelist commented: "No women can be seen in this country of men, but strangely, half of the walking population in the streets is wrapped in black bags from head to the toe without even an opening to breathe." A British orientalist, Clara Rice, observed that "most trades are in the hands of men, such as pottery-making, calico printing, felt-hat making and confectionery. All shops are kept by men.... there is no profession open to women. Art, music and literature may be said to be closed to them. All occupations followed by them [women] call for manual work rather than brainwork."[1]

Yet, these invisible women were capable of action, as in the Constitutional Revolution of 1905–11 when many women gathered in the streets of Tehran took off their veils and shouted: "Long live freedom.... We must...live the way we want!" In the late nineteenth and early twentieth-centuries, Iran was economically backward, politically chaotic,

[1] "Slaves and servants," and "Islamic custom," Javadi, Marashi, and Shekarloo, 124–128 and 134. Astarabadi also opened one of the first elementary schools for girls. See Afari, "[Feminist Movements] In the Late Qajar," 489–491; Jamalzadeh, Jamalzadeh, 106–107; and Rice, Rice, 219.

predominantly *Shi'i* Islam, and a patriarchal society. While leading a secluded life, its women were differentiated by class and were culturally and politically diverse. Focusing on women's lives, this historical chapter discusses women's experiences in the family and their work, religion, and politics at the turn of the twentieth-century. The underdeveloped economy and polity and patriarchal tendencies intimately defined a woman's position, although a few women's political activism culminated in, what might loosely be called, feminism.[2]

VEILING

Women were primarily confined to the household and reproduction. Their three-piece dress consisting of the *chador* (a long veil that covered them from head to toe), the *rubandeh* (a short veil that masked the face), and the *chaqchur* (very loose trousers) that signified their separate world; it assured them space and identity as *zai'feh*, or the weak sex and status as *moti'eh*, or those obedient to men's will. Strictly safeguarded from the public domain or men's world, their houses or rooms had no windows facing the streets and the outside world, and their mobility was severely controlled. Elite and wealthy women seldom went out – the men of their class would not approve. When they did, eunuchs accompanied them or they sat in a closed carriage alone or with other women or children. Feminist activist of the time, and subsequently my school Principal, Badr al-Moluk Bamdad, wrote that in Tehran, after four in the afternoon, the streets would be sex segregated, with men walking on one side and women on the other; should a woman need to cross the street to reach her home, she was required to obtain authorization from the street police. Even then, she would be scolded: "walk faster *zai'feh* and tighten up your veil," the police would say.[3]

Women spent most of their lives in the private world of the family. Indeed, a common name for a wife was *manzel* (the home). Rich or poor, women were confined to, and devoted their entire lives to the family. Affluent men might support an *andaruni*, the Persian equivalent of harem. A daughter of a powerful Qajar prince who grew up amidst her father's harem of eight wives described the intimate dynamics of such a separate

2 "Long live," Malekzadeh, 62.

3 Wealthy women, Rice, 168 and 193. When prosperous women went out, they mostly visited European shops and public baths where their servants carried bathing accessories, food supplies, and musical instruments so they could enjoy their half a day or the entire day. See Haas, 165; and "Walk faster *zai'feh*," Bamdad, Zan-e I, 68.

establishment by noting that "the wives in the compound looked upon each other's children as their own" and "Everyone there was linked with everyone else." It was common for men of royal families to have "100 or 200 or even 300 wives." Some of the wealthy landlords had over "400 servants, half of whom were women." Besides the legitimate wives, an *andaruni* might contain concubines and temporary wives (*siqehs*) as well as children and servants. In lesser households, husbands lived with their families as economic insecurity encouraged monogamous marriages, and many families were forced to share a room. But whether or not she was secluded in separate quarters, a woman's world was that of the *pardeh-neshin*, one who sat inside behind the curtained windows.[4]

From birth to marriage, women experienced disapproval. Unless girls were born into well-to-do families, their birth was less enthusiastically welcomed. Among the less-privileged classes, the birth of a baby girl usually meant disappointment to the father and fear in the mother, who might face abandonment or punishment by her husband or his close relatives or her own father. In some families, it was traditionally a *nang* (social disgrace) to give birth to girls, who were sometimes buried alive inside walls, whereas boys' birth would be celebrated with joy. Wealthier families showed greater tolerance toward their daughters – they provided child care and hired private tutors to teach them reading and writing in Persian, Arabic, and French as well as sewing and embroidery. Regardless of their social background, families required their daughters to remain virgins until marriage. As they grew up, girls learned that their sexuality, reproductiveness, and their labor were their only assets, though in fact, as women they exercised little control over their own body or labor. At puberty, even at the age of nine or ten, with no consideration for their wishes, parents would betroth and marry their daughters. They would then live out the life cycle for which they had been socialized, a life that repeated their mothers' experiences.[5]

The marital system ensured patriarchal domination. Patriarchy denotes a system of male control over women's labor and sexuality, both in the private and public spheres. As in *Shi'i* Islam, permanent marriage is analogous to a commercial transaction, in which the woman, the object of the contractual transaction, is exchanged for the *mehr* (brideprice). The

[4] "The wives" and "everyone," Farman Farmaian, 6–7; "300 wives," Soltanzadeh, 105–106; and "400 servants," *Ibid.*

[5] *Nang*, a story that I recall from my father's mother, Tehran, about 1960; and betroth and married, Bamdad, Zan-e II, 57–58.

brideprice specifies *saman-e boz'* or the price for a woman's sexual organ. The marriage contract approximates a commercial contract in Islamic Law, where *saman* (price) is exchanged for the *mabi'* (object for sale). Marriage is thus a contract for the legalization of sexual intercourse, not for love or even reproduction.[6]

The marriage contract legitimized the exchange – "immediate or deferred, symbolic or actual" – of a price for the bride's sexual organ. The indispensability of the *mehr* to the marriage contract and its interpretation as the distinct claim of the wife over husband, related especially to divorce, will be discussed later. In reality, however, divorces were rare. When they did occur, women's lack of social power prevented them from reclaiming their *mehr*. The marriage contract was in reality executed by two men, the father or the guardian of the bride and the groom or his family, without her consultation but with her consent executed the transaction. In so doing, the father transferred his authority over his daughter to the husband with the payment of a price through which the groom compensated the bride for the loss of her control over her sexuality and became the owner of her sexuality and "by extension herself."[7]

Such transactions or the traffic in women refers to the commercial exchange of women's sexuality between men, which ensures and enforces patriarchal domination while devalorizing women's position. Writing at the turn of the nineteenth-century, a British observer reported that "the men deem it obligatory to make a profound apology whenever they make mention to their companions of a dog, a hog, a donkey, or a *woman*. With them, [a] woman is no more than an idol of sensuality and a slave of passion." Men required women to be submissive, obedient, gracious in walk and speech, patient, caring, and loving. Paradoxically, their most private demands were superficially at odds with this picture. As a Qajar prince in his *Ta'dib-ol Nesvan* (Disciplining Women) instructed women, "in bed, put aside all bashfulness and innocence, move without shame and embarrassment. Do not think it exceeds your fame and reputation. If you do, what is your status then?"[8]

Patriarchal relations and control over economic resources reinforced men's power over women. Islam granted women property rights, but women had hardly any economic resources of their own. Even elite women complained about their financial situation and their dependence on men.

[6] *Saman* and *Mabi'*, Helli, 428.
[7] "Symbolic or actual" and "extension," Haeri, 34–38.
[8] "Slave of passion," Yonan, 18; and Qajar prince, Javadi, 78.

Data is scarce on property ownership, but where there was property, legal inheritance rights favored men. *Shi'i* Islam assigned a daughter a share half as large as her brother's, while a wife's share was one-eighth as large as her son's; the husband's share of his wife's legacy, on the other hand, was one-fourth that of her children. What little information is available points to women's limited ownership and control over economic resources or property.[9]

In sum, despite variations in different classes, women were primarily confined to the private and secluded world of the family. Growing up with little social esteem, most girls gained some economic and social value through the sale of their sexual organ in marriage contracts; in marital life, they became the virtual property of their husbands, paving the way for patriarchal control in the household and over economic resources. Patriarchal power also varied by class. The higher women were on the social scale, the more secluded and less mobile they were. By contrast, less-privileged women were more mobile and less secluded. Class and patriarchy acted together to shape women's lives; together, they affected women's work both within and outside the family.

WOMEN AND WORK

Women's work in the household and in the marketplace is intertwined, not distinct and separate. The narrow methodological approaches often adopted by scholars of Iranian political and economic history neglect the value of women's domestic work for the society and economy because it is wageless and contains no exchange value. Similarly, the scattered economic data offer aggregated information on employment as a whole, thereby failing to provide specific knowledge on the work patterns of women and men. Thus, women's work and their contribution to Iran's economy of the early twentieth-century remain underestimated.[10]

During the early 1900s, Iran's overall economy experienced a slow transformation from a subsistence to a market economy. One of the features of societies undergoing such a change is that household production is still united with production for the market; the two are not separate spheres as they are under advanced capitalist systems. As a result, women's work in the market, to the extent that it exists, remains an extension of their work at home and their reproductive activities. Depending on

[9] "Financial situation," Farman Farmaian, 18–19.

[10] Economic data, Issawi; Bhahrier; Baldwin; Katouzian; Amuzegar; and Looney.

the kinds of work they performed, working Iranian women often combined child rearing with their tasks in the larger economy. Not all women worked outside the family. Those who did, they struggled against poverty, whether single or married, or as child laborers. While these women encountered male domination both in the household and in the marketplace, the economically secure women stayed home and experienced patriarchy more directly there. Gender subordination varied by class insofar as women's work was concerned.

Women's work was diverse. Many poor women worked as carpet weavers, vendors, domestic laborers, and seamstresses. Quantitative data on the actual number of these women and their distribution are unavailable. Scattered sources, however, confirm their participation in paid production. Iranian carpet weavers, especially young girls with nimble fingers, are well known throughout the world. Iranian carpets, famous for their fine and miniature weaves have been traditionally produced by small hands, sometimes of men, but more often of women and children. In the nineteenth-century, in order to maximize profits that were returned to the West, "European firms set up organizations [in cities] for the systematic collection of Persian carpets." The carpet industry helped the domestic economy and it partially "counterbalanced the deindustrialization that took place in those areas of the economy [textile production, handicrafts, and other works involving artisans] which came into direct competition with imports from the West." Women played a crucial economic role for an industry whose growth is described as "fortuitous for the economy."[11] One observer noted:

> Carpet weavers worked under deplorable conditions. The factories were damp and cold; with the looms crowded in back to back, and the workers crouched on a wooden plank shelf or scaffolding. The scaffold is more or less typical picture of a number of small factories, which average from six to fourteen looms with five workers at a loom. Some of the factories are doubtless even worse.[12]

The typical earnings of female carpet weavers cannot be accurately determined from the available sources. But one report indicates that some women received a net wage of not more than two Qerans ($.02) per working day. Another source based on a private memoir suggests that instead of a money wage, some women received other forms of compensation, sometimes to benefit male members of their family. A woman who was an

[11] "European," "deindustrialization," and "fortuitous," McDaniel, 41.
[12] "Weavers," Woodsmall, 268.

adolescent in the early twentieth-century recalled girls from a city that produced prestigious carpets weaved days and nights for wealthy relatives in the carpet business in order to support the schooling cost and business training of their brothers. Such an example fits in with the family economy as it existed in Iran at the turn of the century. Women worked not for their own interest, but for the interest of the family as a whole. Carpet weaving formed an exploitative industry in which weavers worked hard, received little, and experienced no control over the products of their labor.[13]

Not confined to weaving alone, women's work in carpet factories served as an extension of their reproductive tasks. Specifically, responsibility for children's care rested with young working mothers at their work place. One observer noted that "Many of the children have spent most of their lives in the factory, brought in as infants and 'parked' all day by the mothers' looms. In order not to interfere with the speed of the mother, since her wage depends on her speed, the child is usually half-drugged" with opium. Similar drugging practices were reported during the Industrial Revolution in Western Europe. Child rearing in factories complicated the workload of working mothers, while benefiting the industries' owners.[14]

Raised in this unhealthy work atmosphere, children learned the skills of weaving and many became carpet weavers themselves. Indeed, workshops or factories actively recruited both girls and boys, already at ages five, six and seven. Except for the master weavers, it was usually children who produced the finer, superior weaves; hence, the proprietors particularly profited from child labor. In some factories almost one-fifth or more of the workers were under ten years of age.[15] A report from the city of Kerman concluded that children

> work from sunrise till sunset, week in, week out, with but a half day off on Friday for holiday. The work is carried out in ill-ventilated hovels, warmed in the cold winter only by the heat of their bodies, and over-heated in the summer by sheer want of air and space. Thus many fall victim to a very crippling form of late rickets, which affects not only the bones of the arms and legs, but those of the skeleton of the body also. One result is a gross form of knot-knee, which renders walking difficult or impossible, so that many children have had to be carried by their parents to and from their homes.[16]

[13] $.02, Woodsmall, 268; and training of their brothers, private memoir in possession of the author.

[14] "Half drugged," Woodsmall, 267; and Industrial Revolution, Engles; and Thompson.

[15] "Child labor," Rice, 256.

[16] "Work from sunrise to sunset," *Ibid.*

If they survived, girls usually experienced severe damage to their health as they grew older. For many, factory work brought serious injury or death, and for both poor women and their children, the struggle against poverty brought serious health hazards, if not loss of life. But the work of poor women, regardless of their marital status, was often essential to the survival of the household in a fluid subsistence economy.[17]

Women also worked as vendors at the bazaars, the locus of commercial and financial activities in larger cities. Some of these vendors were seamstresses who made garments at home before taking them to market for sale. At the *bazaar*, vendors would "sit on the ground in rows, in their black chadors and with their veils down, almost under the feet of horses and donkeys and men, with their goods for sale in front of them." Such work was not lucrative. It might happen that a vendor sold only one shirt in a whole day. Even when failing to earn much, vendors worked in a marginal economy to help support their husbands, children, and other members of their extended households.[18]

Women's work extended to other areas. Those with superior needle skills produced embroidery and hand-crafted clothes, shoes, and fabrics at home for merchants who supplied capital. Such patterns of putting out system or cottage industry are typical of early market economy everywhere. Many women also worked as cheap domestic laborers for wealthy families, particularly in Tehran and Tabriz. Some earned low wages, many received only food and shelter in return for their services, and a few were sexually abused by the household head or physically punished. In addition, many others begged in the streets for food or money, while a few drew small incomes as fortune tellers, *dallaks* (bath attendants), *rakhtshoors* (laundresses), prostitutes, and dancers and singers for private parties. Some were saleswomen outside of the *bazaars*, selling jewelry, cosmetics, and fabrics house-to-house. More professional women included healers, midwives, and leaders of religious ceremonies. Those familiar with Iranian *Shi'i* practices made a small living by conducting popular religious ceremonies such as the rituals of mourning, *Qoran-khani* (gatherings to read the holy Muslim book), *rouzeh-khani* (gatherings to commemorate religious rituals and history), and participating in *sufreh* (religious

[17] "Severe damage," – whether single or married, women of all ages worked as weavers. Although Iranian men disapproved of factory work for their womenfolk, women's work was essential to the family and the economy. At the Oriental Carpet Factory in the city of Hamedan, many women workers were married, and many were over twenty years of age. Woodsmall, 267.

[18] "Sit on the ground in rows," Rice, 91.

feasts). A few religious women reached the level of *mojtahed* (Islamic scholars).[19]

Thus, Iran was not simply a "country of men." While it is inarguable that the practice of seclusion fostered a certain public invisibility, it hardly impeded the mobility and workplace activity of women engaged in the struggle for survival. The work of these women usually differed from that of men in their families, yet it was part of a joint struggle against poverty. Nonetheless, both husbands and employers controlled women's work. Poor women faced subordination at work in terms of lack of control over production and the products of their labor. Seclusion failed to protect women's work beyond the home; rather the *andaruni* and its more modest equivalents formed a part of an enveloping patriarchal structure that extended from the household to the marketplace. As a result, whatever the value of a woman's work in the market, it was likely to be compatible with her reproductive task, especially children's care. In this phase of Iran's development – as at comparable earlier stages in capitalist economies – household labor and commodity production formed a continuum. Moreover, however limited and unremunerative women's paid work may have been, it should no more be excluded from analysis of the economy than the tasks performed for the maintenance of life and the reproduction of future generations of laborers.

Economically secure women spent much of their time at home. Women with fewer means participated in child rearing and cleaning and sewing. They devoted much of their time and labor to cooking and preparing food, for example, cleaning grain, breaking sugar into lumps, milling salt and spices, and making bread. They also washed family clothes by hand. Although there is little data on the role of servants in this period, even women of modest means had the help of maids in performing their household tasks. Women in wealthier families had fewer responsibilities related to child rearing as their servants performed tasks and managed family activities. Rich women embroidered, made sweets and sherbets, practiced the piano and such traditional musical instruments as the harmonica or the tar, and they read and studied poetry and literature.[20]

Saved from worries about survival, wealthier women endured seclusion at home. If they had an interest in working outside the family – and there

[19] "Putting out system," Tilly and Scott; sexually abused, Sultanzadeh, 105–106; prostitutes, *Ibid.*; and *mojtahed*, Sykes, 96–97.

[20] Preparing food, Sykes, 96–97; and piano, Rice, 198. Given the limited number of educational institutions for women, many had their fathers or elder male relatives as tutors.

is no documentary support for this – Iran's economic backwardness, bare urbanization, and its strict prescription of female seclusion would have provided no rewarding employment. Contrary to the case of poor women, class position prevented these women from joining the market. Spared harsh treatment by employers, they depended on their menfolk; and their familial dependency on men protected them from the bitter realities of the marketplace. Men's control in the household may have also limited their mobility and participation in paid production. Thus, more secluded and less mobile than their poor sisters, patriarchy and class restrained the activities of privileged women. But their work at home was accorded no recognized exchange value – unlike even the patriarchal exchange value acknowledged in the marriage contract and other religious customs.

WOMEN AND RELIGION

As elsewhere in the Middle East, religion and culture powerfully affected women's lives. A "culture continent," the Middle East is often seen in terms of Islam as the "total way of life." In this view, Islam is "the fundamental motivating force behind most aspects of culture [which] has its way in practically every act and moment in life." Thus, Islam is identified as a homogeneous, immutable, fixed, and ahistorical force, one that transcends specific social contexts. Within the monolithic rubric of "Islam," political entities lose their cultural and historical specificity, and religion becomes the greatest determinant of social relationships, particularly the social construction of gender. Such perceptions, however, ignore historical variations in the theoretical and political development of Islam as well as the diverse experiences of women, as determined by such factors as class and politics, patriarchy, and women's struggles.[21]

Islam came to Iran with the Muslim Arab conquest in A.D. 637–651. *Shi'ism* was adopted as a state religion in 1501, though it co-existed with other religions. At the turn of the twentieth-century, there existed a Muslim majority and a non-Muslim minority. The former was itself divided into *Shi'i* majority and *Sunni* minority, but even the *Shi'is* had their own schismatic divisions. Non-Muslims included, among others, Zoroastrians, Jews, and Christians (especially Armenians). Not only was there strife among these religious groups, but whether their adherents

[21] "Culture continent," and "total way," Patai, Chs. 1–5; and "motivating force," and "homogeneous," Gilsenon, 1–28 and Ch. 5.

lived in tribes, villages, or towns, each had its own customs and cultural practices. Iran's religious diversity thus complicated its "ethnic mosaic."[22]

From the sixteenth until the present century, Iranianism and *Shi'ism* blended for many people. *Shi'ism* was "neither a mere reflection of Iranian social relations nor its sole determinant"; rather, it became "inextricably interwoven within Iranian social relations." But both *Shi'ism* and Islam in general have undergone significant changes over time and in various societies. How and why different Muslims adopted their own variations in religious doctrine and practices is a complex task beyond the scope of this study. As it concerns women, one view considers Islam as a "patriarchal system of thought," while another argues that Islam intended to improve women's social position. It is worth noting that "What is special about Islam in regard to women is the degree to which matters relating to women's status have either been legislated by the *Qoran*, which believing Muslims regard as the literal word of God as revealed to the Prophet, or by subsequent legislation derived from interpretations of the *Qoran* and the traditional sayings of the prophet." Both the religious interpreters and the legislators have, of course, always been men.[23]

Revering women, the Prophet Mohammad introduced fundamental and profound changes in tribal practices concerning women. In a *Qoranic* revelation, he forbade the practice of burying unwanted baby girls. He also instructed his followers to respect their mothers, for "Heaven is under the mother's feet." Further, the *Qoran* commanded that: "We have charged men to be kind to their parents – their mothers bore them with hardships and painfully gave birth to them." Significantly, a *Qoranic* injunction highlighted gender equality by specifying that men and women were "created from potter's clay" or "the union of two sexes," as against the *Genesis* account of man's rib. This revelation concurs with the Islamic notion of *Adl* or justice, in which all Muslims, regardless of their sex, are equal before God.[24]

22 "Ethnic mosaic," Abrahamian, *Iran*, 15–18, and 27–28. – Divisions included the Mujahedin Twelvers, the major schisms of Shaikhism and Babism and other sects such as the Isma'ilies, Ni'matis, and Haydaris.

23 Iranianism, Yeganeh and Nikki, 109; "Iranian social relations," *Ibid.*; "patriarchal," "system of thoughts," Azari, 7–9; improve women's social position, Coulson and Hitchcliff; and "God," Beck and Keddie, 25.

24 Burying unwanted baby girls, *Qoran-e Majid* [the Koran], 6.141; mothers bore them, *Ibid.*, 46.15; and "Potter's Clay," "union of Two," and "*the Genesis*," Azari, "Islam's Appeal to Women," 1–7.

When applied to particular contexts, these prescribed notions of equality and justice sometimes seem at odds with gender relations in particular situations. For instance, Islam designated monogamy as a rule for women, but it allowed polygamy to men, although restricted to four permanent wives and limited to circumscribed conditions. To this end, the *Qoran* advised men: "Marry women who seem to be good, just and proper to you, two or three or four, not more; and if you fear you cannot do justice to them, then marry one only." Another section of the same *sureh* (a *Qoranic* chapter) referred to the difficulty of exercising justice among wives. It threatened husbands: "God is well aware of your actions. If you cannot treat your wives justly – for it is beyond your control not to admire the more beautiful and younger wives – even if it is your ardent wish, then, do not discriminate among them. Give your wives equal allowances." This passage seems to enjoin polygamous husbands to treat their wives equally in financial terms, no matter the physical attraction. Thus, polygamy, though conditional, was accorded to men as a right: a limited, but inalienable right. Women had *no* right to polyandry.[25]

Polygamy was practiced in Iran before the Islamic conquest and continued with Islam. Like most religions, early Islam incorporated "polygamy, repudiation, the prohibition of '*Zina*' [sexual union of unmarried couples] and practices to guarantee, physical paternity." Some pre-Islamic Arabian tribes treated women more decently than others in the Peninsula, and some women enjoyed freedom and independence from their husbands. A custom that allowed men to have sexual access to multiple women in Arabic is called the *mote'h*, or its Persian equivalent, the *siqeh* (temporary marriage for a designated time and price). Pre-dating Islam, the *Sunnis* forbade it, but the *Shi'is* legitimized it. At the turn of the twentieth-century in Iran, polygamy was class-based, practiced only by the elite and wealthy men. It is more common in today's Iran, being encouraged by the government, especially after the eruption of the Iran-Iraq War of 1980–88.[26]

[25] "Marry one only," *Qoran-e Majid*, 4.3; and "equal allowances," *Ibid.*, 4.127 and 4.128. A different interpretation is that "Even within the *Quran*... men are told that, unless they fear they cannot treat them (women) equally, they may marry up to four wives; but later in the same *sureh* men are told that no matter how hard they try they will not be able to treat their wives equally – exactly the same Arabic verb for 'equal treatment' is used both times." Yeganeh and Keddie, 113.

[26] *Zina*, Beck and Keddie, 25 who note that "virility- fidelity-son producing ethos, a sexual double standard" existed in the Middle East and other parts of the world prior to Islam. Some women enjoyed freedom – early Muslim women who were related to Mohammad as Fatemeh, Khadijeh, Ayesheh, and Zeynab were public figures and active in politics; *mote'h*, Haeri; and pre-dating Islam, Yeganeh and Keddie, 115–116.

Another contentious subject concerns the marriage contract under Islam. Generally, *nekah* (marriage), as an Arabic term denotes sexual intercourse of a man and a woman. Subject of various interpretations of the *Shari'eh* (Islamic Law), *nekah* is seen as a contract guaranteeing domination over the woman's sexual organ, so that, according to the *Qoran*, the husband "may enjoy affection and relaxation in [his wife's] company." But *nekah* is an oral contract in which the husband realizes the ownership of intercourse at the outset. In the case of a woman slave, the right to intercourse followed from ownership of the slave, without requiring her contractual agreement. In a marriage contract, the woman herself must give her consent for the contract to be legal. The groom pays the *sadaq* (nuptial gift or *mehr*) to the bride.[27] A marriage contract legalizes men's dominance and possession of women's bodies and sexuality. While the contract ensures women's sexual objectification, the brideprice varies according to the class position of bride and groom. Traditionally, the wealthier a bride's or groom's family, the more *mehr* would be required. In the 1960s and 1970s, many urban educated Iranian women had their husbands substitute less expensive and more symbolic objects such as a volume of the *Qoran* or flowers for the *mehr*, thus undercutting what they saw to be a demeaning sale of their bodies. Recent economic hardships have led to the exchange of more valuable objects and money in marriage contracts among women.

Veiling and women's modesty are other debated themes. The *Qoran* instructed women to "cover yourself in the veil so as to be honorably protected from passion-seekers." The Prophet further advised women to:

> Cover your eyes and bodies and not display ornaments and beauty except those that ordinarily appear. Draw veils over face, shoulders and bosoms. Do not reveal ornaments and beauty except to your own husbands, fathers,... sons, brothers,... women... and children unaware of your nakedness.... Do not take steps in ways to show your hidden beauties of legs and feet....

Historian Nikki Keddie suggested that veiling is interpretative, not a mandatory religious practice. The practice, she observes, "is nowhere enjoined in the *Qur'an* [*Qoran*]." The widely held interpretation that women should "cover hair, neck, forearms, and so on is linguistically farfetched." The passages cited, however, suggest that the key concept is "covering." Both the Arabic and Persian versions of the *Qoran* as

[27] "May enjoy," *Qoran-e Majid*, 7.189; and marriage contract, Haeri, 29, and 36, and note 8.

quoted above clearly commands women to cover themselves and their bodies. What is open to interpretation is the extent, shape, and style of the veil, which has taken different forms in different societie at different times.[28]

Like polygamy, veiling did not begin with Islam. The court women of the Achemenian Empire practiced it in the sixth-century. It also existed in the Byzantine and Sassanian Empires before it spread to Muslim Arabs in the seventh-century. During the early twentieth-century, Iranian women were publicly veiled, though they wore different customs in different parts of the country. With the 1936 unveiling decree (*Kashf-e Hejab*), wealthy urban and educated women abandoned the veil, while the rest of the society continued to practice veiling in accordance with its local traditions. From the 1950s to the late 1970s, as unveiling became more acceptable among urban and educated women, especially the more Westernized middle-class and elite women, it gradually made inroads in other parts of the country and other classes. In postrevolutionary Iran, the regime institutionalized the *hejab* and enforced reveiling. Thus, veiling, unveiling, and reveiling are highly political issues, influenced by class, state, patriarchal structures, and cultural mandates. How women themselves have interpreted, accepted, or rejected veiling will be explored later.[29]

Perhaps enjoining male dominance is the most implicit religious revelation. The *Qoran* makes women subject to men, who as husbands and breadwinners have the right to punish them:

> Men have dominating and protecting rights over women because they provide them with subsidy. Therefore, tamed and worthy wives must guard their husbands' rights in their absence... and those women who mismanage their allowance, [exhorting husbands:] admonish them first. If they are not tamed, avoid copulation. If they still refuse to obey, scourge them. If they then comply, seek no more punishment.[30]

Such a *sureh* highlights male dominance over women, who are clearly subordinated to their husbands' will and whims. By controlling and privatizing women, men achieve patriarchal status, gaining power at home and in the society. The postrevolutionary Iranian state, in immediately reveiling women, signaled its larger intention to restore patriarchal power.

[28] "Cover yourself," and "Cover your eyes," *Qoran-e Majid*, 4.31 and 7.189; and "is nowhere" and "farfetched," Keddie in Yeganeh and Keddie, 113.

[29] Byzantine and Sassanian, Keddie, *Roots*, 14.

[30] "Punishment," *Qoran-e Majid*, 4.34.

Ownership and property and inheritance rights are other controversial themes. Although Islam supports private property rights in general, women have fewer rights than men. Women are granted the right to hold private property, and the *Qoran* permitted married and divorced women to keep their dowries. Husbands must give their wives a share of their property. The earnings of married couples are safeguarded, for "to men and women, there is a right in what they have earned." But inheritance rights always favored men, women received much less than men; *Shi'i* Islam assigned a daughter a share half as large as her brother's, while a wife's share was one-eighth as large as her son's; the husband's share of his wife's legacy, on the other hand, was one-fourth that of her children. Single women received even less than married ones although they acquired neither an allowance nor the brideprice. With respect to women's right to hold and control property, especially in regard to the family *waqf* (property assigned to endowments), there have been variations according to time, place, and class.[31]

Over the centuries, *Qoranic* legal rulings supported significant changes in different societies. Although many Islamic injunctions were based on Arabic customs, some of them had analogues in ancient Iran. Even the Islamic legal scholars who believe that the *Qoran*'s original intent was to advance women's social position, agree that "the general Quranic [Qoranic] norms and injunctions suffered progressive dilution...." As a result, the *Qoranic* provisions regarding women's status in the family were "dissipated and largely lost" and "Islamic law continued to reflect the patriarchal and patrilineal nature of society based upon the male agnatic tie." While male domination reinforced religious laws concerning women, pre-established mores – some encouraged by Islam and others prohibited by it – were sanctioned by legislators, *Qoranic* interpreters, or men in positions of power. Thus, religion became a weapon to legitimate men's personal and political power.[32]

Despite the heavy burden of patriarchal authority, some Iranian women found ways to go around the system and assert their interests. A few expressed their protests in particular responses to national and

[31] Dowries, *Qoran-e Majid*, 4.4 and 2.232; "a share of their property," *Ibid.*, 4.4, and 4.5; "they have earned," *Ibid.*, and 4.32; and women's right to hold and control property, Yeganeh and Keddie. Some justify unequal inheritance by arguing that married women receive *nafaqeh* (allowance) and *mehr*, but men will not always provide support, and seldom pay the *mehr*. Moreover, the economic support for single women, at least, theoretically, remains unclear.

[32] "Injunctions," "dissipated," and "male agnatic," Coulson and Hinchcliffe, 37–38.

international politics. This broader stage perhaps fostered women's ability to transcend local customs and cultural pressures. In any case, this reaction articulated women's own aspirations, as well as general political themes.

NATIONAL AND INTERNATIONAL POLITICS

Absolutism ruled Iran during the Qajar dynasty from 1796 to 1925. Of tribal origin, the Qajar kings – in Persian the shahs – and their legions of royal relatives headed the court. Ruling with "total power," they emulated the style of ancient Persian emperors and aimed at glorification of their power. But in order to do so, they had to celebrate and exalt *Shi'ism*. Still, they failed to obtain the sanction of religious leaders who believed that they, not the temporal leaders, should lead the public. Although some members of the religious establishment were willing to identify with the throne, most high-ranking clergymen "remained aloof from the court and interpreted the earthly texts of *Shi'ism* to argue that the state was at worst inherently illegitimate and at best a necessary evil to prevent social anarchy."[33]

The Qajars ultimately succumbed to colonialism and its designs on Iran. The European influences that had begun in sixteenth-century Iran, took the form of competing military pressure by the Russian and the British in the early nineteenth-century. By mid-century, through devastating wars and military expeditions, Iran had "lost its independence and moved into a semi-colonial situation." The British needed Iran to maintain their Indian empire and to secure markets for their exports, while the Russians were interested in annexation and political and commercial domination. The wars were humiliating. They ended in disgracing treaties, which resulted in the loss of Iranian territories, payment of a large indemnity, the granting of several commercial capitulations to Russia and Britain, and general economic decline and poverty. With the help of the colonialists, the Qajars "bled the country dry by selling lands, concessions, privileges, and even peasants into slavery [while] squandering the revenues on palaces, luxuries, pensions, presents, and foreign trips."[34]

Iranians responded to the policies of the domestic despots and their colonial lords. One such reaction culminated in the Tobacco Protest of 1891–92 against the granting of a monopoly over the production, sale, and

33 "Total power," Ashraf, "The Historical," 307–327; and "social anarchy," Abrahamian, *Iran*, 47 and 40.

34 Early nineteenth, Banani, 3; and Ashraf, "The Historical," 322; "semi-colonial," Abrahamian, *Iran*, 52; and "foreign trips," *Ibid.*, 70, note 31.

export of all of Iran's tobacco to the British. As the concession threatened the profits of domestic businesses, massive protests began against the government and the concession. Some prominent *ulama* [religious scholars] led and mobilized the popular movement against the government. Participating in the revolt were *ulama*, reformists with secular tendencies, merchants, and ordinary urban people, including women.

Active in bread riots and other urban uprisings, women continued this tradition in the Tobacco Protest. Zinat Pasha, a woman from the city of Tabriz, who is described as "passionate, brave and enlightened," led a group of armed and veiled women in the *bazaar* against the concession. Their protest closed down the *bazaar*. In a direct Tobacco Protest in proximity to the seat of power, "harem women, broke their waterpipes in front of the king and vehemently resisted his absolutism." Indeed it is reported that Naser al-Din Shah's (1848–96) most influential wife, Anis al-Dowleh, helped spread the riots. Popular resistance eventually led to cancellation of the agreement by the government. While "many of the ulama were bought off by the government and some quiet years followed," as Keddie noted, "the 'religious-radical alliance' had shown its potential for changing the course of Iranian policy.... The basic alliance of *bazaaris* (especially merchants), ulama, and secular or modernist reformers continued to be important."[35]

The colonial impact went beyond the foiled tobacco concession. Iran's economic structure was slowly being corrupted according to patterns typical of colonial rule. This was most evident in the establishment of foreign banks by Britain and Russia, which took control of Iran's financial system, which in turn led these governments to intervene on behalf of the interest of their traders, investors, and nationals who controlled major economic institutions. Foreign trade also adversely affected the economy and especially the middle-classes. Although during the course of the nineteenth-century the total volume of trade increased, the overall trade balance and the trade remained unfavorable to Iran. The British and Russians encouraged exports of cotton, dried fruits and nuts, opium, and carpets, which they promoted through low tariffs and exports to Iran of their manufactured goods. The growth of trade thus undermined Iran's local industry as imported foreign goods superseded Iranian products, and exported

[35] "Passionate, brave," Ghavimi, 104–104. Pasha organized women against the tyrannical king and when she discovered the rich were hoarding the grain stock, especially during famine, she led the revolt of the poor against them. Little data exist on women protesters' background or their lives in the *bazaar*; "harem women," Bamdad, Zan-e II, 5; "quite years," Keddie, *Roots*, 65; and "religious-radical alliance," *Ibid.*, 67, 35, and 65–67.

raw materials replaced manufactured goods. By weakening the Iranian handicrafts and manufactures, the competitive position of Iranian merchants and products vis-à-vis foreign products and commercial agents declined. Simultaneously, an emerging dependent bourgeoisie replaced a failing independent bourgeoisie. Finally, some middle-classes, the urban *bazaaris* who had ties to the clergy, became aware "of its own predicament for the first time and coalesced into one cross-regional grouping," the "traditional middle-class."[36]

Contact with the West, through travel, translations, and modern educational institutions was important in the formation of a new professional middle-class or the intelligentsia. Some of these intellectuals were aristocrats and royal princes, while others were civil servants and army officers, clerics, and merchants. They were persuaded by their understanding of Western history that human progress was possible to attain if they defeated "royal despotism, clerical dogmatism, and foreign imperialism." Desiring to establish a modern and developed Iran, they thought that their goals could be realized through "constitutionalism, secularism, and nationalism." Nationalism, though it had a history in Iran, grew in reaction to Western encroachment. Paradoxically, its new appeal was an "emulation of Western patriotism as a supreme virtue." The 1905–11 Constitutional Revolution incorporated these aspirations; it was a successful popular revolt against colonialism and despotism, a revolt that witnessed the growing participation of women.[37]

THE CONSTITUTIONAL REVOLUTION AND WOMEN'S PARTICIPATION

During the first half of the nineteenth-century, the Qajars responded to Western challenges by inaugurating minor reforms. These included programs to modernize the military; to establish factories, supply the army,

[36] Colonial rule, British and Russian banks also took control of Iran's financial system. See Keddi, "Oil, Economic policy," 15. Foreign trade, Katoozian, 46; trade balance, Ashraf, "The Historical," 325; exported raw, Keddie, "The Economic History," 71; dependent bourgeoisie, Ashraf "the Historical"; and "traditional middle-class," Abrahamian, *Iran*, 50. He indicates that the middle-class was not uniform. A component of the middle-class, the urban *bazzaris*, had ties with the *Shi'i* clergy and is referred to as Iran's "traditional middle-class." Another segment of the middle-class or the intelligentsia and a new professional middle-class who became inspired by Western ideas. Through its modern studies and educational institutions, it learned about liberalism, nationalism, socialism, and other related Western philosophies.

[37] "Royal despotism" and "constitutionalism," Abrahamian, *Iran*, 50, 61–69, especially 62; and "supreme virtue," Banani, 10 and 14–15. Earlier forms of Iranian nationalism date back to the Achamenins, Sassanians, and the *Shi'i* opposition against their Sunni neighbors.

and cut imports; to build Dar al-Fonun, the first secular high school for aristocratic male students; to dispatch male students to Europe for the first time to study military sciences, engineering, and modern languages; and to print the first official newspaper. Amir Kabir, a modernizing prime minister initiated some of those projects. But Malek-Jahan Mahd-e Olya, the powerful mother of Naser al-Din Shah (1848–96) halted his reforms and ordered his assassination. Henceforth, many of the reform programs were scrapped. Those which continued, displayed little impact on Iran's declining political and economic situation that in turn spawned rising social discontent.[38]

This discontent peaked in 1906 when, through a series of protests, demonstrations, and bloody clashes with the royal forces, a coalition of intellectuals, *bazaaris*, the *ulama*, and women compelled Mozaffar al-Din Shah (1896–1906) to accept the constitution. The intelligentsia strove for nationalism, secularism, and constitutionalism. During the Constitutional Revolution, they supported the *ulama* against both the monarch and foreign powers. The *bazaaris* and merchants, angry over economic crisis and especially the king's price policies, also joined the clergy in protest. As the movement grew from 1905 through 1906, the clergy and theology students became increasingly active. Their demands included enforcement of the *Shari'eh* and establishment of a Judiciary Department. Women joined, too. Initially mobilized by the *ulama*, they took part in anti-governmental and anti-colonialist demonstrations and strikes. Later, they incorporated some independent demands, including the recognition of their *anjomans* (societies), the launching of girl's schools and suffrage rights.[39]

The numerous studies on the Constitutional Revolution have concentrated mainly on the role of various male actors. Almost always, women fall outside their purview. "Except for a few isolated references here and there,"one historian wrote, "most available sources hardly mention women." Such exclusionary works create the illusion that "the revolution was strictly a man's affair, expressing only men's nationalist aspiration for freedom and self-expression. It certainly was not." Indeed, women "played a unique role in transforming the essentially political revolution of 1906 into the beginnings of a social revolution." Secluded and veiled women may have exhibited political power that changed the course of history for Iranian women and men.[40]

[38] Olya, Ghavimi, 103.

[39] Intelligentsia, Abrahamian, *Iran*, Ch. 2; and women, Bayat-Phillip, 295–299; and Nateq, 45–54.

[40] "Isolated references," "mention women," and "the Revolution," Bayat-Phillip, 295; and Nateq, 45–54; and "social revolution," Afari, "On the Origins," 69.

Women's participation in the constitutional movement was reminiscent of, though somewhat different from, the Tobacco Protest. Like their predecessors, they were nationalists and anti-colonialists; they wanted an independent Iran, free from foreign hegemony. But, in the early twentieth-century, they also wanted a constitution, education, and enfranchisement. By 1906, some women had organized separate women's societies that were first secret, but subsequently became public. Others participated in demonstrations, street riots, boycotts, and armed clashes. A few made donations to the nationalist cause. Women gave "an unabating moral support" to male revolutionaries and "did much to keep the spirit of liberty alive."[41] Women's initial participation might have been inspired by religious zeal in that, "Most probably [they] were acting upon the *ulama*'s instructions." Other studies substantiate this claim. In 1906, a large number of women protesters stopped the carriage of the monarch, asking him to respect the wishes of the clergy and not succumb to foreign powers. They demanded: "We want the masters and leaders of our religion! The masters have helped us keep our properties! King of the Muslims, ... if Russia and England support you, upon the orders of Muslim leaders, Iranians will declare *jihad* against you."[42]

The revolutionary movement succeeded in compelling the monarch to sign a proclamation to create the *Majles* (the National Consultative Assembly), on October 7, 1906. Shortly after, they propelled him to ratify the Fundamental Laws of the Constitution on December 30, 1906, only a few days before his death. Following the revolutionary triumph to establish a constitutional government, women withdrew slowly their support of religious authorities. As will be discussed later, they became disillusioned with the *ulama* who dismissed their demands for girls' education and legalization of their organizations. Despite this temporary setback, women's commitment to the constitution remained. One of the projects of the first *Majles* was the creation of a national bank, which would reduce Iran's dependence on foreign loans by borrowing funds from the natives. Women responded decisively: women workers invested their small wages, some parted with their jewelry, while others turned in their cash and their inheritances. They also boycotted imported fabrics and wore and encouraged others to use Iranian textiles.[43]

[41] "An unbating," Shuster, 195 and 191.

[42] "*Ulama*'s instructions," Bayat-Phillip, 299; and "*jihad*," Kasravi; and Bamdad, Zan-e II, 6.

[43] Textiles, Bamdad II, 38 and 15; Bayat-Phillip, 299; and Afari, "On the Origins," 69.

Some women took up arms in support of the constitution. In 1911, as Russia occupied parts of northern Iran and presented various demands, including an ultimatum to occupy Tehran within forty-eight hours, the monarchy and royalist forces decided to give in to Russian pressure. While the *Majles* debated the ultimatum, women mobilized in response. They met in a mosque to debate and draw up a plan of action. "Behind the mosque curtains," an observer wrote: "mass meetings of women were held, where fiery speeches were delivered on Iranian independence." One woman announced that "although the law of Islam forbade it, the women would nevertheless take part in a holy war [against the Russians.]"[44]

The women were determined and spirited. As the *Majles* debates continued, "three hundred women marched into the public galleries with pistols hidden under their long veils, and threatened to shoot any deputy willing to submit to the Russian ultimatum."[45] In an eyewitness account, Morgan Shuster, the American treasurer-general in Tehran, corroborated this version of the event:

> Out from their walled courtyards and harems marched three hundred of that weak sex, with the flush of undying determination in their cheeks. They were clad in their robes with the white nets of their veils dropped over their faces. Many held pistols under their skirts or in the folds of their sleeves. Straight to the Majlis they went, and, gathered there, demanded of the President that he admit them all.... In this [the President's] reception-hall they confronted him and lest he and his colleagues should doubt their meaning, these cloistered Persian mothers, wives and daughters exhibited threateningly their revolvers, tore aside their veils, and confessed their decision to kill their own husbands and sons, and leave behind their own dead bodies, if the deputies wavered in their duty to uphold the liberty and dignity of the Persian people and nation.[46]

The *Majles* deputies who received the women's message later said: "the women teach us how to love our country."[47]

This was not the first time women had resorted to arms. As in the Tobacco Protest, in 1908, after one of a series of battles in Azerbaijan between anti-constitutional royalist forces and the local population, "twenty female bodies, clad in men's clothes, were found among the dead." Another young Constitutionalist who had been wounded but had

44 "Behind" and "Mass meetings," Malekzadeh, III, 62; and "holy war," Bayat-Phillip, 303 and 308, especially 38th reference.

45 "Three hundred women," Shuster, 192.

46 Shuster, Shuster, *Ibid.*

47 "Love," Woodsmall, *Muslim*, 364. Despite the protests and popular discontent, foreign pressure eventually brought about the downfall of the *Majles*.

refused to undress and receive medical attention, finally confessed to the crowd and supporters that: "I am not a man, but a woman."[48]

How many women participated in the revolution and their class background is unclear but scattered data suggest that thousands of women were involved. Bayat-Phillip and Shuster agree that a number of these women, particularly those active in the *anjomans* and those who had formed the nucleus of resistance, came from wealthy urban women classes and included daughters and wives of the king, princes, *ulama*, and *Majles* deputies. Sultanzadeh suggests that this women's movement consisted of wealthy women, without any participation by proletariat women. This view differs from Bamdad's description of the small financial contributions made by some working-class women to the national bank. Moreover, the crowd scenes and demonstrations that Malekzadeh, Bamdad, Abrahamian, and Shuster describe might conflict with the idea that active women in the movement were primarily from prosperous families. But in the absence of more concrete information, it is probable that women's class background played a significant role in women's participation – the higher the women's socio-economic background, the more extensive their political activities. There are no comparable studies of the class position of active women in the Tobacco Protest.[49]

Women's participation in the Constitutional Revolution discloses significant information regarding women's lives, their perspectives, national liberation struggles, and aspirations for women's progress. Women incorporated feminism into nationalism and anti-imperialism. Iranian women became "almost at a bound the most progressive, not to say radical, in the world," Shuster wrote. That "this statement upsets the ideas of centuries makes no difference. It is a fact." Despite the persistence of seclusion and gender inequality, women managed to leave their homes, organized the *anjomans*, and participated in the revolution. Torn and caught between the world of tradition and the tumultuous world of change, some women rose against patriarchal polity and society. Although a handful of men supported their cause, the majority of the male drafters of the constitution and the secular and religious revolutionaries – similar to the 1979 Revolution – failed to endorse women's demands. Women's right to suffrage remained postponed.[50]

[48] "Twenty female bodies," Sheikholeslami, 85; and Shuster, 191.

[49] Bayat-Phillip, 300; Shuster, 191; Sultanzadeh, 106; Abrahamian, *Iran*; and Bamdad, Zan-e I, 38.

[50] "This statement"and "ideas of centuries," Shuster, 191. Note that a handful of men who supported women's activites and gender equality during the constitutional era were journalists, writers, poets, and delegates to the Parliament and included Akhund-Zadeh,

REFORMS AND MEN'S, NOT WOMEN'S, SUFFRAGE

Mohammad Ali Shah (1907–09), whose father was challenged to accept a constitution in 1906, promulgated Supplementary Fundamental Laws on October 7, 1907. The main body of the constitution, which was based on the 1830 Belgian constitution, had introduced a parliamentary system of government. It curbed the power of the king by granting extensive powers of representation to the *Majles*, but as a concession, it conferred upon the monarch the authority to appoint senators. It also introduced a "bill of rights." Further, it set out to establish a Western liberal democracy with secular institutions, but without the separation of religion and state.[51]

Iranian constitutionalism "was almost wholly inspired by Western ideas," and the constitutional government was a "thoroughly Western importation." But the 1906 document mandated that all constitutional provisions were "subject to a strict conformity" with the *Shari'eh* and *ulama*'s approval. By trying to blend alien traditions with national practices, the 1906 constitution created a contradiction not resolved until the Revolution of 1979. Regarding gender and politics, few incompatibilities existed between the two different traditions; they both restricted to different degrees, if not excluded, women's participation from public activities.[52]

The 1906 constitution enfranchised men, but not women. It denied women political rights, although it guaranteed equal rights and protection to all Iranians. Article 5 of the 1906 Supplementary Fundamental Law stated that Iranians "are to enjoy equal rights before the law." But equal rights applied to men only; Article 1 of the 1906 Electoral Law

Ali-Akbar Dehkhoda, Mohammad Reza Eshqi, Iraj Mirza, Abdol-Qasem Lahouti, Malkom-Khan, Mirza Aqa-Khan Kermani, Seyyed Hossein Taqizadeh, Haj Sheikh Taqi, and Vakil al-Ra'aya.

51 "Bill of rights" and "separation of religion," Banani, 15–17.

52 "Ideas," "importation," and "strict," Banani, 17 and 15. For years, most Iranians firmly upheld the *Qoran*, *Shari'eh*, *hadith* (the sayings and traditions of Mohammad), the sayings and traditions of the *Shi'i emams* and *ejtehad* and *ejma'* (consensus and judgment based on the *Qoran*). Before the 1920s, there existed three systems of law: Islamic law, secular laws concerning water rights and land disputes, and the edicts of the kings regarding foreign affairs, taxes, and public security. While the constitution created several civil courts such as the criminal court and the court of appeals, it did not establish codes or procedures, and the *Shari'eh* dominated these courts. Prior to 1925, a temporary civil code and a commercial code were established. In 1928, the *Majles* approved a civil code based on primarily the French civil code. By 1940, as the courts were mostly advisory, the new legal system became a mixture of two different traditions, a Western one, and an Islamic one in strict conformity to the *Shari'eh*. See Frye, 95–98; and Browne, E. G., 374 and 356.

identified the electors as men of various propertied and non-propertied classes: it implicitly excluded women. Article 3 of the same law, explicitly prevented women from voting rights by stating that the persons who are "entirely deprived of electoral rights" include "Women;" those "in need of legal guardian;" "Foreigners;" persons with "mischievous opinions;" and "Murderers, Thieves, [and] Criminals," among others. Moreover, the constitution denied women the right to be elected as it recognized them in Article 5 of the 1906 Law and its 1909 Supplement to the constitutional outsiders. Furthermore, Article 2 excluded women's representation in the *Majles* because they failed to be "participants in the economic and political affairs of the country." Not only did the constitution prevent women from citizenship and classified them along with foreigners, minors, criminals, and murderers, but it also excluded them from electoral politics.[53]

Discriminatory laws failed to pacify women. Against men's sense of privilege, women insisted on an educational reform that guaranteed the right of all women to education. As early as 1906, a woman, whose identity remains unknown, petitioned one of the prominent *ulama* delegates to the *Majles* requesting the establishment of girls' schools similar to those for boys. But she was advised that her proposal was legitimate only to the extent that such schools would train girls to become superior mothers and wives. Unable to receive support from the conservative parliament members and that wing of the *ulama* that was antagonistic to their education, as will be discussed later, women turned against the established authorities and began their own independent initiatives without men's help.[54]

Women's next attempt was to file a petition and ask the *Majles* officially to recognize their *anjomans*. In 1908, they submitted their request. But their action created an uproar. A number of conservative *ulama* and wealthy merchants declared the *anjomans* "anti-Islamic" and "heretical." Supporting women, a few liberals argued that women's organizations had existed throughout Islamic history and could not be considered un-Islamic. Echoing their endorsements were the progressive members who debated the need to separate religious from secular laws. But the

[53] "Enjoy equal rights," "deprived of electoral rights," "need of legal guardians," and among others, Browne, E. G., 322–324; "participants," *Ibid.*, 374 and 356; criminals, *Ibid.*, 356 and 386–387; and electoral politics, *Ibid.*, 387, 363, and 377.

[54] *Majles, Parliamentary Proceedings*, First *Majles*; and Abrahamian, *Iran*, 93, note 91. Almost two years later, an uproar erupted in the *Majles* as deputies discovered that the family of deputy Eskandari had founded a school for girls and a society for women. Eskandari was married to Mohtaram, the socialist-feminist, who will be discussed later.

parliament rejected the women's petition. This did not silence the veiled and the so-called secluded women.[55]

Women's subsequent effort aimed at enfranchisement. Using parliamentary tactics, they approached their *Majles* supporters again. They petitioned the parliament through the liberal deputy Vakil al-Ra'aya in 1911. The *Times* of London, which provided the only coverage – in any language – of the *Majles* debates reported that Vakil al-Ra'aya had:

astonished the House by an impassioned defence of women's rights. The Mejliss [*Majles*] was quietly discussing the bill for the next election . . . and had reached the clause that no woman shall vote. . . . the House shivered when Vakil el Rooy [Vakil al-Ra'aya] mounted the tribune, and declared roundly that women possessed souls and rights, and should possess votes.

Vakil al-Ra'aya had then invited one of the powerful *ulama* deputies, Sheikh Asadollah, to deliver a speech in support of his proposal. Shocked apparently, Asadollah responded that he had "never in a life of misfortune had his ears assailed by such an impious utterance." "Nervously and excitedly," as the *Times* reported, "he denied to women either souls or rights," and declared that such doctrine would mean the "downfall of Islam." The debate failed to proceed further, as the Assembly's president called the discussion to end and ruled to exclude the proposal and debates from the Parliamentary records. "The Mejliss applauded!" But for unknown reasons, the *Times* printed a different version of the proceedings later. It construed Asadollah as responding: "We must not discuss this question, for it is contrary to the etiquette of Islamic Parliament." Women must nonetheless be excluded from electoral politics because:

God has not given them [women] the capacity needed for taking part in politics and electing the representative of the nation. They are the weaker sex, and have not the same power of judgment as men have. However, their rights must not be trampled upon, but must be safeguarded by men as ordained in the Koran [*Qoran*] by God Almighty.[56]

The Parliament did not discuss women's suffrage until the 1940s, although women continued their struggles by concentrating on their own specific gender interests. Women had nationalist and anti-imperialist

[55] *Parliamentary Proceedings*, First *Majles*, 483–485.

[56] "Possess votes," The *Times of London*, August 22, 1911; "never in a life," "nervously," "he denied," "downfall," and "applauded," *Ibid.*; and "Islamic Parliament" and "God Almighty," *Ibid.*, August 28, 1911. Asadollah thought women lacked "souls and rights," were a "weaker sex" with inferior "power of judgment." They required men's protection and were incapable of autonomy and independence, *Ibid.*

aspirations similar to those held by male participants in the Constitutional Revolution; however, their own autonomous goals were shared by few of their fellow supporters only. Yet the seeds of a growing Iranian feminism had been cultivated. Women's real struggles had just begun.

FEMINISM

Most specialists have investigated Iran as though kings, the *ulama*, and other male actors were the sole makers of history, and women, except as mothers or wives or queens, were bit players in politics and society. This is an inaccurate generalization. During the middle and end of the nineteenth-century, individual women voiced opposition to their condition. Toward the end of the century, there were sporadic organized activities by women, although in most cases, they were mobilized by men and the clergy. But during the early twentieth-century, and especially during the Constitutional Revolution, for the first time in Iran's history, women organized by themselves, through their own initiatives.

Women activists had no coherent ideology, organizational framework, specific leadership, or large followers. But unlike the 1979 Revolution, some of the turn-of-the-century women's organizations continued their work for several decades. Similar to other women's movements of the time in the developing world, Iranian women mobilized themselves, as nationalists, to free Iran from despotism and imperialism and to liberate themselves, as women and feminists, from patriarchy and tragic conditions of their lives. While the revolution brought into existence a variety of secular political groups, including liberals and social democratic parties, some of which aimed to "Europeanize" or "Westernize" Iran, as well as a number of Islamic reformist organizations, which wanted to incorporate modern ideas into the fiber of Islam's traditions, women also took initiatives to improve their own personal and public conditions. Through their organizations, educational endeavors, and publications, women began to articulate feminist ideas that spoke to their own gender interest, specifically women's good and benefit.

Feminist movements have typically encompassed ideas about women's historic and immediate oppression and exploitation and proposed actions to redress these injustices. Historically varied, feminism refers to women's movements that aim at the erosion of oppression and exploitation within which they live and are situated. Oppression denotes specific subjective and personal experiences that stem from women's positions in patriarchal relations, which are hierarchically structured and sanctioned by culture and tradition. By exploitation, I mean specific objective circumstances of women's lives that are derived from male dominance, whether exercised by a group, class, leaders, states, economies, or a combination of these that are interwoven with social and political structures of a specific society. Specific forms of oppression and exploitation differ through time and by class. How women articulate their ideas and respond as a group to these subjective and objective experiences determine the direction of a particular feminist movement. Iranian feminism, as a very small and sporadic activity, began at the turn of the century. It went roughly through three stages. Women's awakening had started earlier in history.[57]

The first stage of women's awakening can be dated in the first half of the nineteenth-century. At least one woman had proclaimed, publicly and individually, her concerns about women's condition. Named variously Fatemeh, Zarrin, Zakieh, and Om al-Saltaneh, she was better known as either Tahereh or Qorrat al-E'in (1815–51). A poet, orator, preacher, and debater, she was learned in Islamic studies and outspoken against the veil, marital relations, and polygamy. She was also notorious for her conversion from Islam to Babism, a religion considered by Muslims as blasphemous. Qorrat al-E'in came from a respectable religious family and married an Islamic leader, with whom she had one daughter and two sons. But her scholasticism and curiosity made her impatient with the ideas of her husband and father. She left her family and children and traveled from one city to another, meeting with intellectuals, learned religious men, and notables, while preaching Babism. Her knowledge had already gained her many friends and foes. During a debate in the city of Qazvin, she ordered the curtain between herself and the audience to be removed, thus revealing her uncovered face to men. She appeared "face unveiled in public." Whether her unveiling was accidental or purposeful remains unknown. She was assassinated probably by a Babi opponent, in Tehran at the age of 36. Because of her fervent Babism, she left little legacy for many Muslim women.[58]

[57] Feminist movements, Mies, Ch. 1. I have divided the historiography of women's awakening into three stages. My intention is to differentiate women's activities of different periods, although realizing that often women had various interests and their activites overlapped from one field of concentration to another. For example, Astarabadi was a feminist writer and she was also involved in women's education. Because she lived during the early part of the nineteenth-century, I placed her in stage one of women's awakening, despite her multiple and varied experiences.

[58] Qazvin, Bayat-Phillip, 296; and Maud, 1175–1182. Babism was founded in the nineteenth-century as a religious movement with beliefs in spiritual, moral, and political unity of the world. It advocated equality of rights for women and men and called for the abolition of polygamy, the restriction of divorce, the abolition of the veil, and compulsory education for all.

During the late nineteenth-century, a few women became prominent leaders, although their efforts did not culminate in any organized women's groups. Feminist writer Bibi Khanum Astarabadi and the activist woman in the Tobacco Protest, Zinat Pasha, worked individually on behalf of women and the nation, and a number of kings' wives and daughters were politically influential in their respective courts. But the activities of these individual women did not culminate in any organized women's groups. Sporadic movements such as bread riots and the Tobacco Protest witnessed the organized participation of women, usually mobilized by the clergy. These activities had disappeared upon the realization of the immediate demand. It was only during the early days of the Constitutional Revolution – in a way similar to the 1979 Revolution – that many different women's organizations came into existence.

The second stage of women's awakening consists of their educational endeavors during and after the Constitutional Revolution. Prominent leaders of over a dozen women's organizations advocated women's rights, especially women's education. They included Mohtaram Eskandari, Mastureh Afshar, Sadigheh Doulatabadi, Taj al-Saltaneh and Eftekhar al-Saltaneh who were Naser al-Din Shah's daughters, Noor al-Hodah Mangeneh, Mahrokh Goharshenas, Shams al-Moluk Javaher-Kalam, and many others. These women were staunch advocates of education through the establishment of schools for girls and development of political rights for women. Some held socialist and other democratic ideals, while others embraced Islam. Unlike the activists in the nineteenth-century, these women and their organizations did not disappear immediately after the constitution was granted. They continued their struggle and finally won the battle for women's education.[59]

Education was a key to women's advancement and their efforts to restrain patriarchal control. Privileged women knew the value of education from tutorials at home, although they could not use it for public service. Some young girls had received insignificant training through *maktab-khaneh* (the old educational system). Under this system, the clergy taught classes, but most teachers were "nearly illiterate." Teachers offered some lessons from the *Qoran* in Arabic but girls rarely learned to read or

[59] Doulatabadi and Eskandari, Ch. 2 of this book; Taj al-Saltaneh, Ettehadieh and Sa'dunian, eds.; and Amanat, ed. Note that Taj was more active than her other royal sisters, Fakhr al-Saltaneh, Eftekhar al-Saltaneh, and Fakhr al-Dowleh. A poet, writer, socialist, and a feminist criticized patriarchy and called for women's emancipation, she addressed Iran's backwardness and issues related to class exploitation and imperialism. Bamdad, Zan-e II, Sheikholeslami, and Ghavimi.

write in Persian. Before the "impact" of the West, "education had come to be the monopoly of narrow-minded and parasitical clergy." Women's education was considered either un-Islamic or undesirable. It was widely believed that educated women would threaten the morality of the society, for once women learned the art of writing, "they would write love letters" and generally undermine the existing social order. Although most women were unschooled, their education, even minimal, represented a challenge to many men who were anxious not to lose their privilege over women's mind and body.[60]

Confronting the patriarchal system, women decided to establish their own schools for girls. No educational institution existed for Iranian Muslim women at the turn of the century. Learning at home from tutors was primarily available to well-to-do women until the establishment of the first girls' schools. Earlier in 1874, the American Presbyterian Missionary Society had opened two girls' schools primarily for Christian Armenians in Tehran, although Muslim women graduated from the school, and by 1909, 120 Muslim girls attended. Encouraged by the activities of the missionary school and dedicating boundless energy to their cause, Iranian women were finally able to create their own self-financed girls' schools.

Toubi Azmoudeh (1896–1936) was the first Iranian Muslim woman to establish such a school, *Namous* (Honor), in Tehran in 1907. The daughter of a colonel, Azmoudeh married at the age of fourteen and learned Persian, Arabic, and French from tutors hired by her husband. Devoted to women's education, with no financial or moral support from the government, she held the first classes at her own house. Azmoudeh saw no contradiction between women's education and Islamic teachings. She incorporated religious texts and the study of *Qoran* into the curriculum and with the teaching help of her female friends, her school offered women well-rounded education in Persian studies and home economics.

Azmoudeh's opponents soon destroyed her small school and harassed her students in the streets with accusations of immorality and unchastity. Despite her fears, she persisted in her ambitions continuing her break from the social norms and cultural traditions of her society regarding women. Shortly after, she moved *Namous* to a larger building, and even added secondary school classes and evening classes for adult and working women. She expanded the school to six more branches in Tehran, with the help of her supportive husband. In the absence of regular teachers, Azmoudeh invited elderly men as substitute teachers because the employment of

[60] "Illiterate" and "Parasitical," Banani, 85–86; and "love letters," Sheikholeslami, 84–85.

young male teachers would have caused a scandal. In a few years, a number of well-trained and educated *Namous* graduates became Iran's first women's teachers. Relatively unexplored by female scholars in Iran and exile, Azmoudeh was a feminist pioneer in women's education.[61]

The challenge to the old system intensified as more women and men followed Azmoudeh's path. In 1908, a notable, Yousef Khan Reyshahr Moa'ddab al-Molk founded the 'Ecole Franco-Persane at his home for his daughters and those of his relatives. By 1910, more than 50 private girls' schools, literacy and night classes existed in Tehran, most of them established by prominent women who had been supported by men. However, these schools encountered serious obstacles from hostile men, especially conservative members of the religious community who cursed, stoned, and insulted teachers and students in public. Sheikh Fazlallah Nuri, a respected *ulama*, who had himself mobilized women on the first day of the Constitutional Revolution, now turned against both the movement and women's activities and denounced the schools as un-Islamic and a Babi plot. Despite harsh opposition from the devout men, women persisted and succeeded. The first Teacher's Training School for women, which granted ninth-grade diplomas began in 1918 when the Dar al- Mo'allemat (Teachers' School) joined the 'Ecole Franco-Persane. Women's desire to rattle the shackles of patriarchy, despotism, and imperialism would not be forced to a standstill.[62]

In a third stage of women's awakening, journalism heightened the sense of urgency for reform. From 1910 to the early 1920s, women published and edited at least thirteen journals. Like the schoolmistresses, women editors and publishers came from privileged backgrounds. Their publications covered a wide variety of issues that related to women's oppression, patriarchy, the veil, polygamy and divorce, and national and international politics. Some editors expressed a desire to be emancipated like European women, while emphasizing their contempt for Western domination. In order to highlight the concerns of prominent women's publications and the personal and professional perspectives of their editors, I will discuss three newspapers and journals that appeared at the turn of the century. *Danesh* (Knowledge) is significant as the first journal edited by a woman. *Shoukufeh* (Blossom) was the first journal both edited and published by a woman. The third newspaper, *Zaban-e Zanan* (Women's Tongue), was the first publication to use the word *zan* (woman) in its title. This last

[61] Azmoudeh, Bamdad I, 41–43 and Sheikholeslami, 86.

[62] Night classes, Bamdad I, 45 and 62–63; and "Babi plot," Malekzadeh, III, 178–181.

newspaper offered the most interesting, diverse, and original ideas of the three.[63]

Danesh was the first Iranian journal that "aimed at the awakening of masses of women." It printed especially articles that addressed women's concerns and their problems both in Iran and internationally. Qamari Kahhal, a woman occultist, edited the journal and her husband published it in Tehran in 1910. This journal had a very brief history and there is little real information about its specific contents.[64]

Shokufeh was both edited and published by Omid (Maryam) Mozayyan al-Saltaneh, a daughter of the surgeon general of the army. Begun in Tehran in 1913, the journal was at first primarily concerned with issues that directly affected women, such as gender equality, education, and the dangers of early marriage and superstition among women. It also discussed patriarchy by repeatedly calling upon men to treat women fairly. Later, *Shokufeh* became more political, addressing national independence and foreign incursions and asking women to unite and struggle in the national cause. While working on the journal, Mozayyan al-Saltaneh established two girls' schools and a women's organization, which promoted Iran-made industries and women's arts and also provided classes to train women in the arts and sciences. In five weeks after its establishment, this organization registered five thousand women members. Mozayyan al-Saltaneh's journal lasted almost four years and her woman's organization "played an important role in public awakening, especially in raising the social consciousness of women."[65]

Zaban-e Zanan (Women's Tongue), one of the most prominent feminist journals ever printed in Iran, was published by the remarkable Sadigheh Doulatabadi (1884–1962). She was a daughter of a renowned *ulama* who hired tutors to educate her at home. She also attended boys' school, necessarily dressed as a boy. Not only was she well versed in Persian and Arabic, but interested in her education, her mother contributed all her belongings to her education in France. Nonetheless, at her father's order, she was married at sixteen to a doctor much older than she. Her marriage did not last long and after a few years, she was divorced without having had any children.[66]

[63] "Thirteen journals," Sedghi, "Women and Class," Ch. 2, note 60.

[64] "Masses of Women," Sadr-Hashemi, I–III, 266; Kahal, Sheikholeslami, 82–84; and Afari, 491.

[65] *Shokufeh*, Sheikholeslami, 83–88; and Sadr-Hashemi, 7, 80, and 267.

[66] Doulatabadi, *Da'eratal Ma'ref-e*, 1009. But Ghavimi marks her birth and death days as 1879 and 1962, respectively. Because other scholars have referred to Doulatabadi's eightieth birth date, a date that seems to be closer to the one spelled in the Persian

Well versed in Persian, Arabic, and French, Doulatabadi was concerned with women's education and enlightenment. In 1917, she opened a school by the name of *Madreseh-e Madar* (Mother's School). Three months after inception, however, the government closed the school and imprisoned her assistant, Mehr Taj-Rakhshan. A few months later, in 1918, Doulatabadi created the *Anjoman-e Khavatin-e Isfahan* (The Women's Organization of Isfahan). *Zaban-e Zanan* came into being as a newspaper in Isfahan in 1918. The paper carried articles, mainly written by women, to promote their interests and social advancement. Its editor and publisher, Sadigheh Doulatabadi, wrote in her first editorial: "*Zaban-e Zanan* is the first publication that used the name 'woman'; and could be written by a woman about women and for women's interests. Its historical significance derives from its intent to challenge the backwardness and feeble-mindedness of Isfahan [regarding women] at the time." Initially a bi-monthly paper, it printed articles such as "Women and Sciences" and "Women are not Desperate [Dependent]" and later incorporated reports and articles on national and international politics, such as "Long Live Pen [writers]," "Freedom Wins," and "Down With Dictatorship."[67]

In its second year, with a circulation of two thousand and publishing as a weekly, the government censored *Zaban-e Zanan*. Even before this action, the government had searched its publishing house and the malicious neighbors and public had cursed and stoned its small staff several times. Reacting to these attacks, Doulatabadi wrote:

> If they [the government and the hostile public] want us [to] stop enlightening the public, if they think we are frightened, if they wish us to bloc our writings and cover up the truth, if they think they can force us to lie or to forget Iran, or to currying up favors, they are wrong. They live in a world of dreams and hallucination.

As the government was suspending the paper, the chief of Isfahan's police wrote to the editor: "Madam, you are born 100 years too soon."

Encyclopedia, I rely on the later date. Her mother, *Nur al-Elm*, 8; and "France," Pirouz, 26. Pirouz is a pseudonym for one of Doulatabadi's relatives who graciously gave me her time and documents in Tehran in 1991.

[67] French, *Nur al-Elm*, 8; School, Ghavimi, 97 records the name of the school as *Maktab Khaneh-e Shari'yyat* (School of Religious Studies). However, Piruz refers to the school under the name of *Madreseh-e Madar* (Mother's School). Because of other problems with Ghavimi's work as cited earlier, I rely on Piruz's reference. Isfahan, Sadr-Hashemi, III, 6, dates *Zaban*'s publication in 1919. However, Sheikholeslami, 89, traces the publication date to 1918. Because the latter is more consistent with the lunar calendar's translation, I assume it is more accurate. "Dictatorship," Sheikholeslami, 97–98.

Doulatabadi responded in a column: "Sir, I am born 100 years too late; otherwise, I would not have permitted our women to be chained so viciously and violently by you men."[68]

Forced to abandon her publication in 1920, Doulatabadi fled to Tehran and then to France to study educational psychology. Upon her return to Iran in 1927, she took off her veil, put on a European hat and went to work unveiled. The first woman to publicly unveil herself, Doulatabadi continued to go unveiled for almost nine years before the unveiling act of 1936. Indeed, in Tehran she had a position in the ministry of education as head inspector of the school system, all the while continuing to promote women's interests. She then became involved with *Kanun-e Banovan* (Women's Center), which later promoted national unveiling. Twenty-one years later, in 1941, she published a journal in Tehran under her beloved title: *Zaban-e Zanan*. It lasted until her death.[69] Sheikholeslami wrote:

> Doulatabadi is the founding mother of Iranian feminism. She was a nationalist, progressive and a determined woman who dared to tell the truth and to struggle against foreign domination of Iran. Nor did she fear to speak alone and to act alone. She knew how backward the condition of women was in the country and she spoke against it vehemently. She condemned the society that had all its doors closed to its women. She made her earnest efforts to enhance and advance their lives.[70]

Another commentator observed, "*Zaban-e Zanan* was the only oppositional paper in Isfahan that had severely attacked the 1919 unpopular ... treaty with Britain. It was one of the very few papers that had openly discussed socialism and democracy." Another biographer pointed out that "despite her religious background, Doulatabadi had rebelled against cultural traditions and religious prejudice and ... fostered their struggles against ignorance, darkness and dictatorship."

"I want to die while I am at work," Doulatabadi wrote in her will. "If God, the merciful, blesses me with this wish, I would be the most fortunate woman of my time." Her instructions to women mourners were precise and unrelenting: "Please, if you are veiled, do not attend my funeral. I'll never forgive you."[71]

[68] "Hallucination," Sheikholeslami, 97–98. The premier was Vosuq al-Douleh; and "Madam" and "violently," Pirouz, 30.

[69] "Unveiled," Pirouz, 30. Although Doulatabadi was harassed on streets, Reza Shah's government supported her unveiling initiatives; for Doulatabadi's unveiling prior to 1936 see, Sadr-Hashemi, III, 6–10.

[70] "Founding mother," Sheikholeslami, 89.

[71] "Socialism and democracy," as cited in *Nur-ol Alam*, No. 5; "Dictatorship," *Ibid.*; and "I want to die," Sheikholeslami, 99.

Following World War I, repression had largely destroyed an incipient Iranian feminism. Although Doulatabadi and a few other women had introduced feminism, there was no light at the end of the tunnel. Reza Shah Pahlavi replaced independent women's movement with "state feminism" and coercively enforced unveiling. Women had spoken out against imperialism, the state, and patriarchy. The renewal of free feminist debate and activity would wait until the near disappearance of the state after the abdication of Reza Shah Pahlavi in 1941.

PART II

WOMEN IN THE KINGDOM OF THE PEACOCK THRONE

2

The Pahlavi Dynasty as a Centralizing Patriarchy

He "was the very embodiment of a traditional masculine character." So Ashraf Pahlavi remembered her father Reza Shah, founder of the Pahlavi dynasty. "Although I feared my father, I shared some of his qualities: his stubbornness, his fierce pride, and his iron will," wrote his powerful daughter, the twin sister of Mohammad Reza Shah, the second and the last Pahlavi ruler of Iran.[1]

Reza Shah left behind no autobiographies, but as Amin Banani notes, he "had to perfection the politician's talent for opportunism." While still uncertain in his power, for example, "he knew how to play upon the religious emotions of the people." He was "antagonistic toward the clergy," although he was "basically apathetic to religion." There was also "a definite ideological motivation" in his political actions. Dedicated to nationalism and statism, he sought a rapid adoption of "the material advances of the West [by] a breakdown of the traditional power of religion and a growing tendency toward secularism." He built a modernizing, Westernizing, and centralizing state in Iran, a state that was based on a strong army and repression, not the consensus of the governed.[2]

Reza Shah introduced policies that altered the lives of Iranian women. For the first time, some women entered into the modern sectors of the economy, public and non-sex segregated schools were established, family laws were modified, and unveiling was enforced forcibly in 1936. But critical of state authoritarianism, a small number of women who had

1 "Embodiment" and "iron will," Pahlavi, *Mirror*, 61 and 14.

2 "Opportunism," Banani, 39; and "religious emotions," "antagonistic," "apathetic," "ideological," and "secularism," *Ibid.*, 44–45.

participated in the Constitutional Revolution continued their political and feminist activities. In the 1930s, Reza Shah's response was to ban all independent women's organizations, as he did other dissident groups, and replaced them with a state-sponsored *Kanun-e Banovan* (Ladies Center), composed primarily of privileged women.

This chapter explores the downfall of the Qajar dynasty and its replacement by the Pahlavis, with a particular attention to state-gender-clergy relationships from Reza Shah's reign to the 1953 Central Intelligence Agency (CIA) coup. It views the state-clergy contest for political power through the importance of gender and women's issues. I argue that state intervention in women's lives challenged private patriarchy in households and transferred some of its authority to the domain of the state as public patriarchy. Unveiling and other gender policies restricted and challenged some of male dominatory tendencies, specifically the cleric's control over women's sexuality and their labor. Thus came the Pahlavi state's drawn out battle with the clergy concerning women and gender relations, a power struggle that lasted until the 1979 Revolution.

REZA SHAH: POWER AND POLITICS

Born in Mazanderan around 1879, Reza Shah seized power in an atmosphere of political chaos in an Iran dominated by European interests and torn by the Qajar dynasty.[3] The events that brought Colonel Reza Khan, the commander of Qazvin Cossack Brigade, to power in 1921 have been recounted elsewhere. This book requires only a brief political biography and explores his political and economic goals, particularly as they pertained to women.

Disorder and discontent that had marked the early twentieth-century Iran provided a ground for Reza Khan's ascendance to power. Mohammad Ali Shah Qajar's (1907–09) reign had been increasingly weakened by the upsurge of popular dissatisfaction and constitutional forces. With the help of the Russian Cossack Brigade, the royalist coup dissolved the *Majles*, incurring substantial bloodshed in Tehran. A civil war, in which many women joined with men, finally assured victory for the constitutional forces and the king sought sanctuary in Russia. His twelve year old son, Ahmad Shah succeeded him (1909–25). A new *Majles*, representing predominantly the interests of liberal forces introduced European-style reforms in the areas of law and order, financial, administrative and

[3] Reza Khan, Ghani, Chs. 1–5.

governmental organization, the judiciary, and education. In 1914, it approved the establishment of a teacher's college for women and the introduction of a uniform curriculum and textbooks for all schools. The relative tranquility was short lived, however. With the outbreak of World War I, anarchy grew rampant again. Iran's central government lost its authority to rule and Parliament suspended its work until 1921. Although the war was not literally fought on Iranian soil, it brought instability and destruction as it divided the country into "spheres of influence," with parts occupied by Russian, British, and Turkish troops.[4]

In order to prevent Iran's disintegration, Reza Khan led a bloodless and unopposed coup on February 21, 1921. Having soon acquired the post of *Sardar-e Sepah* (the army commander), he turned his attention first to foreign policy and then to domestic issues. In an attempt to restore stability, he revoked the much detested and exploitative 1919 Agreement with the British, and signed a friendship treaty with the Soviet Union. In an effort to consolidate his military and political power, he defeated local gendarmeries or internal security forces, tribes, and separatist movements. He then merged the Cossacks with gendarmes in order to fulfill his dream of a new and strong army. By late 1923, he became prime minister, and in early 1925, the Parliament granted him the title, Commander-in-Chief of the Armed Forces. In December 1925, in a bold move, he convened the *Majles* to secure the deposition of Ahmad Shah and to obtain the throne for himself. At the age of forty six, Reza Khan, the son of a small landowner, peacefully and within *Majles'* power, became the first king of the Pahlavi dynasty, named after an ancient Persian language. An English writer who attended the ceremonies described Reza Khan's crowning of himself to the Peacock Throne:

> Escorted by his generals and his ministers bearing jewels and regalia, the aigrette in his cap blazing with the diamond known as the Mountain of Light, wearing a blue cloak heavy with pearls, the Shah advanced towards the Peacock Throne. The European women curtsied to the ground; the men inclined themselves low on his passage; the mullahs shambled forward in a rapacious, propriety wave; the little prince [Mohammad Reza, the Crown Prince], frightened, possessed himself of a corner of his father's cloak.... With his own hands he removed the cap from his head, with his own hands he raised and assumed the crown, while two ministers stood by, holding the dishonored tiaras of the Kajar [Qajar] dynasty. Then from outside came a salvo of gun, making the windows rattle, proclaiming to the crowds in the streets that Reza Khan was King of Kings and the Centre of the Universe.[5]

[4] New *Majles*, Abrahamian, *Iran*, 112.
[5] "Escorted," Sackville-West, 133–134.

STATE-BUILDING, WESTERNIZATION, REPRESSION, AND EMASCULATION

Inspired to build a strong army and a centralized state, Reza Shah was imbued with notions of Westernism or Europeanism. Westernism meant the separation of religion and politics, but more significantly, the curtailment of clerical power. Reza Shah's vision for Iran was that of a society with secular educational institutions comparable to those in Europe; unveiled women wearing European clothes and attending schools, teaching, and working outside the home; men wearing Western clothes instead of the traditional garb and hats; a modern economy with industries, banks, roads, railways, cars, telephones, and other communication networks; a powerful military with uniforms and powerful armaments; and a modern bureaucracy and judiciary. Ending the dominance of foreign forces, he attempted to build state capitalism during the 1930s. But he was intolerant of dissent and brutally crushed the opposition, secular or religious. He also relied on court patronage, while making himself the richest landowner and the wealthiest person in Iran. Thus, Westernism and repression presented two sides of the same coin in Reza Shah's state-building efforts. It is within that context that changes in women's lives should be understood.[6]

Westernization implied emulation of and identification with Europe as a model for Iran's progress and modernization. Reza Shah's objective was to meet Europeans on equal terms and to Europeanize Iran. He advocated altering daily habits of life. Ashraf Pahlavi wrote that the "Persian style of eating was done with hands, with bread used as utensil. My father, however, lean[ed] more toward the Western ways he associated with progress, [and] wanted us to learn Western eating habits." He also ordered an Iranian musician to Westernize traditional Iranian music.[7] Reza Shah never visited Europe, although Mostafa Kemal Attatürk's modernization projects in neighboring Turkey provided an impetus for his visions of change. He admired Turkish programs and imputed his desire to use them as models for Iran's development. European influence had been already long felt in Iran, but like Attatürk, he desired to create a capitalist Iran, to eliminate foreign incursion, and to dismantle religious authorities. But unlike Attatürk – who sought to construct a secular state and civil society through a complete break with the past – the Pahlavi monarch made

[6] Westernization and Europeanization, are used interchangeably here; and court patronage, Abrahamian, *Iran*, 135–149.

[7] "Persian style," Pahlavi, *Faces*, 17; and "Iranian Music," Wilber, 233 and 160.

Iran's imperial and monarchic history the basis of his nationalism, and for purposes of political legitimacy, he exploited the Iranian *Shi'i* tradition as a phenomenon unique in the Islamic history of the Middle East. Thus, in a sharp departure from Attatürk, Reza Shah never completely divested the clergy of power. Nor did he build a civil society based totally on secular norms and ideals. In a further contrast to Attatürk, the Pahlavi ruler based his power not on a social class, but on the military, with its monopoly over the coercive use of state power.[8]

Westernization was a correlate of centralization and repression. Centralization meant the building of a strong military force, both for strategic purposes and the consolidation of state power. Although Reza Shah restored law and order, eventually the military state turned against its own civilians. Secular and intellectual forces, varying in class background and ideological persuasion, some of them supporters of Reza Shah's rise to power were silenced. He then banned all opposition groups, political parties, independent newspapers, women's organizations, and trade unions; restricted the activities of ethnic minorities; transformed the *Majles* into a rubber stamp parliament; and destroyed the powers of rural communities and tribes, as well as the urban commercial and industrial classes. The newly created Pahlavi state, thus, deprived itself of a class base upon which to build its political institutions.[9]

Westernization also meant the suppression of the power of the religious establishment, although state-religion relations underwent significant changes. Prior to his self-coronation, Reza Shah sought the *ulama*'s support, for example, by abandoning the idea of republicanism as practiced in Turkey in favor of the clerical's preference for monarchism as a safeguard against secularism. He thus received the support of a powerful faction of the *ulama*. Initially, he was still conciliatory when he was consolidating his powers: he capitulated to the clergy's demand for exemption from military service and from wearing uniform clothing. But once he believed that he no longer needed the clerics, whom he viewed as obstructions to his secularization and modernization schemes, he turned completely against them. His deep contempt for the clergy made it possible to neutralize that rival center of power, which traditionally exercised an enormous political hold on ideology, institutions, and women. Yet state-clergy relations remained Reza Shah's most difficult challenge, crucial as

[8] Capitalist Iran, Keddie, *Roots*. Ch. 5; and Abrahamian, *Iran*, Ch. 3, especially 148–149.
[9] Class base, *Ibid.*, Ch. 3, especially 149–165.

it was to his Westernization policies, and formidable as was the power of the religious establishment.[10]

Emasculating the clergy through women's emancipation was perhaps one of Reza Shah's effective weapons against the clerics who wielded considerable personal and public authority over gender relations and the family, specifically women's conduct. Although Reza Shah's educational reforms and dress codes for both women and men provoked great discord with the *ulama*, researchers of the period shed little light on the significance of women's emancipation for neutralizing religious power. Women supporters of the monarchy ignore the link between gender reforms and state-clergy conflict. In contrast, feminist opponents of Reza Shah view his treatment of women in the context of state-building projects or repressive measures.[11] But emancipation was not only a reflection of modernization and state-building, it was also an attempt to disempower the clerics whose social, cultural and political power on women and gender relations was formidable. Their hold on societal ethical and moral values enabled them to define women's behavior, including their sexual obligations to their husbands, the upbringing and socialization of children, and their public conduct. In addition, they interpreted rules regarding marriage and divorce, education, property relations, and traditions pertaining to personal and social honor or men's *namous*. Moreover, their teachings not only reinforced male domination and female subordination, but provided a degree of personal security for men in their private family lives that might have counteracted the tensions arising from class hierarchies, poverty, backwardness, and the arbitrary rule of despotic monarchs.[12] Thus, by defining and manipulating the norms and institutions that shaped women's lives, religious authorities exercised enormous influence in Iranian society.

Reza Shah stripped much of clerical power from controlling women's labor and sexuality. By so doing, his Westernization schemes came full

[10] Deep contempt for the clergy, Akhavi, 36. Restrictions on clerical power had already begun during the constitutional movement, yet the *ulama* still wielded considerable influence rooted in the constitutional declarations that *Shi'i* Islam was the religion of the land. While silencing oppositional clerics, Reza Shah sought the alliance of a number of senior *ulama*. He established state's hegemony over religion but he could not totally divest the clergy from their hold over society as the *Shari'eh* and religious customs dominated many aspects of Iranian life, especially patriarchal and property relations.

[11] Dress codes, Chehabi, 213; great discord, Akhavi, *Religion*, Ch. 2; women's emancipation, women supporters, Bamdad I and Bamdad II, and Ghavimi; and feminist opponent, Najmabadi, "Hazards"; and Sanasarian.

[12] Despotic monarchs, Wilber, *Riza*, 36.

circle: women's emancipation meant state exploitation of gender as a measure to combat and contain religious forces and their *bazaar* supporters. A masculinity symbol, Reza Shah himself was a patriarch and presumably understood male domination and its social and political implications; conversely, it is possible that he knew the meaning of emasculinity and its disempowering effect. Ashraf Pahlavi stated that she dared not dine with her father in sleeveless clothes or request equal treatment with her brother, Mohammad Reza, especially an equivalent education. Women's emancipation also signified the building of a legitimate foundation for Westernization, as well as bolstering the monarch's "modernizing" image in the outside world, particularly in the Middle East region. Put differently, the emancipation of women as a public policy instrument provided the state with a new form of power: the ability to use gender to emasculate religious authorities and transfer patriarchal power from the domain of the clergy to the realm of the state, and further, to utilize gender to accomplish its Europeanization policies. This was manifested in the gradual entrance of women to the labor force and educational spheres.[13]

WOMEN'S WORK, EDUCATION, AND LEGAL REFORMS

Reza Shah imported Western science and technology in order to excel in the types of achievements of Western civilization. His economic programs included generating state revenues by increasing oil production and royalties; creating investment capital through foreign trade, state monopolies, modest income taxes, and deficit financing; and industrializing. Economic development changed the structure of production. It created modern working-class, service sector employment, and it promoted urbanization. More visible in the service economy and as the state's employees, women's work outside the home acquired more legitimacy as they began to appear in public.[14]

Iran's major source of revenue was oil. Its discovery at the turn of the century and the formation of the Anglo-Persian Oil Company (AIOC) in 1908 failed to produce income. Through the purchase of most of its shares, the British government made AIOC essentially a British enterprise, insuring itself high profits. Despite high productivity and growing oil exports, Iran experienced deficits in the crude balance of visible trade between 1909 and 1921. Reza Shah reversed these policies in the 1920s, raising income

[13] Pahlavi, *Faces*, 23–24.

[14] Economic development, Banani, Ch. 7; and Abrahamian, *Iran*, 146–148.

from oil and putting these revenues to governmental use. Setting aside a budget for industrialization, he spent much of the oil income on arms and building a strong army. He promoted statism: the state became the dominant investor in the fields of banking, transportation, and construction; it provided subsidies and financial and technical assistance to privately owned plants; and it initiated many other new infrastructure projects, including the construction of roads, telephones, a railroad, automobiles, modern schools for men and women, a university, and a women's training college in Tehran.[15]

The structure of production underwent rapid changes as the Pahlavi monarch encouraged industrialization according to a strategy guided by the philosophy: the more, the better. Julien Bhahrier described Reza Shah's notion in practice: "more factories are better than fewer factories;... state factories are better than private factories;... big plants are better than small plants; and... capital intensive products are preferable to labor intensive products." In the early 1900s, manufacturing activity had been confined to small workshops and there was no state industry. The chief urban productive classes were the *bazaar* merchants and artisans. By contrast, between 1934 and 1938, new plants were built, and the move toward larger factories was accelerated. Moreover, the share of capital formation in the Gross National Product (GNP) climbed from 8 to 9 percent in the first quarter of the century to 15 to 20 percent during the 1930s and 1940s. As a result, for the first time in Iranian history, "A modern working-class had been born."[16]

The service sector grew too. In 1900 this sector was an insignificant part of the GNP. By the 1940s, its contribution was much higher because of the growth of such industries as banking, energy, communications, transportation, and public service. By contrast, agricultural production

[15] Oil, Keddie, "Oil, Economic Policy"; and Nirumand. Trade, Bhahrier, 113; and infrastructure projects, Wilber, *Riza*, 141. The state also intervened in other areas of the economy. In 1931, in response to the worldwide economic depression that had adversely affected Iranian exports, Reza Shah introduced the Foreign Trade Monopoly Policy. As a result, he reversed the Qajar dynasty's foreign trade policies, ended capitulations, regained tariff autonomy, and used protective tariffs. He also encouraged foreign capital investment in the mines and in the construction of dams and irrigation.

[16] "More factories," Bhahrier, 87 (although Reza Shah emphasized state factories, he also ventured into private industries); GNP, *Ibid.*, 55–56; and "modern working-class," Abrahamian, *Iran*, 147 (while Reza Shah himself had "thoroughly milked the country," his policies led to the growth of still other classes. His "activities enriched a new class of 'capitalists' – merchants, monopolists, contractors, and politicians – favorites, [while] inflation, heavy taxation, and other measures lowered the standard of living of the masses).

declined as the state gave agricultural development a low priority. Whereas in 1900 agriculture constituted 80 to 90 percent of the GNP, in the 1930s and 1940s, it fell to about 50 percent. Displaced, many agricultural producers moved to the cities and urban centers. Between 1900 and 1950, the number of small towns and cities grew from 100 to 186.[17]

Economic changes had significant implications for women's work. Data are limited for the industrial sector, although many women continued to weave. One survey of twelve cotton spinning and weaving plants operating in 1936 suggests that the number of male workers declined. Unlike early industrialization in some Western countries, women did not replace these men, children did. This survey ignores women's participation in carpet weaving, and its usefulness is limited for our purpose. However, data for subsequent years show a relatively high rate of participation by women, who comprised almost 16 percent of the industrial labor force by the mid-1950s. Exactly when such a gender shift in the industrial labor force occurred is not known with certainty, given the unavailability of accurate figures for either the pre-Reza Shah period or his reign. Because World War II with its adverse impact on Iran could not have produced a significant increase in women's industrial activities in the immediate post-Reza Shah period, one must look to the early 1950s to account for a gender shift in the industrial sector.[18]

Interestingly, women's participation in agriculture declined, whereas their work in the service sector increased. This shift corresponded with a significant decrease in the agricultural labor force, as already noted in connection with urbanization. In 1900, 90 percent of the population worked in agriculture; in 1930, 85 percent; and in 1946, 75 percent, a trend that continued in subsequent years. By contrast, more women joined the service sector. At the turn of the century, few people were engaged in the distributive trades or in public and private services, but by the early 1950s, labor force participation in the services was much higher. Although reliable data for Reza Shah's period are unavailable, it is possible that more women sought employment as teachers, nurses, charity workers, midwives, and seamstresses than in earlier decades. Statistical figures for 1956 reveal that 24 percent of the population worked in the service sector

[17] 1900, Bhahrier, 7, 61, and 59–60; and Abdullaev, Z. Z. as cited in Issawi, ed. *The Economic*, 47.

[18] Cotton spinning, Statistical Center of Iran, *Salnameh-e Amari-ye* 1352; 64; and Ministry of Interior, *Sar Shomari-ye Amari-ye* 1335, 26; children, Bank Markazi, *Bulletin* no. 17, 1; and Bhahrier, 178; industrial labor force, Statistical Center, *Salnameh-e*, 1352, 64; and women's industrial activities, Ministry of Interior, *Ibid.*, 26.

and that urban women accounted for 23 percent of all employed service sector workers. This means that approximately 52 percent of all working women in urban areas had service jobs, and that this 52 percent is much higher than women's corresponding participation in industry, which was 40 percent.[19]

The development of a quasi-capitalist system and economic expansion, in conjunction with such "modernization" policies as women's emancipation and secular education in the 1930s, help explain the growth of women's employment in the 1950s. In France and England, industrialization was spurred by private capital, with relatively little interference by the state. In Iran, though partially dependent on foreign capital and investment, the state used its control of oil and Western technology to promote industrialization and invest in the growth of various institutions and services. The expansion of the service sector required both greater investment in these areas and a larger labor force to fill newly formed occupations. The creation of this new labor force would have a political impact by boosting the state's efforts at Europeanization. It would also require more schooling, and women's emancipation necessitated girls schools and female teachers. Furthermore, uniform and secular education, as Reza Shah wanted, would need state intervention in girls' schooling.

Educational reform was perhaps Reza Shah's greatest achievement. During his reign, many schools were established, the enrollment of both girls and boys increased, and women officially entered institutions of higher education and taught. Women teachers contributed to the economic infrastructure and fostered the state's Westernization policies. As students and teachers, women were officially, if perhaps unintentionally, empowered to challenge the institutional and social powers of religious authority over the educational system and opposition to women's education. Although this new policy began to create an environment that would counteract the tradition of prejudice toward educated women, their schooling lagged behind that of men.[20]

Ushering in secularism, Reza Shah established state hegemony over the old school system dominated by clerical authorities. In 1910, Parliament

[19] Participation in agriculture, Statistical Center, *Salnameh-e Amariy-e* 1351, 64; service sector, *Ibid.*; and 1956, Ministry of Interior, *Sar Shomari-ye* 1335, 26. As noted above, this has little statistical significance. The aggregated data provide insufficient detail on women's work and their specific activities.

[20] Reform, Woodsmall, *Women and the Near*, 84–85.

had already created a Ministry of Education and embarked on a number of innovative measures to reform the educational system. But the clergy's influence had remained intact, in fact in 1911, legislators had passed a bill insuring the dominance of religious schooling. Reza Shah broke with this tradition, in 1921 empowering the Ministry and its supervisory High Council of Education to secularize the educational system and to separate it from the religious domain. With this mandate the Council prepared a curriculum for a coeducational teacher's college, used the *vaqf* endowments (resources available to the clergy) to finance and build public schools, and proposed to reform the religious schools or *maktab khaneh*. The government also allocated a large sum to the Ministry to create a curriculum for secular elementary and secondary schools and to reform and "modernize" the old religious curriculum. Many reforms showed Western influence. On the model of the French Lycee, the Ministry introduced French texts and scientific curricula and it organized programs to train teachers as professionals. The University of Tehran hired European professors and the government sent male students – not women – abroad, as far as the United States.[21]

Women's schooling was well under way by 1935 and 70 women were admitted to the University of Tehran in 1936–37. But most women's schools were private and set up by women without governmental assistance. In contrast to 1910, when 167 girls enrolled at 50 private schools, literacy, and night classes, in 1929, 11,489 girls studied at 190 schools, and by 1933, 870 schools registered 50,000 female students. The figures were even more impressive in 1940, a year before Reza Shah's abdication and exile: 4,907 girls received sixth-grade certificates, and 451 obtained high school diplomas. Despite the mushrooming of education for girls, Reza Shah's state still paid greater attention to boys' education; by the early 1930s, Iran had four times more boys' schools than girls'.

[21] 1911, Banani, 90; curriculum, *Ibid.*, 108–109; and Akhavi, *Religion*, 38 and 40–45 (A 1928 law required an examination for students in religious schools and licenses for teachers of religion. In 1931, the Ministry of Education established a syllabus for religious schools, and in 1935, a Faculty of Theology at the University of Tehran was established under state supervision. Sums were also allocated by the state to eliminate the more popular aspects of religious teaching, such as the narrative accounts of the lives of *emams*). University of Tehran, Banani, 89–95 (drawing on European models, technical and industrial co-education was introduced. Although memorization as a pedagogical technique remained, universities borrowed European methods. The extensive educational reforms that were planned during the constitutional era were now advancing, though in a more secular direction and under an autocratic ruler).

Moreover, more than one quarter of girls' elementary education took place in private schools, and private girls' secondary schools outnumbered public ones four to one. Overall, women's independent activities in schooling and teaching was enormous; one of the graduates of Dar al-Mo'allemat (Teachers Training School), Badr-al Moluk Bamdad, my schoolmistress, in the 1950s inaugurated the coeducational primary school that I attended.[22]

Educational reform, especially women's education, had significant implications for state-clergy relations. Although Reza Shah himself was uneducated, even illiterate, the transformation of the educational system served his overall goal – a "modern" state and economy. Viewing religious beliefs as incompatible with his Westernization schemes, he thought that secular education could directly undermine the power of a clergy who had a substantial hold on Iran's educational life and intellectual substance. Indeed, Reza Shah's distaste for the religious establishment was so great that he sent his eldest daughters and the Crown Prince to Tehran's Baha'i elementary schools rather than schools run by Muslims. During his reign, enrollment at traditional religious schools declined drastically.[23]

Yet educational reforms did little to overcome discrimination against women. There is no evidence that women's entry into the educational sphere weakened the patriarchal structures of society. Vehemently against their daughters' education, many families preferred to marry them off. Reza Shah forbade the foreign education for his daughters that his son enjoyed. When Ashraf Pahlavi made such a request while already abroad in Switzerland, her father's response was "'Stop this non-sense [nonsense] and come home at once.'" Another well-to-do woman recalled the harassment she experienced as a student when antagonistic men and women who opposed women's education scolded, cursed, and stopped her and her classmates on the streets. Students and teachers were continuously intimated and threatened. Women were not totally passive in the face of hostile and abusive bystanders. Sometimes female students took their

[22] 1910, 1929, and 1933, Woodsmall, *Moslem*, 146; and Sedghi, Feminist Movements, 492; 1940, Banani, 108; private schools and public ones, *Annual Report of the Ministry of Education* as cited by Woodsmall, *Moslem*, notes 2 and 3; and Bamdad I, 62 (Dar al-Mo'allemat was founded by the government of Mirza Hasan Khan Vosuq al-Douleh in 1918–19).

[23] Baha'i schools, Banani, 109, 87, 111, and 96; and decline in traditional studies, Abrahamian, *Iran*, 144–146.

books from under their *chadors*, threw them at men, or hit them on their heads.[24]

Although the consequences of Reza Shah's educational reforms on women cannot be fully assessed, it was in that period that women's education was institutionalized and legitimized for the first time in Iran's history. Permitted to be students and even to obtain a university education, women could also teach officially. The generation of female pupils and teachers of the Reza Shah era were instrumental in subsequent years in training and inspiring the new generation of women who became the pioneers and activists of Iranian feminism during the late 1970s and early 1980s. Nevertheless, the absence of equally profound changes in family laws undermined the impact of these educational reforms on women's lives.

Westernization affected both the secular judicial system and the *Shari'eh*, altering existing features and introducing new provisions, especially in family relations. Rather than attempting to document changes in the overall structure of the judiciary system, I will address those aspects that concerned women, notably legal reforms relating to marriage, divorce, and household relations. Like other policies enacted under Reza Shah, the reformed legal system was yet another effort to disrupt the clergy's power by modifying some of the Islamic laws governing family matters and challenging other legal provisions that defined men's direct control and ownership of women. Because the new statutes lacked effective mechanisms for implementation, the net effect of Reza Shah's family reforms was limited in terms of women's daily lives.

Theoretically, these reforms secularized some aspects of marriage and divorce laws, yet at the same time, they upheld other stipulations that complemented religious principles. Marriage and divorce were now to be registered; and registration was to take place in civil bureaus, not in religious courts. The issuance of marriage licenses became mandatory as well. Marriage age was also slightly modified: whereas the *Shari'eh* recognized the age of female puberty as 9, against 15 in males, a 1931 law required that a marriage contract be based on "physical aptitude" for marriage rather than age. A 1935 law then clarified it further by promulgating 15 as the legal age for women and 18 for men. The new marriage law recognized an agreement between the bride and groom as a prerequisite for marriage; it permitted the cancellation of an engagement even

[24] Ashraf, Pahlavi, *Faces*, 23; well-to-do and bystanders, Bamdad I, 66.

after the arrangement of the *mehr*; and it authorized women to marry aliens, but with government permission. These reforms overshadowed the power of a clerical-dominated legal system, which delegated responsibility for marriage and divorce to Islamic jurists or *Shari'eh* courts. In practice, however, the new provisions were more fully applied in cases involving wealthier urban residents than among the poor and those in the countryside.[25]

In the spirit of clerical interpretations, sexual objectification of women continued. The new injunctions divided the rights and obligations of married couples into two categories: material and non-material. A wife's material rights included her independent right to own property and to use it accordingly. A husband's material obligation consisted of duty to support his wife or wives with food, clothing, and shelter. This duty applied only to permanent wives, not a *siqeh* wife, once the temporary marriage was terminated. Unquestionably, a wife's non-material obligation to her husband was in line with patriarchal notions of sexual control. A woman's "wifely duties" committed her to be sexually submissive to her husband; correspondingly, it was the "husband's right" to receive "sexual gratification at times of his choosing," regardless of a wife's wish. This stipulation constituted a de facto approval of a husband's absolute ownership of and control over a wife's sexuality.[26]

New laws granted women minor rights. They empowered women to institute divorce proceedings. But in conformity with the *Shari'eh*, the husband retained an absolute authority to divorce his wife or wives. Other provisions of the new civil code legitimized male supremacy. Legally, children belonged to their fathers and in separation cases, custody was his. Inheritance laws, the use of a surname and guardianship were all codified

[25] Agreement between the bride and groom (Articles 1062, 1064, and 1070), cancellation (Article 1045), and aliens (Article 1060), Banani, 81–83; and Filmer, 370–371 and 374. Some provisions of the new Civil Code concerning marriage continued to uphold the patriarchal system by following the *Shari'eh* (Articles 1056–1057 legalized temporary marriage, Articles 1050–1051 forbade polyandry, Articles 942, 1046, and 1048–1049 allowed men four permanent wives as well as an unlimited number of temporary wives, Articles 1042–1043 required a father's permission for the marriage of daughters, but not of sons, and Articles 1075–1077 allowed Muslim men to marry aliens who were not isolators, and unlike their female counterparts, no governmental or religious permission was necessary).

[26] New injunctions (Articles 1102–1118), Banani, *Ibid.*, 83–84; and sexual gratification *Ibid.* In conformity with Islam, Reza Shah's reforms granted women private property rights but women remained subordinated to men's will. Theoretically, the foundation of the family was based upon the "harmonious coexistence" of husband and wife, but practically, the husband's dominant role was unchanged.

in conformity with Islamic Law. In matters of employment, a husband's permission was essential, as a "husband may forbid his wife to accept a job that is degrading to him or her." In short, the new secular laws confirmed the patriarchal and patrilineal nature of the society, though somewhat differently from the *Shari'eh*.[27]

The 1925 Penal Code implicitly alluded to the importance of the control of women's sexuality by men as well as punishments for women who would challenge men's sexual hegemony. Article 180 embodied the *Shari'eh* view and stated that:

> If a man kills his wife and/or her accomplice while in the act of adultery, he is exempt from punishment; if he kills his daughter or sister and/or their accomplices under the same circumstances, he is punishable by one to six months' imprisonment.[28]

An adulterous man, however, received short-term imprisonment. Legally, men were granted the right of life and death over women.

Despite secular legal reforms, many aspects of women's lives remained in strict conformity with the *Shari'eh*. The influence of Western-inspired laws was considerable, as was the expansion of state power in the sphere of religious laws. Yet changes introduced in the legal status of women, especially in marriage, divorce, and family relations, were slight, especially in comparison to the state's encouragement of women's education. As Reza Shah attempted to Westernize the legal system, he also contradicted

[27] Divorce and "husband may forbid," Banani, 82–83, notes 51–52. Article 1133 of the 1935 civil law stated that a "husband may divorce his wife any time he wishes." Similarly, in conformity with the *Shari'eh*, Articles 1057–1058 in specifying causes for divorce included the provision of "triple divorce," whereby a divorced woman was allowed to remarry her husband. But in order to ensure that a woman was not pregnant at the time of divorce, Articles 1150–1156 specified a waiting period for her remarriage. The same waiting period was imposed on widows. The intention of the waiting period was to persuade or prevent a pregnant woman from obtaining a divorce; it was also to ensure that the child was legitimate and belonged to the husband's lines of descent, another patriarchal practice. However, in order for the triple divorce to be legal, a special stipulation maintained that the wife must marry another man (or a *mohallel*) and enter a consummated relationship with him first. After requesting divorce from the second husband and obtaining it, she can then remarry her first husband. The second husband often enters this relationship for a fee. But the problem arises when *mohallel* refuses to divorce the wife; in this case, it is difficult, if not impossible, for the wife to obtain divorce. The intention of triple divorce is to provide sufficient time for the couple to assess the viability of their marital relationship.

[28] Article 180, *Ibid.*, 80–90 (Articles 207–210 define penalties for "adultery, polyandry, homosexuality, statutory rape, rape, prostitution, and conspiracy to promote prostitution"); see also Sedghi, "Women in Iran."

the state's purpose and intent, by incorporating religious laws into state structures. The state had rid itself of the clergy as a potent authority, yet the legitimacy of religious mandates could not be ignored, particularly in laws pertaining to women and gender relations. Although women were given some minor rights, they could not be widely implemented in the patriarchal society. In response, politicized women took independent actions despite being vulnerable to the state's manipulation and coercion.

INDEPENDENT WOMEN'S ACTIVITIES AND "STATE FEMINISM"

Women's activities during Reza Shah's reign underwent two distinct phases: their independent but small movement of the 1920s; and subsequently the 1930s movement from above. A significant feature of the women's movement in the early 1920s was that it was almost free of interference. Continuing to stress earlier themes, women spoke out against the government, the intervention of foreign powers, and their own unequal status. During the 1930s, however, as Reza Shah became increasingly repressive, dissident individuals and organizations, including women and their activities, came under attack. The state co-opted women's undertakings, presenting itself as the champion of their emancipation; it drew on female supporters of the monarchy, and banned the initiatives of oppositional women. The rise of the strong state, thus, made women's autonomous activities obsolete as it exploited women's earlier efforts for its Westernization and centralization policies. This was manifested in a new, state-sponsored "feminism."

Feminism in the early twentieth-century was a direct result of women's growing consciousness, arising out of their attempts to challenge and struggle against domestic tyranny and foreign incursions. Mostly from privileged backgrounds, they came from the same generation of women who had participated in the Constitutional Revolution. Their activities in Tehran included organizing a small association and publishing five short-lived magazines with fairly limited circulation. They adhered to a variety of ideologies and belonged to several small organizations. Concerned with their nation's defense, these nationalist and anti-imperialist women were fascinated by the simultaneous eruption of women's movements in the Soviet Union, Turkey, Egypt, China, Japan, England, and the United States. Disappointed with their own lack of recognition and support by post-constitutional governments, and encouraged by women's successes elsewhere, they continued to struggle for change, independent of support by the government, political parties, or influential men.[29]

This feminism was profoundly new to Iran. Activist women had come together – both covertly and openly – to debate and struggle not only against internal and external pressures, but against their own oppression, while encouraging male supporters to defend their rights as women. For these women, feminism aimed at the improvement of women's condition, which was integral to changing the patriarchal society and freeing Iran from imperialism. Feminists' fundamental demands focused on unveiling, education, reform of marital and divorce laws, and the right to vote and citizenship – all of which required reforms both within the polity and society. Those who assert that "Iranian feminists . . . stress[ed] their non-political demands [such as education, marriage and divorce laws, hygiene, and children's and women's health]" are mistaken. These "non-political" demands were, in fact, essentially political, involving as they did power relationships between men and women, as well as between the state and civil society and international politics.[30]

In order to highlight the independent feminist activities of Iranian women during the earlier period of Reza Shah's rise to power in the 1920s, I will sketch the personal, professional, and political concerns of two remarkable women with diverse backgrounds and activities: Mohtaram Eskandari, a socialist, feminist, and the founder of an important women's organization that had the longest history of any such organization; and Fakhr Afaq Parsa, an educator and a journalist who dared to oppose publicly religious practices responsible for women's backward status.

Mohtaram Eskandari (1895–1925), a contemporary of Doulatabadi, held a socialist and a feminist perspective. A nationalist and constitutionalist as well as a champion of women's struggles, Eskandari advocated women's emancipation both in private and in public by establishing a women's organization, publishing a journal, and opening schools for women. She was the daughter of Prince Ali Khan, known as Mohammad Ali Mirza Eskandari, a liberal and a constitutionalist, an intellectual, an author of articles on women's rights, and a founder of a law society. Her education began at home under the supervision of her father. As she grew older, she studied history, literature, and French under the tutelage of

[29] Nationalist and anti-imperialist women, Sedghi, "Third World." See also Jayawardena; and Sedghi, "Feminist Movements," 492.

[30] "Iranian feminists," Sanassarian, 46.

Soleiman Eskandari who was a close friend of her father and subsequently the leader of Iran's Socialist Party. Socialized in politics from childhood, Eskandari attended her father's meetings, participating in debates on gender and politics.[31]

Determined to elevate women's position, Eskandari founded and chaired the prominent women's organization, *Jam'iyyat-e Nesvan-e Vatankhah* (The Patriotic Women's Society, 1922) which was a division of the Socialist Party. Its members included such remarkable women as Doulatabadi and Parsa, as well as a number of men who had been pioneers in the constitutional movement. The Society campaigned for legislation to help women, organized consciousness-raising plays, and arranged adult literacy classes for women. Even before the founding of the Society, Eskandari was headmistress of one of Tehran's few girls' schools, campaigned against laws that discriminated against women, and lectured on women's oppression. Despite a severe back ailment, she worked hard and tirelessly and encouraged women to stand up for their rights. She articulated her ideas in the Society's journal, *Nesvan-e Vatankhah* (The Patriotic Women), which published ten issues between 1923 and 1925. The journal played a prominent role in women's awakening as it printed articles on women, their status, education and emancipation, as well as national politics. In addition, The Society launched adult literacy classes for women (*Madreseh va Akaber- le Nesvan*). It also organized a consciousness-raising play, "the Apple and Adam and Eve in Paradise" with support from spouses of enlightened notables in 1923. But the performance was stopped by the police as a preacher insinuated that unveiled women were to congregate at the play.[32]

The Society's objectives were numerous, if not always complementary. It intended to educate women, endorse and promote national industries and organize cooperative societies on their behalf, care for orphaned girls, build a hospital for poor women, and assist nationalist women, materially and spiritually. Despite its status as an independent organization, it declared that "when and if appropriate," it would seek governmental financial assistance. Given its close alliance with the Socialist Party, this

[31] 1925, Bamdad I, 49; and Ghavimi, 116–118 (Ghavimi recorded Eskandari's death date as 1924 but later registered it as 1923. Because of Bamdad's greater attention to Eskandari and Ghavimi's several inaccuracies, especially on dates, I rely on Bamdad); and education at home, Ghavimi, 116–117.

[32] Society, Sheikholeslami, 143; and Play, Sedghi, "Feminist movements," 493. Spouses of notables included: Vosuq al-Douleh, Yahya Doulatabadi, and Adib al-Saltaneh Sardari. The preacher was Mirza Abd al-Lah Wa'ez.

position of the Society was ambiguous. According to one account, Reza Shah secretly supported the organization, an allegation that cannot be verified without independent data.[33]

Although a socialist organization, the Society purported to honor Islam and its laws, perhaps less as a matter of principle than out of political expediency. But Eskandari was often subjected to "criticism, denunciation and admonition by religious authorities." An *akhund* (a low-ranking clergyman) once condemned the Society for its support of unveiling. Shortly after, Eskandari was stoned and harassed on the streets. Still, she did not abandon her struggles, despite the urgings of those like Haj Aqa Jamal, a religious man who told her that, "[you must] stay home to sew . . . [clothes]. Once you do, sell them, and then, give me the *khoms* (religious alms giving). Thereafter, make a pilgrimage to Mecca."[34]

Eskandari's commitment to women's causes, as well as her Society and journal were formidable. She used every opportunity to advance her feminist cause. In a demonstration that she organized with the help of her supporters and members of the Society at one of Tehran's largest squares, *Sepah*, as was traditional, she set a fire by burning a number of her journals in public. This drastic action intended to arouse passion and heighten tension in public, while exploiting the spectacle to publicize women's issues. Arrested and taken into custody, Eskandari proclaimed to the authorities: "we want to protect and defend the rights of your mothers and sisters." "Like all human beings," she claimed, "we have brains, too. We are not insidious, [we are protecting our rights]." After this speech, she was released, without charges. Eskandari died young in 1925, hardly thirty years of age. Such feminists as Noor-al-Hoda Manganeh, Fakhr-Ozma Arqun, Mastureh Afshar (Eskandari's successor as the Society's President), Sadigheh Doulatabadi and Fakhr Afaq Parsa continued Eskandari's tradition of activism and the Society to promote her views.[35]

Other women besides Eskandari used journalism to counter patriarchy. During the 1920s Iranian women published and edited at least six journals, one of them in Berlin. Although they had fairly limited circulation, these publications covered many of the women's issues that had been raised a decade earlier. Some devoted space specifically to female authors writing about women. In the vanguard was *Jahan-e Zanan* (Women's

33 Governmental assistance, Bamdad I, 47–48; secret support, Sheikholslami, 143–144 (perhaps like various other groups, including the Socialist Party, the Society accepted Reza Shah's backing, but became oppositional when he became dictatorial).

34 "Criticism and denunciation," and "Mecca," Sheikholeslami, 147 and 146.

35 "Sisters" and "brains," Bamdad I, 48; and feminists, Sheikholeslami, 152–162.

World), which was first edited by Fakhr Afaq Parsa with her husband's assistance (1890–1971) in the religious city of Mashhad in 1921. Parsa's bi-monthly journal was a pioneer in its non-partisan struggle against religious prejudice and those who opposed changes in women's status. After it was charged with being anti-Islamic by the clerical establishment and the *bazaaris*, the government suspended the journal and the Parsas were exiled to Qom.[36]

From a religious family of modest means, Parsa was trained by her mother, an embroidery teacher. Her mother encouraged her to pursue Islamic studies by enrolling her at a traditional school, against her stepfather's will who opposed girls' schooling. Upon the completion of primary school, Parsa's covert schooling was discovered by her stepfather, who angrily threatened to kill her if she continued her education. The same year, at the age of nine, Parsa was made to marry her schoolmaster – marriage being a means to transfer responsibility for a daughter, especially for fathers who felt threatened by the fear of potential social disgrace. Nonetheless, with the help of her husband and tutors, Parsa finished the ninth grade. She then became a school teacher, joined Eskandari's Society, and began to work on Women's World. Parsa used pages of her journal to campaign against veiling as a symbol hostile to women's progress, lobby against gender inequality, and encourage women's education. In the first issue, Parsa explained the journal's objectives by announcing that it "follows Islam and its laws. We shall endeavor to attain our goals and whatever we want" and we "seek refuge from God, who will protect from harm by those who envy and resent our endeavors." The first four issues covered a variety of subjects, such as women's education and status, child-rearing, cooking, superstition, famous women, and women's status in the world.[37]

The government suspended the fifth issue.[38] The banned journal, as earlier issues, had advocated emancipation and invited women to unite with men to meet political and social challenges. One article spoke against veiling and favored the building of schools for women. The same piece

[36] 1921, Ghavimi, 182–189. In 120n1, she cites an interview with Fakhr Afaq Parsa, which took place in 1971. Because no other information on Parsa's life has been accessible to this author that might provide a different account, I assume that Parsa lived through 1971. Non-partisan struggle, Sheikholeslami, 104; and exiled, Sadr-Hashemi, *Tarikh-e* II, 184 (states that Parsa was the first woman who went into exile at about 1921).

[37] "Islam and its laws" and "seek and refuge," Sadr-Hashemi I, 266–267 and 6–10.

[38] Sadr-Hashemi, *Tarikh-e* II, 185 and 181, and Sheikholeslami, 106.

attacked Iran for keeping women backward because of religious prejudice; in comparison it noted:

> ... Afghanistan, which hitherto had not taken any step to improve women's condition, is currently taking important steps to educate women and to free them [from traditional bondage]. Aren't they Muslims? Aren't they more religious than we? We see that this newly civilized nation [of Afghanistan], is far ahead of Iran, which has 6000 years of civilized history....

Another article raised the question: how do clergymen become prominent when they cannot even perform their duties effectively? Charged with being anti-Islamic, the journal was closed down immediately. Leaving her three sons behind with her mother, Parsa escaped to Tehran with her husband. In Tehran, the journalist gave birth to a daughter, Farrokhru Parsa, who became the first woman minister (of education) under the second Pahlavi monarch, but was subsequently executed by the 1979 revolutionary government.[39]

Parsa was deeply committed to her journal. In Tehran, she resumed its publication in 1922, retaining similar goals. However, as the journal and its editor gained in reputation for their critical outlook, they could no longer survive in Tehran. Once again the journal was denounced; this time Parsa was exiled to Iraq. On the way, she settled in Qom, where she heard that followers of the Baha'i faith had been murdered in Iraq. Rumor had it that Parsa was Baha'i. While in Qom, she heard that she had been identified as the enemy of Mohammad; it was then that Parsa sent a message to the journal's readership, announcing the end of publication: "unfortunately, we are stopped by lack of freedom of press and freedom to express and criticize men." The journal formally closed in 1922. With changes in the Tehran government, Parsa returned. There she was cheered by journalists and other supporters. Reviving the journal again in 1930, this time Parsa faced censorship by Reza Shah's government. Unable to confront the repressive state power, Fakhr Afaq Parsa ended her feminist initiatives.[40]

The rise of a strong state undermined these independent women's initiatives, which had managed to co-exist with a weak state earlier in the

[39] Government suspended, Sadr-Hashemi, *Tarikh-e* II, 185 and 181; "Afghanistan," Sheikholeslami, 106; and clergymen, *Ibid.*, 107–108.

[40] "Unfortunately," *Rooznameh-e Iran* [Iran's Newspaper] 1301/1922 as cited in Sheikholeslami, 110–112. About the same time, the alumnae of the American Girl's School published the Women's Universe (Alam-e Nesvan) which ran from 1921 to 1933 in Tehran. See, *Ibid.*, 120–141.

century. The 1930s thus presented a profound discontinuity from the past and the loss of women's independent activists. Under an all-pervasive state, the beginning steps toward independent women's movements were channeled into state-sponsored women's organizations. While many feminist leaders of the constitutional and post-constitutional eras had died or been stopped by the obstacles they faced on all fronts, some began to cooperate with the state in the hope of fulfilling their long overdue dreams. Consequently, the 1930s remain important to the course of Iranian feminism because the state co-opted prominent feminist organizations as well as such distinguished feminists as Doulatabadi and Parsa.[41]

One of the women's organizations that went under the state's umbrella was Eskandari's Patriotic Women's Society. Both the Society and its nearly eleven year old journal, terminated operation in 1932. After Eskandari's death, one of the Society's organizers was Mastureh Afshar, daughter of Majd al-Saltaneh Afshar, a nationalist and intellectual from the city of Rez'aieyyeh. Educated in Russia and learned in Turkish and French, Afshar was a nationalist and feminist who closely followed the ideas and activities of her predecessor. In her endeavors, she received help from other activists, Nur-al-Hoda Mangeneh, Homa Mahmudi, Fakhr Ozma Argun, Sadiqeh Doulatabadi, and Fakhr Afaq Parsa. In 1932, the government invited Afshar to assist in organizing and inaugurating the Second Eastern Women's Congress in Tehran from November 27 to December 2. On the Society's behalf, she accepted, perhaps not anticipating the implications for her organization.[42]

Ashraf Pahlavi chaired the Congress, although she had no experience of working with or on behalf of women. Participants to the Congress included women from Afghanistan, Australia, China, Egypt, Greece,

[41] Besides the 1920s feminists, some women were not involved in public activities, but dared to express themselves in the male-dominated society and to infiltrate men's domains. One such woman was Parvin E'tesami (1907–41), the first woman who published a poetry collection, thus breaching a world formerly reserved to men in Iran. Although her political views were not stated categorically, it seems that before Reza Shah consolidated power, in the mid-1920s, E'tesami had refused to cooperate with his Court. Because of her reputation for mastery of literary knowledge, Reza Shah had extended several invitations to reside in his palace and teach literature and language to the Queen Mother as well as read aloud Iranian history books to both the King and the Queen. E'tesami had declined. In the early 1930s, she took a more conciliatory approach, briefly joining *Kanun-e Banovan* (Sheen, 255–257). E'tesami's view on veiling was also a shifting one. She called for women's emancipation and changes in women's lives through educational reforms. With Reza Shah's unveiling edict in 1936, she condemned the veil as a form of attire but proclaimed her admiration for virtuous women (Bamdad I, 54).

[42] Afshar, *Salname-ye Pars*, 86–89; and Mangeneh and others, Sadr-Hashemi II, 1969–70; and Bamdad 1, 48, 152–162.

India, Indonesia, Iraq, Iran, Japan, Lebanon, Syria, Tunisia, Turkey, and Zanzibar. Inspired by advances made by European women, they discussed their movements and condemned the backward situation of Persian and Arab women, including female illiteracy and the tyrannical domination of husbands and abuse of their wives. The Congress passed a resolution with twenty-two articles advocating women's suffrage, equal opportunity in education, occupation and wages, family reform laws, and abolition of polygamy and prostitution. But the Congress's accomplishment, brought the downfall of the Society. After the meeting ended, the Patriotic Women's Society stopped its activities; the state took it over.[43]

An official "feminism" was now to be promoted from above. In 1935, Ali Asqar Hekmat, the Minister of Education, called on his own initiative a number of Court women, leading female educators, and veterans of the women's movement from the 1920s and early 1930s to form *Kanun-e Banovan* (The Lady's Center) on October 14. Hajar Tarbiat was appointed as its director. Reza Shah pledged his support and appointed his older daughter, Shams, to preside over the organization. Its board members included Afshar, Argun, Bamdad, Esmat-al-Moluk Doulatdad, Doulatabadi, Parvin E'tesami, Taj al-Moluk Hekmat, Akhtar Kambakhsh, Sams-al Moluk Javaher-Kalam, Parsa, Fakhr al-Zaman Qaffari Bayandor, and Pari Hosham Sahidi. The Center actively campaigned against what Bamdad called, the *kafan-e siah* (a pejorative reference to the black *chador*) and encouraged all participants to attend its meetings unveiled. In 1937, the Center was transformed from a women's association to an adult and young women's educational and welfare center with Doulatabadi as its director. Promotion of unveiling became the most important focus of the Center's activity. The Center provided the organizational apparatus for propagating the idea of unveiling and its implementation. It encouraged unveiling in a variety of ways. It provided moral support for women who had to convince their families of the importance of abandoning the *chador*. It rewarded any new female member who attended Center meetings unveiled with a front-row seat, which was normally reserved for female academicians. It also received the police's cooperation to guard unveiled women in public who would be verbally abused and humiliated, in particular attacked by stones and sticks in empty streets and poor neighborhoods of Tehran. In order to avoid public disgrace, women commuting from those areas of the town would be veiled, then would unveil under police protection once they arrived in wealthier sections. Although unveiling had been

[43] Congress, *Salname-ye Pars*, 86–89; and Bamdad I, 60 and 59.

feminists' avowed dream, it now seemed to be the strong state that was achieving it with the cooperation of women who aspired to this symbol of autonomy.[44]

The Center's activities in many ways remained consistent with the intentions of earlier feminists. Although the evidence, which would fully explain women's cooperation with the state is missing, the history of women's rights movement in Iran may shed some light on their motives. Some women may have feared the state's power and its vicious and brutal activities that they had observed. On the other hand, they probably thought that they could win their battles by working with a state that intended to Europeanize the society and emancipate women. It is also possible that feminists' nationalist ideology played a role in their readiness to collaborate with the state that had achieved national sovereignty. Driven by personal and political ambition, some women undoubtedly saw an advantage to side with a state that appeared willing to respond to some of their concerns. A more complex picture is required than the contention that "Ideologically, [the Center] was proestablishment and too [moderate] on feminist issues... the Center's work was geared toward social and charitable activities for women." In particular, the 1930s feminists exerted little choice but to coordinate their activities with the state that was promoting unveiling. As positive gains were achieved, women referred to expanded educational and some employment opportunities as examples. On the negative side, women's unveiling came through coercive means. Thus state intervention shaped the nature of Iranian feminism in the 1930s.[45]

UNVEILING

Scholars of Reza Shah's reign refer to the unveiling edict as an extension of his reforms, as the influence of Attatürk and his gender policies, as a project in state-building, or as a manifestation of repression, or

[44] Official feminism does not refer to the state's interests in representing and promoting women's interests. Nor does it connote the idea that the state is gender neutral. Here, it refers to the state's actions in promulgating measures that helped improve women's position, which benefitted state's interests, first and foremost – see subsequent chapters, and to some extent, women's suffrage. Asqar Hekmat, Hekmat, 85–102; and Doulatabadi was offered, Bamdad I, 52 and 58; and Sheikholeslami, 113 and 120. The Center's aims included women's education and training; teaching them home economics and childrearing; encouraging them to engage in sports and athletics; establishing charity organizations for poor women and foster children; and inspiring women to live within modest means. See Bamdad I, 88–91.

[45] "Ideologically," Sanasarian, 68.

in terms of women's emancipation. One study denied the emancipatory nature of unveiling: "But in a society where men themselves were helpless objects of manipulation by the organized lawlessness of the state, would it not be grotesque to regard this act of persecution of women as their emancipation? . . . would women be emancipated by going out without [veils]?" My focus is on the centrality of unveiling to Reza Shah's policy and politics. I view unveiling in the context of state-building, state-clergy relations, and women's responses to them. As indicated earlier, Reza Shah's aims were to Westernize and strip the clerics of their power, in particular over women, at first slowly, then more swiftly in the 1930s. Many women resented authoritarianism in silence, while a minority fervently embraced the monarch and his gender policies.[46]

Unveiling was a gradual process as the *chador* was not abolished overnight. Reza Shah formulated his policy of banning the veil after his state visit to Turkey in the summer of 1934. But Reza Shah's campaign was integral to his Westernization policies which had begun long before his trip to Turkey. At the beginning of his reign, he introduced somewhat modest changes in women's status but later, he stepped up changes – especially those concerning women's public appearance. In 1926, he provided police protection for women who chose to appear unveiled publicly, but with a scarf or a hat to cover their hair. In a dramatic episode in 1928, the monarch attacked and humiliated religious authorities who had admonished the Queen for exposing part of her face in the holy shrine at Qom. In 1928, the Law of Uniformity of Dress outlawed men's traditional garb in favor of Western clothing though some religious authorities and *chador*-wearing women were exempt. When police began to enforce the 1935 rules pertaining to men's hats in the holy city of Mashhad, bloody clashes occurred between officials and the crowd who had other political grievances as well. There were many casualties, with hundreds dying.[47]

[46] Reforms, Banani, 39; gender policies, Abrahamiam, *Iran*, 144; state-building, Najmabadi, "The Hazards," 53–54; and Chehabi, "Staging," 209–229; repression, Azari; emancipation, Bamdad, *Zan-e* I, 94; and "persecution of women," Katouzian, 127.

[47] Turkey, Hekmat, 87–102; and Filmer, 367–368; Qom, Banani, 84; and Akhavi, *The Politics*, 42; and Law of Uniformity, Chehabi, "Staging." The Law of Uniformity assigned uniforms that were to be made with domestic fabrics for the army, schools and institutions. It outlawed the tall hats and traditional headdresses that men wore and replaced them with the new "Pahlavi hat," which resembled the French military cap. It also encouraged European-style suits, already worn by wealthy men in the capital, especially in the Court. In 1935, a second hat directive introduced a style modeled after Turkish men's hats. Resembling the French brimmed chapeau, it was not welcomed by all men, especially not the clergy, who found that it hampered their touching the ground with their foreheads during daily prayers.

Public mixing of women and men, prohibited by the clerics, became part of the unveiling campaign. After the Qom incident, the government issued police regulations to guard women who attended cinemas, theaters, restaurants, and other public places in men's company. Women were also permitted to speak to men in the streets and to ride with them in carriages – of course, with the carriage hood down. In 1935, the ruler's daughters inaugurated women's cultural centers in Tehran, and the wives of high officials and cabinet members appeared unveiled in a tea party given by the Prime Minister. Later, at a reception in Golestan Palace, Reza Shah "condemned the superstitions encouraged by mullas (mullahs)" while criticizing the *chador* "by contemptuously mimicking the gestures of a woman covering and uncovering her face as a man approached."[48]

Unveiling became a state policy upon Reza Shah's address at a ceremony held in Tehran Teachers College on 17 Day 1314s./January 7, 1936, thereafter known as *Hefda-he Dey* or *Rooz-e Azadi-ye Zan* or Women's Emancipation Day. An advance order had been issued to all women teachers and wives of ministers, high military officers, and government officials to appear in European clothes and hats, rather than *chadors*. Prior to the ceremony, Reza Shah admitted to his family that the unveiling decision was "the *hardest* thing I've ever had to do." He then asked his daughters and wife to attend the ceremony unveiled and "serve as an example for other Persian women."[49] He then announced his proclamation of women's emancipation. He said that:

> Previously Iranian women could not exhibit their talents and render services to the country.... But now, they can enjoy other advantages on top of their remarkable duties as mothers.... We must not forget that in the past half of the population was unemployed and was not taken into account. At no time women's potential was utilized.... You ladies should take advantage of the opportunity to work ... and to educate.... you have now entered the society, have moved ahead to guarantee your own happiness and to contribute to the welfare of your country. Remember, your duty: work.... Be good educators of the future generation and train good students.... Serve your country. Save, avoid luxuries and be useful to your nation....

An eyewitness reported that some older women who were showing their faces for the first time were so embarrassed that for most of the ceremony

[48] Public mixing, Filmer; 367, and Frye, 6; and mimicking, National Archives, American Ligation Dispatch 613, October 3, 1936, as cited in Wilber, *Riza*, 168.

[49] *Hardest* [Emphasis added], and "serve," Pahlavi, *Faces*, 25.

they hugged and stood in front of the walls, perspiring and hiding their faces from men. Other women cheered.[50]

With outlawing the veil, European fashions replaced Iranian women's clothing in public. Soon after the unveiling proclamation, by order of the state, schoolgirls paraded in the streets in Western athletic costumes, unveiled female teachers appeared before their classes, and medical and law schools admitted women. Business boomed for seamstresses and beauty salons, and shops specializing in European hats became noticeable in Tehran's streets. A trade commission was sent to Europe to buy quantities of clothes and hats from France and Germany.[51]

Unveiling edict was implemented ruthlessly. The state dismissed high-level officials whose wives appeared in public in *chadors*. It fined low-ranking government employees if their wives accompanied them veiled. It also prohibited veiled women from cinemas and from public baths, the only bathing places available for a large majority of women. An eyewitness interviewee from Tehran recalled that even a woman who wore a scarf in public was stopped by police who would joke with her and then without explanation, pull off the scarf or tear it into shreds. Another eyewitness commented that, without prior notice, officials would sometimes break into private homes or search door-to-door and arrest women wearing *chadors* in the privacy of their homes. A report from the city of Tabriz stated that only unveiled girls could receive diplomas or their degrees with honor.[52]

Many women resented the unveiling act. The veil symbolized the "sign of propriety and a means of protection against the menacing eyes of male strangers"; thus, "for the majority of Iranian women, removal of the veil meant committing a major sin and disgrace." But the meaning of the veil changed according to social class and local traditions. Generally,

[50] Women's emancipation, Amuzegar, *Maqam-e Zan*, 483–487; and Sadeghipoor, 41; and eyewitness, Bamdad I, 94.

[51] Parade, Filmer, 378; salons, Bamdad, I, 94–96; and trade commission, Wilber, *Riza*, 174.

[52] Eyewitness, Sedghi's interview with Shahjoun Alavi in Huntington, New York, November 25, 1992; another eyewitness, Sedghi's conversation with her mother, Afsar Shishehchi in Baltimore, Maryland on February 16, 1992; and Tabriz, Woodsmall, *Moslem*, 151. To begin to understand the impact of forced unveiling, one might imagine the following allegorical tale: one day as American women stepped out of their homes to go shopping or take a bus or taxi to work, they were arrested on the spot by local police. Store managers and drivers were made liable to pay fines if they served these women. Charged with disobeying new laws requiring women to appear nude in public, they were told that neither they nor their husbands would be entitled to collect their salaries unless individually or in the company of their husbands, they appeared nude at the payroll office!

urban women wore the veil, whereas rural and tribal women covered their hair with long and wide scarves. Unveiling was primarily enforced in larger cities as centers of Westernization and capitalist development; it had little effect on tribal, small town, and rural women, who wore different costumes than urban women. Except for a few affluent and educated women in larger cities, most urban women abhorred the new policy as creating a space between women and the cosmos; the *chador* gave them protection and security, and physical comfort. While the majority of urban women felt psychological and physical safety with the *chador*, unveiling, by contrast, symbolized insecurity and estrangement, perhaps in the way nudity would for many Western women.[53] Thus, one interviewee questioned: how could women be stripped of their clothes overnight? How could women who had no power to defend themselves against the state and police bear the disgrace and humiliation? The same interviewee recalled that women protested in silence and sought refugee in their homes. Another interviewee indicated most women went out only to visit the public baths once a week; they did so, at night, in their *chadors*, taking long routes and passing through frightening, dark and narrow alleys, hoping to remain unnoticed by police. Many older women refused to accompany their husbands in public, sending their daughters instead.[54]

Some women liked the unveiling edict. Less culturally and personally attached to the veil, the generation of daughters exhibited a greater tolerance toward unveiling than their mothers; many of them were happy to abandon their *chadors*. Most of the women who immediately took advantage of the new rulings came from privileged backgrounds; some had resided abroad and had already abandoned the *chador* in favor of European clothing. Similarly, Westernized, middle-aged, educated and elite women, including a number of participants in the constitutional movement, welcomed unveiling. Some ignored the brutal means by which the edict was implemented and proudly referred to it as *Farman-e Bozorg* or the Great Order.[55]

Unveiling may have seemed in some ways even more catastrophic to men than to women, although some men favored it. Photos from the 1930s portray men with their unveiled female family members. One interviewee

[53] "Sign of Propriety," and "sin," Nashat, *Women*, 27. Regarding nudity, see note 52, above.

[54] Same interviewee, Sedghi's interview with S. Alavi; and another interviewee, Sedghi's discussions with her mother, who recalled her older sister, not her mother, accompanying her father in public.

[55] Daughters, Sedghi's discussions with her mother; and Order, Bamdad I, 94.

recalled that her uncle was so ebullient that he took his three daughters, unveiled, out to the streets immediately when he heard the proclamation of unveiling. But for many men, their honor had long been associated with their hold on women. The source of a man's personal power, indeed his masculinity, resided in women's seclusion, restrictions on their physical appearance, and control over their sexuality and labor. At the time, many men resented the edict, yet they abided by it publicly. A governmental interpreter stated that the king had "made much progress [regarding women], but he went too fast. Persia needed a dictator, it was already too late to go slowly. There was too much to do. People were angry in their hearts, but they had to advance." Bystanders continued to harass and humiliate unveiled women in the absence of police. Available sources do not reveal much information on men's behavior toward women at home. But on a deep emotional level, unveiling must have produced a sense of personal fearfulness and powerlessness on the part of many men: fearfulness over losing control over women; and powerlessness for being unable to neutralize the power of the state.[56]

Unveiling represented a critical blow to clerics' power. Privately, they shared with other men the power to control women through the household, family, sexuality, and the socialization and training of children. What men concealed was now being revealed; what was private for them was now public; and what men owned was now being taken away. Publicly, the clergy had already lost some control over institutions that held power over women, for example, the educational system, and to a lesser degree, marriage and divorce laws, and property relations. Unveiling further challenged the clerical domination over women, and especially their power over female sexuality. The religious communities in Tehran, Tabriz, and Mashhad waged drawn-out battles to recover social legitimacy and control over women and the state, although all their attempts were ruthlessly suppressed.[57]

In sum, the state succeeded in its unveiling initiatives. Unveiling transferred some patriarchal power of the clergy to the state, and the state itself assumed the role of patriarch. Although Middle Eastern patriarchy falls within the patterns of the classical model, Iranian patriarchy was immutable. It transcended specific social and political contexts as some of it shifted from the men's domain to that of the state's in the 1930s. Indeed,

[56] Photos, my relatives' photos in possession of the author; interviewee, Sedghi's interview with M.S. in New York City, January 1999; and "dictator," Woodsmall, *Women*, 50.

[57] Tehran, Bamdad I, 96; and Nashat, 27.

unveiling was carried out more coercively than comparable clothes and hat policies for men. Hardly a feminist or a champion of women, Reza Shah "was never subject to feminine influence, and never displayed a sentimental affection for the fair sex," his daughter acknowledged. His gender reforms did not intend to undermine women's actual oppression and exploitation.[58] His primary aim was the establishment of a centralized and superficially Westernized state that required emasculating the religious establishment. Women's emancipation was thus a means, not an end. Nahid Yeganeh indicated that Iranian feminist critiques of "traditionalism" and patriarchy were forcibly challenged by the powerful actions of the state and wielded against the clergy in an effort to weaken its power. Since gender policies required neutralizing the clerics' power, women who had long been active against the veil and their backward situation, found themselves confronted with the possibility of "emancipation" and unveiling overnight. Unveiling became the symbol of the clergy's "emasculation" and women's liberation from clerical patriarchy. Yet unveiling was a far cry from real democratic change. Women still remained subordinated. Thereby Reza Shah became his own gravedigger, as World War II began.[59]

WORLD WAR II, DYNASTIC CHANGES, AND NEW FEMINISMS

The Allies invaded Iran in August of 1941. Iran provided a strategic route to the Soviet Union, and the Allies sought to protect oil installations and avert pro-German activities. Unlike the constitutional period, foreign invasion provoked little popular resistance. Given his alliance with the Germans during the war, the Allies pressured the monarch to relinquish power in September 1941. Within three weeks, they deported Reza Shah to South Africa, where he died in 1944. Reza Shah abdicated in favor of his twenty two year old, Swiss-educated son, Mohammad Reza (1919–80), who retained the crown until the 1979 Revolution. The abdication brought an end to autocracy and state control of society, at least

[58] Middle Eastern patriarchy, Kandiyoti, *Women*, 1–21; and fair sex, Wilber, *Riza*, 236; and Pahlavi, *Faces*, 23–24. It is unclear whether Reza Shah had a distinct idea about what constituted a "Western" state and society; in many ways, he promoted autocracy, which paralleled many developing societies of his own time. Nor was he sympathetic to women, especially his own daughters who could not even choose their own schooling or select their own husbands.

[59] Yeganeh, Yeganeh, "Jonbesh-e Zan."

until the overthrow of Dr. Mohammad Mosaddegh's government by the CIA in August 1953.[60]

World War II and the Allied occupation nearly destroyed the Pahlavi state. The influence of capitalism and Western politics and culture grew along with those of communism and the Soviet Union. While the United States tried to incorporate Iran into its geopolitical orbit in conjunction with Greece and Turkey, the Soviet Union helped to form the Azarbaijan and Kurdish republics in northern Iran. Meanwhile, the wartime chaos intensified social and political conflicts, reintroducing old rival political groups, but simultaneously creating an atmosphere that fostered the emergence of new activities and movements. In the absence of an overpowering state and a decrease in the legitimacy of monarchy, different groups and power contenders began to reassert themselves, and gender issues became a major source of controversy, in particular between the conservative and modernist forces. The conservative clerical establishment and the newly formed fundamentalist organization of the Devotees of Islam (*Fe-da'in-e Eslam*) demanded a return to the veil and attempted to block women's suffrage as initiated by progressive groups and liberal forces in the National Front. On the other hand, women themselves became organized and articulated liberal and leftists' agendas, as will be discussed later. The *chador* reappeared concurrent with the closing of girls' schools, a process that happened sooner in smaller towns distant from the capital where customs and patriarchal dominance had been more strongly persistent. But even the streets of Tehran and other large cities were eventually filled with veiled women. Resources necessary for an adequate explanation of reveiling are unavailable. The growing power of the religious establishment might provide an explanation, although the clergy never regained the position it had held prior to Reza Shah's consolidation of state power. Reveiling also allowed some women to declare their own choice of clothing, and from this perspective, it was hardly a symbol of subordination especially, in the absence of a coercive state.[61]

[60] CIA, Gasiorowski, 261–286. In 1948, an attempt was made on the life of the Shah, and in 1951, Premier Razmara was assassinated. Both incidents are attributed to the growing power of the clergy after Reza Shah's abdication. Allegedly, Ayatollah Kashani's supporters who had grown increasingly impatient with the Shah and his court were behind both actions. See Akhavi, *Religion*, 68.

[61] Consolidation, *Ibid.*; and *Religion*, 90 and 60–72. During this period, old folk also came back, along with such outlawed religious practices as *ta'zieh* (passion plays) and *rozeh khani* (recitals).

The unstable political condition provided an opportunity for some women to pursue their own gender interest. A few were more willing to combat injustices, whether protesting the closing of girls' schools or the resurgence of old prejudices against women's rights. Others engaged in professional and educational endeavors or journalism and organizing, while many raised daughters who later claimed autonomy and became feminist activists in the late 1960s and 1970s. Women's organizations tended to be more specialized, often drawing their membership from particular professions. This period also saw the participation of independent feminists, as well as the formation of a number of women's associations, and an explicitly partisan political organization for women, the Tudeh Party's *Jame'y-e Democrat-e Zanan* or the Democratic Union of Women, which will be discussed below.[62]

Fatemeh Sayyah (1902–48) was one of the independent feminists of her time who exemplified the emergence of highly educated women in Iran. Born in Tiblis to an Iranian father and a German mother, she received a doctorate in literature from Moscow University. Although not many university professors had doctorates, initially the government was unwilling to let her teach in higher education. It was only with the insistence of university officials that she was employed by the University of Tehran, first as an adjunct, then as a regular, full-time professor in 1942. The first female professor at the University of Tehran, Sayyah taught literature. While fluent in Persian, Russian, French, and German, Sayyah's interests extended to broader social concerns such as women's struggles and socialism.[63]

The author of many articles and a frequent lecturer on women's issues, Sayyah co-founded (with Safiyyeh Firuz) *Hezb-e Zanan-e Iran* (The Women's Party of Iran). The goal of the party was to promote women's education and social status and awareness. In 1944, when the issue of electoral reform was discussed in the *Majles*, the party lobbied for women's suffrage. She also founded, edited, and published *Zanan-e Iran* (Women of Iran), which focused on women's rights, especially suffrage. In 1945, Sayyah was the only Iranian woman to participate in a U.N. meeting. She also represented Iranian women at the Peace and Women's Conference in Paris. In 1946, the party was transformed to *Shora-ye Zanan-e Iran* the Iranian Women's Council. Sayyah died, only seven years after arriving in

62 Associations, Ghavimi, 169.

63 Sayyah, Bamdad II, 77–78 (Sayyah was married for three years. When she divorced, she had no children.

Iran. Yet her importance was memorialized by the chairman of the Department of Literature at her university: "The University of Tehran has lost one of its most distinguished scholars. This loss is an inestimable tragedy, not only for the university, but also for the world of Iranian women. Perhaps many years will pass and no one will be able to attain the literary status of Professor Sayyah."[64]

Another important voice for women was that of Fakhr Ozma Arqun, a *Kanun-e Banovan* member, who was also a poet and mother of a noted living female poet, Simin Behbahani. Arqun established a secondary school for women in Tehran and, aided by her second husband, published and edited the journal *Ayandeh-e Iran* (Iran's Future), and later the journal *Banovan* (Ladies). There were also a number of professionally diverse women's organizations. The *Jam'iyyat-e Zanan* (the Women's Society), founded in the early 1940s, which after the war and the founding of the United Nations became *Sazeman-e Zanan-e Tarafdar-e E'lamiyy-eh-e Huquq-e Bashar* (The Women's Organization in Support of the Declaration of Human Rights). Concerned with women's education and literacy, legal matters, and suffrage, these organizations joined five other women's associations after 1943. Some of these organizations were formed on professional lines, for physicians, civil servants, and educators. They issued a joint statement and declared that "educated and progressive Iranian women of today cannot consider themselves isolated from the rest of the society. They must go forward and struggle for their own rights." In response, the government censored the liberal newspapers and feminist publications that had printed their declaration.[65]

The most active organization of women in this decade was the *Jame'y-e Democrat-e Zanan* (The Democratic Union of Women or the Union), women's branch of the pro-Soviet Tudeh Party. The party began focusing on women in 1943, culminating in one group for female party members and another for sympathizers. The two groups merged in the Tudeh's Democratic Caucus of Women in 1949. Most members were middle-class women associated with party leaders or Eskandari's Society, or

[64] Firuz, and chairman, Bamdad II, 38; "University," Bamdad I, 103–105; and Paidar, 126–127.

[65] Organizations, Bamdad I, 103–105. Other women's organizations included: *Anjoman-e Mo-Avenat-e Zanan-e Shahr* (The Association of Cooperating City Women), *Jami'yyat-e Rah-e No* (The Society for the New Path), *Anjoman-e Banovan-e Farhangi* (the Council of Women in Education), and *Kanun-e Banovan-e Pezeshk* (The Female Physicians' Center); joint statement, Abrahamian, *Iran*, 335; and "progressive," Royanian, 23.

had achieved professional prominence. Activists included Zahra and Taj Eskandari of the renowned progressive family; Maryam Firuz, a notable feminist, political analyst, and a member of the party's advisory board; Dr. Khadijeh Keshavarz, a well-known lawyer and author of a book on women's legal rights; Dr. Akhtar Kambakhsh, an acclaimed gynecologist and writer of a book on childrearing; and Badr-Monir Alavi from a prominent activist's and writer's family. The Democratic Union published a feminist journal *Bidari-ye Ma* (Our Awakening), edited by Homa Houshmandar, a high-school teacher.[66]

With the Democratic Union of Women, a women's organization for the first time coherently linked issues of class oppression and gender, while also placing a greater emphasis on improving the position of working-class and underprivileged women. The Union campaigned around such concerns as women's education, mobilization of women for political activities, prostitution, the exploitation of women and girls in factories (demanding hour limitations, equal wages, paid holidays, and sick leaves), day care centers, workshops to train women, and promotion of women's journals. It criticized Reza Shah's reforms for women as "modeled after fascism, which aimed not at true equality but at 'placing women in the home as wives, mothers, housekeepers, and cooks.'"[67]

It is unclear how the Democratic Union of Women financed itself and whether there were internal differences of opinion among its members. However, its apparent control by the Tudeh's male leadership may help to explain its silence on such gender-specific and patriarchal issues as marriage, polygamy, and divorce. This interference by men marks a crucial difference between the Union and previously discussed women's groups, which focused more on women-specific issues than on class conflict and were headed by women. Perhaps Afsaneh Najmabadi was thinking of the Tudeh group when she commented that, during the 1941–53 period, women's issues "became [incorporated into] broad political utopias, with packages for social change, rather than issue-centered, for instance, around female education and family laws, as had been the case during the constitutional period." Yet despite its subordination to the Tudeh party, the Union backed Mosaddegh's Nationalist Front government (1951–53), actively supporting him by "selling national government bonds and raising funds." Assisted by the Tudeh Party, the Union's women

[66] Democratic Union, Abrahamian, *Iran*, 323 and 326.

[67] "Housekeepers," Abrahamian, *Iran*, 323.

succeeded in helping place a suffrage bill before the *Majles*, certainly here meeting the criterion of a gender issue.[68]

DEFEAT OF WOMEN'S SUFFRAGE, MOSADDEGH, AND THE CIA COUP

From 1944 to 1952, Parliament was presented with three bills to enfranchise women. In 1944, the Democratic Union of Women openly challenged the government to extend the vote to women. For the first time in Iran, a women's organization collected over 100,000 signatures in favor of the reform. Introduced to the *Majles* by Tudeh deputies, the bill stirred less of an uproar than had been raised in 1911; yet it again was defeated. In 1946, Prime Minister Ahmad Qavam agreed to submit a women's suffrage bill. Challenged from within by his own Democratic Party as well as by the clerical opposition, his refusal to withdraw the measure resulted in the resignation of members from his party and the bill's defeat. Crucial in the bill's defeat was opposition by the clergy who found women an expedient issue for mobilizing its supporters. Uniformly the clergy opposed women's enfranchisement. The two issues that preoccupied the clergy in the 1940s and early 1950s were in fact women's suffrage and communism.[69]

The clergy utilized a two-pronged strategy to thwart women's suffrage in particular and feminist demands generally. First, make the battle public by bringing it into the streets, then challenge women in the halls of power. In 1948, fifteen high-ranking *ulama* issued a *fatva* (religious decree) forbidding unveiled women to shop in the *bazaars* and markets. In a feeble response, the government, still reeling from the aftermath of the war, asked Tehran's leading Ayatollah Mohammad Musavi Behbahani to curb public attacks and harassment of women by zealots. Furious with both the decree and the weak government response, the Union condemned the *fatva* as a "deprivation of all women's rights."[70]

The clergy's second strategy employed legislative skirmishes. Dr. Mohammad Mosaddegh, the nationalist Prime Minister, failed to include women in a 1951 electoral reform bill, which intended to increase the

[68] Financed, Abrahamian, *Iran*, 336; and Najmabadi, Najmabadi, "Hazards," 57–59.

[69] Signatures, Tudeh Party, "Proposals for," 336; 1944 defeat, Abrahamian, *Iran*, 230 and 244; and 1946 defeat, Akhavi, *Religion*, 63 and 69. Despite internal differences on politics, ideology, and the relationship to the state, the clergy's position with respect to women remained basically unchanged since the constitutional era. See Doroshenko, *Shiitskoe Dukhovenstvo*, 78 as cited in Akhavi, *Religion*, 63.

[70] "Deprivation of all women's," Abrahamian, *Iran*, 268–269.

representation of the urban population. Upon the recommendation of his advisers in 1952, one of his supporters in the *Majles* introduced a motion to extend the vote to women, arguing that it was within the spirit of the Iranian constitution and its supplementary laws. One deputy opposed women's enfranchisement on the grounds that it might create an uproar in Parliament. Proceeding with heated exchanges, the *ulama* countered the motion claiming that the *Shari'eh* restricted the vote to men. The prominent Ayatollah Abol-Qasem Kashani, a leading conservative cleric, maintained that women's place was at home and their duties were bounded by motherhood and childrearing. It is possible that in order to prevent further clashes, the *Majles* speaker had argued that the motion was improperly placed on the calendar; he ruled the motion out of order.[71]

Clergy-liberal-left strife over women's suffrage continued. Five days after the inception of the first debate, the *Majles* re-opened the floor for a discussion of women's suffrage. Once again, the *ulama* asserted that existing laws protected women and that any deviation from them would "create political disorder, cause religious decline and social crisis." Finally, after more heated debates, two high-ranking Ayatollahs, Mohammad Hossein Burujerdi and Behbahani, both strong collaborators with the Pahlavi state from 1953 to 1959, forced Premier Mosaddegh to withdraw the bill. Women's suffrage was not proposed again until 1959, after Mosaddegh's downfall.[72]

Mosaddegh, a European-educated aristocrat and a constitutional lawyer, who became the most prominent Third World nationalist leader through his challenges to foreign incursions and monarchical privileges, nationalized the Anglo-Iranian Oil Company (AIOC) as the key to Iran's development, sovereignty, and independence. Yet nationalization led to the West's economic boycott of Iran. Despite a positive trade balance, the blockade resulted in a shortage of foreign exchange and decline in governmental revenue. Although a popular leader, Mosaddegh was unable to consolidate his powers. He was the first Iranian premier who openly criticized the monarch for "violating the constitution" and took "the constitutional issue directly to the country." But the traditional wing of his supporters, primarily the *bazaaris* and the clergy, were threatened both by his economic reforms and by his support for women's suffrage. Conflicts

[71] 1951, Narimian and Safa'i, 2–3; The *ulama*, Kashani, "A Message," as cited in Abrahamian, *Iran*, 276; and *Majles* speaker, B. Jalali. Another Ayatollah, Ali Akbar Borqe'i, who was considered a "leftist," had supported the enfranchisement bill. But Borqe'i had little political influence.

[72] "Political disorder," Akhavi, *Religion*, 63; and bill's withdrawal, Abrahamian, *Iran*, 170.

between various wings of the National Front led to splits, with Mosaddegh losing some of his supporters.[73]

Ashraf Pahlavi secretly helped the planning of a coup. Not a Mosaddegh admirer, the CIA and the British government induced her to help with his downfall. In Italy, she met with Kermit Roosevelt, one of the architects of the coup. Although forbidden by Mosaddegh to enter Iran, Pahlavi arrived in Tehran covertly and met with Soraya, the Shah's second wife. Placed under house arrest, Pahlavi was again deported to Europe. In operation BEDAMN and AJAX, the CIA realized Mosaddegh's overthrow on August 19, 1953. This act of American foreign policy profoundly affected Iran's politics and economy, and thereby altered women's lives as will be discussed later. With Mosaddegh overthrown, the Shah returned from exile and was reinstated to power. Mosaddegh's ouster and the elimination of Britain's preferential position in Iran opened the way for American participation.[74] The United States became involved in exporting Iran's oil and incorporating it into its sphere of influence. After the coup, it sent $127.3 million in aid to Iran. By the mid-1950s, Iran appeared to be urbanizing and well on the road to integration into the world capitalist system.[75]

The coup and the Shah's return brought repression, modernization, and women's suffrage. Political parties went underground, members of the religious and secular opposition were arrested, and some were sentenced to life imprisonment. Similar to his father, the Shah seemed to be consolidating the state. This time Ashraf Pahlavi herself took the responsibility "to create a framework for . . . [Iran's] women's movement," by amalgamating eighteen women's groups in the High Council of Women's

[73] "Violating," and "constitutional," Abrahamian, *Iran*, Chs. 3–4. Mosaddegh also introduced land reform and taxation measures that tried to weaken the power of the landed upper-class and the royalist supporters of the Shah.

[74] Pahlavi, Pahlavi, *Faces*, 135–136; Roosevelt, K. Roosevelt; oil, Nirumand, 93–94, 100; and post-coup, Pahlavi, *Faces*, 154. Aid specialists and U.S. military experts arrived in Tehran to build up the army. The National Iranian Oil Company ratified a new contract with an international consortium comprised of Western oil companies. Foreign investors rushed to Iran; they constructed large-scale projects and established banks.

[75] Integration into the, Bharier, *Economic*, 27–28. Between 1900 and 1950, the number of urban localities grew from 100 to 186, a net increase of eighty-six towns. Similarly, in 1900, the total population was 9.86 million, and in 1956, it was 20.38 million, a growth rate of 2.20 percent. Urban population grew too. It grew from 2.07 million in 1900 to 14.06 in 1956; and the rural population increased from 7.79 million to 14.06 for the same years. These figures show that the compound rate of population growth from 1900 to 1956 was 4.40 percent for urban and 1.40 percent for rural areas.

Organizations in 1959[76] and, subsequently, the Women's Organization of Iran (WOI) in 1966. Once again, feminism would be directed from above. But fewer women wore the veil and more joined the rapidly expanding labor force as Iran's economy became increasing integrated in the global political economy.

[76] "Create a framework," Pahlavi, *Faces*, 154–155; Woodsmall, 1960, 83; and Paidar, 138–139.

3

Economic Development and the Gender Division of Labor

"Since American military and other aid has brought my country such important direct and indirect benefits," declared Mohammad Reza Shah in an autobiography written a few years after the CIA returned him to the throne, "I hope I shall not sound ungrateful if I state my conviction that we have been receiving glaringly inadequate amounts of it." In fact, the Cold War brought American military and economic aid to Iran by the late 1950s, helping the Shah consolidate his power against communism and the secular and religious opposition. He expressed his own preeminence in a 1973 interview with Oriana Fallaci: "Where there's no monarchy, there is anarchy, or an oligarchy or a dictatorship."[1]

Iran's integration into the world market and the ensuing economic growth based on rising oil revenues bolstered the state's power. Unleashing the unpredictable forces of change and expediently defending the throne with either co-optation or repression, the state launched several projects that changed the structure of the economy, the labor force, and the gender division of labor. Urban communities expanded with migration from rural areas, and the enlarging industrial and service sectors absorbed even more workers. More women, unveiled and educated, followed Western fashions and joined the growing labor market. Many began working in gender mixed occupations, while experienced the "double day," working both inside and outside the home. But empowered by the new economic environment and the gradual loosening of traditional ties, a few middle- and upper-class women gained a degree of freedom

[1] "American military" and "inadequate amount," Mohammad Reza Shah Pahlavi, *Mission*, 312; and "dictatorship," Fallaci, "A Shah's," 24.

and control over their own lives and sexuality. In essence, the earned income gave women an increasing power to negotiate their relationships to patriarchy, necessarily restraining its power, especially in the household. Unable to land rewarding and secure jobs, most working-class and lower middle-class women worked in meager jobs and made minimal wages.

Thus, economic development and state policies of the 1960s and 1970s provided opportunities for women to join the labor market and gain some autonomy and financial independence. But women's work involved both old and new forms of subordination: as employees by employers, as women by men, and as women by women in positions of power. It is my argument that the increasing absorption of women in the economy not only generated shifts in the division of labor, but it also met part of the demand for the expanding labor force of the rapidly developing Iran during the 1960s and 1970s. Women entered the sphere of production while they experienced the double day and gender inequality in the labor market. This chapter focuses on the impact of economic changes on the gender division of labor within the context of Iran's integration into the world political economy. It considers women's labor both inside and outside the home, especially according to the division of labor by gender, class, education, marital status, and life cycle.

INTEGRATION INTO WORLD CAPITALISM

Iran's growing integration into the global market was a typical example of the post-colonial political and economic relations between developed and peripheral developing states rich in natural resources. In their search for oil and markets for manufactured commodities and military equipments, Western governments and multinational corporations facilitated trade between Iran and the industrial world.[2] Iran's relations with the West were also formed within the context of Cold War containment policies. The West wanted to maintain stability in Iran, while it was also interested in preventing the communist states from having access to Iranian oil and political processes.

Western interest was first and foremost defined through oil. In Iran, the West made significant economic gains from the country's petroleum wealth: in 1971–75, multinational oil company profits increased substantially, and by 1977, the several American multinational oil companies that

[2] Search for oil, Nirumand.

marketed large consortium sales earned even greater profits. After the CIA coup, the formation in 1954 of an oil consortium between the National Iranian Oil Company (NIOC) and an international oil cartel ensured Western petroleum companies, especially British and American, access to Iran's oil. The new agreement also gave Iran a greater share of profits. In the 1960s and 1970s, Iran achieved some measure of economic prosperity through the Organization of Petroleum Exporting Countries (OPEC). Whereas in 1950 oil revenues totaled $91 million; in 1960, they reached $285 million; in 1970, $1.3 billion; and in 1974, they rose to $20.6 billion, after a quadrupling of world oil prices. In the period of 1973–77, the cumulative oil income reached over $71 billion. With increasing oil revenues, the state made considerable investments in development projects, although Iran remained vulnerable to the West.[3] The state also welcomed a market for Western manufactured goods as imports to Iran grew to high levels: from almost 16 percent of GNP in 1961 to 24 percent in 1972, and over 25 percent of GNP in 1974 – a rate almost without precedent among developing countries.[4]

Although the United States became an economic power in Iran after the coup, Iran maintained a diverse pattern of economic ties with Western European and Japanese firms, primarily in capital-intensive, rather than labor-intensive industries. In oil production, a highly sophisticated capital-intensive industry, American and to a lesser extent British companies, became dominant. Western countries established other modern capital-intensive industries with a minimum of 51 percent national ownership. Having welcomed and relied on the outside world for its development projects, the Shah's state had little of a domestic manufacturing and

[3] Economic gains, Keddie, *Roots*, 178 and Storke, 54–55. For 1950, 1960, and 1970, Rustow and Mugno, 131; 1974, Bank Markazi Iran, *Gozaresh-e Salnameh*, 1353(1974), 14; 1973–77, Bank Markazi Iran, *Gozaresh* Salnameh, 2434/1975, 10; Department of Commerce, *U.S. International*, December 1977, 6; and Looney, *The Economic Development*, 16–18.

[4] Imports included machinery and transport equipment, food, and live animals. Nonmilitary items accounted for over 89 percent of Iran's total imports. See Issawi, "The Economy: An Assessment," 48–50; Looney, *A Developmental Strategy*, 56–58. Market and import-substitution, International Labor Organization. *Employment and Income*, 50. Scientific studies are unavailable about the effects of imported goods on women. Having grown up in Iran during that time, I believe it would be revealing to research the impact of substantial imports of Western clothing, fashion, make-up, and hairstyles on women's perception of themselves, their public role, and changes in traditional gender relations. Current data only illuminate the volume of imports, Iran's dependence on the world market, and the economy's tilt toward consumerism and import-substitution industrialization.

technological base upon which to build Iran's economy and productive capabilities.[5]

In pursuit of its interests, the West also provided political and technical aid – an integral part of the Cold War strategy. In 1949, the Truman administration, with the Shah's agreement, introduced the Point Four program. After Mosaddegh's downfall, foreign aid brought large numbers of U.S. officials, advisers, and technical experts to Iran. Joined by American investors, they stimulated the development of the Iranian banking system, even as American economic and technical experts helped draft Iran's Second Development Plan of 1955–62. The Iranian government itself introduced the 1955 Law of Attraction and Protection of Foreign Investment in order to inspire foreign firms to invest in the country. Direct American private investment in Iran grew from $20 million in the early 1960s to $98 million in 1975, $125 million in 1976, and $700 million in 1977. These incentives that Iran offered to foreign investment, Robert Looney stated, were not available to Iranian firms, they "allowed U.S. and Western European firms, to preempt markets that local firms could have supplied."[6]

Thirdly, massive American military aid and sales accompanied the U.S.'s interest in offering economic assistance. In 1955, the British and American governments encouraged Iran to join the Baghdad Pact (later the Central Treaty Organization or CENTO), and in 1959, Iran and the United States formed a bilateral military treaty through which "Washington committed itself to take, in case of aggression against Iran, 'such appropriate action including the use of armed forces as may be mutually agreed upon.'" In the case of outside aggression, notably by the Soviet Union, this included the right to land troops in Iran "directly and indirectly." The Nixon Doctrine then provided even greater military support for Iran and

[5] After the coup, Ivonof, *Tarikh-e Novin-e*, 247; American, U.S. International Commerce, 1977, 3; and 51 percent national ownership, Halliday, *Iran: Dictatorship*, 255–256. Japan established a strong presence in petrochemicals, France in building nuclear power plants and automobile industries (Peugeot in Mashhat, Renault in Tehran, and contracts for building the Tehran subway system), England and West Germany in automobile production, and later in cement and steel. Both Japan and Western Germany retained competitive positions with the United States in their export to Iran.

[6] 1955–62, The Department of Commerce, May 1966, 10; American private investments, The Department of Commerce, *U.S. International*, October 1977, 6; 1976, *Ibid*; The Department of Commerce, *U.S. International,* October 1978, 8; The Department of Commerce, *U.S. International*, September 1978, 7; and Falk, "Iran and American Geopolitics," 41–56. "U.S. and Western European Firms," Looney, *Income Distribution*, 152. Looney also states that Direct American private investment in Iran grew from $20 million in the early 1960s to $700 million in 1977.

the Shah; the United States would sell the monarch "virtually any conventional military hardware he wanted" – a policy that continued until the Shah's downfall. In the words of a 1978 report to the Joint Economic Committee of Congress, "American support" of Iran "spans six American Presidential administrations, going back to early 1946."[7]

Iran's integration into the world market not only promoted Western interests and influence, but also its own economic and military projects. Under its 1973–78 Five Year Plan, Iran devoted 31 percent of all its monies for national development on military and intelligence expenditures. In addition, assisted by the Israeli Mossad (the Institute for Special Intelligence Tasks), the CIA and FBI (the Federal Bureau of Investigation) in 1957 it established the infamous secret police that came to be known as SAVAK *Sazeman-e Ettela't va Amniyat-e Keshvar* or the Organization of Intelligence and National Security. While building a powerful military and intelligence machinery, the Shah introduced policies that generated shifts in the structure of the economy and the labor market, both of which had important consequences for development and women's work.

THE SHAH AND ECONOMIC DEVELOPMENT

It is difficult to disentangle Iran's development and the role of the state from that of the Shah. Identifying himself as the state, and at other times as the country's head according to constitutional mandates, the Shah reigned and ruled simultaneously. The state was not only an institution with a monopoly over the use of coercion, but from the early 1960s until the 1979 Revolution it was also the dominant force in regulating the economy and fostering change.

Initially, the road to state-building and economic development proved difficult for the young Shah. By the late 1950s, the Shah's power appeared consolidated, although there was a recession and rampant inflation. The stagnant economy of 1960–63 created unemployment and a balance of payments deficit. Subsequently, the ensuing state repression resulted in popular discontent, and it seemed that the severe social, economic, and

[7] CENTO, Saikal, 57; "Washington committed" and "directly and indirectly," J. Cooley, "U.S. Faces," 10; the Nixon Doctrine, Hurewitz, J.C., 45; and military support, Contrell and Hanks, "The Future," 547. Note that U.S. foreign military sales to Iran expanded from $800 million in 1950 to $2.8 billion in 1977 (The Department of Defense, *Security Assistance*, December 1980, 1–2); other military figures are even higher: over $15 billion in 1973–77. See Stockholm International Peace Research Institute, *U.S. Military Sales*, 16, 21, and 27.

political crisis was moving the country almost to the brink of a revolution. In response, the Shah strengthened the undemocratic state while launching economic development programs that set records for growth in the Middle East and in the world.

Interested in Iran's development, the Shah aspired to twin goals – modernization and Westernization, which he referred to as "our welcome ordeal." His "mission" for Iran was his "vision" of a "Great Civilization" that would ultimately revive the ancient Persian Empire as ruled by Cyrus the Great. In the Shah's modernization tableau he would be Iran's Emperor Napoleon, his third wife, Farah Diba, the Empress or *Shahbanu* (shah's wife) and later the Regent. Like his father, the Shah would crown himself on the Peacock Throne. He alone, in his condescending, pretentious, and patriarchal self-image, would represent the Persian empire. What served Westernization – as he understood it – served the monarch: even a degree of women's emancipation and their participation in the labor force. In his father's footsteps, he followed secularization, co-optation, and repression. Unlike his father, however, the Shah wanted his programs to affect the vast majority of Iranians throughout the country, not only the urban administrative and military apparatus and economic organizations. Taking an active interest in building a quasi-capitalist economy, he launched a semi-industrialized economy that was based on capital-intensive and import-substitution.[8]

The Shah's major reform program came with the 1963 White Revolution. He called it the "Revolution of the Shah and People." The intention was to contrast it with the "Red" or Bolshevik Revolution and the "black" or clergy-instigated upheaval. The Kennedy administration was then encouraging its allies in the developing world, including Iran, to carry out reforms to combat popular discontent. The White Revolution's six tenets were: land reform, nationalization of forest land, sale of state-owned industries; profit-sharing in industry, enfranchisement of women, and establishment of an education corps for literacy programs in villages. Politically, it aimed at the suppression of dissidents and the achievement of long-term stability, especially through the promotion of land reform by gaining the support of the peasantry, the inarticulate majority of the population. Socially and economically, it set to transform the economy by promoting growth and capitalism in both rural and urban areas and by fostering the participation of foreign and domestic businesses in development

[8] "Welcome ordeal," "Mission" and "Great Civilization," Pahlavi, *Mission* and Pahlavi Mohammad Reza, *Besu-ye Tamaddon-e Bozorg*.

projects. However important, the White Revolution might have had only a tangential relationship to women. To the extent that it did affect official gender policies, I will discuss it in the next chapter.[9]

By the mid-1970, Iran's rate of economic growth was unprecedented in the world. Investments with oil monies boosted capital formation. Together the rapid increase in oil revenues and capital formation provided dynamic economic growth, as reflected, for example in the GNP. In terms of constant prices, the GNP rose by 8 percent per year in the 1960s, by 14.2 percent in 1972–73, by 33.8 percent in 1973–74, and by 41.9 percent in 1974–75. Moreover, the structure and distribution of the GNP exhibited an impressive change. The highest priority went to the growth of industry and services at the expense of traditional agriculture. An insignificant factor in 1900, industry accounted for about 14 percent of the GNP in 1959, 19 percent in 1965, and 22.9 percent in 1975. This was an indication of the great dynamism of industrial growth, both in terms of productivity and number of factories.[10] The service sector also showed substantial growth. Accounting for only 10 to 20 percent of GNP at the beginning of the century, it increased to 38.3 percent in 1959, rose to 39.5 percent in 1965, and retained its large share in 1975. As discussed later in this chapter, this sector absorbed the largest number

[9] 1963 White Revolution, Pahlavi, *The White Revolution*, and Pahlavi, *Answer to History*. Domestic private capitalists remained dependent on the state but continued to play an active role in Iran's industrialization. The activities of this class, coupled with state initiatives and foreign capital contributed to the implementation of Iran's economic development. See Ashraf, "Historical Obstacles," 33; Graham, *Iran*, 47–9; and Looney, *The Economic Development*, 20.

[10] Capital formation, in simple terms, is investment by another name. It is the amount of investment that is added to the old capital stock. Calculating capital accumulation is complex; here, I have measured it in terms of capital formation, the GNP, and employment/unemployment relations. From 1955 to 1961, during Iran's rapid accumulation, foreign aid and investment helped economic growth. The post-White Revolution was the second period of rapid accumulation. The rate of capital formation at 1965 constant prices grew at an extraordinary annual average of 10–15 percent from 1955 to 1977. See table 4 in Sedghi, "Women and Class" and Bank Markazi, *Annual Report and Balance Sheet, 1351* (1972), 141; *1352* (1973), 139; *1353* (1974), 143; and *2534* (1975), 50. Most state investments went into heavy industry – steel mills, gas pipelines, automobile, petrochemical, and oil plants – and development banks. Government also built roads, ports, dams, energy power, and communications systems. Industry (including manufacturing and mining, construction, and water and power generation) enjoyed spectacular growth. GNP, table 5 in Sedghi, "Women and Class" and Bank Markazi, *1349* (1960), 117; *1351* (1972), 143; *1353* (1974), 143; and *2534* (1975), 48. GNP growth, Bank Markazi, *1351* (1972); 144, *1353* (1974), 142; and *2534* (1975), 48; and the share of GNP components, Bank Markazi Iran, *National Income of Iran 1338–1344*, 21; Bank Markazi, *1351* (1972), 143; *1353* (1974), 142; and *2534* (1975), 48.

of women workers, especially in urban areas. Despite an absolute increase in the agricultural sector, agriculture experienced a decline in terms of its contribution to the GNP. Agriculture constituted 80 to 90 percent of GNP at the beginning of the century, its contribution was about 33 percent by 1959, 27 percent by 1965, and 10 percent in 1975. By contrast, oil, which was almost insignificant in 1900, by 1959 accounted for 10.8 percent of GNP. By 1965, its share was 14.5 percent, and by 1975, 38 percent.[11]

Despite tremendous growth, Iran's economic development encountered serious obstacles. As industrial production concentrated on the assembly of finished goods in the petrochemical, electronic, automotive, and consumer areas, reliance on imported parts discouraged both domestic manufacture and the formation of domestic technology. In addition, the service sector grew much faster than industries or agriculture, although it attracted a larger portion of the labor force and was important to women. Another impediment to Iran's development was the expenditure of large sums on food imports – \$2.6 billion worth of food in 1977, in part due to population and income growth. Finally, the Shah's agricultural and land reform policies led to setbacks. New land distribution policies introduced changes in property relations in the countryside as well as changes in market relations. But the displaced and unemployed rural laborers migrated to the cities, in turn contributing to urban unemployment and exasperating urbanization problems and developmental processes.[12]

URBANIZATION

The rapid growth of modern urban centers, typical of capitalist industrialization, was fully evident in Iran. Investments increased employment opportunities in capital-intensive industry, and as major centers of production, cities offered a site for capital concentration. The vast service sector also served a variety of political, economic, cultural, and bureaucratic functions, creating new occupations not only for the growing urban population but also for some rural migrants. It was in cities that middle- and upper-class women would replace their *chadors* with hot pants, jeans, mini-skirts, and other kinds of Western clothing; attend universities; and find new jobs along with working-class women who covered or revealed their hair.

[11] Agriculture constituted, and oil, Looney, *The Economic*, 1–25.
[12] Land reform, Khamsi, "Land Reform," 20–28 and Moghadam, *From Land Reform*.

Faster than elsewhere in the developing world, Iran experienced rapid population growth and large-scale rural-urban migration between 1956 and 1976. Iran's total population, almost 19 million in 1956, reached 25,078 million in the next decade; by 1976, it was 33,662 million, for a growth rate of 32 percent from 1966 to 1976. The growth rate of urban population was almost twice as large – 62 percent in 1956–66 and 61 percent in 1966–76. Urban population, almost 5,953 million in 1956, rose to 9,754 million in 1966 and 15,797 million in 1976. In part, rural migration contributed to accelerating the urban population. The land reform programs of the White Revolution and Iran's rapid and uneven economic development triggered this migration to cities by disproportionately decreasing rural compared to urban income and employment opportunities. Rural unemployment, the class transformation of the countryside and a relative decrease in agricultural productivity were other factors. Finally, the policies of farm and agri-business companies contributed to the dislocation of agricultural workers and motivated their migration to cities. However important, a detailed discussion of rural changes is beyond this book's scope.[13]

Urban areas were themselves attractive, especially their concentration of capital and employment opportunities in the industrial and service sectors. Tehran, the largest locus of population and Iran's political, economic, administrative, and cultural center, became the central point of the new economy. By the mid-1970s, it accounted for 51 percent of all manufactured goods, for example, shoes, clothes, automobiles, plastics, textiles, rubber, and electronics. Tehran also served as Iran's educational core, with public, private, and Western universities and colleges, technical schools, high schools, kindergartens, and day care centers. Culturally, it offered theaters, a symphony hall, cinemas, museums, discos, parks, sports and bowling clubs, and restaurants. Americans and Europeans almost outnumbered Iranians in the northern and wealthiest parts of the city, as though these sections represented Western colonies.[14]

[13] Population growth, Sedghi, "Women and Class," table 8, Ministry of Interior, *Sar Shomari-ye 1335* (1956), 207–208; Statistical Center of Iran, *Sar Shomari-ye 1345* (1966), 34–35; and Statistical Center of Iran, *Nataye-je Sar Shomari-ye Omumi 2535* (1976), 52–53. The latter is based on 5% sample – Rural population growth was 17 percent in both periods of 1956–66 and 1966–76. Urban income, ILO, *Employment*, 24–25 and Langer, Frederic and Editors, 13; and rural unemployment, Khamsi, *Ibid.*

[14] Colonies, Graham, 24. Although in many ways Tehran was unique, the kind of expansion that took place there was imperfectly reproduced in most of Iran's major cities, which increasingly became centers of production and services.

Diverted by the pace of rapid change, governmental authorities overlooked Tehran's shanty towns and its slums. For many migrants and displaced rural people on the lookout for work, home and survival, Tehran was brutal: it provided no cultural ties, no job training, and no sense of community. Many became homeless and began their new lives on the edge of the city or underground within cardboard or metal walls (*halab-neshinan*). The city officials, charities, and other kinds of social organizations abused and ignored them. Falling back on their *Shi'i* consciousness and religious allegiance brought from the countryside, many of the urban poor took refuge at cities' mosques where they received spiritual and financial help from the clergy. In mosques, they met their future organizers, employers, and political leaders.[15]

Overall, Iran's integration into the world market created a dual or an "uneven economy." Industry and service sectors grew rapidly, while the agricultural sector withered slowly. Likewise, modern cities grew but population growth and migration outpaced the capital's ability to absorb them. The pool of surplus labor was reflected in urban unemployment and ever rising unemployment in the countryside. With oil revenues, however, the Shah strengthened his autocratic powers, launched the White Revolution and embarked on economic development. Such processes generated major shifts in the gender division of labor both in the unpaid sphere of the household and the paid labor market.

THE GENDER DIVISION OF LABOR: THE HOUSEHOLD

In Iran, economic development swept all corners of the society, introducing changes in the nature of the household and making it more vulnerable to the market's needs. During the last two decades of Pahlavi rule, more women abandoned the household and its male dominance for the labor market. Depending on their class and access to resources, women continued their work at home, while many transformed their activities from primarily household production to consumption and labor force participation. Feminist scholarship explains the role of reproduction and the dominant/subordinate relations between women and men in households as determinants of women's labor force participation and the gender division of labor. They argue that participation in production can be direct or

[15] Homeless, as depicted in Dariush Mehrjooyi's film, *Dayereh-e Mina* that was produced in Iran during the 1970s but was banned.

indirect. The former consists of paid work and the latter includes unpaid activities such as household work.[16]

Traditional cultural restrictions and women's seclusion are crucial to households. A woman's first and foremost responsibility consists of serving her immediate family. As we saw in Chapter 1, religion assures men's economic support of women, in return for women's obedience to husbands' whims, and it exercises authority over the individual through the traditional patrilineal, patrilocal, patriarchal, and endogamous extended family. But secular codes also legitimate the father, or the husband, or the brother to be the household's head, controlling decisions pertaining to a woman's place in the society. In Iran, the control of women's sexuality validates the man to interfere with women's work outside the home. Thus, seclusion, veiling, male dominance, and control of women's sexuality often go hand in hand with women's role in reproduction, women's work at home, and the gender division of labor.

State policies and economic development can challenge and alter the traditional gender division of labor. Concerned with Iran's development, the Shah encouraged women to leave the household for the labor market. During the 1960s and 1970s, official proclamations and family laws challenged some of men's power over women's sexuality, bolstering women's work outside the home. In addition, motivated by the drive to project a "modern" image of the state, as well as of himself, to the West, the Shah declared that to meet part of the demand for labor, "greater use must be made of the enormous existing pool of women." He announced that:

> [M]ore facilities for part time work . . . will permit fuller use of housewives and provide them with the opportunity to play a *worthy* role in the work of social reconstruction *even* while administering and supervising the home. . . . Women . . . make up a great force whose effective participation in activities is an essential requirement for all development and progress. [Emphasis added.]

But critical of women's abilities, the monarch told the Italian reporter, Oriana Fallaci:

> In a man's life, women count only if they're beautiful and graceful and know how to stay feminine. . . . [Women] may be equal in the eyes of the law, but not . . . in ability [.] [Have women] lacked the opportunity to give history a great cook?

[16] Participation in production, various articles in Young, et al., *Marriage*; and Beneria and Sen, "Accumulation." This book uses the following terms interchangeably: "labor," "paid producer," "wage laborer," "employed," "employee," and "working population."

> [Women] have produced nothing great, nothing! [They are] ... schemers ... evil. Every one ...

Premier Amir Abbas Hoveyda refined the royal statements: "Woman's emancipation does not mean her estrangement from the family; on the contrary, it means the deepening of her roots in the family."[17]

But as economic development was generating substantial income inequality and consumerism, it was inducing women to leave the household for work in the market. Both urban income and consumption levels grew, especially from 1969 to 1975. With the rise in urban consumption, the relative income from wages as a percent of total income declined. This meant that wages alone did not compensate for consumption and expenditure in struggling families or those who attempted to maintain their previous standard of living. The conundrum was exasperated by the growing income inequality and high inflation rate for the period of 1969–75, specifically after 1973, when oil income quadrupled. Under such circumstances, more members of urban families, namely wives and daughters, had to enter the labor market, for the economic cost of remaining in the home was increasing sharply. In part, therefore, the consumption patterns of households, their income, and class position helped women to seek employment.[18]

By the mid-1960s, consumerism was rampant. It created new demands on women's household activities – to abandon some traditional tasks, but to work more and consume more. Instead of producing and preparing food at home, many middle-class women began to spend time and money purchasing goods, processed foods, and ready-made household items from such newly built supermarkets as Tehran's *Iran-Super*. Instead of sewing at home, many bought finished clothes from Western-like chain stores, such as *Furushgah-e Ferdowsi* in Tehran. Working-class women generally shopped at small neighborhood stores. Gradually though, large numbers of urban households began to consume and buy purified water; acquire refrigerators, radios, tape recorders, and televisions; and utilize

[17] "Pool of women" and "worthy role," Sanghvi, et al., 3–17; Fallaci, "A Shah's," 24; and "Women's emancipation," "Hoveyda: Azadi-ye Zan," *Keyhan-e Havai'i*, 3.

[18] Rise in urban consumption, Bank Markazi Iran. *Natayej-e Barresiy-ye Budjeh-e Khanevarha-ye Shahri-ye*, 2533/1974. Sec. I, table 18; and Sedghi, "Women and Class," table 15; relative income, *nataye j-e*, 2533, Sec II. 70; and Sedghi, "Women," table 16. Wages, Bank Markazi, *Gozaresh-e Salnameh*, 1353/1974, 20; and Sedghi, "Women and Class," table 17. Note that profits constituted a great portion of income rise, not wages. Also consult Sedghi, "Women," tables 18, 19, 20, 21, 22.

such labor-saving devices as gas and electric stoves. The privileged households obtained dishwashers, laundry and drying machines, freezers, and other luxurious and modern commodities like cooling and heating systems. The consumption of these commodities not only created new tasks for women within the household, but also linked domestic work to the market.[19]

Women had different reasons for abandoning the household for work in the labor market. A small number of middle-class women wanted employment to be financially independent, use their educational training, and significantly, construct a different life from that of their mothers. Others sought paid work to supplement the income of their husbands, naturally, subject to their approval. In contrast, working-class women exercised no such options. Poor women entered the labor market as a necessity to maintain household subsistence and help their families to survive; they had less alternatives than wealthier women. Thus, the household gender division of labor shifted, not because men attempted to share the burden of family tasks, but working women increasingly took a greater responsibility to contribute to the families' income.[20]

Women's support was crucial to women who entered the labor force. Many middle-class women hired maids to perform domestic tasks. Some were part-time, others were not. By the late seventies, many former servants had joined the growing industrial and service sectors and there was a smaller supply of household assistance, not for the wealthy, but for middle-class women. Some women sent their children to nursery and preschools. In the event that maids or nurseries were inaccessible, women relied on traditional networks – mostly relatives and mothers – for child care and babysitting. If help was unavailable, a few husbands would sometimes assist with shopping but not with cooking, cleaning, and washing. During the booming economy, many women referred to themselves as "wageless maids."

Among the poor families, the elderly women, younger daughters, and relatives assisted with domestic tasks. Daughters' help was especially crucial. The poorer the household, the greater the daughters' responsibilities. In the northern towns of Iran, I saw girls from the age of 6 who fastened

[19] Consume and buy, Bank Markazi, *Natayej-e*, 1353, table 18; and Sedghi, "Women," table 15.

[20] Working women, Moser-Khalili, *Urban.*, and Keyhan Research Associates, *The Employment of Women.*

their younger brothers or sisters to their backs while doing household chores, carried buckets of water, and prepared food for their siblings. The working mother prepared the meals when she arrived home, squeezing cleaning and washing into odd moments. In the absence of daughters' help, the mothers took the younger children to work or made arrangements with their own mothers, relatives, or neighbors to look after the children. Thus, low income women entered the labor market by depending on their traditional and personal network relationships. This was necessary because subsistence was based upon wages, and class inequalities were formidable. Intermeshing two kinds of work led to the creation of a new form of subordination for women – the double day: as unpaid domestic workers and consumers in the household, and as paid workers in the gender segregated labor market.

THE GENDER DIVISION OF LABOR: THE LABOR FORCE

Any industrializing country will experience a transformation of its laboring population and labor market. Similar to the early stages of European industrialization, Iran's development led to the creation of new kinds of occupations, and laborers, skilled and unskilled, women and men who joined the labor force. There were also the urban unemployed in search of jobs and the migrants who had lost their means of subsistence in the countryside. As I will discuss in the next chapter, through its active interference, the state altered family legislation, encouraged greater secularization and cultivated liberal attitudes toward women's public appearance, in particular, gender relations and women's work even in sexually mixed occupations.

As capitalist industrialization was on its way, Iran's labor force expanded significantly from 1956 to 1976. In 1956, 6 million people, ten years of age and over, were economically active, compared to 7.5 million in 1966, and almost 10 million in 1976. Women entered into the labor market, although there was a disparity between their labor force participation and men's. The number of economically active men increased from 5,491 million in 1956, to 6,584 million in 1966, and 8,288 million in 1976. For women, growth was from 575,000 in 1956, to 999,000 in 1966, and to 1,452 million in 1976. During the same period, however, the percentage of active men dropped from 83 percent of the total male population in 1956, to 77 percent in 1966, and 70 percent in 1976. Conversely, the percentage of active women rose from 9.2 percent of total female population in 1956, to 12 percent in 1966, and 13 percent in 1976. Iran did move ahead of many other Middle Eastern countries but stayed behind Latin America in female labor force participation.[21]

The urban labor force increased at an even more rapid rate than did the overall country. It increased from 1,893 million in 1956, to 2,768 million in 1966, and 4,294 in 1976, moving the urban labor force from 46 percent of all workers in 1956–66 to 55 percent in 1966–76. Economically active urban men went up from 1,705 million in 1956, to 2,449 million in 1966, and 3,807 million in 1976. For urban women, growth was 187,000 in 1956, 300,000 in 1966, and almost 500,000 in 1976. Thus, the labor force participation of urban men expanded almost three-fold in numbers as against a two-and-half-fold increase for their female counterparts.[22]

Economic growth and labor market expansion generated unemployment, although it was less in urban areas that had a greater capacity to absorb or reject workers, including rural migrants and women. The employment/unemployment pattern can be understood by Iran's particular form of development that geared toward capital-intensive and import-substitution industries. Capital-intensive economic growth retarded the market's ability to draw on the supply of available labor and created fewer jobs than a labor-intensive industry would have. Nonetheless, despite its rapid expansion and extraction, two decades of growth were hardly sufficient for building a healthy and sustaining economy that would generate sufficient resources for expanding the labor force participation, in particular that of women. But entering the market exhibited important challenges for women as they experienced significant variations in the industrial and service sectors.[23]

[21] Labor force expanded, Ministry of Interior, *Sar Shomari-ye 1335* (1956), 207–208; also Statistical Center of Iran, *Sar Shomari-ye 1345* (1966), 34–35; Statistical Center, *Natayeje 2535* (1976), 52–53; and Sedghi, "Women and Class," tables 8–9. The percentage of active women, Sedghi, *Ibid.*, table 8. And Latin America, Youssef, *Women*, 74.

[22] Labor force increased, Sedghi,"Women and Class," tables 11 and 8.

[23] Unemployment, Sedghi, "Women and Class," tables 10 and 12 and Chs. 4–5. Note that because of problems in unemployment data, I assume a higher rate of unemployment than what actually appeared in the data. During the period under the study, unemployment rose from nearly 3 percent in 1956 to 9.6 percent in 1966 and 9.7 percent in 1976. Urban areas experienced less unemployment and its pattern was somewhat stable during the 1956–76 period. Women's unemployment, while lower than men's, increased steadily from .03 percent in 1956, to 1.2 percent in 1966, and 2.5 percent in 1976. Men's unemployment as a percentage of the economically active population went up from 4.9 percent in 1956 to 5.3 percent in 1966, but declined to 3.8 percent in 1976. Similar figures for women indicate a steady increase from .07 in 1956 to .4 percent in 1966 to .7 percent in 1976. Also, the relationship of unemployed men to the total economically active population increased from 2.6 percent in 1956, to 8.4 percent in 1966, then decreased to 7.1 percent in 1976.

DIVISION OF LABOR BY MAJOR ECONOMIC SECTORS AND CLASS

Iran's economy prompted greater employment opportunities for women in the service than the industrial and agricultural sectors. From 1956 to 1976, the percentage of the urban female labor force in the service sector increased from 52 to almost 59 percent, in industries it decreased from 39 to 31 percent, and in the overall agriculture sector it experienced a decline from 3 to 2 percent. Men's labor force participation exhibited similar patterns. Compared to women, their absorption by agricultural and industrial sectors declined, however, their participation in the service sector increased slightly.[24]

As in other class-based societies, in Iran, one's place in the occupational structure related strongly to her/his class position. Some Iranian studies scholars have adopted a class approach to the study of politics and society, but they have ignored the gender category. In general terms, class refers to one's relation to the mode of production, and as a concept, it is an abstraction with broader parameters than occupational categories and it is intrinsically integrated with gender. Methodologically, the specific case of Iran poses another challenge, typical of that encountered by scholars of repressive societies. Often, respondents to data collectors felt restrained to speak openly. One official study of working-class conditions concluded that "factory workers are not allowed to freely talk because they are always accompanied by supervisors during interviews." Nor do Iranian census data provide sufficient information for a systematic analysis of class, gender, and work. Despite these difficulties, a study of women's participation in the industrial and service sectors provides an explanation for women's work during the last decades of the Pahlavis.[25]

[24] Major economic sectors, Sedghi, "Women and Class," T. 23. Note that men's labor force participation rose especially in construction, commerce, and transportation, those areas most exclusively dominated by male workers.

[25] Classes, Bill, *The Politics*; A. Ashraf; and A. Banuazizi, "Classes in the Pahlavi Period," 677, 691. During the Shah's reign, substantial investment was made in data collection. Yet some of the data are not trustworthy because of the presence of SAVAK at some official interviews and sometimes because of governmental pressure on data collectors and researchers to produce more favorable results. Many researchers and scholars that I encountered during the course of my interviews and field research, especially at the Plan and Budget Organization in 1975 and the Bank Markazi in 1977 echoed unreliability of the data. But there were also those who believed that government pressure pertained to sensitive data only. They included such figures as GNP and GDP, which were often revised and changed in subsequent years. "Factory Workers," The Office of Women's Studies Research, "Bar-resi-ye Ejmali-ye Sharayet-e Kargar-e Zanan," 13.

The Industrial Sector and Women

Women's work in the industrial sector consisted of their participation in "traditional" and modern factories and small workshops. While the majority of urban women workers were in the service sector, and secondarily in industries, most rural women engaged in what is known as traditional industries, or weaving and agriculture, respectively. Little accurate and specific information is available about women and their working condition in the industrial sector, although tales of Iran's "wretched of the earth" are abundant. Continuing the work of earlier generations of women, many women worked as carpet or gelim weavers, or knitters, and most were illiterate. Others worked in a variety of small and large, public and private, and traditional and modern industries. These included food, tobacco, wood and cork, printing, chemical products, oil and coal products, non-mineral activities, steel products, machines, and assembings. The majority of women worked in textiles, clothing, and shoe-making industries.[26]

Parallel to women's work at the turn of the twentieth-century, women's participation in the industrial sector constituted a struggle against poverty. Sometimes as sole wage earners in female-headed households, women undertook the responsibility of feeding children by themselves, and other times, they worked to compensate for their husbands' or fathers' low wages. Generally, they spent long hours on appalling jobs in unhealthy environments to earn an income in the midst of urban poverty. Because many women lived far away from their jobs, their six-day-a week work day, including unpaid commuting time, might run 12.5 to 13.5 hours per day. Whether working as adults or child laborers, women received exceedingly low wages and experienced discrimination.[27]

Wages varied somewhat by type of work and age of the worker. One study suggested that women frequently earned more than their husbands by working longer hours. Another nationwide research on industrial women's wages in 13 large factories (500 plus workers) and smaller workshops (some owned privately) found that most women earned 100–150 rials [$.13–.20] per day, an absolute wage less than their male co-workers. A third study of 31 large and small, public and private factories and workshops in Tehran and Isfahan, where most industries were concentrated,

[26] Women's work in industrial sector, the Plan and Budget Organization, *Degarguniha-ye*, 77–79; weaving and agriculture, Moser-Khalili, *Urban*, 20; and the variety of small and large, and majority of women, Rastegar, E., "*Sokhanrani*," [A Lecture], 1354/1975, 26.

[27] Low wages, Rastegar, "Tose'eh-e," 20.

revealed that women's wages varied with job categories, which differed from men's. Generally, when women performed machine-related jobs, such as those in shoe, clothing, and textile factories, their wages were almost identical with men performing similar tasks; however, when they completed simpler and manual jobs, such as packing in glass and chemical factories, their wages were lower than men's, perhaps because of women's reduced bargaining position at that level. The study concluded that women's wages were higher than the minimum wage because they worked overtime. With overtime, women's wages were highest in electrical factories (74 rials [$.09] daily), in chemical factories (61 rials [$.08] daily), in tobacco (60 rials [$.08] daily), in textile factories (55 rials [$.07] daily), in food (52 rials [$.06] daily), in shoes and clothing (50 rials [$.06] daily), and in paper and glass factories (35 rials [$.04] daily).[28]

Exploitation of child labor and girl children as cheap laborers continued despite the Shah's rhetoric of "modernization." Girls below the age of 16, most as young as 9 or 10 worked in Isfahan's larger glass and paper factories. Their wages were a pittance. Factory owners often justified the situation by claiming that the girls lived with their families and thus needed no meaningful wages. Violating labor laws, some owners refrained from paying these girls their holiday pay of 18 days and some refused their consecutive holidays.[29]

Knitting and sewing workshops exhibited a different pattern of exploitation. A study of 24 workshops with 406 employed women described a group of employed women averaging about 30 years of age, whose wages varied from 45 to 250 rials [$.06–.33] a day. Larger workshops, perhaps because they were under greater governmental scrutiny, abided by the legal age limit of 12 years old and offered women wages and insurance as set out by the 1958 labor legislation. By contrast, smaller workshops paid lower wages and were more exploitive. Operating in homes and based on the putting-out system, they employed many girls and paid minimal wages (there are no exact wage reports). These workshops did not meet minimum legal standards with respect to wages, working hours, or age restrictions. Women and young girls hired by these small workshops reported to work every day, took an order, and brought it home to complete. Their homes or rooms were also their workplace. Their

[28] One study, Rastegar, "Tose'eh-e," 12; nationwide study, The Office, "Bar-resi-ye Ejmali," 1–14 and 17; and third study, as cited in The Office, *Ibid.*, 16. Note that I calculated the rate of exchange on the basis of seventy rials per one dollar, as it was in the 1970s.

[29] Exploitation, The Office, "Bar-resiy-e," 21.

piece-work wages were less than those received by men doing similar tasks.[30] Wool-making and *ketira* (special dye) workshops, essential for weaving, sewing, and textile disclosed the worst pattern of exploitation. The same survey included 16 workshops, which employed 650 women.[31] Their work was done entirely by hand and these workers were older, averaging about 45 years of age. Under 50 percent of these women were married. Their husbands typically had low-paying and low-skilled jobs, were unemployed, or too old to work; others had abandoned their family. Less than 50 percent of these women were widowed, and a small number were single. Most women had at least 4 children; a few had more than 4, though some had fewer or even none. These women's wages varied between 24 and 35 rials [$.03–.04] daily, and employers failed to pay them health insurance or holidays. In its analysis of Isfahan and Tehran workshops, the study concluded:

> Having the worst working conditions, these workshops are unhealthy workplaces. Women's working hours are irregular, sometimes they work all day, sometimes their work is seasonal when workshops close down. Workers have no lunch break and they eat a small amount while continuing to work. Most often mothers bring along their young daughters for help with their own work or to babysit for their infants.[32]

These women were *Zaqeh-neshin* or dwellers of Tehran's worst shantytowns; they lived in one room, paying 250–350 rials [$.33–.46] monthly rent – almost higher than their earnings – with no running water or electricity. This study concluded that although on average these women made higher wages than carpet weavers, their work condition was harsher and they worked harder to finance the high cost of food and housing in the slums.[33]

Working conditions in workshops depicted a gloomy picture, hardly improved since the turn of the century. A study of 15 carpet workshops in an urban shantytown, Isfahan's Moft-Abad, revealed that subcontracted

[30] A study of 24, The Office, "Bar-resi-ye," entire article.

[31] Survey, The Office, *Ibid.*

[32] "Infants," cited in The Office, *Ibid.*, 24–28, and 27–34.

[33] This study, The Office, "Barresiy-e," 24–28 and 27–34. Note that carpet workshops or weaving tents exist all over urban, rural, and tribal Iran. Generally, rural female weavers exceed those in the cities and there are more female than male weavers. Although master weavers tend to be men, men are not generally professional weavers; they joined the industry when they could not locate other jobs especially in concentrated urban areas. Traditionally the main laborers in this industry, women and children have been the backbone of weaving, and city weavers have been younger than rural ones.

homework was the norm among these workshops. Entering into contractual relations with a wealthy businessman, a middleman would hire a few assistants to purchase the raw materials for weaving. They would set up workshops in various homes with no attention to health and work standards. Generally dark, workshops were too cold in winter and too hot and damp in summer. Old and cracked scaffolds made the work dangerous and more difficult. One workshop was supervised by a woman who lived on the premises, and who oversaw 4 to 8 girls, aged between 4 and 14. Working from dawn to dark, weavers could devote only a few minutes to eating lunch. Although weavers' wages varied by skill level and their urban or rural residence, their wages were much lower than those of other factory or workshop workers discussed above, 3 to 10 rials [$.03 to .10] daily. Children's wages were paid to their parents.[34]

Women workers also experienced discrimination in the workplace. A study of 13 factories found that employers thought women were undisciplined because of "pregnancy, child delivery, and menstruation"; disturbing to the work environment because they had "verbal contacts with male workers"; and unqualified because they were "unable to work in night shifts." Alleging that women's interest was primarily in the household, not in wage work, employers argued against training women, fearing that women might leave upon marriage. Moreover, employers refrained from offering jobs that required heavy labor or needed technical training like electricity, steel, and machine repair to women because they considered women biologically weak, incompetent, unskilled, uninterested, and unintelligent. Ironically, employers' willingness to hire women was itself related to stereotyped attitudes, namely the beliefs that women were "careful and disciplined, especially in precise and elegant work"; that women were "patient and cooperative"; that women were "obedient" and "uncritical about wages"; and that as co-workers women "produced a better psychological environment for male workers."[35]

[34] A study of 15, Rastegar, *Sokhanrani*, 4.

[35] Study of 13 factories, Rastegar, *Sokhanrani*, 2, 6, and 14–15. Note that workers consisted of 1,083 females and 15,367 males. Rastegar interviewed 50 men and 50 women. He found that women were discriminated against, in part because of the widespread belief that in Iran menstruation made women weak both mentally and physically. Physically weak women were considered incapable and less intelligent than men. Also, the arbitrary classification of jobs as "light" or "heavy" provided superior qualities to men and inferior ones to women. Even if women had jobs equal to men's, they would still be seen as less productive because they had lower technical knowledge and intelligence. Furthermore, the use of such adjectives to describe women as careful, patient, and obedient relegated women to the world of subjectivity connected to their role as homemakers, as against

Discriminatory attitudes were not limited to employers. One study found that among 39 married male workers, only 3 approved of their wives working in the labor market. The rest indicated that women's primary responsibility lay at home, that Islam did not approve of women's contact with men, and that women should stay home because they lacked skills. Also, men felt guilty about their wives working, especially when they were ill and had to continue to work. Significantly, men related their superior position in factories to higher work productivity as a result of their higher physical strength. Such misguided beliefs use general categories like biology to disqualify women. While biology determines childbearing, it does not require women to stay home bound, nor does it give the prerogative of higher productivity to men because of their access to machinery or technical knowledge. Unequal access to jobs and wage disparities encourage differential treatment and reproduces gender divisions in the labor process. This pattern existed not only in industries, but in the service sector where more women were concentrated.[36]

The Service Sector and Women

Iran's increasing integration into the world market and its own specific developmental strategy as discussed earlier explain the growth of its services as well as the attraction of this sector to women. Because of Iran's large and growing web of commercial and financial transactions with the West, and the opportunities it provided to investors, many positions in the service sector such as secretaries and clerks in hotels, cinemas, theaters, supermarkets, restaurants, insurance companies, banks, various corporate enterprises, and educational systems opened up to women. As international capital searched for cheap and disciplined labor in the developing world and as domestic employers operated on similar motives, those jobs welcomed women's candidacy.[37]

Many of the newly created positions were "modern." They provided the appearance of a more egalitarian work environment to women; for

the public position that is considered men's space. These views might in part explain why women were prevented from obtaining more rewarding jobs. Employers' unwillingness, Rastegar, *Sokhanrani*, 13–15; and Rastegar, "Tose'-ye," 15. Note that despite employer's many excuses, women showed enthusiasm to undergo training but their plea was rejected.

36 This pattern, *Ibid.*.

37 In discussing the service sector, I recognize different levels of hierarchies as may be broadly defined by class; however, the concept of class cannot be systematically operationalized, here, because of the lack of data. See also note 38, below.

some Iranian women, it was even a status symbol to work for such establishments as Phillips. However, because of their low bargaining position in the market, those jobs tended to offer relatively lower wages to women. Thus, the expansion of services served the needs of foreign as well as Iranian capital, while it assigned to women a crucial role in Iran's economic development particularly in urban areas. But the predominance of women in this sector posed a striking difference between Iran and Western European countries during their respective early stages of economic development. In the early phases of Western industrialization, women participated primarily in industry, due to higher levels of investment and capital accumulation in this sector. It was during the later periods that women became predominant in the service sector. In the developing world, women's absorption in the service sector can be explained in terms of its relatively greater expansion or insufficient demand for women's labor in industries. The growth of the services and the availability of new jobs pushed more Iranian women to join the service sector.

The service sector encompassed a plethora of jobs in business, transportation, communication, finance, insurance, and real estate. It included doctors, lawyers, engineers, teachers, administrators, health workers, tailors and seamstresses, cooks, waiters, bartenders, barbers and beauticians, launderers, dry cleaners, ushers, clerks, secretaries, phone operators, and salespeople. At the bottom of the service-based jobs, the informal sector consisted of petty commodity producers who produced goods at home and peddlers who sold their goods in the *bazaars* or in the streets. They were domestics, *dallaks* (women or men who worked in public baths but sometimes visited homes to assist with bathing and massaging), *band-andaz* (threaders going to homes or working in beauty parlors), and sexual service workers in Tehran's red light district. Thus, service jobs cut across class lines and occupational categories.[38]

[38] Commodity producers, Keyhan Research Associates, *The Employment*, 8–10; various occupations, H. Sedghi, "Women," table 25. Secretarial and clerical jobs can also be considered as "crowded" service-based occupations. Sexual service workers, *Vaz'e Zanan-e Ruspigar*, as cited in *Setam Keshidegi-ye Zan dar Iran.* [Women's's Oppression in Iran]; and service jobs, Statistical Center of Iran, *Sar Shomari-ye Omumi-ye Nofus*, 2535 (1976), i and g. I have also incorporated various other studies in this list. They include: The Plan and Budget Organization, *Degarguniha-ye* and WOI, *Naghsh-e Zan dar Barnameh*, 2535 (1976). Further, based on my own observations, I have modified these data to incorporate the informal sector of the services. Like the industrial sector, a class analysis of the services poses some difficulties. Note that while service sector employees were income earners, their class position was diverse: for example, doctors, who provided a variety of services, earned high incomes, and were located in the upper echelons of the

Women's participation in the services consisted of gender-typing positions. In urban areas, women accounted for more than half of the urban labor force in nursing and health services (65 percent) and secretarial positions (50.1 percent), and about one-third in teaching (34 percent). These data suggest that "the largest percentages of all employed women were not in the teaching positions." In fact, the teaching profession did not absorb the largest number of women. But if "women's jobs" are defined as those in which more than half the employees are women, then over 50 percent of urban Iranian women were concentrated in health and secretarial jobs. Entering the modern sectors of the economy but then clustered into certain occupations, women experienced stereotyping. Early in the century, women struggled for education as a key to self-determination and emancipation; in the 1960s and 1970s, many more women emerged from their homes and joined educational institutions, while others enlisted the labor force in other capacities. But women were now lumped together in gender-typing occupations and were marginalized. Because educational institutions incorporated many women as teachers, students, and administrators, and provided an atmosphere for them to develop their ideas and participate in social change, I will highlight teaching in order to illustrate gender inequality and stereotyping.[39]

During the 1960s and 1970s, more women became literate in Iran. Women's literacy rate increased from nearly 8 percent of the female population in 1956, to 17.4 percent in 1966, to 26.3 percent in 1971. Similarly, urban women's literacy rate rose from nearly 22.4 percent in 1956, to 38.3 percent in 1966, to 49.4 percent in 1971. By 1977, one out of every 10 rural women and 5 out of 10 urban women were illiterate, although equal numbers of girls and boys attended urban high schools and one-third of rural primary schools were filled by girls. One study found that many women failed to pursue education, especially in rural areas because of their involvement in physical work; household and reproductive activities; ailments caused by early and multiple pregnancies; social

middle-class, but domestic workers and many low-paid secretaries (some secretaries came from privileged classes; they wanted to work, not for the money though) were at the bottom of the service category and may be classified as working-class members. Both class and occupational categories intersect with service jobs.

39 "Women's jobs," Sedghi, "Women and Class," table 26. Although nursing was almost exclusively a female-dominated field, women were mostly concentrated in secondary positions. In a survey of 13 hospitals in urban areas, there was only one female director of nursing and 2 female heads of units. Jobs became exclusively female dominated the further down the medical hierarchy one went: out of 153 head nurses, there were only 2 men, and among 664 nurses, two were men.

prejudice; women's own lack of motivation; men's antagonism and harassment of female students; and families' preference for educating sons rather than daughters. Although many of these problems went beyond women's control, literacy data alone cannot provide a valid criterion by which to measure social awareness and real educational growth. In 1976, I suggested that "The Iranian educational system continues to concentrate on the 'banking' type of education, training students to memorize instead of teaching them to develop their critical faculties."[40]

Over the years, more educational institutions opened their doors to women. Women entered schools and universities as students: from 71,718 in 1943–44, to 725,300 in 1963–64, and to 1,816,560 in 1973–74. As cities welcomed more private and public schools, women looked into teaching as a career option. But the higher the grade level, the fewer women were employed, as I experienced in my all-girls high school. Of the total number of secondary teachers, there were 23,513 (47 percent) women and 26,404 (53 percent) men; of primary school teachers, there were 66,865 (54 percent) women and 56,903 (46 percent) men; and of pre-school teachers in the country, there were 5,999 (99.9 percent) women and 3 (.05 percent) men. At universities, gender segregation was more prevalent, as they generally offered women the lowest and least admired positions. In a survey of 7 universities, almost all the top administrative positions, including chancellors and their deputies, deans of faculty and their assistants, were male. In a study of public school systems throughout Iran, women held 3,394 or 16.5 percent of the total administrative positions, whereas men held 17,214 such posts or 83.5 percent. Overall, women's representation in the more respected university administrations was negligible, whereas their place in less prestigious teaching positions was relatively greater than men's.[41]

University faculty had the worst representation of women. Private universities and colleges scored higher than the public ones in female faculty employment. In a 1975 survey of 7 universities, out of 500 full-time faculty, 3 were women. Fewer women were hired as part-time staff in

[40] Women's literacy rate, Soltani, "*Bar-resi-ye* Amuzesh va Eshteghal," 2536/1977, 8; one study, *Ibid.*, 5, 8, and 19; "The Iranian educational system," Sedghi, "Women in Iran," 225. Note that in 1982, Sanasarian, *The Women's*, 109, made an identical remark indicating that "educational system in Iran was based on memorization," however, my earlier work was not acknowledged.

[41] Women entered schools, Keyhan Research, *The Employment*, 67 and 12; survey of 7 universities, Fakhr Sadat, "Zan va Amuzesh," 2535 (1976). 17; and study of public schools, Keyhan Research, *The Employment*, 12–13.

these institutions: 254 women out of a total of 1,512. More discriminatory, state-run universities had 600 full-time female professors out of the total of 4,200 full-time teaching staff and 248 part-time female faculty out of 2,355 part-time teaching staff. In 1975 when I sought a faculty position at Tehran University's Department of Political Science, I was told by the Dean that "the University would be delighted to have you on the staff, but you will have a difficult time with male students who would not take you seriously and would challenge your authority as a professor," he added, "because you are a woman." Indeed, greater stereotyping existed at the higher academic echelons than it did in most other positions in the service sector.[42]

Women worked in the service sector for various reasons. Work had social and personal significance because of its economic benefits and the reward of a paycheck. An extensive survey of 313 female government employees, mostly in Tehran, corroborates this assertion. Sixty percent of those women indicated that they enjoyed financial security and intended to keep their jobs, for work elevated their place in the society and contributed to their psychological well-being. Other women had different preferences. One of my own interviewees who considered herself a middle-class woman contended: "I'd like to stay at home but I have 12 years of government employment credit toward my retirement. I can make it a total of 30 years and then get the full retirement income." While proud of her managerial position, another woman considered her earnings as supplemental to that of her husband's, "it is difficult to run the family with his professorial salary alone," she said. For single women, earning an income meant "freedom to buy according to personal need" as well as exercising a greater voice in the household, including placing a break on patriarchal authority.[43]

Despite personal pleasure, financial concerns constituted the greatest impetus for women's work. Almost 95 percent of respondents in the above governmental survey cited acknowledged the importance of their work to the family income, while only 5 percent considered it mainly for their own advancement. Most women spent their income on household maintenance and children's schooling, about half of them hired maids, some relied on

[42] 1975 survey, Keyhan Research Associates, *The Employment*, 12–13; and Dean, my interview at the University of Tehran, 1975.

[43] Survey of 313, Sazeman Radio va Television, *Masa'el-e Zanan-e Karmand-e*, 66–67, 29, 12, 16, 20, 28–29, and 56; and my own interviewees, Tehran, 1977. Note that in some of those families, women's jobs provided the extra cash for a child's schooling, or hiring help with the household.

their mothers' help, and a few remained without assistance. Interestingly, almost 80 percent of the respondents received some cooperation from husbands at home. More strikingly however, 40 percent maintained that if they had financial security, they would abandon their jobs and devote more time to mothering. Perhaps discriminatory and unsatisfactory environment accounted for some of women's resentment toward work. Many women complained that their male colleagues perceived them as "inferior" and "failed to respect them as employees." They also believed that they could not "compete for promotion" because the workplace was "unhealthy and insincere" and there existed "social inequality between the sexes that was sanctioned at work and in the society in general." Wage discrimination, especially in relation to their husbands' salaries, underlined some women's hostility toward work. All women interviewed in the above survey indicated that – though their incomes varied – they earned less than their husbands: almost 10 percent earned about 5,000 rials [$7.00], 82 percent, 5,000–20,000 rials [$7.00–27.00], and the rest made 20,000–30,000 rials [$27.00–40.00] monthly. By contrast, about 6 percent of the husbands earned 5,000 rials [$7.00], 50 percent earned 5,000–20,000 rials [$7.00–27.00], and the rest earned 20,000–30,000 rials [$27.00–40.00] monthly.[44]

Whether participating in industries or in the services, working women experienced subordination that was more gender specific than class-bound. Even women who enjoyed some luxury and comfort due to higher earnings and greater financial independence, like the majority of Iranian women, they drew their social status not from themselves as women, but from their relationship to men: as married women from their husbands, and as single women from their fathers or brothers. As wage earners, the motives of women in the services for joining the labor market were almost identical to women in industries – all wanted economic security, all desired increased consumption, and all valued empowerment. Perhaps the difference was that the middle-class women's incomes supplemented their husbands' and they held more rewarding jobs, whereas the working-class women rarely received financial backing from their men and worked

[44] 95 percent, Sazeman-e Radio, *Masa'el-e*, 23, 34–35, and 37. Most of these women were high school graduates, and about one-third had some university education, some worked as technical engineers and office supervisors, and many as nurses, receptionists, analysts, secretaries, and clerks. They earned less than their husbands, *Ibid.*, 23, 34–35, and 37. Some of these women had additional incomes from second jobs such as sewing and knitting, others as beauticians, and a small number had rental earning from properties. *Ibid.*, 18, 22, and 42–43.

at low paying and very difficult jobs. But women's lives were more complicated as there were other variations in the division of labor by marital status and age. In both regards, Iran's female labor model was different from elsewhere in the world.

DIVISION OF LABOR BY MARITAL STATUS AND LIFE CYCLE

The division of labor is not only based on gender and class, but also on marital status and age. In the West, during the early stages of capital accumulation, the labor force participation of single women was higher than that of other women. Marriage and especially children's births caused a decline in women's labor force participation that lasted as long as children were young and remained at home. But in Iran, married women's labor force participation surpassed that of other women. As a percentage of the total female labor force, the share of married women was highest at 51 percent, followed by single women at 36.5 percent, widows at 9.4 percent, and divorcees at a mere 2 percent. The same pattern held in urban areas. Among all urban female workers, 131,000 (41 percent) were married, 122,000 (39 percent) were single, 47,000 (15 percent) were widowed, and 16,000 (5 percent) were divorced.[45]

The division of labor also correlates with age and life cycle patterns. In Latin America, women's participation in formal employment declined with age, especially after 25, while it increased in the informal sector. In contrast, in some African, Middle Eastern, and Asian countries (for example, Libya, Morocco, Turkey, and Pakistan), women's rate of employment rose after the age of 35. Iran demonstrated an atypical pattern, in that women's level of employment according to age varied from urban to rural areas: in the country, it was highest among women aged 10 to 24, while among urban women it peaked between ages 20 and 29, especially among married women, a pattern that was consistent with the high share of married women in the total labor force as discussed above. Data on the figures for labor force participation by age and population, as well as by marital status and age, allow inferences about labor force participation by age and marital status keeping in mind that all data are unverified.[46]

[45] Share of married women, Sedghi, "Women and Class," table 29.

[46] Age and life cycle patterns, Sedghi, "gender and aeging," 1–12; Latin America, Arizpe, "Women," 29; age of 35, The Plan and Budget, *Degarguniha-ye*, 75; and atypical pattern, Sedghi, "Women and Class," tables 30–31.

Labor force participation of urban women exceeded that of other women in the age group 20 to 29 in 1976. Among this age group, married women ranked highest. Thus the labor force participation of married women between the ages 20 and 29 surpassed that of other women in urban Iran. Younger women continued to work, although their labor force participation decreased if they enrolled in school. Women who worked beyond the age of 30 because of financial needs discontinued or decreased their work as they grew older. Iran in the 1970s provides a specific case where female labor force participation was highest among women in their twenties.[47]

Why was Iran atypical? What factors made it possible for married women to combine their tasks in production and reproduction? Marriage at an early age (often 15 years old, sometimes younger with parental permission) among urban working-class women increased their availability for labor force participation, especially during the period of economic growth and market expansion. In their early 20's, these women relied on oldest daughters or mothers and neighbors to help care for younger children and the household. For these women, then, personal and traditional relations, as discussed earlier in this chapter, facilitated their entrance into wage labor. Middle-class women who often married somewhat later, depended mostly on maids and servants, though sometimes on their mothers as well. Thus, the tradition of early marriage, economic growth, and class background contributed to higher labor force participation of married women between the ages of 20 to 29, which became possible during two decades of boom in Iran.[48]

In sum, Iran's integration into the global political economy and its unprecedentedly rapid economic growth generated shifts in the structure of the labor market and the division of labor. Capitalist development, characterized by limited industrialization and dependence on import-substitution industries, separated producers from the means of production, increased consumption, and absorbed more women in the labor force, especially in the services. By the mid-1970s, economic structure and its labor force were radically different from the early 1900s when Iran was hardly distinguishable as an economic entity and its production processes were exclusively male-dominated. Therefore, women's lack of

[47] Labor force participation, and specific case, Sedghi, *Ibid.*

[48] Marriage at an early marriage, in 1975, the legal age for marriage for girls was eighteen, but prior to that time it was fifteen; although with parents' consent, younger girls could be married too.

participation in production outside the home, their seclusion, and veiling paralleled the stagnant economy of the early twentieth-century, and conversely, the rise in women's labor force participation, education, and unveiling practices during the later decades corresponded to Iran's rapid economic development and its changing place in the international division of labor.

State policies accommodated those alterations in the economy and the gender division of labor. Specifically, in order to consolidate his powers, through the encouragement of the Kennedy Administration, the Shah launched the White Revolution and silenced the opposition. Daughters growing up in the 1960s and 1970s experienced a different life than their mothers had, especially in urban areas. In urban areas, many wore Western clothes, attended private or public educational institutions and learned English and French. Unveiled women and women in head-scarves cut some of the strings of patriarchal control and left their homes for the labor market as they took advantage of the available opportunities. Thus, state policies exerted a powerful impact as is absorbed women in the work force. Yet in the process, the state left untouched the traditional cultural and legal precepts and practices that had sustained gender inequalities for centuries. The next chapter will discuss various legislation and family reform laws and their outcome for women and gender equality.

4

The State and Gender

Repression, Reform, and Family Legislation

"I don't underestimate [women], as shown by the fact that they have derived more advantages than anyone else from my White Revolution," stated the Shah. Whether or not the monarch was sincere when he said so, he was taken at his word by the Ayatollah Khomeini who denounced the Shah's reforms and Family Protection Laws as "anti-Islamic." They were "intended for the break-up of Muslim families," maintained the Ayatollah. Those responsible for the laws are "condemned by Islam; women who utilize those laws and divorce are not legally divorced and if they remarry, they are adulterous and their children are illegitimate and disinherited...."[1]

The White Revolution marked an intense state-clergy strife that temporarily led to the supremacy of the state over religion but also over its secular opponents. Although the clergy did not uniformly oppose the state, the Shah succeeded in winning over the religious opposition while himself appropriating more firmly the ideological imagery of "God, the Shah, and the nation." Proclaiming that his reforms exemplified "justice and equality," he claimed they were compatible with the "true religion of Islam." Through women's suffrage and his gender policies, enacted despite the clergy's jurisdiction over family and gender relations and their opposition, the Shah promoted his modernizing posture, especially in the Western hemisphere. In his legal reforms, he was more triumphant than his father

[1] "White Revolution," Fallaci, "A Shah's," 24; and "anti-Islamic," "break-up," and "condemned by Islam," Khomeini, Ruhollah Musavi, *Resalleh-e Tozihol-Masa'el*, entire, especially problem no. 2836, 583–584.

in shaking the power of the religious establishment by depriving it of a major source of strength over nearly thirteen centuries: the theoretical, and to a lesser extent, the actual privatization and control of women.[2]

Abundant in Persian and English, legal studies address changes pertaining to women from both Islamic and secular perspectives.[3] Yet they shed little light on these shifts within the context of state formation and economic development. I argue that the changes in the structure of the economy paralleled a gradual shift not only in women's work but also in state gender policies that played an active role in shaping women's lives. In this process, the state created a dialectical tension for women: it liberalized secular and religious laws that restricted women's mobility and autonomy and increased the demand for women's labor; however, it upheld some laws that restrained women's sexuality and denied women full equality and protection relative to men. Discussing repression and reform under the Shah, this chapter focuses on the state's interference in matters of family relations, criminal codes, and labor laws insofar as they concerned women. It examines various pieces of legislation that were enacted in the 1960s and 1970s, and assesses the consistencies and/or contraditions between the official proclamations of change and their implementation. Thus, it explores the relationship of the state to gender.

THE STATE AND GENDER

Through legislative policies, the state can exert a powerful influence on gender construction and women's lives. I view the state through its gender policies, and conversely, analyze gender through a state lens. Although conceptualized variously, this book sees the Iranian state as an organization involved in the exercise of political domination and hegemony, including its monopoly over coercive apparatus of the political and social system. Relatively autonomous at times, the state embodies its own interests, ideology, and structures. These components may undergo changes because the state is fluid as it responds to its environment in different ways. However, depending on its goals, the state's activities transcend its

[2] "God," I recall seeing and hearing this statement all over the country as I was growing up; and "justice," and "Islam," *Ittela' at*, 11 Sharivar 1331/1952 as cited by Akhavi, *Religion*, 99.

[3] Legal studies, Motahhari; *Nezam-e*; Sadr; Hasan, *Huquq-e Zan dar Islam*; Zamani, *Payman-e Zanashu'i*; Taj (Langarudi); Mohammad Mehdi, *Dastan-e Zanan*; Bagely, R.C. "The Iranian Family Protection Law of 1967"; and Pakizegi, entire.

role in the accumulation process and thus, its predominantly *political* aspect aims at state formation, legitimation, and conflict resolution.[4] States are not gender-neutral, rather they are gender-centered.

In Iran, the state incorporated gender in its policies and by so doing, it restructured some patriarchal relations in the family, the labor market, and educational institutions. Little agreement exists on the nature of the Shah's state. Most studies generally miss a recognition of the importance of gender to policy making and the functioning of the state. But the state has historically exemplified gender interests as well as class interests, and consequently any analysis of the state requires an investigation of its class and gender content. Second, women's positions *depend* on their relationship to the state and their own responses; that is, the state promotes or prevents women's work or sets an agenda for the control of particular classes of women or their activities. It encourages and discourages emancipation via policy, legislation, and other forms of governmental and social control. The next chapters will fully examine women's responses to the state.[5]

Third, manipulating gender issues as a source of legitimacy, and sometimes as a response to its constituencies, the state draws on some women's support in order to strengthen and consolidate its power and build its particular image to the outside world. Both Pahlavis, for example, politicized unveiling to boost their Westernizing and modernizing image and to triumph over religious powers. A related point is the issue of gender and class and the state's representation of its particular supporters. States build alliances with different social classes of women, especially in their policies of mobilization. Conversely, different classes of women respond differently to a state, its ideologies, and policies. For instance, the Shah's state mainly responded to the interests of upper-class and some middle-class women, who were the primary beneficiaries of his legislative policies, although they were not without consequences for the poor, some of whom had taken low-paying jobs.

Fourth, the state uses women as a source of conflict resolution, sometimes in conjunction with its policies on sexuality, and other times with its mobilization policies. Under the Pahlavis, women's emancipation or subordination depended, in part, on on-going political conflicts between

[4] Conflict resolution, Gramsci, *Selections From the Prison*; Buci-Gluckmann; Skocpol, *States;* Hudson; and Charrad and Deitch.

[5] Shah's state, see Introduction to this book and Ashraf, "State"; Jazani; and Akhavi, S. "Shi'ism"; and Gender content, MacKinnon, 184–188; Mollyneux; and Sedghi, "Women, The State," 113–126.

the male leaders of the state and clergymen and their different perceptions of gender and sexuality. Hence, specific ideologies of gender differentiation, for example, secular versus religious, assumed significance as they acquired strength through the state power. A case in point can be made from various veiling policies. The monarchical state considered veiling as antithetical to modernization, Westernization, and emancipation, whereas under the current regime, unveiling is adversarial to Islamization and decontrol of sexuality. Yet each of these measures acquired political significance through a specific quest for political power. But understanding how the Iranian state interfered in gender construction requires an analysis of the power struggle between the state and the clergy.

STATE-RELIGION CONFLICT

In the post-1953 era, in an attempt to consolidate the state power, the Shah used both co-optation and repression to respond to political contenders. Taking a firm stand against the secular opposition, especially the intelligentsia, he cautiously avoided clashes with the landed aristocracy and the *bazaaries*. Led by Court supporters, he encouraged the formation of alternative political parties. He also strengthened his cooperative relationship with such prominent religious leaders as Ayatollah Ozma Seyyed Mohammad Hossein Burujerdi and Ayatollah Mohammad Mousavi Behbahani, and released the less-renowned Ayatollah Abol Qasem Kashani from prison. But political and economic crisis were even more widespread. Corruption was rampant; revenues could not pay for the Shah's ambitious economic plans; and there was little freedom and democracy.[6]

The religious authorities had their own specific concerns. Having expressed discontent over the 1959 land reform bill, they were especially alarmed by the growing power of the state and their own relationship to

[6] Secular opposition included the intelligentsia, the Tudeh Party, and the working-class. See Abrahamian, *Iran*, entire; Kashani, because the government had suspected Ayatollah Kashani's participation in the 1948 assassination attempt on the Shah's life, it sent him to exile in Lebanon. Upon his return to Iran three years later, Kashani was arrested and imprisoned because of his alleged association with the *Feda' iyan-e Eslam* (the Devotees of Islam), who were charged with the assassination of Premier Ali Razmara in 1951. Kashani was released from prison after he promised to disassociate himself with the *Feda'iyan*. He remained active and continued to play a key role in Iranian politics; for example, he declined to support Mosaddegh's nationalization attempts – Abrahamian, *Iran*, Ch. 9; and Akhavi, *Religion*, 65–70.

political authority and the society. Ann Lambton argued that the clergy's antagonism

> was probably due not only, or even mainly, to obstructionism and reaction but rather to an instinctive feeling that the whittling away in one field by the temporal Government... of personal rights guaranteed by the divine law and the Constitution is likely to weaken their position all along the line.[7]

The clerics were also critical of the growing corruption and autocracy of the Shah and his reign.[8] Although tyranny existed throughout Iran's modern history, it is doubtful whether, by itself alone, it could have triggered the state-clergy strife.

Of paramount importance were the clergy's material interests and their control over women, both of which were threatened by the Shah's drive to consolidate his powers. The religious establishment managed and administered the *vaqf* (endowed land and property) out of which they drew income to spend on mosques, religious schools, and ceremonies, as well as their own salaries. As Islam authorized the holding of private property by clerics, they judged the state's interference in those matters unjustifiable. Significantly, the clergy was alarmed by the Shah's intention to enfranchise women. As indicated before, the clergy had opposed a women's suffrage bill in 1911, 1944, 1948, and 1952. When Mosaddegh's son-in-law introduced a similar bill in 1959, the *ulama* again agitated against it. Ayatollah Burujerdi vetoed the government's plan to have a women's rights parade in Tehran. The Shah's commitment to land reform and women's suffrage legislation appeared as formidable catalysts for intense opposition to the monarch among the clerical leaders.[9]

Thus, the political conflict between the state and the clergy began to take shape under the second Pahlavi ruler. Having indefinitely dissolved the Parliament in 1961 on the grounds that elections were rigged, in January 1962, the Shah's cabinet approved a revised version of the land bill. In riots at Tehran University, protesters denounced the Shah's actions as unconstitutional. Authorities arrested a number of leading religious leaders, some of whom had been pro-regime, and the police crushed and detained their followers. The Shah, however, remained cautious not to totally alienate the clerical leadership. In an attempt to "preempt *ulama* countermaneuvers that might lead to a consolidated landlord-*ulama* alignment," he ordered the release of some clergy after a time.[10]

[7] Lambton, "Persia," 82.
[8] Reign, Akhavi, *Religion*, 95.
[9] Property, Rodinson, entire, and; Tehran, Akhavi, *Religion*, 95.
[10] "Preempt *ulama*," *Ibid.*, 94.

Opposition to the Shah continued to grow among other groups and classes. In December 1962, Mosaddegh's National Front leaders openly attacked the Shah. They wanted free elections and freedom to speak, act, and organize: they called for the restoration of the constitution. The government not only rejected their requests, it soon ordered their arrest and imprisonment. But repression backfired. The more discontent was inspired, the more people poured into the streets. Popular dissatisfaction manifested itself in strikes, peasant rebellions, and demonstrations by students, teachers, and urban intellectuals.

Political disorder alarmed not only the Shah but the Kennedy administration which saw Iran being destabilized. The U.S. government was committed to safeguarding its military and corporate stakes in Iran, whose "socio-economic development and foreign policy objectives [had become] . . . closely tied to the interests of the capitalist world." In order to protect its position in Iran and other Third World countries, the United States had urged its allies in the developing world to carry out the necessary reforms to "stave off" popular unrest. This was the background to the White Revolution – the backbone of Iran's development in the 1960s and 1970s.[11]

Thus, the state consolidated its powers. To establish stability and bolster his own popularity and legitimacy, in 1962 the Shah introduced other changes in the land reform to create a six-point package known as The White Revolution (in 1964 and 1967 he added other reform points). The Shah organized a nationwide plebiscite, in which, according to the official announcement, almost 100 percent of the voters endorsed the package, incuding women's suffrage, in January 1963.

THE WHITE REVOLUTION AND THE OPPOSITION

The immediate impact of the White Revolution was an escalation of protests against the state. Dr. Mosaddegh's National Front boycotted the vote on the grounds that only a freely elected parliament had the authority to legislate reforms. Almost six months after the plebiscite, during the *Shi'i* mourning month of Moharram, thousands of teachers, students, women, *bazaaries*, National Front supporters, clergymen, civil servants, and workers demonstrated in the streets against the Shah, his reforms, repression, and corrupt rule. Protesters responded to calls by the secular opposition leaders, and significantly, to the message of a new religious leader, Mojtahed Ruhollah Khomeini.[12]

[11] "The U.S. government," Saikal; and "Stave off," Katouzian, *The Political*, entire.

[12] The White Revolution, see Ch.3 of this book.

Divisions had increased among the *ulama* leaders after Ayatollah Burujerdi's death in 1961. This book will not discuss the rifts, although suffice it to indicate that the squabblings among those leaders created room for the entrance of the junior Khomeini to *Shi'i* leadership. Considered a young associate by his colleagues, Khomeini had relatively few writings. In his major 1943 work, he argued for an Islamic government. Although he criticized Reza Shah's harsh policies against the clerics, he did not yet reject monarchy. But he remained a non-activist until 1962–63. With the weakening of the Tudeh Party and the National Front by the Shah, and especially, after Burujerdi's death, he became vocal. During the early 1960s – when many of his colleagues denounced the Shah's land reform and women's enfranchisement – Khomeini opposed women's suffrage only once in 1962. Instead, he focused on more general problems, including Westernization and Islam's decline, economic slide of the peasants and merchants, corruption, capitulation to foreigners, constitution and electoral improprieties, the state's interference with universities and the press, oil sale to Israel, and the bureaucracy's expansion. He did not yet call for the overthrow of the monarchy.[13]

Riots swept major cities by June 1963. Massive upheavals shook Tehran, Qom, Shiraz, Isfahan, Mashhad, and Tabriz. Hundreds, if not more, were brutally killed and thousands were injured as the Shah's police and the army responded violently. Buildings and streets were burned and universities and shops closed down. After three days of intense clashes between the state and the opposition, the former triumphed. The Shah was able to consolidate his powers again. The National Front leaders were arrested as was the sixty-four-year-old Khomeini, who was exiled – first to Turkey and then, in 1965, to Iraq. In 1978, he went to France, to return in 1979, when renewed upheavals finally put an end to the White Revolution and its accompanying gender legislation.[14]

THE FAMILY PROTECTION LAWS

Political changes often accommodate economic shifts. Throughout the 1960s and most of the 1970s, Iran's economy moved toward an increased integration with the economies of the more advanced capitalist countries of the West. The inauguration of the 1963 White Revolution represented

[13] Junior Khomeini, Algar, "The Oppositional Role"; writings, Akhavi, *Religion*, 101–104; women's suffrage, Paidar, 142, 121 and 144; see also Khomeini's major work, *Kashf-ol Asrar* (The Secrets Revealed) and his *Zendigi Nameh*.

[14] Abrahamian, *Iran*, 426.

a turning point in Iranian industrial development and the expansion of its labor market. Reinforcing the needs of the rapidly expanding economy, public policies addressed gender issues. This growth paralleled the enactment of laws to free women from the household and to facilitate their entry into paid production. The Family Protection Law (FPL) of 1967, which was subsequently revised in 1975, addressed age restrictions for marriage, divorce, child custody, and polygamy.

Law is politics by another name. Politics is the process of who gets what, how, and when. State policies as manifested in legislative politics are both rooted in the class structure of a society and gender. In most societies, including Iran, state policies, especially those pertaining to women, are launched from above. Praising her brother's role in promoting women's emancipation, Ashraf Pahlvai stated: "Equality between women and men has been truly realized under the laws of my King brother." And she anticipated that he would "provide the framework for women's social and economic activities." The Shah assigned the task of organizing women to a state-sponsored Women's Organization of Iran (WOI), with his twin sister as its president. Chapter 5 delves fully into that organization. Here, it suffices to indicate that the monarch expected the WOI "in achieving its progressive aims to prepare women to the fullest extent for Iran's advancement." Ashraf Pahlavi declared her own intention to "integrate women into every aspect of society and to create the condition of equality our female ancestors [in pre-Islamic Persia] had enjoyed centuries ago." The WOI, not independent or autonomous women's organizations, played an instrumental role in the drafting of the FPL.[15]

Legal codes are frequently partial, although they are important vehicles for the state to construct and regulate gender relations and women's lives. The Iranian family laws reflected inegalitarian tendencies as they sanctioned male authority, often insuring women's vulnerability. From a theoretical perspective, the FPL intended to restrain some of men's powers in marital relations, although as Haideh Moghissi indicated, the state "not only did not adopt far-reaching changes, remaining faithful to the principles of Islamic legislation, but its failure to foster and to promote the preconditions of change such as women's economic independence from men helped the oppressive character of the family to be maintained."[16] An alternative view may be that although certain aspects of religious

[15] Politics, Lasswell; "King brother," and "framework," Notq-e Vala Hazrat; "Iran's advancement," "Farmayeshat-e Shahanshah," 11–12; "integrated women," Pahlavi, *Faces*, 154; and WOI, Bagely, 57.

[16] "Far-reaching changes," Moghissi, "Women, Modernization," 210.

teachings were excluded from the FPL, legislators failed to consider the implication of the new laws for most women; the majority of women remained unaffected as the main female beneficiaries came from the more privileged classes of urban Iran.

One of the FPL provisions was a new set of minimum age restriction for marriage, from 15 to 18 for women and from 18 to 20 for men; exceptions were granted to women aged 13 and above and men aged 15 and above.[17] But these age restrictions failed to prevent early marriages for women as parents perceived their daughters as sexual objects, child bearers and too expensive to keep at home. Cultural norms, as discussed in Chapter 1, degraded women's sexuality and only assigned value to them when they fulfilled men's sexual passions. Similarly, because many parents forbade their daughters from working outside the home to earn a living, they considered them as economic overhead, and consequently, they had to be disposed of (to be married) in order to minimize family expenses. For centuries, early marriages existed as an intimate part of Irano-Islamic mores. Even in affluent families, many women preferred to marry young; society belittled those beyond the age of 19 as *torshideh* – as aged as a pickle.

Official statistics documented the ineffectiveness of age restriction in marriage. A study of marriages after the 1967 enactment of the FPL pointed out that in 1971, almost 1 percent of all women between the ages of 10 and 14 were married, with a higher frequency in the rural than urban areas. Another study conducted in greater Tehran showed that 41 percent of married women were under 18 years of age. These figures show the futility of the legal system as well as the persistence of cultural mores that continued to support early marriages.[18]

In most parts of Iran, the age at which women married reflected their class backgrounds and social customs, not the public laws. In general, the higher a woman's class position, the older she was at marriage. Although many wealthy and secular middle-class women married before the age of 20, some postponed marriage after that age in order to study or work. Traditional middle-class women followed social custom and married at an earlier age. The majority of women, those of the working-class and rural backgrounds, married young, too. These women married early because

[17] Age restriction, Pakizegi, "Legal," 219; and Mo'ini-Araqi, "Bar-resi ye," 41. Exceptions were discussed in Article 1031 of the Civil Code.

[18] Study of marriages, General Department of Civil Registration as appeared in the Plan and Budget Organization, *Selected Statistics*, 1972/73, 14; another study, The Ministry of Justice, *Bar-resi-ye Amari-ye Ezdevaj*, 2533/1974., 2, T. 1; and Sedghi, "Women and Class," 431.

their poverty stricken families were financially unable to keep them at home or pay for their education.[19] Perhaps this was also the main reason for the higher participation of these women in low-paying jobs, as discussed in the previous chapter. Overall, despite the legal change at marriage, the majority of women – the impoverished and the poor as well as many women of other classes – failed to benefit; they continued to be treated as sex objects in a marriage market.

In contrast, the divorce provision of the FPL was a step forward toward realizing women's rights, although most beneficiaries were economically advantaged women. A departure from the Islamic tradition, the new divorce law required that all divorces be decided by the newly established Family Protection Courts, not Islamic jurists. But compatible with the *Qoran* and the *Shari'eh*, the new law required that the Court's duty was to encourage the reconciliation of the troubled couple. Only if the differences were irreconcilable would divorce be granted.[20] Unable to divorce at will, as had been customary, men now needed to present valid reasons when petitioning for divorce. Whereas women previously had few rights to divorce, now their rights were comparable to men's: they had equal rights in submitting valid divorce requests.

Although it is unclear who initiated them, data indicate that in 1971, out of the total of 18,000 divorces, 15,000 took place in cities and 3,000 in villages. The same study reveals that most divorces in greater Tehran occurred because couples were incompatible or the wives "hated" their husbands. My own observations suggest that most divorced women in Tehran came from the middle- or upper-middle-classes. These women had lost affection for their spouses or had been verbally and sometimes physically abused along with their children or had experienced unfaithfulness. Less-privileged women who might have chosen to divorce remained either uninformed or felt socially disgraced or were too dependent on the wages of their husbands to obtain divorces. The application of divorce laws thus tended to be mainly middle-class based and urban, although currently, more lower-middle-class and poor women apply for divorce.[21]

[19] Poverty stricken families. Often early marriages were justified on religious grounds and cultural traditions, regardless of women's class background. Because of their greater financial worries, however, many poor families ceased upon appropriate opportunities "to give away" (or to marry) their daughters. In this regard, these families exhibited more concerns with their own survival than with religious beliefs and teachings.

[20] Court's duty, Kamankar, Article 18.

[21] Greater Tehran, General Department of Civil Registration, 14; and currently, Mir-Hosseini's documentary video, "Divorce."

Data on the employed divorced women divulge interesting information. Among female workers in greater Tehran, most divorces were among clerical, technical, professional, and service workers, respectively.[22] As indicated in Chapter 3, urban economic development provided new work opportunities for women, especially those with higher education. The ability to earn an income and obtain a decent education relate positively to women's increasing feminist consciousness, their self-esteem, and their articulation of interests as women. Affected by family reforms, the working and educated women could contemplate to free themselves from the patriarchal tradition of remaining wives with their oppressive husbands. It is also possible that the divorce laws, mostly used by middle-class women, were more accommodating to the needs of the growing labor market, especially in the services. The fewer restrictions women experienced in the household and marital relations, the greater their availability to participate in the market.

The FPL also addressed child custody. Religious law permitted a mother to have custody of a boy to the age of 2 and a girl to age 7; thereafter, the children would go to the father. The FPL transferred jurisdiction to the Family Protection Courts. Newly instituted, these Courts applied the FPL, not religious laws, to marital and divorce cases, if that was a woman's desire. Moreover, before the family reforms, the children's custody went to the father's relatives in case of the father's death; however, the new stipulations recognized the mother as the legal guardian of her child(ren) in case of the father's death.[23]

The implementation of the child custody reforms varied by women's class position. Some affluent women considered their divorce settlements, alimony, and child support awards reasonable. They would often either send their children abroad to boarding schools or hire nurses or governesses to care for them. Still, the Court could not always enforce its decisions when, for example, a husband ran away or threatened his ex-wife. Some less-privileged women complained against their husbands for refusing to make payments despite the Court's injunction. Lacking the financial resources to pursue their cases, these women had to seek additional work opportunities or intensify their long work. Women who received a small amount from their husbands spoke of their financial dependence on a man despite freedom from marriage. For these women, economic dependence meant subordination not through marriage but

[22] Female workers, The Ministry of Justice, *Bar-resi-ye Amari*, 12, table 12.

[23] Custody, Kamankar, 175; and Family Protection Courts, Bagely, 58 and 60–64.

through divorce.[24] The impact of the child custody law thus reflected ambivalence on the part of the state: it undermined gender equality for poor women because legal implementation was difficult for them to obtain. Despite these obstacles, the right to child custody, even though not absolute, was a step in the right direction for women.

Another FPL provision aimed at restricting polygamy, but did not abolish it altogether. Theoretically, legislation in both 1967 and 1975 discouraged polygamy – permanent marriage of one man to four women and the practice of *siqeh* or temporary marriage. The earlier law required that a man obtain Family Court permission for a co-wife or wives by demonstrating that he was financially able to support more than one wife and that he was able to treat them equally and justly. That law also required the first wife's consent. This stipulation was somewhat similar to Islamic injunctions, as discussed in Chapter 1. But the 1975 law further empowered the first wife by underlining strongly her agreement, provided that she had fulfilled her sexual obligations and was fertile. In a study of 64 cities in 1973, 7.4 percent of 1,164 women (or 86 women) had marital problems with their polygamous husbands and sought counseling. In the same study, 9.1 percent of 262 responding women (24 women) actually obtained divorces on grounds of polygamy. Another study of rural areas, based on interviews, concluded that most men favored monogamy, although they admitted that if they had the financial means, they would marry more than one woman. Rural men perceived polygamy positively, the study concluded.[25]

The meaning of polygamy varies regionally and culturally. In one study on Africa, a husband's wives represented additional economic resources. Other African research viewed polygamy as an institution for the containment of women's power, or explained it in terms of control of social reproduction in societies where women (presumably from the upper-class) were secluded in ways similar to the Middle East. Iranian specialists have focused on temporary marriages. But little attention is given to polygamy under the Shah, which may be due to the fact that polygamy was not widespread in Iran at the time. My own experiences, particularly

[24] Subordination, Sedghi's interviews with Dokhi, Jaleh, and Parvin, Tehran, 1974.

[25] Co-wife, Kamankar (this provision of the FPL is similar to the *Qoranic* verse that conditionally approves *Mot'eh* as discussed in Chapter 1. What is different is that the FPL required the wife's permission for another marriage of her husband, whereas the religious law allowed men to use their own judgment for entering into another matrimonial pact. Polygamy, Women's Organization of Iran, *Bar-resi-ye Masa'l va Moshkelat-e*, 1343/1974, 30, tables 26, 32, and 29; and rural men, Ghiasi, 10–11.

in urban Iran, suggest no occurrence of polygamy among the upper and middle-classes. Men of these classes had little interest in losing control over their wives' wealth or risking their own social prestige; instead, they chose mistresses, not additional wives. They exercised such practices as Westernized men acculturated in Western values. In contrast, a small number of wealthy traditional men and working-class men who managed on low budget, engaged in polygamy.[26]

Restricted by legislation, polygamy underscored Iranian women's dependency on male wage earners and men's control of their lives and sexuality. Although the 1975 FPL was an improvement, it had little effect. A woman's lack of financial independence, her husband's threats with divorce, and worse, her fear of social stigma attached to being divorced, frequently left the first wife no alternative but to consent to her husband's remarriage.[27] Thus, polygamy was sanctioned not under the *Shari'eh* but under secular legal reforms; in this respect, the state granted women minimal rights, although it upheld men's social and familial powers.

The state legalized abortion in 1973 in a major policy proclamation and implementation. One report indicated that women in Tehran experienced 20 to 30 unauthorized abortions per 100 live births in 1972. Simultaneously, the rapid rise of population had been a serious governmental concern since the late 1960s. It took a few years before authorities decided to launch an aggressive policy to curb population increase. Along with voluntary and non-governmental agencies, the government established family planning centers and imported and distributed modern contraceptive devices and methods. Due to their improper use, contraception failed to reduce the widespread tradition of abortion. Perhaps desperate at its inabilities to limit population growth, the state had decided to sanction abortion as another legal alternative. Married women obtained the right to lawful abortion, with the consent of their husbands, and unmarried women could undergo abortion up to the eighth week of pregnancy.[28]

[26] Husband's wives, Boserup; polygamy, Mernissi, *Beyond*. XVI; and sociology of polygamy during the early years of the Islamic Republic see Haeri, *The Law*. There is very little research available on the subject under the Shah, probably because polygamy could not enhance the state's image of modernization; as a subject matter, it could not receive sufficient encouragement and support.

[27] Social stigma, Pakizegi, 221.

[28] 1973, Mossavar-Rahmani, 253–255. Afkhami, however, states that in 1975, abortion was permitted to married women with the consent of the husband (see her "Women in Postrevolutionary Iran," 192, note 22); population growth, Ch. 3 on growth rate of population; and lawful abortion, Afkhami, "*Ibid.*," 192, note 22. Data are scarce on the impact of abortion laws.

But the enactment of abortion, it was widely believed, intended to address population growth rather than women's interests and women's choice.

Overall, the FPL accommodated the state's triumph over religion and in some ways Iran's economic growth. But the impact of these reforms was contingent on class. Except for the divorce statutes, which were used by women of diverse backgrounds, the FPL primarily benefited wealthier and more educated urban women. Understandably, elite women were most instrumental in the FPL's drafting.[29] Yet legal reforms were in force for too brief a time to have a lasting impact. The history of state-clergy conflict and the monarch's modernizing schemes made it possible for his challenge to the religious leadership and his success in securing a Westernizing image to be more significant than genuinely improving women's status. I am not suggesting that the Shah was unaware of the clerics' ability to exert control or shape women's position and gender relations. Rather his main interest lay in Westernization and secularization, which in many ways required gender reforms. Although land reform met vehement protests, from an ideological and political perspectives, the worst blow to the clergy came from their diminished power over women and their sexuality. In this bitter contest over women's sexuality, a process which had begun under Reza Shah, but continued more harshly under the Shah, more of men's power was transferred from the religious realm to the state's domain. Still, religious ordinance prevailed in some criminal areas concerning men's abuse of women.

ADULTERY, RAPE, AND PROSTITUTION IN THE PENAL CODE

In its modernization drives, the state failed to win all its battles against the clergy. One of its greatest concessions to the religious establishment concerned upholding Article 179 of *Qavanin-e Jaza'ie* (the Penal Code) of 1940, which addressed adultery and punishment. The Article stipulated that if a wife was discovered in an adulterous act, she could be murdered by her husband, brother, or father. "Whenever a husband sees his wife with a strange man in a compromising position," the Article stated, "and thereby murders or injures one of the parties or the two of them, he is exempt from punishment." Thus killing or injuring an adulterous woman was legally justified. But if the wife is not murdered, is over 18 years of age, and has consented to the sexual act, Article 207b of the

[29] Elite women, Afkhami, "Iran: A Future," entire.

Code made her "liable from 1 to 5 years imprisonment." In this respect, murder is punished less than adultery.[30]

As virginity is highly valued for women, but not for men, the laws assigned severe sanctions for assault on a virgin woman. Article 207a of the Penal Code stated that "if a man forces a virgin woman [over the age of 18] to sexual intercourse or enters her vagina (*farash*), ... he is sentenced to 3 to 7 years of imprisonment." But if the virgin woman was over 18 years of age and consented, Article 208, Section 2 made the man punishable by 1 to 2 years of imprisonment; she was not to be punished. This could possibly mean that an adult virgin woman could willingly have sexual intercourse, and perhaps continue it if she was not murdered and she was not seen performing such acts. Nowhere do the injunctions discuss punishment of women engaging in unlawful sexual acts or prostitution, although those who encouraged it were punished.[31]

Women had no equivalent recourse in the case of an unfaithful husband. Article 212 of the Penal Code stated that "if a married man is engaged in adultery, *if proven*, both he and his female accomplice are subject from 6 months' to 3 years' imprisonment." But a wife who took revenge (acceptable for a husband under Article 179) she would be sentenced to long imprisonment. For example, one woman who murdered her husband's companion received 15 years' imprisonment. Had she also murdered her "master" or husband, she would have received life imprisonment.[32]

The state's bias against women and in favor of husbands was also extended to fathers and brothers. Article 179 of the Penal Code gave fathers and brothers similar rights to those of husbands: "If a man sees his daughter or sister with a strange man in a compromising position, and thereby murders her or both of them, he is punishable by 1 to 6 months' imprisonment, but if he injures them, he is liable for 11 to 60 days of

[30] "Whenever a husband," (note that if the husband kills his wife, he is exempt from punishment; however, if the father or brother kills the same woman-as a daughter or sister-his crime is, punishable by 1 to 6 months' imprisonment), Kamankar, 82; and "liable from 1 to 5," Article 207b, *Ibid.*, 82 and 88–89; and also Mazlooman, *Zan Koshi*, 13–72. It may be useful to compare these aspects of the Penal Code with some traditional and religions customs as discussed in Chs. 1 and 2, above.

[31] "If a man forces," Kamankar, 82; Article 208, *Ibid.*, 90; and prostitution, *Ibid.*, 91, Article 210, 93–95, and Articles 213–214.

[32] Article 212 (emphasis added), *Ibid.*, 92–93; and "Master," Mazlooman, "Zan Koshi," 32–33 – for Article 179 see the following discussion.

incarceration."[33] This may possibly suggest that murders, in this contest, are preferable to injuries.

A proponent of Article 179 justified men's "natural" response to events that injured their "pride, compassion, chastity, honor, and prejudice." Yet, as analyst Reza Mazlooman points out, such a rationale implies that women in similar situations would respond differently. In other words, those assumptions ascribe different characteristics to men and women: men are motivated by pride and prejudice, whereas women are not.[34] Severely critical of this law, Iranian feminist lawyer Mehrangiz Manoochehrian wrote:

> In defense of Article 179, some say that men have freedom while women have husbands. Thus disillusioned women have no option but to tolerate and acquiesce in [the behavior of] their deceitful and disloyal husbands until their old age and death. Others say that because women are kinder and more nurturing than men, they are more interested in the well-being of their children and the upkeep of the family. For the same reasons, they assert that women cannot be violent and therefore cannot be permitted, as men are, to punish their spouses. But we say, women's kindness must not fasten their hands and feet like chains. On the other hand, if lawmakers can think of women only as kind individuals, how could they even conceive of women as murderers, much less execute them?[35]

Daily newspapers often printed articles on husbands who murdered their alleged unfaithful wives. For example, the *Havades* (Accidents) section of *Ettela'-at* reported that in one incident a suspicious man tore open the stomach of his wife with a sword, ripped her chest, and drank her blood. In another instance, the man not only severed his wife's head, but also those of his children. In a third case, the man cut open the stomach of his pregnant wife and cut off her head and those of his two children. In a fourth case, a 46-year-old man killed his wife with a nail. According to *Keyhan*, another man shot his wife and her companion to death. Data are scarce on the background of these men, and it is possible that these events might have occurred in poor urban areas or by psychotic individuals. It is also conceivable that educated middle-class men usually divorced their disloyal wives, because divorces were somewhat compatible with their secular beliefs. But elite and wealthy men generally refrained from publicity and divorce; in conformity with social values. They pardoned

[33] Article 179, Kamankar, 82.

[34] Different characteristics, Mazlooman, "Zan Koshi," 29–35.

[35] Manoochehrian, *Enteqad: Qavanin-e*, 89–106, especially 99.

the unfaithful wife in order to maintain social prestige. By contrast, most rural husbands preferred to divorce or permit governmental authorities to decide on the appropriate punishment for their deceitful wives. Only 5.8 percent of rural husbands interviewed by the Plan and Budget Organization saw murder as the only viable solution.[36]

Daily newspapers also printed columns on murderous fathers and brothers. *Keyhan* contained many stories of brothers and fathers who killed sisters or daughters because they had failed to respect the men's *namous* (honor). A case in point was a suspicious brother from a modest background who cut his sister into pieces with a knife; he "proudly" accepted five months' imprisonment as the price for preserving his *namous*.[37] Middle-class men might make threats of death, but most did no more than restrict the public mobility of their daughters or sisters. Thus, laws corroborated social practices. Gender biased codes endorsed men's patriarchal control, especially among more impoverished and traditional families.

Available data do not reveal information on women who killed men. Women generally reacted passively to unfaithful husbands. Wanting security, many women hoped to provide for the well-being of their children. In addition, fearful of abandonment in a male-dominated society, terrified of physical abuse by their husbands or relatives, dependent on the income of the head of household, few women committed criminal acts against their adulterous spouses. Instead, women would put up with their disloyal husbands; if the relationship was unbearable and the women were legally conscious of their rights and had financial means, they might seek divorce. But the destiny of divorced women was not any better. Repudiated as "second hand commodities," these women were disgraced socially. They were usually poorer because their alimony (if they received any), or other financial support from their husbands or families was less than when they were married.[38] In contrast, the more privileged divorced women would have a few more options such as entering the workforce or going

[36] Ettela'-at, *Ettela'at* 14039 (1351/1972), 22; *Ettela'at* 14230 (1352/1973), 18; *Ettela'at* 14275 (1351/1972), 13; and *Ettela'at* 13945 (1351/1972), 78 as cited in Mazlooman, "Zan Koshi," 15, notes 2, 15, 3, 27, and 2, respectively; Keyhan, *Keyhan* 8522 (1350/1971), 22 as cited by Mazlooman, "Zan Koshi," 27, note 1; and rural husbands, Qiasi, "Bar-resi-ye," 1.

[37] Proudly, Mazlooman, "Zan Koshi," 62, and 41–42.

[38] "Second hand," a cliche that I often heard; and alimony, although divorced women were legally entitled to their *mehr*, many men refused to fulfill their financial obligations, and they got away with it.

abroad or remarrying. Thus, the effect of legislation on women varied according to their social class.

Overall, adultery codes had substantial social and economic ramifications. Not only did they assign a greater value to men's lives than to women's, but they instituted severe punishments against women, upheld men's power over women, and left little options for battered or injured wives. Those laws would also pit men against women instead of providing ways of reconciling their differences or curbing men's compulsive passions.[39] But the Penal Code reflected larger class and gender inequalities in the society. Although in theory adultery laws confirmed men's violent actions against women, in practice the codes primarily justified the criminal behavior of men, not women. Moreover, the laws provided no legal protection for women of lesser means against the harsh consequences of men's behavior. The more affluent women enjoyed greater choices as they opted for divorce and could seek employment opportunities particularly in the growing service sector. The labor legislation facilitated this transition, although women continued to be treated unfairly.

WOMEN AND LABOR LEGISLATION

Labor statutes may be viewed as yet another attempt by the state against its religious opponents. By encouraging women to join the workforce, labor laws signified women's empowerment but the clerics' lesser control over women's labor and their confinement to the household. Compared to other legislation affecting women, these laws remained contradictory in theory and practice. While some women benefited from these laws, many continued to experience exploitation in the workplace. Thus, the new labor acts reinforced class-based subordination of women workers and strengthened legal gender bias and male domination.

Accelerating women's entry into the workforce, the 1960s and 1970s labor laws loosened certain traditional and legal restrictions against

[39] Compulsive passions, because of their inferior economic status and lack of better opportunities, some psychologically disturbed men would resort to violence as a means to realize an illusionary sense of empowerment in the society that is marked with wide class disparities. As workers, they remained powerless and insecure in the workplace and frequent unemployment further eroded their self-confidence. Such men might look to their wives for the chance to prove their worth and power, even to the extent of murdering them. Ironically, while wealthier and more powerful men exercised political influence, and middle-class men obtained some deference and respect in their jobs, poor men who had neither political or economic clout over other men might displace authority onto women – specifically, their own "adulterous" wives.

women's employment. These had been set down in *Qavanin-e Madani* (the Civil Code), enacted in 1930 and 1935, and revised in 1939, which incorporated much of the *Shari'eh*. Article 1117 of the Civil Code extended to husbands and fathers the legal power to forbid their wives or daughters wage work that they thought was disreputable or inappropriate to their status, honor, or to the welfare of the family. Modifying this statute, Article 16 of the 1967 FPL made it more difficult for a husband to prevent his wife from employment, requiring that he obtains an injunction from the Family Protection Courts on the ground that his wife's job was "disreputable." But the wife had no similar legal power to prevent her husband from engaging in "disreputable and inappropriate" work.[40]

Article 18 of the 1975 FPL awarded equal privileges to the wife by allowing her to stop her husband from inappropriate work. But the laws added "that the Court shall uphold [a] woman's request to prevent her husband from disreputable work only if it decides that man's cessation of work will not interfere with the family's income and affairs."[41] In reality, however, the special conditions of Article 18 made it unlikely that a woman would exercise her rights in keeping with Article 16. As the legal head of household and as the family's main financial provider, the husband was socially and culturally obligated to support his family. A woman had fewer opportunities to meet the financial requirements of the entire family, regardless of how qualified and skilled she was in the marketplace.

Yet the reforms benefited women by challenging traditional social mores and values toward women's work outside the home. Some enjoyed their work and the sense of achievement and some appreciated the opportunity to contribute financially to their families (Chapter 3). Many educated women actually took pride in being economically independent and socially mobile; for them, the life of a career woman was more liberating than what their mothers had experienced at home. Socially and psychologically, however, women's lives were confined to the household, and many envisioned themselves hardly as productive individuals beyond the high walls of their homes. For some women, work meant helping their family to survive; for a few others, it brought new disappointments and rewards, or a different way of perceiving and controlling life. Yet many privileged women disparaged the idea of wage work, preferring to be their own boss at home, where they could spend their time on the family and

[40] Article 1117, Mo'ini Araqi, 46; and Article 16, Bagely, 58 and 63.

[41] Article 18, Mo'ini-Araqi, 35.

children and attend salons and luxury parties. Thus, women's attitude toward work varied according to social class.[42]

Men had different attitudes toward women's work. Many preferred to have women confined to the household, as was in keeping with their legal powers as head of the household. For psychological and cultural reasons, women's work constituted a threat to the family's or men's power and prestige. Some men discredited women's work as appropriate to the poor, prostitutes, and other dishonorable persons; and a few perceived women's work as an attack on their feelings of masculinity. "When I die my wife can choose to work," one man asserted. Yet unprosperous men had little choice but to rely on women's economic contribution. More open-minded and educated men respected their wives' or daughters' sense of achievement and self-sufficiency. "My daughter can do what she pleases," a proud father insisted.[43]

Despite the statutory endorsement of gender equality in the labor market, there was little power of implementation. A case in point was Article 23 of the 1958 Labor Law that stipulated equal pay for equal work, regardless of gender. Notwithstanding the law's liberal appearance, its enforcement varied according to the nature of the work. For example, female machine workers in some modern factories that manufactured textiles, shoes, and clothes received wages equal to men doing similar work. However, equal wages did not prevail in such modern factories as those that produced electrical equipment or lightbulbs in the electric appliance industry.[44] In discussing wage discrimination by gender, a female interviewee who was a treasurer at the Pars Electric Factory in Tehran stated that:

> . . . . women who have similar jobs to men receive lower wage than men. Employers justify wage discrimination by saying that due to family obligations to wives and children, men have higher expenses. Is this legal? At the time of hiring, a single male worker is classified at rank three, four and five, whereas women are assigned to rank one, and therefore receive the minimum wage for a year.[45]

[42] Educated women, Hamideh Sedghi's interviews at the University of Tehran and with acquaintances, Tehran, 1973 and 1975; productive individuals, see Keyhan Research Associates; and luxury parties, Sedghi's interviews, 1973 and 1975.

[43] "My daughter," Hossein Sedghi's comment in reference to me, and my interviews that I conducted in Tehran at the Plan and Budget Organization of Iran, 1975. The views expressed by these interviewees corroborated my own observations. Also see Chapter 3 of this book, especially references to Rastegar.

[44] Equal pay, The Ministry of Labor, *Qavanin-e Moqarrarat-e Kar*, 23; and female machine workers, WOI, "Bar-resi-ye Ejmali," 16 and 24–25.

[45] Pars Electric, Rastakhiz-e Kargaran, 17.

Other modern factories practiced similar discrimination. In 1974, in the city of Rasht, women at a lightbulb factory went on strike for higher wages. Their wages were raised from 55 rials ($.73) a day to 80 rials ($1.06), but men's wages for similar work was 130 rials ($1.73). While women's militancy won them a wage increase, they continued to receive less pay than men. Though limited data are available, contradictions existed between labor laws and practice as they concerned equal wages for equal work regardless of gender (as was fully discussed in the prior chapter).[46]

Inconsistencies between legislation and practice also existed with regard to the minimum age of workers. Article 16 of the Labor Law forbade employment of workers' below the age of 12, and Article 58 stipulated severe sentences for infractions. In reality, however, a number of factories and workshops employed children under age 12. Indeed, a study of traditional industries such as carpet manufacturers in Isfahan pointed out that "most workers are girls between the ages of 9 and 10." Employment of children was widespread in factories with environmental hazards, such as wool, color, dyes, threads, and carpet workshops. For example, in the 15 carpet workshops in the Moft-Abad section of Isfahan, all workers were girls between the ages of 5 and 12, who worked from sunrise to sunset. Their very low wages, which often varied with their age, would go to their parents. Maltreatment of workers often went unpunished; data fail to shed light on circumstances, if any, under which employers might have been penalized.[47]

The exploitation of young working girls had implications that went beyond material imperatives, and that bear upon women's socialization and subordination. Both parents and employers exercised authority over women and their property, making it difficult, if not impossible, for women to develop any degree of independence. Brought up as subservient individuals, outside forces exerted profound influences on many women's lives. It is possible that such upbringing explains partially why the state failed to enforce the minimum age law. By predisposing unprivileged

[46] Rasht, Zafar-Dokht, "Bar-resi va Tahlil-e Madh-e Dahom"; and women's militancy, Tavraf-Chian; and Vafa, *Dar Bareh-e*, 21. To the extent that women's militancy did not threaten the stability of organizations or offices or the state itself, they were not harmed by the system. But if they were oppositional and threatening like A. Dehghani and others (Chapter 5), then they would be intimidated by the state.

[47] Article 16, Mo'sesseh, *Qavanin*. Vol. I, 20, and 48; and low wages, WOI, *Barresi-ye Ijmali*, 16 and 24–25.

women dependent on authority, the state not only socialized women into a passive position, but it also allied itself with and supported male establishments.[48]

In contrast to laws that appeared egalitarian philosophically but not practically, the text of other laws reflected definite gender inequality. A case in point was Article 17, which prohibited night shifts (from 10:00 P.M. to 6:00 A.M.) to women, except in the case of traditionally recognized "female" occupations such as nursing. Nursing is a labor-intensive job that is regarded generally as a woman's job in Iran. As nursing required women to work at night, Article 17 – strictly interpreted – discouraged women from performing that task. The law also promoted wage differential by gender, especially that Article 21 of Labor Law assigned a 35 percent wage increase for night shift workers – more men worked at night than women. Furthermore, because nursing as a profession could be viewed as an extension of household work, Article 17 possibly encouraged gender-typing occupations.[49]

In addition to its discriminatory and paternalistic nature (for example, the fear for women's safety), it was profitable to prevent women from working night shifts. Although men's salaries were relatively higher than women's, the law made it obligatory for employers to provide extra facilities for women, especially if they brought children to work. Many women would have needed such facilities at night. Article 18 prevented pregnant women from working in the period from 6 weeks before childbirth to 4 weeks after delivery; during this period employers could not dismiss them. Article 19 also entitled women to 30-minute breaks with pay for every 3 hours of work, so that they could nurse their infants. As a result, many employers preferred not to hire women or excluded them from night work. My interviews with a number of factory owners confirmed this point. They thought that even if they could legally justify their need for women workers for night shifts, they would still be unwilling to hire them because of the high costs of nurseries as well as the wages paid to women for nursing during night shifts.[50]

[48] It should be noted that *not* all women were trained as subordinates. As this book has shown, women remained active, although they shifted the boundaries of their lives as they had to make adjustments. See Chapters 5 and 8.

[49] Night shifts, Mo'sesseh, *Qavanin*, 20; and Article 21, *Ibid.*, 22–23; and Sedghi, "Women and Class," Chapters 6–7.

[50] Articles 18 and 19, Mo'sesseh, *Qavanin*, 20–21. Article 19 also mandated that if there were more than 10 infants at a workplace, employers were required to establish day-care centers and nurseries at the job; See also Sedghi, "Women and Class," Chapters 6–7.

The night shift law supported the state's ability to regulate working people through its control of women's roles in household maintenance. Women's presence was indispensable at home, especially at night when children and the husband were present. Women working at night would also be unavailable to their husbands for sexual services. It is possible that the night shift injunction intended to legitimate women's role in reproduction as well as preserve the family structure[51] and control women's participation in the labor market. In this way, the interests of both male employers and the state coincided: women were subordinated to men as both heads of households and employers (as discussed in Chapter 3).

Yet when men were unavailable for night shifts, employers' looked to women, not hesitating to violate night-shift mandates. Nor did the state intervene to enforce its laws. For example, women were hired for night shifts in a large textile factory in Isfahan because of the low productivity and unavailability of male workers. The owner explained the men's low productivity as due to the fact that textile and carpet factory work took secondary importance to jobs in better paying and more prestigious establishments such as steel mills and the military located in the vicinity of Isfahan. Because there are significant differences in Isfahan's economy as compared to the rest of the country women filled workforce shortages, despite legal violations.[52]

Other laws presupposed a stipulated gender inequality in work. For example, Article 20 restricted women from "difficult"[53] and "harmful," as opposed to "light" jobs. These categories reflected the gender division of labor in "masculine" factories such as those that made brick and wood, and "feminine" jobs such as clerical into which women were crowded. By so doing, they restricted women's occupational mobility and promoted gender inequality.[54] In sum, while labor legislation ran counter to traditional mores by legalizing women's right to work in public, it also reinforced women's subordination. The laws were contradictory: they represented progress in challenging household-related patriarchy, but they also supported the commitment of the state and employers, male-dominatory values. In that sense, some of men's powers shifted from religious domain and the household to the sphere of the labor market and the secularizing

[51] Family structure, Pakizegi, 223.

[52] Isfahan's economy, WOI, *Barresi-ye Ejmali*, 15–16.

[53] Difficult, Mo'sesseh-e, *Qavanin*, Vol. I, 21.

[54] Article 20, Mo'sesseh, *Qavanin*, 21–22; and Sedghi, "Women and Class," Chapters 6–7.

state. In so doing, gaps remained between the theoretical promulgation of the Labor Law and its implementation.

Concomitant with the White Revolution, the state consolidated its powers and defeated the secular and religious opposition. It sponsored repression, while at the same time, its economic strategies shook the fabric of the society and absorbed the pull of women into the workforce. Public policies modified gender issues with respect to marriage and divorce. Addressing adultery, legislation failed to alter adultery, statutes that had been encoded many years before and reflected the spirit of the *Shari'eh*. Despite the introduction of some emancipatory measures, gender equality remained a dream.

The Shah's state, like that of his father, both challenged and affirmed the religious basis of Iranian society, claiming to be the true representative of Islam. It is not surprising that in this process, the state acted ambivalently. On the one hand, it passed a number of laws that facilitated some women's entry into wage work and political office, as will be discussed in the next chapter. On the other, it promulgated and maintained laws, such as family legislation, which promoted religious and other traditional mores and enjoined women's subordination. In this way, while the state conferred limited secular legal status on women, it also supported their subordination. The new legislation increased middle-class women's options. It also strengthened legal gender bias and male-centered institutions, especially for less empowered women.

Reform, therefore, liberalized family laws and labor legislation while it reinforced institutional male domination, though in a secular way. As the White Revolution was an antecedent to the state's actions in Family Protection Laws, the Penal Codes, and Labor Legislation, it was women who became actors supporting the state or opposing it through their formal and informal political activities, and through their own networks and organizations.

5

Women and the State

Ashraf Dehghani, the only woman in the Central Committee of the underground opposition, the Organization of Iranian People's Feda'i Guerrillas (OIPFG), was twenty-two years old in 1971, when she was arrested. Her memoirs recall her prison experience: "The thugs strapped me to a bed.... whipping the soles of my feet.... they gave me electric shocks using [a] truncheon-shaped electrode," then they "strapped me to a bench, face down. The shameless vermin dropped his trousers and assaulted me...." Resisting SAVAK and the state's vicious rapists and interrogators, Dehghani's defense was to maintain silence. Having so provoked and diminished her abusers, she was transferred to Tehran's infamous Evin Prison, where still more cruel "professional" torturers attempted to force a confession. There, she remembered, "they picked up a pair of tongs, gripping and twisting my flesh" and "they began compressing my fingers in a vice. They said they were going to pull out my nails...." But she persisted in her resistance while wishing her own death under the state's torture. Iranian scholars and feminists alike have largely ignored Dehghani's tale. She had a unique life and experiences: she was a nonconformist, militant, and defiant political actor.[1]

In contrast, many other politically active women made their accommodations with the state, representing its class and political interests.

1 "The thugs," "strapped me," and "picked up," Dehghani, *Torture*, 22–23 and 29–30. After escaping from prison in March 1973, she continued her work with her organization. Dehghani's tale, Najmabadi, ed. *Women's Autobiography*, Introduction. This latter study excludes Dehghani's memoirs.

One such woman was Mahnaz Afkhami, the Secretary General of the Women's Organization of Iran or WOI (1970–79) and Minister of State for Women's Affairs (1970–78). Concerned with raising women's political consciousness, especially the housewives, and mobilizing them behind Iran's only political party, the pro-Shah *Hezb-e Rastakhiz* or the Resurgent Party, Afkhami contended, "it is the duty of every Iranian woman to show her political and social growth by participating in [the 1976 parliamentary] elections." Many Iranian women "fail to participate in politics" because they "lack [political] consciousness." In order to educate women in their "national duties," she authorized the WOI to assign its voluntary members to go from house to house "to inform women," "to advertise campaigns" on the radio, and to set up special television programs to introduce female candidates. Such strategies, she believed, would allow a female electorate to "vote for the candidate of her choice with full awareness."[2] Afkhami was a conformist and remained a strong advocate of the state until the 1979 Revolution.

Through its modernization drive, the Shah's state instituted gender policies and promoted women's suffrage. Its economic policies reverberated in politics and culture, altering the gender division of labor and family laws. The state also engaged in conflict, competition, and cooperation with the opposition, specifically the clerics. At stake was control over political power, wealth, and even women's sexuality. Whether exercising repression or accommodating co-optation, the state claimed new property relationships over its inhabitants, in particular women. Women responded as active agents. They were not merely passive recipients or "grateful beneficiaries of the state."[3] Some collaborated with governmental institutions and others questioned the existing patterns of political power, structures, and ideologies. Occasionally affecting politics and inscribing their own feminisms, women did so in different ways, to different degrees, and following different political persuasions. How women obtained enfranchisement, how they articulated their goals in support or rejection of the state, and how they set limits to the state's behavior in the 1960s and 1970s will be my focus.

It is my contention that the state can modify, eradicate, and restructure institutions of political rule and through it, gender and patriarchal

[2] "It is the duty," "fail," "lack," "national duties," "inform," "advertise," and "vote for the candidate," WOI, *Bulleton-e Haftegi*, No. 386 (1354/1976), 2, and 14.

[3] "Grateful beneficiaries," Najmabadi, "Hazards," 58–63.

relations and women's lives. But women's responses and resistance and, more generally, women's political activities and movements can itself constrain and subvert the state's behavior. This chapter will view the state in terms of its relations to gender and simultaneously examine gender politics through its interactions with the political system and structures. It will thus bring to light the end of the aberrant secular era of the Pahlavi dynasty with its changing nexus of state–clergy, state–gender, and clergy–gender relations.

WOMEN'S SUFFRAGE AND POLITICAL INEQUALITY

Originating in the West, suffragist movements were relatively latecomers to the Third World, where they emerged from multiple struggles as anti-colonialism and nationalism, and were sometimes combined with women's struggle for emancipation. Occasionally, these movements were not advanced by women themselves, rather by male nationalists, revolutionary leaders, or under state patronage.[4] Suffragists generally demanded the promotion of women's rights and the improvement of women's position in their respective societies, although the circumstances that led to their success differed. In many parts of the West – whose suffragists were primarily drawn from white or dominant elite women – these movements occurred when their societies were undergoing capitalist transformation. The women's rights movements in the developing world had more heterogeneous paths to victory.

In Iran, public policies, economic backwardness, and state–clergy discord delayed women's suffrage. During most of the twentieth-century, women's initiatives and their desire for enfranchisement depended, to a great extent, on the resilience of the state. The weaker the state, the more independent, diverse, and creative were women's assertiveness as during the early twentieth-century and post-Reza Shah abdication. Conversely, the stronger and more repressive the state, the more dependent were women activists on the state as under Reza Shah and Post-WWII reign of the Shah. Women's quest for inclusion in the public sphere also reflected challenges of developmental processes, which often entailed tensions in the rise of the modernizing state with opposition groups, in particular the dominant religious establishments. As these frictions intensified over time, especailly under the Shah, the scope of state–religion contests

[4] State patronage, Sedghi, "Third World Women."

expanded to comprise land, distribution of resources, and equally more importantly, women's emancipation.[5]

Spawned by the White Revolution, women's suffrage came almost a decade after the CIA coup and Iran's increasingly close ties with the United States. Attempting to consolidate his power, the Shah launched his major economic and political project, the top-down White Revolution. Through this project, the state fostered economic growth and won an impromptu victory over the opposition, in particular, the dissenting clergy. On January 9, 1963, the monarch announced women's enfranchisement as one of the White Revolution's six points of action. The clergy immediately denounced it and declared women's suffrage unconstitutional and harmful to Islam. Two weeks later, the religious establishment organized violent demonstrations in the *bazaar* and neighborhoods of south Tehran where its power base remained strong and their impact more invincible. "One of [the protest's] specific aims," Hafez Farmayan maintained, "was to strike against the growing popular acceptance of feminine [female] participation in the [White Revolution] referendum."[6]

Passionately reacting with counter-demonstrations, women went on strike on January 23, 1963. Women teachers, nurses, and public and private employees poured into the streets, calling on women to challenge the 1906 constitutional mandate that had categorized them as aliens and criminals. Protestors marched peacefully and gathered outside one of the Shah's palaces, *Kakh-e Marmar*, to express their demand for enfranchisement. It is unclear whether the state had mobilized women or they organized themselves, but women's response to the patriarchal culture and the cleric's desire against women's suffrage must have had the Shah's support. The next day, on January 24, 1963, magnifying his own grandiose self-image and boasting his masculine and military powers, the Shah declared in Qom: "We are done with social and political parasites; I abhor the 'black reaction' [the clergy] even more than the 'red destruction' [the left]."[7] Two days later, on January 26, 1963, the referendum on the White

[5] Women's emancipation, note that with the absence of a strong state at the turn of the century and in the early 1940s (and later during the early part of the 1979 Revolution), women's initiatives and struggles as well as their varied goals and aspirations created an atmosphere for the development of autonomous organizations, despite the persistence of patriarchy.

[6] "Feminine participation," Farmayan, "Politics," 104–109; and Akhavi, *Religion*, Ch. 3, 63–65, 95, and 97 where he discusses the split among various factions of the clergy and the pro-women's suffrage activities of Ayatollah Borqei'e. Also see Paidar, 140–146.

[7] "Black" and "Red destruction," *Ketab-e Salnamey-e* as cited in Farmayan, "Politics," 105.

Revolution was held and passed without difficulties. Women were now citizens.

Although a predominantly symbolic act, the suffrage denoted different meanings for the state, the clergy, and women. It served the state in three different but related ways. It affirmed the state's victory over the intransigent clergy. As discussed earlier, one of the greatest blows to the clergy's influence came from the loss of some of its control over women's sexuality and labor. The enfranchised, more publicly visible and freer women would potentially choose different lifestyles and careers outside the traditional household and would unquestionably pose challenges to male authority, specifically that which was sanctioned by the religious establishment. Thus, gender was temporarily beneficial for state formation, producing a short-lived lull in the historical rift that had marked monarchy–mullah relations. As earlier in the Pahlavi period, the state manipulated gender to "emasculate" religious power, and negate their hold on politics and society.

Second, women's suffrage contributed to state formation in an Iran that was increasingly characterized by secularism, economic growth, and a gradual integration in the world capitalist market. Women's enfranchisement boosted the state's image abroad and bolstered state legitimacy by enhancing its developing, "democratic," and equalitarian posture internationally, in particular in the United States. The *New York Times* applauded the ceremonious event at the Parliament and lavished attention on their majesties: "The royal couple drove in state from the palace to the Parliament building in a gilt coach, escorted by the imperial Lancers." Saluted by crowds, "Women[,] schoolgirls, laborers[,] and representatives of farming families who lined the route cheered, clapped[,] and shouted 'Long live the Shah! Long live Empress Farah!'" At the *Majles*, according to the report, "The presence of the Empress Farah at the opening ceremony and of women in the Parliament emphasized the newly acquired right of Iran's women to vote...."[8]

Third, emancipation encouraged a state–gender alliance. When the referendum on the White Revolution was to be held, Radio Iran announced that women could vote. Women and men would vote in separate ballot boxes, and women's votes would be tabulated but not counted in the national total ballots. The government "was very cautious in its handling" of women's votes. Of the almost 5.5 million voters, only 4,000 voted

[8] "The Royal," "Farah," and "Iran's women," "Iran Parliament," *The New York Times*, (October 7, 1963), 7.

against the referendum; counted separately, the women's vote amounted to almost 271,000. How many women casted negative votes and how many of them voted without pressure by the state remains unknown. Bamdad referred to the enormous enthusiasm of both rural and urban women's participation in electoral politics. Carefully orchestrated, the White Revolution legitimized women's new political rights. It formally emancipated women, and accorded them the legal rights of citizenship. In so going, the suffrage engendered the state by bringing women into the state's domestic and international orbit.[9]

Moreover, suffrage connoted a different meaning for the clergy. Divisions that existed among the religious establishment earlier in the century continued during and after Mossadegh's cabinet. It is not the intention of this book to focus on dissensions among the clerics, but it is noteworthy that Ayatollah Ali Akbar Borqe'i supported women's suffrage, whereas many other prominent clerics, such as the Grand Ayatollah Burujerdi, Ayatollah Behbahani, Ayatollah Kashani, and Ayatollah Ruhollah Musavi Khomeini denounced the state's plan for women's rights. The White Revolution referendum, Khomeini remarked, purged Islam and the *Qoran* and instead, "gave women the right to vote and participate in elections." But, he argued, this is merely "a slogan or propaganda by the state to mask its dictatorial and fascist face with democracy and liberalism, and as the builder of the country of free men and free women." Referring to the Shah as "the wild and bloodthirsty wolf," Khomeini accused him of being a duplicitous "snake" – with beautiful skin but deadly poisonous fangs – who is "now carrying the message of freedom." "To speak of women's liberation and equality [being granted] by the dependent colonial regime" of the Shah, he asserted, "serves only to mislead the uninformed masses and to cover its crimes."[10]

Finally, the meaning of the suffrage for women is difficult to assess. Enfranchisement legitimized women's political participation. It also extended formal representation, electoral rights, and the right to hold political offices to women. While the poor and working-class women had little means to represent themselves, some middle-class and elite women

[9] "Cautions," *Ettela' at-e Salnameh*, (1963/1342), Sec. I, 50 as cited in Farmayan, "Politics," 105–106; and Bamdad, Bamdad I, 12, who states that because of women's overwhelming enthusiasm to vote, women were allowed to vote, but separate ballot boxes were employed for women and men voters. She does not explain why women and men had to vote separately.

[10] Suffrage, Akhavi, *Religion*, Chs. 3–4; Chs. 2–4 of this book; and Abrahamian, *Iran*, 425 n 10; and "gave women," "a slogan," "the wild," "snake," "freedom," "women's liberation," and "crimes," *Zendegi-nameh-e Emam Khomeini*, I, 62–63.

forged a new alliance with the state as its representatives, ideologues, and policy planners, in particular regarding gender matters. The Shah's proponents wrote the most eyewitness accounts of the period and there is little evidence on oppositional views. The former viewed enfranchisement as the extension of the Shah's democratic will to recognize women's rights. One feminist's impassioned praise stated that "the great dam which prevented women's participation in legislation for many years" is now crushed by "the unshakable will of the Iranian leader [the Shah], and democracy has now acquired a real meaning." Bamdad noted that the right to vote was the culmination of "The great transformation of Iranian women's destiny during the Pahlavis, which will be written in golden scripts." Hailing Iran's democracy, Sanghvi exalted the ruler as a democrat and stated that the Shah's White Revolution was a "scheme to impart a new life to Iran's democracy within the defined framework of constitutional amendments." He "cannot accept that half the work force of the country be deprived of its legitimate [political] rights."[11]

Actually, the Shah himself provided a different perspective on women's rights in an interview with Italian reporter Oriana Fallaci. She quoted him as saying:

> In a man's life, women count only if they're beautiful graceful and know how to stay feminine.... This Women's Lib business, for instance. What do these feminists want?... [Women] may be equal in the eyes of the law, but not... in ability.... [Women have] never produced a Michelangelo or a Bach. [They have] never even produced a great cook. And don't talk of opportunities.... Have you lacked the opportunity to give history a great cook? [Women] have produced nothing great, nothing!...
>
> ... All I can say is that women, when they are in power, are much harsher than men. Much more cruel. Much more blood thirsty.... [Women are] heartless when [they]'re rulers.... [They]'re schemers,... evil. Every one of [them].... [12]

Yet two years later, in an address to the *Majles* that coincided with the 40th anniversary of unveiling and the beginning of International Women's Year, the Shah stated that he issued "the [enfranchisement] decree on the equality of political rights of men and women [because] Iranian women had achieved the maturiy and capability to be given this right."[13]

Both electoral politics and women's political representation were new to Iran. While elections were increasingly rigged, women in the position

[11] "The great dam," "The unshakable will," and "the great transformation," Bamdad I, 18 and 11–31; and "scheme" and "rights," Sanghvi, et al.

[12] Fallaci, "A Shah's," 24.

[13] "Decree," *Keyhan International* (January 5, 1975).

of policy making were rare. The Shah and SAVAK appointed and/or approved nearly all of the *Majles* or *Sena* (the Senate) members.[14] Prominent, wealthy, and educated women occupied some high-level positions: no one represented the poor or rural women and men. By the end of 1963, 6 of the total 197 deputies were women. They included such figures as Dr. Farrokhru Parsa, Fakhr Afaq Parsa's daughter, Hajar Tarbiat, Dr. Mehrangiz Doulatshahi, Nayereh Ebtehaj-Sami'i, Nehzat Nafisi, and Shoukat-Malek Jahanbani. Also highly educated were the 2 women out of the total of 60 senators in 1963: Dr. Shams-ol Moluk Mosahab and the feminist attorney Dr. Mehrangiz Manoochehrian who had published more than 28 books in law, gender codes, and sociology.[15] Although a few more women were elected as deputies during the subsequent elections, the change was negligible. At the ministerial level, Parsa served as Education Minister (1968–74) and Afkhami as minister without portfolio. Gender representation remained highly unequal in governmental offices.[16] Having obtained suffrage 55 years later than men, only a few privileged women attained high-level positions.

The right to citizenship was a mixed blessing for women. Whereas suffrage gave some women political visibility, formal recognition, and an ability to participate in governemntal decision-making, it signified little value for the majority of politically disadvantaged, disempowered, and

[14] Sena, Farmayan, "Policies," 105.

[15] 197 Deputies, Vezarat-e E'tela'at va Jahangardi, *Fehrest-e Nam va Onvan-e Maqamat*, 1354/1975–1355/1976; Sedghi and Ashraf, "Dynamics"; and *Who's Who in Iran 1979*, entire, especially 303. After being a deputy for 2 consecutive terms, Tarbiat became a senator. See also Esfandiari, "Iran: Women and Parliaments." My interviews with a female senator in Tehran in 1971 and 1991 reveal that while critical of the Shah's regime, the late senator, who wished to remain anonymous, indicated that all elections had to be approved by *Darbar* (the Court) and SAVAK, and that all "representatives" or appointees were essentially window dressing.

[16] Gender representation, *Ibid.* and Keyhan Research, *The Employment*, 49, 10, and 50. Sedghi, "Women and Class," Chs. 4–6, and tables 50–52. Similar patterns of unequal representation existed throughout the government. The higher the post, the lower the representation of women, in particular such high-level political and administrative posts, as judges, diplomats, and members of Urban Arbitration Councils, Rural Houses of Equity, and Provincial, District and City Councils. Among 106 undersecretaries, only 3 women were appointed in 1975. In 1975, none of the 23 governor generals or 154 governors were women. There were only 2 female and 436 male mayors. The ratio of men to women departmental directors was 447 to 18; by 1977, this gap had somewhat narrowed with an increase of 21 women. Like the sex-typing occupations discussed in Chapter 3, the concentration of women was relatively high in the Ministry of Education, but there were no women in such traditionally male-dominated ministries as Economic Affairs; Finance; Foreign Affairs; Commerce; Post, Telegraph, and Telephone; Justice; Roads; Welfare; Industries and Mines; Labor; Interior; Housing; Energy; and Agriculture. Thus, political equality for all women remained a sham.

anti-establishment women. We will never know how democratic representation and pluralism might have developed had the Iranian secularizing state lived longer. But given the state's authoritarian nature and its class and gender biases, the chances to attain genuine representation and political parity remained doubtful. Still, this phase of Iranian history witnessed some strength in women's political agency.

WOMEN'S AGENCY

What little has been written on Iranian women during the Shah's period has a pro-monarch bias. As discussed, studies that supported the regime's gender policies, ignored women's agency. More generally, they suffered from a lack of theoretical analysis and the treatment of women remained mainly descriptive, statistical, and legalistic. But those available data offer insights into the complexities of women's activities: the 1960s and 1970s witnessed a dialectical tension between two diametrically opposed groups of women, both committed to politics and political activism. While female supporters of the monarchy entered into alliance with the state and its institutions, the same process denied participation to women who denounced the state and its national and international politics. Still, despite vast political differences, common interests pertaining to women sometimes intersected.

Women were active and proactive agents: they affected public policies and to some extent, they promoted their own interests. Focusing on agency allows the observer to conceptualize women as dynamic actors and escape the straightjacket of women as victims. Although patriarchal culture and mores exerted important influences, depending somewhat on women's class and educational background, they responded differently to political and social issues, especially those that directly concerned their lives. Many urban upper-class and educated middle-class women broke away from traditional lifestyles and sometimes from the cultural restraints of their time. In contrast, most of the rural and poor urban women sought to achieve power through their sanctioned place in male-dominated households and the centuries old network of local and religious institutions.

Active women were diverse. The diversity among them included variances in ideology, politics, and feminism. Depending on their political perception and relationship to the state, these women consisted of conformists and nonconformists, each with its own subdivisions and overlapping interests. Classifying women into groups has advantages and disadvantages: dichotomies allow the researcher to draw distinctions among different political actors, while they can obscure common interests that may exist among them. I consider women's agency in terms of conflicting and intersecting interests among active women. Conformist women were those members of the royal family, the women's Organization of Iran (WOI) or *Sazeman-e Zanan-e Iran*, and state officials who formally participated in politics and actively supported the state and monarchy. Because their political position was somewhat identical, I will not address ideological differences among them. In contrast, nonconformist women were those whose political involvement remained informal and took place outside existing state structures. They denounced the state, its officials and policies, and regarded the Shah as despotic and dependent on the West.[17] Not holding a monolithic oppositional stance, nonconformist women were further subdivided into secular left, secular independent, and religious groups.

Despite ideological and partisan differences, common interests pertaining to women sometimes overlapped. Primarily from urban areas, many active women experienced patriarchal influences that they struggled with, in their personal and public lives, in different ways, and to different degrees. Many were secular and believed in unveiling. They also gave broad support to women's emancipation and gender equality. Although these common interests existed among active women, they never acknowledged them. Nor were those interests sufficient to generate a political alliance among ideologically and politically divided women.

Social class, as might be anticipated, had a definite effect on women's agency, in particular their political participation and perception. Conformist women typically derived status from their fathers, or through marriage, or close association with the royal family, or through their mastery of political cunning.[18] Some of these women held honorary political and social positions, or headed powerful governmental offices. When they received an office, as trustees of the state, they were endowed with distinguished titles, staff of experts, and recognition. Publicly visible and unveiled, these women wielded power, allegedly advancing pro-establishment politics and sometimes feminist concerns. Less-privileged

[17] The term "conformist women" will be used interchangeably as pro-state, pro-monarchy, pro-Shah, and pro-establishment women; the term "nonconformist women" will be used to refer to oppositional women, who were anti-state and/or anti-monarchist – see the following discussions.

[18] There is no hard data on women's wealth and salary in Iran. My assessment of women's salary is based on personal observations as well as my extensive study of Iran's communication industry as a result of one summer of internship at that organization in 1977. See Sedghi, "Women and Class," Ch. 6.

women were not always treated so well, even if conformists. The monarchist women served the King of Kings well in his consolidation of power and quest for national and international legitimacy. By bolstering the state's objectives, conformist women fostered their own prestige and legal reforms that advanced feminism from above.

Nonconformist women came predominantly from the middle or lower-middle class but, sometimes from families with lesser means, both from large and small urban centers.[19] Coming to prominence in the 1960s, as individuals or organizational members, their opposition to the state included its autocracy and repression. They showed little deference to state feminism, although undoubtedly, they must have resented and been affected by patriarchal tendencies. As secular individuals, women raised their voices in tracts and poetry; however, fearing retaliation, they expressed their political discontent in a symbolic, abstract, and indirect way. As members of secular revolutionary or religious organizations, women presented the ideological and political objectives of their respective groups. Because they stood for abolishing monarchy, many of them operated clandestinely and many were imprisoned or died under torture. Whether conformists or nonconformists, women did not respond uniformly to the state; class background, ideology, individual or group affiliation, and the level of their feminist consciousness mattered.

CONFORMIST WOMEN

Visible as deflators of the religious establishment and symbols of modernization and Westernization, the conformist women exercised some control over their own sexuality and their relations to men. They enjoyed freedom of movement unusual for women in their culture. Some participated in political decision-making, in particular, policies related to gender issues. Yet many symbolized the "Queen Bee Syndrome." They thought they were "special" and "have unique qualifications that allow them to get high ranking positions normally denied to women." For them, "nondiscriminatory policies become threatening" and they tended to dissociate themselves "from the fundamental issues of equality for women." Ironically though, because of their "access to power and male favor," they

[19] Nonconformist women. In her biography, Dehghani describes herself as a member of a working family, born in Iran's city of Azerbaijan to a father who was a *mirab* or a water distributor. For another biographical account of a nonconformist woman see Fatemeh Amini, *Hamse-ye Yek*. Some nonconformist women, especially those who were active in larger cities or in exile, came from middle-class backgrounds.

were "in the best position to advance the cause of women," but they failed to do so. The Queen Bee allies herself "with the establishment and proselytizes for the status quo."[20]

My own interviews with some Iranian Queen Bees who had attained high political positions indicated that they primarily embodied the interest of elite men in power. They ignored any possibility of female solidarity across class lines and they appeared elitist and condescending of women of other classes and ideological persuasions.[21] Here, I consider three categories of conformist women: elite women, high-ranking female officials of the WOI, and the media. Elite women are significant because they held powerful national and international posts. High officials of the WOI also deserve attention because the organization contributed to the formulation of gender policies and promoted the state's posture abroad. Finally, powerful women in the media industry or *Sazeman-e Radio va Television-e Melli-ye Iran*, the National Iranian Radio and Television (NIRT) are illuminating because the organization helped advance the state's ideological interests.

Elite Women

With the exception of scant references to Ashraf Pahlavi and the three official wives of the Shah, almost all studies of Iranian elite under the Pahlavis are male-centered. There are no definitive studies on the wealth and possessions of women or men, although some elite women owned and had access to substantial resources and power. The quality of available records is uneven, but memoirs, speeches, interviews, and secondary data allow us to sketch a picture of their lives and activities. Elite women consisted of female members of the royal and non-Court related prosperous families. This study will only address the most powerful women who were closely associated with the Shah.

Publicly visible, some Pahlavi women wielded considerably more power than any other women. Many owned property – land and industries, corporate holdings, and shares – sometimes through direct ownership, sometimes through the Pahlavi Foundation; and many had domestic

[20] "Queen Bee Syndrome," and all the other quotations in this paragraph come from Satines, Tavris, and Jayarante, "The Queen Bee," 55–60; and "status quo," Keyhan Research, *The Employment*, 49; and Sedghi's interviews, NIRT, 1977.

[21] Female solidarity, Sedghi's interviews, NIRT, 1977. The Queen Bees' work relations to other women resembled occupational segregation of women by class, as discussed in Chapter 3.

and international bank accounts. Some studies estimated that the Pahlavi's wealth ranged between 5 and 20 billion dollars; Pahlavi women held a portion of those holdings too. Their fortune stemmed from inheritance, kin-relations, or close relations to men in the Palace or men of wealthy families.[22] Besides their involvement in charity work, they dispensed political power through their appointments.[23] Often they designated trusted relatives or associates to sensitive governmental, institutional, and business posts and, other times, they assigned themselves to highly prestigious domestic and international offices. Through their activities abroad, they attempted to present a positive state image. At home, they were severely criticized – more so than the male members of their family for their nepotism, lavish lifestyles, and extravagant parties and clothes. Ashraf Pahlavi, Soraya Bakhtiari, and Farah Diba stand out.

The most powerful Iranian woman, Ashraf Pahlavi, drew authority from her father, the founder of the dynasty, later, her brother, the Shah, and her own sense of power and politics. She recalled her father's wish that she had been born a boy. "I never liked what I saw in the mirror," she wrote. Although, her self-critique had another perspective, namely that of the West, she wanted "fairer skin and more height," something that many Iranian urban women lacked, and men liked. But she also had a grandiose self-image, as psychoanalyst Karen Horney might say, a distorted self-image to compensate for the insecure self. She imagined herself a "panther," "turbulent, rebellious, [and] self-confident." She matched herself with her father, "stubborn," "proud," and with an "iron will." Like him, she married three times.[24]

Comparing her memoirs with those of her contemporaries, Pahlavi appears more independent, ambitious, and hard-working. She applied to national and international politics a sense of Machiavellian politics that other Court women lacked. Less preoccupied with fashion and jewelry

[22] Fortune. For an informative list of 5,500 biographies of influential and wealthy Iranians see *Iran Who's Who*. For information related to the wealth and status of various Court members consult, *The Autobiography of H.I.H. Princess Soraya*, entire, especially 95, where the author stated the Shah's salary was $ 750,000.00 annually, and made indirect references throughout to the Pahlavi's wealth. See also Abrahamian, *Iran*, especially, Ch. 9; and Graham; Branigin; and Chittenden.

[23] Appointments. There is no definitive study on appointing powers of elite Iranian women, but inferences may be made from various sources related to Iranian politics and economics, some of which are listed in this study, and other listings that appear under Diba in *Iran Who's Who*; A. Pahlavi's "Declaration," her *Mirror*; and Vezarat-e Ettela'at, *Fehrest-e Nam*.

[24] "Mirror," "fairer," "self-confident," "stubborn," "proud," and "iron will," Pahlavi, *Mirror*. XV, 14 and 43; and Horney, entire.

than women around her, she vigorously pursued power and remained highly active until the 1979 Revolution. Though an instrumental force in legitimating gender reforms and the WOI, Pahlavi's gender philosophy was not particularly introspective: "I confess that even though since childhood I had paid a price for being a woman, in terms of education and personal freedom, I had not given much thought to the specific ways in which women in general were more oppressed than men."[25]

Ashraf Pahlavi was the most influential woman of her time. She headed various charitable, educational, health, cultural, and business organizations: she was the president of High Council of the Iranian Women's Association and subsequently, the founder and president of the WOI. She also assigned her three husbands and two sons to sensitive and powerful positions. Mention should also be made of her prominent role in the 1953 CIA coup as discussed in Chapter 3. Joseph Stalin recognized her importance with the gift of a sable coat prior to her visit to Moscow on behalf of the Soviet Red Cross. Internationally she held several prominent positions, and in different capacities, she helped enhance her brother's modernizing efforts and the regime's image abroad. Representing the Iranian government, she served as a delegate to the United Nations, chaired Iran's United Nations Human Rights Commission and the Commission on the Status of Women, and led delegations to various international conferences, including the First World Conference on Women held in Mexico in 1975. Together with the monarch, they donated large sums to American universities, for example, to the Johns Hopkins University, the University of Michigan, and Princeton University, among others. Pahlavi's repute as human rights spokesperson often drew criticism because of her active role in Iranian monarchical politics. Likewise, she was the subject of animosity especially by men, because of her unbridled lifestyle and alleged heroin trafficking.[26]

Almost as if competing with her brother for the throne, Ashraf Pahlavi's influence on the Shah's marriages was tremendous. Rumor has it that because the Shah's first official wife, Fouziyeh, the sister of Egypt's King Faruq, could not bear a son as heir to the throne, Pahlavi sought the divorce of her sister-in-law in the hope of persuading her brother to amend

[25] "Price for being a woman," Pahlavi, *Mirror*, 153.

[26] Soviet Red Cross, Pahlavi, *Mirror*, 77, 79–80, 82, and 88; and Mo'tazed, *Fowziyeh*, II. While holding various posts, Ashraf Pahlavi was severely criticized, see Boyle (who wrote in response to Ashraf Pahlavi's Op Ed in the *New York Times* on January 5, 1976), "Sisters of the Princess," *The Nation*. And Pahlavi's repute, Mo'tazed, *Fowziyeh*, II, especially 781–782.

the constitution and declare her the heir to the throne. Soraya Esfandiari Bakhtiari, the monarch's second official wife, noted in her autobiography, that "Ashraf was after [her] position" as "first lady of the Court." Although the king's twin sister was jealous of the Queen, Bakhtiari ultimately proved to have less influence than her. This was so even though she was the Shah's most beloved wife, and even though her father was head of the prominent Bakhtiari tribe.[27]

Soraya Pahlavi sought to establish an independent power position in the Court. She allied with Shams Pahlavi, the older and a full sister to Ashraf, and the Shah who had been a matchmaker for Soraya and her brother. Her miscalculation was to have ignored the Queen Mother and her powerful daughter, Ashraf. In her memoirs, Soraya acknowledged her astonishment at the power of royal women. Although they had "no rights of any kind, in practice they knew a thousand tricks and dodges for getting their own way, and sometimes I had the sensation of living in a thorough-going matriarchy."[28] Soraya Pahlavi's sex appeal was effective in building the Shah's image. Her husband drew pleasure from having her company on royal trips to Europe and America that were aimed at building Iran's international prestige. It is also possible but not definite, that she had convinced her husband to support the CIA coup.[29] But after eight years as queen, Pahlavi's royal powers ended because she could not bear a successor to the throne. Ruling-class status derived from her husband was insufficient to keep Soraya Pahlavi in her power position in the face of dynastic failures and inner-court intrigues. Yet her personal influence brought large, regular sums from the Shah.[30]

[27] Rumor, *The Autobiography*, 73 and 72; and "first lady of the Court," *Ibid.*, 71 and 112–118, where Soraya Bakhtiari expressed her interest in women's "emancipation" as consisting of sponsoring a girls' camp in order to encourage their participation in sports.

[28] "Thorough-going matriarchy," *Ibid.*, 118.

[29] Coup, Pahlavi, *A Mirror*, especially last chapter; and throne, "Queen of Iran," 4; and *The Autobiography*, 72–74.

[30] Personal influence, *Ibid.*, 159. Verifiable sources on Bakhtiari's wealth and her alimony are unavailable and existing memoirs provide conflicting information. In her memoir, Bakhtiari denied receiving any allowance from the Shah after 1958. However, A. Alam, the Court Minister and a close associate of the Shah, indicated in his memoir that as late as 1976, the former queen continued to request and receive large sums from the Shah. See Alam, 460 and 518. In a 1958 interview she stated that because the Shah "has deemed it necessary that a successor to the throne must be of direct descent in the male line from generation to generation, I will with my deepest regret in the interest of the future of the State and the welfare of the people in accordance with the desire of His Majesty the Emperor sacrifice my own happiness, and I will declare my consent to a separation from His Imperial Majesty." In 1976, she requested and received a $6,000.00–7,000.00 monthly allowance, a villa in Paris, and a payment of $1.5 million for hardship. See Alam,

Farah Diba was the Shah's third official wife. In 1967, for the first time in Iran's history, a woman was declared a Regent, meaning that in the event of the Shah's death, she would assume the throne until their son was twenty. Not unlike the Shah's own background, she was not from a royal heritage, rather she was the daughter of an army sergeant. She became one of Iran's most powerful women, especially since she gave birth to two boys. Less significantly, she had two girls. In keeping with her queenly posture, she spent lavishly on clothing: *Women's Wear Daily* reported her purchase of forty-five ensembles of Valentino's new couture in 1978, most of its $160,000 sales in Tehran.[31] She acted as patron of many welfare organizations, and appointed friends and close relatives to sensitive positions. The national media's head was her ex-fiancé and cousin, and the WOI's vice-presidency went to Farideh Diba, her mother.

An architecture student who halted her studies due to marriage, Farah Pahlavi expanded her authority in an area she valued – the arts. Restoring traditional Persian art, she converted several old buildings and gardens such as the beautiful Bagh-e Ferdows in Tehran into a cultural center. In Kerman and Shiraz, she created museums; in Tehran, she built the Carpet Museum, the Museum of Modern Art, and Negarestan Museum, as well as the Farah Pahlavi Foundation, which she sponsored. Inaugurating the annual Shiraz International Cultural Festival at the ruins of Persepolis was another event that she sponsored – the wealthy, prosperous youth, domestic and foreign artists, and some academicians regularly attended it. Finally, she presided over national and international symposiums and headed Farabi University in Tehran and Iran's first women's institution of higher learning, Farah Pahlavi University. Compared to her women contemporaries, Pahlavi was unique in her use of prestige to promote the arts and artists. She expanded the horizons of queenly powers to new territory.[32]

Farah Pahlavi consistently supported the Shah's policies.[33] In agreement with his rhetorics, she declared that: "no competent and talented

Ibid. Although alienated from the throne and the Court, Soraya Bakhtiari continued to be a strong proponent of the state and the Shah.

[31] *Women's*, "Shah Enough," 4 (as queen she commanded a staff of 40 with a $5 million budget); see also, "Zanan dar Daneshgah-e Farah Pahlavi," 8; and Pirnia, *Salar-e* presents a partisan account of the Regent's life.

[32] Museums. She also supported international film festivals and received such actors as Tony Curtis and Frank Sinatra. Pahlavi University, Razavi, "Empress Reveals," 1.

[33] Shah's policies, acknowledging that she "always felt like an ordinary person," in one interview, Diba indicated that she was compassionate toward the poor and was sympathetic with the plight of working women. See "Farah: The Working Empress," 36; Mansureh Pirnia, "Mosahebeh Ba Oliya-Hazrat Shahbanuy-e Iran, [Interview with Iran's Empress]; and *Keyhan*, 21 Mehr, 1354/October 13, 1975, n.p.

woman remains jobless"[34] and that women had "absolute freedom" to compete with men for the highest seat in government. She claimed that this freedom "owed its lot" to the Shah.[35] Despite her advocacy, in a televised interview with American anchorwoman Barbara Walters, the Shah embarrassed his wife who was simultaneously being interviewed, with the comment that she could not reign as well as he. As loyal to her disloyal husband as her predecessor had been, similar to Soraya Bakhtiari, she dedicated herself to elevating the international image of the Peacock Throne: at New York's Asia Society, with dignitaries, including the Shah's friend, Nelson Rockefeller in attendance, she received the "humanitarian" award of the Organization of Appeal and Conscience.[36] Actually before the trip, one student publication noted that Pahlavi intended to win support for her husband and hoped with the U.S. government to prepare American public opinion for the Shah's next visit.[37] Overall, the activities of Farah Pahlavi and other Court women fell within the parameters of authoritarianism and Iran's class society. Yet some Pahlavi women provided vital support to other women who, in turn, encouraged gender initiatives as articulated in the official women's organization.

Women's Organization of Iran

Like other gender-related topics associated with the Shah's period, the WOI has not been thoroughly and critically assessed. The creation of this organization brought Reza Shah's gender policies full circle: the

[34] "Jobless," F. Pahlavi as cited in "Hameh-e Rah-ha-ye Fa'liat," 7, where she noted that "all roads of activities are open to [Iranian] women," and women could now institute "divorce proceedings" and enjoy "equal rights." See also Razavi, "Empress," 1.

[35] "Owed its lot," *Ettela'at-e Banovan*, 1977, 10–11; and Walters, "Empress Farah Talks," entire, 1978. Yet F. Pahlavi believed in limited personal relations between women and men because frequently changing relaions was harmful to building happy family relations. In comparison to the Shah's other wives, F. Diba enjoyed greater recognition. She showed deference to other royal women, especially Ashraf Pahlavi, thereby built a respected political space for herself. Her position as Regent also protected her from political challenges – when the Shah was suffering from cancer, he relinquished many political responsibilities to her. These responsibilities included speeches, attendance at important political ceremonies, and official trips, for example, to Beijing in 1972.

[36] "Humanitarian award." In her acceptance speech, she boosted Iran's history while scourging oppositional students abroad: Iran had been able "to preserve its more than thirty centuries of distinct culture and history," she insinuated, yet some of "our students overseas have cut themselves off from their cultural roots and have become complete deviants." See "Iran Hoveyyat-e Tarikhi," in *Kaeyhan Hava' ie*, 1978, 2.

[37] Student publication, *Resistance* 4, no. 6 and 1.

complete transformation of women's initiatives into a loyal organization. In his attempts at consolidation and mobilization of larger members of the society, the Shah completed his father's goal and assigned the task of organizing women to a state-sponsored and multi-purpose organization. Under Ashraf Pahlavi's auspices, the WOI would mobilize women and prepare them "maximally" for Iran's advancement,[38] although it ignored the voice of dissident women.

Ashraf Pahlavi played a pivotal role in the formation of the WOI. She expected the organization to "integrate Iranian women into every facet of society and to create the conditions of equality that our female ancestors had enjoyed centuries ago [and that had been lost with the Islamic conquest of Iran and the subsequent influence of Islamic Arabs.]" The occasion for this pronouncement was the consolidation of the late 1940s and 1950s women's organizations into the state's orbit. Explaining her actions, she alleged that the existing, narrowly based women's groups must go through an "evolutionary process" in order to encompass a broader and more extensive program for women's activities. This process would occur under her aegis. Bringing together representatives of 18 organizations, she formed a federation called the High Council of Women's Societies of Iran or *Shora-ye A'li-ye Jam'iyyatha-ye Zanan* in 1959. Pahlavi presided over the Council, and seven years after its founding, she transformed it into the much more powerful WOI.[39] This royal patronage marked the beginning of the state-sponsored women's rights movement.

Top officers of the WOI included Court women. Ashraf Pahlavi was its President, and Farideh Diba, Farah Pahlavi's mother, served as the Vice President. The Supreme Board of the organization was comprised of Farrokhru Parsa, the Minister of Education and nine men who held various political, judicial, and ministerial posts, as well as the chief of police. Following Homa Ruhi, Simin Rejali, and Heshmat Yousefi, Mahnaz Afkhami was appointed as the Secretary General in 1970 and remained in the post until the 1979 Revolution. When the organization was first founded, the Tehran branch of the WOI had a membership of almost 4,500 individuals, with 33 secular and religious organizations as

[38] "Maximally," "Notq-e Vala Hazrat Shahdokht Ashraf," entire.

[39] "Arabs," Pahlavi, *Faces*, 154; "evolutionary process," *Salnameh-e Zanan-e Iran*, 141–142; and High Council, Pahlavi, *Faces*, 154. As pointed out in the *Salnameh-e*, *Ibid.*, 41–42, the Council included 18 women's organizations. Not available in current studies, a comprehensive and systematic history of women's organizations in the 1940s and between the 1953 CIA coup and 1959 is in order. Also see, Bamdad I, 106–107.

institutional members.[40] The WOI's constitution mandated the expansion of the organization as one of its objectives. By the late 1970s, it enlisted the membership of 48 women's societies and centers nationwide; with almost 400 branches, its total institutional and individual membership was almost half a million. Ashraf Pahlavi's goal had been achieved: the establishment of a growing organization and the inclusion of all women's groups under one umbrella, that of the state.[41]

The WOI played a significant role in the political process. It merged some of its activities with those of the Resurgent Party, the only legal political party. High-powered WOI political appointees were given powerful offices within the Resurgent Party. Afkhami, the WOI's Secretary General and the Minister of State for Women's Affairs, was such a person.[42] As the Vice President of the Resurgent Party's Political Bureau, Afkhami played a key role in merging the Party's mobilization function with that of the WOI's. Her speeches, which in 1976 were frequently printed in the official WOI weekly, *Zanan-e Iran* (Iranian Women), stressed mobilizing women for the party's interest. Obviously disappointed at women's low party membership, Afkhami refused to give up: "we should never compare the [relatively lower] political participation of Iranian women with other countries because we have many opportunities in Iran, and we must only compare Iran with our own ideals, not with any other countries." Emphasizing the importance of the WOI in mobilizing women for the Resurgent Party and the White Revolution, Afkhami stated in 1976:

> The second Congress of the nation's Resurgent Party can be counted as a new stage in the Iranian [White] Revolution and in the effective participation of women in party politics.... Plans for the political and social education of women and girls

[40] Supreme Board, Paidar, 149. Little written information is available on Ruhi, Rejali, and Yousefi. For a brief sketch of Afkhami see, *Iran Who's Who 1976*. The Tehran branch of WOI included the Society of Women in Education, the Welfare Society of Armenian Women in Tehran, the Society of Women for Peace, the Society of Women Civil Servants, the Society of Jewish Women of Iran, the Society of Iranian Nurses, the Union of Women Lawyers, and the Women's Center of Physicians. See *Salnameh-e*, 100–101.

[41] WOI's constitution, *The Constitution* (because WOI's logo appears in this booklet as it does in most of its publications, I assume that *The Constitution* is a WOI publication); membership, *Tarikh-cheh va*; and *Mihan-e Ma*, 36–40; and Pahlavi, A., *Faces*, 154. The exact relationship between the WOI and other women's organizations and centers (i.e., progressives, religious, minority groups, etc.) is unclear. Figures on membership are also unverifiable. English-language WOI literature gives different figures than the above listing – perhaps for publicity abroad: 36,000 members, 54 affiliated organizations, and 216 branches, as in *The Women's Organization of Iran*, n.d.

[42] Afkhami, *Iran Who's Who 1976*; and Afkhami, G. R. and Nasr. eds., 12.

will be made so that the force of the youth, to the greatest possible extent, can be used for the realization of the goals of the Iranian nation's Resurgent Party.[43]

From exile, Afkhami continued to defend the WOI's activities.[44]

Besides its mobilization function, the WOI stipulated six areas of interest: women's welfare, legal reforms, publications, social concerns, international affairs, and organizational necessities. Its many publications provided elaborate accounts of the organization's domestic and foreign interests. One of its reports described family welfare centers in Tehran and the provinces that had set up daycare centers especially for low-income families, literacy classes for mothers, and vocational training for women to develop marketable skills; and provided family counseling, legal assistance, and health relief. Through its research department, the organization studied issues related to family welfare, women's work and literacy, and various gender laws. Another WOI report devoted much space to its international endeavors and its role in elevating domestic political participation through party headquarters, mobilization units, and other committees. The same communication noted that it was preparing a project on urban women's desire to continue to wear the *chador*.[45]

The WOI, not women at large, influenced the promulgation of some gender policies. It was behind the formulation of the 1975 Family Protection Law. It also lobbied successfully to secure a right to abortion with a husband's consent, or for an unmarried woman up to the eighth week of pregnancy, as was discussed in Chapter 4.[46] Over approximately thirteen years, the WOI's initiative – albeit in a limited way – highlighted issues of concern to women, challenged certain patriarchal tendencies, and built its own organizational apparatus to promote some women's interests. But the WOI occupied an ambiguous position in Iranian women's history in that its activities were intimately tied to and represented the interests and domination of the state over civil society.

43 "We should never," and "The second Congress," *Bulleton-e Haftegi-ye*, 384, 2535/1976, 3; and *Bulleton-e Haftegi-ye*, 456, 2535/1976, 8 and 7.

44 Exile, Afkhami, "A Future." In that article, she did not provide information pertaining to her role in promoting the domestic and international image of the state, nor did she discuss how she was appointed to the WOI, or how she maintained her position as the WOI's head for so many years. Nor did she mention what her ties were to the Pahlavis or what was the organization's source of the fundings and the amount of its fundings.

45 *Chador*, WOI, *Gozaresh-e Fa'liatha-ye Sazeman-e,*" entire and especially 104.

46 Pregnancy, Afkhami, "Women in Post-Revolutionary," 192, note 23. As of this writing, there have not been other testimonies or studies to corroborate or reject Afkhami's assertions with respect to WOI's lobbying activities.

This representative function appeared evident in the WOI's role in the elevation of the throne's international image. Its publications reveal that the WOI devoted much energy and resources to public relations efforts, in particular its activities abroad. One of its reports dedicated a greater coverage to the WOI's international experiences, such as the occasional participation of its leaders at various conferences abroad and/or official visits by representatives of other countries that its officials hosted, than to any other accomplishments. Further, one of the WOI's "global responsibilities" was to partake in international women's forums and interact with international women's organizations and women's associations in other countries. As a participant in international gatherings, the WOI's intention was "to introduce" Iranian women to the world and "to cultivate" close relations with women's organizations throughout the globe. Building the state's image through Iran's support for women's issues worldwide, the WOI's publications also featured many stories and pictures of Farah Pahlavi and Ashraf Pahlavi and their popularity in the West and Western media.[47]

The extent of funding devoted to the creation of the international activities of the WOI and an "emancipatory" image of Iran's ruler and the state remains unclear. Foreign reports, however, estimate the WOI's yearly budget at almost $20 million to $50 million in the late 1970s. Afkhami acknowledged the WOI's success in "channeling substantial financial aid to U.N. programs for International Women's Year" in 1975. Specifically, the WOI President, Ashraf Pahlavi, presented a check for $2 million and pledged greater support for future U.N. women's activities. In addition to expending large sums on publicity and public relations abroad, it is reasonable to surmise that in conformity with its usual methods, the state skillfully used gender issues to win more friends, especially Western women, abroad. It did so by recruiting and assigning women as active and loyal agents.[48]

Although some women benefited from the WOI's version of top-down reform and the organization welcomed their entry, the WOI remained inaccessible to dissenting women. The leadership of the WOI, for example, refused to grant office appointments or to meet with women who potentially offered different perspectives on gender and politics in

47 International experiences, "global," "introduce," and "cultivate," *Gozaresh-e Fa'liatha-ye*, 34–36.

48 Foreign reports, Dopoulos, 24; Friedan, 104; and Afkhami, "A Future," 336; and million, this amount was printed under a picture where A. Pahlavi presented K. Waldheim with a check. See Pahlavi, *Faces*, 173.

Iran.[49] These strategies were consonant with the tactics of the state, which had sought legitimacy through co-optation or repression. An elitist, hierarchical, and extremely insular organization, the WOI acted as an arm of the Pahlavi state, helping to neutralize nonconformist women. Of course the WOI's methods were bound to be somewhat contradictory, divided as it was by conflicting aims and loyalties. As an extension of the state involved in promoting "feminism" from above, it occupied an ambivalent position in Iranian women's history. While it represented the Pahlavi state, through its research, welfare, and legal activities, it had the potential to inspire in women a new consciousness of their subordination. This historical paradox resembled the experiences of other conformist women, for example, those who obtained power in the state-controlled media industry, and those women who remained advocates and supporters of the system.

Women in the State Apparatus

The National Iranian Radio and Television (NIRT) and its subsidiary, the Central Office of News and Information (CONI), illustrate the relationship between class and gender and the attitudes of Queen Bees toward other women in a state-run organization. Women's roles in the NIRT occupational structure was closer to that in other modern governmental organizations such as the Plan and Budget Organization of Iran than the case was in more traditional ones, for example, the State Organization for Employment and Administrative Affairs or the General Department of Civil Registration. These organizations, in contrast to the more traditional offices, were more recently established: they had quasi-Western bureaucracies, a relatively large pool of educated employees, major research departments, and women in various ranks especially in top positions. NIRT was a modern organization and it was unique ideologically: as a case study, it illustrates the potential impact of powerful women on the media's presentation of women, gender roles, women's attitudes toward

[49] Leadership, none of the WOI literature makes references to oppositional women. Some nonconformist women that I interviewed in 1975 and 1977 told me that they made several attempts to interview high officials of the WOI, but they were not given any appointments, nor did M. Afkhami care to return their calls or receive them in her office. The oral history collections that were organized and compiled with the help of M. Afkhami and her husband in exile, excluded all dissidents, with the exception of one political activist. See Afkhami, G.H. and S.V.R. Nasr. eds., *The Oral History*, especially 40.

their female subordinates, and issues related to sexuality – a significant subject, but one that this book cannot fully cover.[50]

The NIRT was established in 1971, when National Radio (established in 1926) merged with National Television (established in 1966). A government-controlled organization, various state and non-state officials and SAVAK representatives produced and monitored NIRT's programs. The Shah, his wife, and their trustees directly appointed or approved its executives. NIRT's head was Farah Diba's close relative, and – as in the WOI – a number of high-level personnel assumed posts in the Resurgent Party, SAVAK, the Office of the Prime Minister and other powerful political organizations. High-level NIRT appointees thus served as linkages between the state, its security organs, and other key public offices.[51]

Ideologically, NIRT's main objective was its "indispensible" role in "national development" through ensuring that political, economic, cultural, and educational programs fulfilled "national aims." More than other Iranian media, "NIRT influenced and addressed a large number of people"; it was hence given a mandate to promote "national developmental plans and ideologies." A news service subsidiary of the NIRT, CONI was largely responsible for implementing the ideological function through its particular involvement in "political education" programs. Presenting academic and political discussions on "the Resurgence of the Iranian People" (i.e., the Shah's Resurgent Party), it attempted to explain "ideological trends" as well as the meaning of "national unity" for Iran. More directly, these programs intended to explain the "inadequacies of communist systems; contradictions between Marxism in theory and practice"; and "Communism within the context of world totalitarianism" in order to discredit alternative ideologies to capitalism and Western ideas of development. Within the Iranian context, this meant the promotion of the ideology of "national development" in order to foster "public participation in the destiny of the Resurgent Party." Such an orientation encouraged financial help from the World Bank.[52]

[50] NIRT, for a more in depth study of the NIRT and CONI's occupational structure, see Sedghi, "Women and Class," Chs. 5–6.

[51] NIRT appointments, Sazeman-e Radio va Television-e Iran, *Gozaresh-e Salnameh-e Sazeman-e Radio Television-e 1353*; "Seeing the Future" section 7; also Sedghi, "Women and Class," Ch. 5.

[52] "Indispensible," "influenced," "national development," resurgence," and "inadequacies," Sazeman-e Radio, *Gozaresh-e Salnameh-e*, "CONI" Sec. 17–18; *World Bank Annual Reports*, 3; Hamideh Sedghi's interviews at the NIRT, 1977; Personnel Records at the Administrative Affairs, NIRT, Tehran, 1977; and Sedghi, "Women and Class," Ch. 5.

The NIRT had several experienced, capable, and highly educated women, including some with Ph.D.s. But with the exception of 3 female executives, it excluded women from the highest posts: director and above. Given the modern orientation of the NIRT and the Shah's agenda, it was unclear why the organization's top ranks failed to represent more women. Personnel records, statistical data, and my interviews indicated that the NIRT rarely promoted women to leading positions; and the organization prevented highly educated women from attaining high posts that remained open to less educated men. CONI middle-class, educated women holding the position of analysts emphasized that the major reason for their and other women's slow rate of professional advancement was a "lack of connections to authorities in higher echelons." In the Iranian context, this meant a lack of elite connections.[53]

Gender bias was also responsible for the exclusion of competent women from high positions. Women interviewed indicated that discriminatory attitudes prevented them from promotion. An influential CONI male executive that I interviewed expressed his definite preference for employing men rather than women when their qualifications were similar. He stated that men were more reliable and more experienced than women – of course, women generally had fewer opportunities to gain this experience. He also variously attributed the low number of women in top jobs to different reasons such as their unavailability for serious, responsible, and demanding positions; their lack of dedication, discipline, and ambition; their inability to make correct decisions in a timely fashion; and their deficient professionalism related to their preoccupation with the family. Somewhat corroborating his assertions, one study concluded that whether a woman was single or married, she was viewed as a bad investment: if single, she would quit her job once she was married; if married, she was always thinking of her children and household. But the same executive related the success of the 3 NIRT female executives not only to their individual competence, work experience, and educational background, but most significantly, to their social class, or "extenuating circumstances."[54]

53 "Lack of connections," Sedghi, "Women and Class," Ch. 5. Note that beyond class bias, women interviewed indicated that gender discrimination was responsible for their lack of progress. Therefore, they had few incentives to apply for or work toward promotion; even if they did, some contended, their male superiors and colleagues would not take them seriously.

54 One study, Amuzegar, *Maqam-e Zan*, especially Ch. I, Sec. B and in particular, notes 29–30, 367–416, 390, 398, 373, 374, 362, 346–348, 354, 362–363, 381, 398, 406, 409, 432–442, and 36; and "extenuating circumstances," Sedghi's interviews, CONI, 1977.

NIRT Queen Bees were definitely different from other women in the organization. The educational background of the 3 NIRT female executives, like most of other women in the industry, ranged from high school diplomas to bachelor degrees; all had long work experience and were referred to by interviewees as disciplined and hard-working women. The only differentiating factor that seemed to explain why these women were executives rather than news analysts or others was their class background. Despite their competence, these executives would not have achieved higher posts if not for their class position. All were married to men in high public offices, and the most powerful of these executives was married to the NIRT's president, the Queen's relative. Once in top ranks, capable women – from elite backgrounds – performed similar tasks to men in high-level positions. Thus, for a woman, ability was necessary but not sufficient to attain a high rank at NIRT; an elite background was a prerequisite. My findings corroborated the analysts' comments.[55]

Most top NIRT male executives, by contrast to their female counterparts, had middle and lower middle-class backgrounds. Many of these men, according to those interviewed, had strong connections to the Shah's family, the Court, SAVAK, and the Resurgent Party. A process of cooptation, which continued throughout the 1970s, explained the rise of many men to high positions. Specifically, "the Shah and the political elite [had] developed a policy of offering incentives, particularly of an economic nature, to those who challenged the system." Therefore some male executives attained top ranks because of their allegiance to the ruling family or their co-optation within the system, a process that involved integrating NIRT's specific functions to reinforce official ideologies

This executive believed that women had to "prove" their competence before a high-ranking post would be offered to them; however, he remained silent when asked about the ongoing corruption of men in powerful and sensitive positions. He showed little understanding of the fact that women were held to different standards than men, which might have led him to acknowledge that this disparity kept women in inferior positions. (This is based on my interviews at CONI, 1977). Both male and female executives appeared to be in agreement on the prerequisites for women's appointment to high-level positions, obstacles to women's progress, and the widening of opportunities for women. They concurred on the issues of competence, capability, and preferential treatment for men. Personnel Files, *Personnel files*, CONI, and the Section on Mechanized Information, the Office of the Administrative Affairs, NIRT, Tehran, 177.

[55] My focus on class background does not ignore the significance of the work experience and the capability factor in attaining high positions by women. Clearly, these women were qualified for the high-level positions they held. Without their class background, however, they would not have likely obtained those positions; and married, my study of personnel files and data at the NIRT.

and policies. Not many women were entrusted with those responsibilities.[56]

NIRT powerful women also perceived their own tasks and those of other women and men differently. My 1977 interview with a Queen Bee was instructive:

Q. Why is it that in Iran, and specifically at NIRT, the number of women in high posts is so low?

A. Because of governmental policies and lack of opportunities for women.

Q. Under what circumstances are women appointed as NIRT's directors?

A. Personal skill and qualifications such as higher education, executive competence, and ability to plan for short- and long-term policies.

Q. What factors at NIRT prevent women from progressing to higher positions?

A. Women themselves. Women have a lower resistance to problems than men. They are closed minded and have not been able to separate household activities from work responsibilities.

Q. Are men at NIRT prejudiced against women's employment, and especially against their appointment to high-level ranks?

A. All societies are patriarchal and Iran is no exception.

Q. Should NIRT increase the number of its female employees? Are there vacancies for women?

A. It is not necessary to employ women simply because they are women. The organization needs qualified people be they male or female. Capable women are yet to be seen at NIRT.

Q. How do you perceive your job?

A. Very time-consuming and much underpaid.

Q. If your job is time-consuming, how do you, if you do, manage your household activities?

A. To look after children and to have two responsibilities is very difficult. I am lucky to have help with the housework; it allows me to devote time and attention to my job.

Q. Of course, many women employees are not so privileged.

A. True. They do have problems.[57]

[56] "Shah," Bill, 1, 30, and 140. The reference here is not to technical experts of the organization, rather the study is based on the background and activities of those executives who were involved in the production of the ideological functions of the NIRT; and male executives, Keyhan Research, *The Employment*, 29, 28, and 26.

[57] Sedghi's interviews, 1977.

Queen Bees held diverse views on other women. Some displayed a condescending attitude toward women, in particular toward women of other classes or those with different ideological persuasions. They attributed the myth of "incapability" to women who had not "made it" to high ranks. Some perceived themselves as "aggressive" and more hard-working than men in similar positions. Two women I spoke with appeared so proud of their Western infatuation that they preferred to conduct the interview in English rather than Persian. Some regarded themselves as subordinates to men who held more powerful positions; for example, one woman said that she "would do whatever she is ordered to do" and another indicated that she "would not take any actions" until she received orders from "a man with superior powers." In a different instance, an interviewee indicated that she would "leave her position if her male chief left." These women saw themselves as superior to other women but deferred to men.[58] Obviously, interviews with a broader range of women might reveal more varied opinions. But the extent to which elite women in high positions saw themselves as part of the male establishment is noteworthy. The Queen Bee Syndrome arose from this tendency of elite and powerful women to view themselves as separate from other women and united with men.

Thus, there existed a chasm between powerful and powerless, elite and non-elite women that reflected sharp divisions among women by class and ideology. As a new organization, the NIRT had 3 female executives but it excluded competent non-elite women from important decision-making positions. NIRT's patterns were consonant with the state's tactics and other state-affiliated organizations, including WOI, which attempted to gain legitimacy through the inclusion of conformist women in high posts while barring other women, even though qualified and competent. But the class friction that existed among NIRT women was vividly apparent in attitudes and work relations: contemptuous and arrogant toward everyone – other women included – the Queen Bees worked hard but were aloof. They dined, for example, at the exclusive club for top officials, their guests, and foreign consultants. NIRT's female underlings performed at a high level, but ate sandwiches at their desks and expressed resentment

[58] Elite, Sha'bani, and Mo'tazed, entire, especially 790–793; Pirnia, *Salar-e Zanan-e Iran*, and her *Safar Nameh-e Shahbanoo Farah*; and Alam. When the Queen Bees held honorary or powerful positions in such international organizations as the United Nations Commission on the Status of Women or national offices as the Women's Organization of Iran, like male politicians, they spoke on behalf of equality and the underprivileged and strongly vowed to address inequalities.

at the power establishment, men and women – a topic that I explored elsewhere.[59]

In all, conformist women played a paradoxical role in Iran. As the state's advocates, they lobbied to integrate women in political processes, and attempted to raise Iran's international image and legitimacy. But, they also helped to undermine the state by delegitimizing it in the eyes of the domestic opposition and critical women in particular. Ultimately, conformist women's activities must be weighed against those of nonconformist women. Whereas the former exercised unduly power and privilege in the undemocratic system, many of the latter were silenced, executed, imprisoned, or went into exile. What is vital for this study is that dissident women behaved differently from loyal women. For all their wealth, power, and prestige – which proved limited and ineffectual – monarchical women would be confronted by the challenges which oppositional women posed to the state. The success of nonconformist women would await the unexpected 1979 Revolution which swept through the entire society.

NONCONFORMIST WOMEN

With the exception of those who wrote under a pseudonym or anonymously, nonconformist women of the Shah's era left fewer records than mainstream women. With the exception of a few references, oppositional women have been largely ignored in Iranian politics and gender studies. Mostly urban, middle-class, and educated, nonconformist women included students, teachers, writers, poets, civil servants, and such professionals as doctors, lawyers, and nurses, as well as housewives. Critical of

[59] Chasm, The Keyhan Research Associates as discussed in Sedghi, "Women and Class," Ch 4. This study of women's employment in Iran reached similar conclusions as this chapter. Based on extensive interviews with women in the higher echelons of the public and private sectors, it concluded that these women viewed their achievements as personal triumphs. Moreover, they regarded themselves as closer to their male counterparts, not "a part of the larger female community." They preferred to deal with men because of their alleged ability to make decisions more rapidly and their greater inclination to respect women's professional competence. The study also found that women also regarded themselves "in a class apart from other females," asserting that "girl packers are satisfied to remain packers and girl clerks are satisfied remaining clerks." Another finding was that "the professional struggle to 'make it,' or the desire to shed the traditional female image, seemed to be sufficiently preoccupying to leave little room for wider concerns." One consequence was that upper middle-class women "rarely [made] a reference to working class women." It concluded that "The chasm between the two remains considerable." For a wider coverage of middle level and lower level female personnel at NIRT and CONI, see, Sedghi, "Women and Class," Chs. 5–6.

monarchy, they implicitly questioned patriarchy for "the fight against dictatorship was also a fight against male chauvinism."[60] They challenged the power structure, and in so doing, they tacitly broke the traditional attachments to the family and gender segregation, by entering the public world, sometimes visibly, sometimes not.

Nonconformist women differed from the women's rights activists of the Constitutional Revolution era. Born to a modernizing and quasi-capitalist economy with educational and employment opportunities, they stepped beyond their household's boundaries to seek a different world and alter the status quo. In this respect, their actions and interests overlapped with conformist women. But unlike the latter, many nonconformist women dedicated themselves to radical social transformation, an experience which they did not share with their active mothers and grandmothers. Not embracing a monolithic critical and feminist stance, anti-government women sharply disagreed on women's oppression, women's emancipation, gender relations, and women's role in reproduction. They participated as independent activists, group members, or spontanuously in large numbers. Before and during the 1979 Revolution, they collaborated with men to achieve their goals. Iranian men had never experienced the potent power of women in solidarity and political struggle, and politically inclined groups, in a pattern similar to that of the Algerian Revolution, needed and sought women's support. Women followed their gut feelings and political inclinations in their desire to augment progressive change.

Nonconformists' manner of political participation remained outside the prevailing rules and structures, as they were unable to participate in the existing political channels.[61] Invisible, cautious, and sometimes underground in the face of reprisal, nonconformist women were factionalized. Divided, they followed different paths, although the state was their common enemy. Some participated in group activities, whether secular or religious. While many served organizations with various leftist

[60] "Fight against dictatorship," F. Sanat-Carr, "Khomeinism," n.p., n.d., 31.

[61] With respect to political participation of nonconformist women it should be noted that, there is no definitive record on the number of women participants or nonconformist women. However, there are numerical accounts of the killed guerrillas. Abrahamian notes that between 1969 and 1979, of the total of 341 dead guerrillas, there were 39 women: 22 women Fedai'e, 7 Islamic Mojahedi, and 2 other Marxists. See his *Iran*, 481. Moghissi's figures are slightly higher. She states that among the 341 dead Fedai's, there were 39 women including 14 housewives, 13 college students, 9 teachers, 2 doctors, and 1 office employee. She also states that many more women had been fighting as members of the Feda'is. See her *Populism*, 115.

ideologies – Marxism, Maoism, Trotskyism, or some variant – others joined Muslim organizations. A small number of independent women who believed in some mixture of socialism and feminism expressed themselves in abstract writing and poetry, or became sympathizers of one or another existing group. Disconnected from the political system, the nonconformists' immediate political impact was indirect and went largely unnoticed; the 1979 revolutionary upheaval which finally brought down the monarchy modified the course of their destiny.

Nonconformist women's active presence made a permanent mark on Iran's women's history. An understanding of them during the Shah's period will shed light on the revolutionary and postrevolutionary activities of women who are currently constructing new forms of feminism. Based on the available data and my own knowledge and participation in the 1979 Revolution, I will highlight the three categories of nonconformists: women of secular left groups, secular left independents, and the religious opposition.[62] Secular left and secular independent women are significant because they both had some socialist tendencies and contributed as rank and file members of various oppositional organizations, or individually as writers, poets, or critical activists. Religious women are also illuminating because similar to other groups, they cooperated with men in massive political protests and by wearing scarves or *chadors*; they recreated a space for the veil as a protest symbol, which I will explore in the next part of this book.

Secular Left Women

Most studies of Iranian social and political movements that covered the Shah's Period, ignored women's experiences as women in those movements. Although a small number of pamphlets, articles, collections of essays, and books published in the West prior to the Revolution discussed women's oppression, a critical analysis of women's situations and their activism under the Shah came during and after the Revolution.[63] The oppositional activities of women under the last Pahlavi monarch illuminate the systemic attempts of nonconformist women to challenge the state,

[62] The available data, see note 61, above; and Abrahamian, *Iran*, his "The Guerrilla Movement"; his "Shariati"; and his *The Iranian Mojahedin*, 232–235.

[63] Pamphlets, *Setam Keshidegi-ye*, entire; Dehghani, *Torture*, entire; Nashat, ed., *Women and Revolution*; Tabari and Yeganeh. eds., *In the Shadow*; Azari, ed., *Women of Iran*; Moghissi, *Populism*; Paidar, *Women*; and Shahidian, "The Iranian Left."

despite the efforts of such powerful organizations as the WOI to mobilize women behind the Resurgent Party and the throne, SAVAK, and the police to neutralize the dissidents.

In the 1960s and 1970s, many urban women became politically active by joining different Marxist and progressive groups. Their aim was to eradicate class inequality and oppression, overthrow the Shah's regime, and to eliminate U.S. imperialism. Although they were divided on tactics, many advocated armed resistance as the only route to liberate Iran. As single women, wives, or sisters of oppositional men, nonconformist women followed the path of their male associates and acquired respect as revolutionary participants and nurturers. But membership in left organizations did not confer an equal status in organizations that practiced gender bias in their structures and political work. Most secular groups ignored the importance of gender analysis, which might have unveiled the roles of patriarchy, women's oppression, and sexuality in Iranian history.[64] But oppositional politics and collective actions provided a meaningful channel for some women to depart from traditional boundaries of both public and private spaces. Although women did not explicitly acknowledge it, it is likely that their activism against state authoritarianism implied a parallel struggle against patriarchy and gender inequality. In their silent resistance against male-domination, nonconformist women received no recognition from conformist women. The experiences of several progressive women demonstrate not only diversity among them, but also political differences between nonconformist and conformist women. One such woman is Ashraf Dehghani.

Ashraf Dehghani – a leader of the Feda'i, the most known and active guerrilla progressive organization – can be seen as representative of oppositional women. Her memoirs, one of the very few written, provide a theoretical analysis of politics in Iran as well as a dissident woman's struggles with prison torturers, SAVAK, and the police. Most of Dehghani's autobiography focuses on heart-breaking stories of her brutal tortures in various prisons as well as her understanding of resistance and strategies to overcome obstactes. The introductory chapter to this work refers to her, not as a woman, but "Comrade Ashraf Dehghani," whose "heroic resistance

[64] Gender bias and gender analysis, Moghissi in her *Populism* criticizes the left for their "sexism," 114–38. See also various issues of *Zanan Mobarezeh Mikonand* [Women in Struggle], published and distributed by the Committee of the Iranian Women Association in North California in the mid-1970s. During the late 1960s and 1970s, active women in exile called for "sisterhood" and advocated struggle against "chauvinism."

[is] an example of [the] courage and determination of the Iranian revolutionaries."[65] Her identity as a woman leftist is masked.

Born in 1949 in a poor working family in Iran's Azarbaijan province and influenced by her parents' memories of the establishment of an independent Azarbaijan in 1945–46, Dehghani was socialized from early childhood in a progressive environment. As she grew older, she was mentored by her brother, Behrouz, who later became a comrade. As a student, she enjoyed raising the political consciousness of her classmates. When she wrote a critical essay on the Pahlavi rule for a friend, her teacher, who was also an informer, reported her to SAVAK. Brought in for an interrogation, she signed a letter that she would never partake in politics again. Close to her brother, she subsequently came into contact with Behrouz's friends, notably, the renowned social, political, and art critic, Samad Behrangi, who was murdered by the Shah's mercenaries in 1968. Her revolutionary politics drew her toward the Feda'in, where her brother was an active member; she probably joined in the late 1960s, becoming the only woman in its leadership.[66]

An unwavering will made her a spirited guerrilla fighter against the Shah and his state and an advocate of overthrowing the monarchy. The history of Iranian guerrilla warfare began when Feda'ies struck against the gendarmerie post on February 8, 1970 (Bahman, 19, 1349) in the northern village of Siahkal on the outskirts of the Caspian Sea in order to release one of the group members who had been arrested. Although the Shah responded to the armed attack with military force, the "Siahkal incident," as it is known, inspired other secular and Muslim groups who continued their activities until the revolutionary upsurge was sweeping the streets of Tehran.[67] Following the Siahkal incident, Dehghani continued her clandestine and guerrilla activities, only to be arrested unexpectedly in Tehran on May 13, 1971 after a harsh and brutal clash with a group of "police and SAVAK thugs." She was sentenced to ten years in prison.

[65] Dehghani, *Torture*, 5–11. "Comrade" is not feminine in Persian as in some languages; and "comrade" and "heroic," *Ibid.*, 10.

[66] Behrangi, Behrangi, *Kend-o Kav* [Delving]. For an account of Behrangi's life, his activities, and torture and death, See Dehghani, A., *Torture*, 10–11; leadership, Abrahamian, *Iran*, Ch. 10, especially 480–489. He does not include any women among the thirteen Feda'ies who inspired the Siahkal incident. However, Dehghani's account reveals that she had joined the armed struggle from "the beginning," which could possibly mean that she participated in the incident. See her *Torture*, 14.

[67] "Siahkal incident," Dehghani, *Torture*, the entire text.

Dehghani's autobiography reveals a woman writing under the most extreme circumstances. In this respect it is very different from those written by Court women. Dehghani's narratives disclose a history of resistance not only in real life but in prison. It is a history of struggle and determination. While incarcerated, she was interrogated, whipped, strapped down, given electric shocks, stripped and raped, handcuffed and assaulted, and tied to the bed against her torn and wounded back. Her fingers were compressed and her flesh was twisted with tongs, and snakes (non-poisonous) were released to crawl all over her body. She was threatened with broken bottles and boiling water. Female guards pulled her hair and slapped her; her nose bled constantly. Uninterrupted tickling was another form of torture. But the worst agony came when she heard her brother's suffering moans; she was told his bones had been broken and twisted. She then received pots full of his blood.[68]

Empowered by revolutionary zeal, Dehghani resisted. Nor could torture bend her determination. "By talking to the enemy," she believed: "I would be serving the despotism of the Shah." Under torture, "I was like a mother delivering a baby," she said. "The pain is there and [continues]. Nothing can be done but wait for the birth of the child. And in that situation, the birth of the child was the arrival of death. I had to wait for that," she asserted. But death did not come, and she continued to live. Perhaps she received strength from her revolutionary thoughts that she wrote about: a firm belief in the justice of the Revolution, hatred of the enemy and the love of others, a "Marxist historical" perspective that argued resistance would eventually succeed, a philosophical analysis of "freedom" and "captivity" especially under torture, an understanding of the enemies' method of torture in order to "neutralize" it, and "an unshakable faith in human will-power," and memories of Iranian and other freedom fighters. Her own categorization of "vermin" guards must have helped too. She must have convinced herself that her enemies were "weak" if their violence could not produce results. She must have strengthened herself by reading citations, poems, and revolutionary works to herself, then denying her own significance by excising self-referential phrases. "In my brain," she explained, "there was no room for the word 'self.'" Her resistance paid off. On March 13, 1973 she escaped the prison. Hidden under a *chador*, she walked out along with other veiled women visitors.[69]

[68] Blood, *Ibid.*

[69] "Enemy," "baby," "Marxist," "freedom," "Captivity," "neutralize," "brain" and *chador*, *Ibid.*, 48, 130, and 126–131.

As a Marxist-Leninist, Dehghani believed in historical materialism, class struggle, and the eradication of a regime that the United States supported and safeguarded. "The Shah's regime," she stated, "deployed all possible means to suppress the [people's] struggle with increasing repression and intimidation. . . ." The government used "money and 'position'" as incentives to move "The venal SAVAK and police ruffians" to "arrest and torture revolutionaries." Applying a class analysis to the women she met in prison, she argued that prostitutes and wealthy women (accused of fraud) were both products of the same class society. They received different treatment as prisoners: the prostitutes were badly abused, whereas the affluent women who were convicted of fraud were given their own private, furnished rooms. Dehghani noted that when Ashraf Pahlavi visited the prison: "All the poor, unfortunate women in prison hated her; especially the addicted women who knew very well that this evil [drug importer] woman was responsible for their miseries."[70]

Dehghani's gender perspective – although not developed – derives from her class analysis: women have been dually exploited, by the class structure (together with men) but also by men. However, she suggests that each woman must have a male companion in order to abolish the class nature of the society. She states, "when a woman attains class consciousness, together with a man who has also gained class consciousness, an understanding that leads them to uproot the class structure, then she is no longer the 'woman' of reactionary standards and values but a 'human being.'" Analyzing the Feda'in's theoretical and practical position on women and referring to the above citation, Haideh Moghissi suggests that "Dehghani explicitly accepts women's weakness," and "considers those who have not joined the class struggle to be on the side of reactionary forces." But there is an apparent effort on Dehghani's part to juxtapose "woman" – as a narrow notion – with "human" – as a broader, full perspective. In this juxtaposition, Dehghani permits no space for reactionary women as human beings.[71] Dehghani distinguished between women with reactionary values and women as human beings. The human being according to her,

> helps to build a structure, a society, in which human beings regain their just and glorious place. To that end, she steps on the path to freedom, freedom for all.

[70] "The Shah's regime," *Ibid.*; Dehghani, *Ibid.*, 48, 130, 126–131; and "addicted," Dehghani, *Torture*, the entire text, especially 29–30, 143–45, and 62. Nirumand, *Iran*, entire.

[71] Gender perspective, Dehghani, *Torture*, 31; "human being," *Ibid.*; and "reactionary forces," Moghissi, *Populism*, 117.

She helps to build a society in which all human beings, men and women, have attained true freedom, and for the progress of which, women and men work side by side.

These statements appear immediately after Dehghani's description of torture by snakes. "They [her tormentors] expected me to be frightened," because they could only "imagine 'women' as weak and cowardly."[72]

It is believed that Dehghani is in Germany, although very little is known about her personal life after her prison escape. Her memoir presents a woman's history of struggle, passion, and commitment to humanity and revolutionary ideas. Her memoir never reached the supporters of the authoritarian state as it was first published in London in 1975, and was banned in Iran until the outbreak of the Revolution. Whether or not her ideas, especially those regarding women and class relations, had an impact on other progressive women and men is not known with certainty; yet some of the women's organizations that sprang up during the revolutionary upheavals bear interesting resemblances to Dehghani's ideas.[73]

Roghieh Daneshgari was another prominent revolutionary woman. A contemporary of Dehghani, Daneshgari was also a member of the Feda'in organization. Although it is not clear whether Dehghani was her mentor, she described Daneshgari as a "courageous fighter," one who was subject to tremendous humiliation and torture and – like her – was sentenced to ten years' imprisonment.[74] She participated in clandestine operations and guerrilla activities, and was committed to promote the interests of the organization. Critics such as Moghissi believe that due to the Feda'in's male dominatory tendencies, Daneshgari was assigned to be an "adviser," a less prestigious status than Dehghani's. Daneshgari left no memoir or autobiographical writing behind and there is little information about her life, experiences, and views on gender. But it is widely believed that she was an admired and respected member of the Feda'in who held important posts in the organization. As nonconformists, other secular women acted independently, as individuals, or sympathizers with other organizations

[72] "Side by side," Dehghani, *Torture*, 31; and "cowardly," *Ibid.*, 20, 30–31 and 126–128.

[73] After escaping the prison, Dehghani continued her political activities. Disagreements pertaining to the nature of the postrevolutionary regime in Iran led her to split from the Feda'in. She then formed her own "Minority" Fedai'n organization that would be committed to armed struggle against the Islamic Republic; and ideas, the document section of Tabari and Yeganegi, eds., *In the Shadow*; and Paidar, *Women*, Chs. 6 and 9.

[74] "Courageous fighter," Dehghani, *Torture*, 151.

both in exile and Iran. Secular independent women were also highly critical of the monarchy and its establishment.

Secular Independent Women

Primarily professionals, many women became independently involved in the politics of opposition both inside and outside the country. Influenced by protests against the war in Vietnam, the global anti-imperialist movement, and the American Civil Rights and women's movements, a large number of female college students found themselves tirelessly absorbed in the anti-Shah and anti-American struggles. This was particularly true of those studying in exile in the United States and Europe. Not only did they risk the lives of their immediate families in Iran, but as protesting students in the United States, they placed themselves in an adversarial position vis-à-vis the American Federal Bureau of Investigation and the Immigration and Naturalization Service. Women's experiences during this period merit attention, although this book, primarily considers women's activities inside Iran.

What little informaton is available on nonconformist women, as group members or as independent activists, generally portrays women as martyrs and heroines. The documentation is rarely neutral or value-free, and the totality of women's experiences is mostly ignored.[75] Women more likely became a subject of attention when they were glorified after death or imprisonment, or if they underwent torture, as though this earned them status and recognition. The record ignores many of women's personal and feminist activities. It is also possible that many articles, pamphlets, and leaflets about oppositional women were written by oppositional men, many of whom may have been more interested in the "heroic," for example, masculine-oriented activities of women than in their personal, professional, and political lives. For security reasons, women used pen names.

The limited data also present confusing records on the "who's who" of the Iranian female opposition. Women's identity remains unknown and there may be an overlap between female group members and independent women. For example, an Iranian group in the United States with Trotskyite tendencies, the Committee for Artistic and Intellectual Freedom in Iran (CAIFI), published, held news conferences, and released

[75] Documentation, Moghissi, *Populism*, 117.

information concerning oppositional Iranian literary circles, women, and men who were harshly treated by the state. Perhaps, more than any other dissident exile group, they exposed the Shah's regime maltreatment of women activists. They publicized the plight of women-as-martyrs and women-as-heroines. But it is unclear whether these women were independents or only CAIFI members. Nor is there information on the feminist activities of these women or their life experiences. Whatever their organizational affiliations, scattered reports corroborate earlier assertions in this book: independent women acted as both political actors and reactors. Women who slightly and indirectly criticized the state in their studies or those whose research focused on governmental inattentiveness to the plight of the poor were arrested or tortured in the late 1960s and the 1970s. These women include Chirin Moazed, a scholar who was put in solitary confinement, tortured, and died in prison; Atefeh Gorgin, the literary critic who was imprisoned and executed; Dr. Simin Salehi, who was pregnant when she was tortured and who died in prison; Tahereh Sajjadi Tehrani was sentenced in a secret trial to 15 years' solitary confinement; and Manijeh Ashrafzadeh was executed.[76]

Another dissident, Dr. Vida Hajebi Tabrizi, was a sociologist at the University of Tehran. She was a researcher on the condition of the peasantry in Iran, a subject that was sensitive to the government because it represented poverty and exploitation, not Westernization, modernization, and development. Hajebi Tabrizi was arrested while driving home in July 1972 and was rarely heard from since. She was booked and tortured, and according to a report, "lost any sense of feeling in her hands and feet, [and] has developed a bad heart, bad blood circulation, meningitis, and no longer menstruates." The Iranian government never acknowledged Hajebi Tabrizi's arrest, nor were the charges against her ever announced. Outraged at her treatment, American intellectuals and feminists protested her treatment throughout the 1970s. In 1974, Columbia University sociologist Alan Silver took a letter of protest signed by the Canadian Association of Sociologists and his own department to the Iranian Embassy in Washington, D.C.; he was told that his letter could be accepted only if it was mailed through the U.S. Postal System. American feminist Kate Millett, the National Organization of Women representative

[76] Feminist activities, Committee for Artistic and Intellectual Freedom in Iran. "Defend Women Political Prisoners in Iran"; and Committee for Artistic and Intellectual Freedom in Iran, "Women in the Shah's Prison: The Case of Vida Hadjebi Tabrizi."

Ann Roberts, Amnesty International representative David Weissbordt, and other concerned U.S. citizens publicly denounced the brutal activities of the Shah's government against Iranian women. The WOI and the Court women remained silent. Other nonconformist women also expressed their dissent through their writings and abstract poetry.[77] Simin Daneshvar, Simin Behbahani, Furuq Farrokhzad and others are noteworthy. Because of her pioneer work at a critical time, my focus will be on Farrokhzad.

Furuq Farrokhzad's (1935–67) success was far greater than that achieved by other critical women. No other professional Iranian woman has been so widely discussed, whether with admiration or abhorrence. Using her pen to rebel against gender subordination and oppression, Farrokhzad focused on women's lives and the impact of patriarchy, thereby agitating the men's world. As she grew older, much of her passion and talents went into political poems that revealed contempt for the class inequalities of the existing social and political order. "If she happens," as Hillman observed, "to be Iran's most famous poetess in history, and one of Iran's most controversial women, then so much the better." Farrokhzad criticized all that was considered "convention" or "tradition," both in her personal and professional worlds. Iran's most celebrated secular progressive woman and feminist, she dared to cross sexual boundaries, becoming one of her country's most acclaimed poets and social and political critics.[78]

Farrokhzad was born to a middle-class family in Tehran. Her father was a colonel in Reza Shah's army. An authoritarian father, he supported the artistic and intellectual curiosity of his children, while his wife maintained smooth relationships in the family. Inquisitive and fascinated with reading, Farrokhzad wrote verses at eleven. By her mid-teens, her perception of herself as unattractive made her uncomfortable with her looks. Perhaps because of this sense of inadequacy, she fell in love with a distant relative who was 15 years her senior and insisted on marrying him. Married at

[77] "Lost any sense," and in 1974, *Dagens Nyheter* as cited in The Committee for Artistic and Intellectual Freedom in Iran, "Defend Women"; and Thurgood, "Iranian Police Tighten Screws" in *Manchester Guardian*; and a letter to the editor signed by many critics. It was entitled: "Iran-Time for Protest," *The Guardian* January 31, 1976. This was also distributed by and reproduced by CAIFI. See K. Millett, A. Roberts, D. Weissbordt, and A. Silver in "Transcript of the Press Conference," 1–30.

[78] Talents, Hillman, *A Lonely Woman*, 137 and 147; and "famous" and "tradition," Hillman, *Ibid.*, 1–3.

16 and divorced at 19, she was left with a son but was unable to obtain custody.[79]

As traumatic as the entire experience was, one year later, she published "The Wedding Band," in which a marrying woman questions the meaning of the wedding ring for which she has earned many cheerful congratulations. Years later, she referred to it as "the ring of slavery and servitude." Still torn by the turbulent failed marriage, many years later in 1962, she wrote that "That love and ridiculous marriage at the age of sixteen shook the foundations of my life" and she noted that "Whatever I have, I've gotten from and by myself.... I want to begin again."[80]

Like many Iranian women, burdened with the power of patriarchal life, Farrokhzad remained self-critical. Although as a poet she exposed her feelings and experiences as a woman, she persistently disapproved of herself. Farzaneh Milani observes her as saying : "I am lazy," she said, "I always escape from what is positive in me and succumb to the negative." While one part of her was self-tormenting, the other part searched for her true soul: "I search for something inside myself," she explained, and "in the world around myself." Commenting on her conflicts, Hillman wrote that Farrokhzad's poetry "reveals the problems of a modern Iranian woman with all her conflicts, painful oscillations, and contradictions" and "women who seek self-expression and social options in a culture not entirely accustomed to them." Notwithstanding her tumultuous world, Farrokhzad's poetry "established 'feminine culture' in Persian poetry" despite severe rejection by many male literary critics.[81]

As Farrokhzad grew older, the self and the poetry became politicized: the personal became political. She wrote five volumes of poetry, as well as poems and articles in magazines. In 1955, her first published volume, *Asir* [the Captive] portrayed the life of a woman who is imprisoned in a "cage," that is, a wife at home, a mother who weeps for her lost child and, significantly, a sensuous woman who loses herself in the world of sexual intimacy. Unable to maintain control or a balance between her personal, motherly, professional, and sexual life, and beset by confusion and enormous grief, Farrokhzad suffered a nervous breakdown and was

[79] Married, Hillman, ed., *Forugh Farrokhzad*, 2. Her son, Kaveh, died while photographing the Iraq War in 2004.

[80] "Ring," Hillman, *A Lonely*, 44; and "Ridiculous marriage," *Bargozideh-e Asar-e Furuq*, 1356/1977, 11–12 and 8.

[81] "I am lazy," "I search," and "Myself," Milani, *Veils*. 137; "contradictions," and "self-expression," Hillman, *A Lonely*, 159, 74, and 84; and "feminine culture," *Ibid.*, 3 and Ch. 3.

hospitalized. But she continued to be troubled by societal pressures on her life as a woman. In 1956, Farrokhzad published her *Divar* [the Wall] which expresses the plight of a woman caught in an unjust society, while also reflecting her passions and amorous desires. She saw the wall as a metaphor that powerfully masked, controlled, and inhibited women's lives by confining them to the home – most Persian houses are walled. One of *Divar's* poems, the *Gonah* or the sin, about sexual intimacy, became "perhaps the most scandalous poem of the post-World War II period." *Osian* [Rebellion] came in 1958. These poems – some angry, others pessimistic – are somewhat different from the previous ones. In 1958, Farrokhzad's life changed. She fell in love with a married film-maker, painter, writer, and critic Ebrahim Golestan. One observer noted that she "drew on Golestan's energy, self-confidence, and independent manner." But Farrokhzad's work prior and subsequent to her relationship with Golestan was exemplary. Expanding her interests, she traveled to Europe to study film production and upon her return to Iran, she edited and directed short films.[82] She also continued to write critically and forcefully on politics and consciousness, class relations, corruption, the mosque, the veil, the clergy, and other important topics of the day. Then came her 1964 *Tavallodi Digar* [Another Birth], which included one of her most celebrated feminist and political poems, "The Windup Doll." A part of this poem reads:

> More than this, ah yes,
> one can remain silent more than this.
> For hours and hours
> with the vacant stare of a corpse
> one can gaze at cigarette smoke,
> at the shape of a tea cup,
> at a faded flower in a carpet,
> at an imaginary line on a wall. . . .
> . . . In the powerful embrace of a man,
> one can be a beautiful, healthy female . . .
> with a body like a smooth leather table cloth,
> with two large, firm breasts.

[82] "World War II," Hillman, *A Lonely*, 34–35; *Osian*, and her "*Osian-e Khoda*" [God Rebels] in *Bargozideh-e*, 121–123; Golestan, Hillman, *A Lonely*, 40; and films, Farrokhzad's first edited film was her 1959 *The Fire*. Thereafter, she produced two short documentaries and her 1961 film, *Water and Heat*. She then produced and played a part in another film, *The Sea*, which she never completed. In 1962, she made her documentary on a leper colony in Tabriz, *The House Is Black*, which has won several international awards. See Hillman, *A Lonely*, 43.

In bed with a drunk, a mad man, a vagrant,
one can contaminate the purity of love. . . .
One can genuflect a whole lifetime
with bowed head at the foot
of a saint's cold sarcophagus.
One can find God in a nameless grave
One can find faith with an insignificant coin.
One can rot in the precincts of a mosque
like an old prayer reader. . . .
Exactly like a windup doll,
one can see one's own world with two glass eyes. . . . [83]

Farrokhzad's interest in bringing her poetic reflections into the world of politics grew. Perhaps her wounded internal self was slowly healing and she was also experiencing her own rebirth. Her political awakening appears strongly in "O Jewel-Studded Land:" this poem describes Iranians under the Pahlavis as individuals who have developed a false consciousness and an uncritical sense of security about Iran's past or, more bluntly, its long monarchical history. In person, too, Farrokhzad expressed her dismay at the ruling elite as, for example, at a private party at the Prime Minister Hoveyda's, when Ashraf Pahlavi and the Shah's daughter, Shahnaz Pahlavi, arrived without prior invitation. Responding to Hoveyda's congratulatory remarks on Iranian politics, outspokenly and without fear of revenge, Farrokhzad negated Hoveyda and criticized the government. Similarly, in "To Ali His Mother Said One Day," she portrayed the vast gap between the world of poor Tehrani residents and an ideal world. She presented her alternative to the prevailing political rule in "Someone Who is not Like Anyone." She wrote: "I've had a dream that someone is coming" and "I've dreamt of a red star. . . ."[84]

Despite a tormented life as an original, talented, independent, expressive, political, and hard-working woman, and the society's and her male colleagues' rejection, she remained proud as a woman. In a 1964 radio interview, she was asked about the "feminine" quality of her poems. She responded that: "If my poems have a bit of a feminine character, . . . it is very natural. I am fortunately a woman. But if the concern is with artistic criterion, then I think gender cannot be a standard. . . . The important thing is to be a human being, not a man or a woman." This last statement resembles Dehghani, although there is no evidence that she

[83] "Windup Doll," Hillman, *A Lonely*, 82.

[84] "O Jewel," "Ali," "Someone," and "dreamt," Hillman, *A Lonely*, 47–55, 62–63, and 65–68.

was affiliated with any left organization. Farrokhzad revealed an awareness of her powerful voice and soul in "It Is Only Sound That Remains" and "Why Should I Stop, Why?" On February 14, 1967, this remarkable woman died from injuries suffered in a car accident. She was buried in Tehran's Zahiroddowleh Cemetery. Thus ended the life of Iran's feminist/political heroine, a woman who resisted the dominant personal, political, and professional dictates of her society. But her message remains compelling and eloquent. No other secular nonconformist woman had such a powerful impact as Farrokhzad on Iranian women's history. The influence of women acting from religious persuasion under the Pahlavis was far less.[85]

Women of the Religious Opposition

Common to all active women was the act of breaking their ties from the traditional lifestyle and participating in male-dominated political and public life. Yet they were diverse – some supported and others resisted the state. The nonconformists themselves included both secular and religious women. The latter were increasingly drawn into the political orbit, where they became active against the state during the 1970s. Religious women included many Muslim women, mostly of the *Shi'i* sect, and many fewer representatives of other minorities, for example, the Christians, Jews, and Baha'is. Here, I briefly highlight Muslim women because of their active involvement shortly prior to, during, and after the Revolution – the next part of the book will devote a greater attention to them.

In the late 1960s and 1970s, Islamic studies were expanding in popularity in Iran. Many urban Iranians, especially women in their early twenties, studied the diverse philosophical *Shi'i* texts. These texts discussed sexuality, gender relations, and women's position with respect to the family, work, and politics from a variety of perspectives specific to Iranian *Shi'ism*. The most influential ones included the works of Ayatollahs Ruhollah Khomeini and Morteza Motahhari and Dr. Ali Shari'ati.[86] No woman had written a major treatise on women. Studying these and other

[85] "Feminine character," Furuq Farrokhzad in a 1964 taped interview with Iraj Gorgin, "She'ir-e Emruz," [Today's Poetry]. Tehran: 1964; and "Why," Hillman, *A Lonely*, 160–162.

[86] Ayatollah, Khomeini, *Touzioh-ol*; Ali, Shari'ati, *Zan-e Mosalman* [Muslim Women]; and his *Fatima is Fatima*; and Motahhari, *Nezam-e Huquq.*, and his *Mas'aleh-e Hejab* [The Hejab Problem]. Tehran: Sadra, 1365/1386.

works helped raise religious consciousness. Amidst general discontent and protests against the Shah's regime, many women became firm believers and embraced Islam as an alternative to the system that was becoming increasingly tyrannical and unjust.

In Shiraz, Isfahan, Mashhad, Kashan, and Tehran, women, some of whom of seculer backgrounds, attended religious classes; they met in gender segregated spaces and they studied the *Qoran*; they listened to sermons, lectures, and interpretations; they went to religious gatherings and ceremonies in mosques and in private homes; and when opportunity arose, they marched, demonstrated, and chanted loud slogans glorifying the faith and defying sinners and heretics. A very popular activity in Tehran for young women was attending the lectures of Dr. Ali Sharia'ti, who was regarded as a major ideologue of the Iranian Revolution, and listening to his tapes while engaging in intensive discussions of his ideas. His tapes were also distributed in exile by various Muslim student organizations. Still many Muslim thinkers advocated not only family values and motherhood, but also women's participation in the liberation of the state and society from corruption, secularism, Westernism, moral degeneration, and decadence. Devout women searched for devout husbands in the hope of beginning a "new" Muslim family, training pious children, and constructing a new ideal Islamic society for the future.[87]

Prior to the revolution and immediately after, women joined different organizations or became participants in a variety of activities. Some women joined the ranks of such Islamic activists and groups as the oppositional clerics and the more clandestine Mojahedin-e Khalq-e Iran (the National Council of Resistance of Iran or MEK), loosely defined as Islamic modernists. Following their oppositional male counterparts, active female members began to reject Iran's integration into the world market, imperialism, corruption, repression, class inequalities, secularism, sexual objectification of women, and the spread of sexual immorality and immodesty. They saw Islam as an alternative to the immoral rule of temporal political authority, and regarded their faith as an antithesis of the Westernization and secularization that had offered little, if any, meaning or hope in their

[87] Heretics, I observed these changes in Tehran in 1971, and especially between 1973 and 1977; decadence, see documents on various views and organizations of Muslim women, in Tabari, and Yeganeh. eds., *In the Shadow*; Abrahamian, *The Iranian Mojahedin*, especially 230–242; and "new" Muslim family, the document section of Tabari and Yeganeh, eds., *In the Shadow*.

lives and social values. Shortly after consolidating its powers, the revolutionary government banned their activities.[88]

Other *Shi'i* women, primarily of traditional middle-class background, especially in urban areas, followed their male relatives and their activities against the Shah's regime. They included women who were associated with the more traditional *bazaar* traders, crafters, producers, or distributors. Some middle-class women, too, in search of a new response to a life they found alienating fell back on Islam. Many were students and teachers; others worked for the state bureaucracy or health or insurance services. Some formerly secular and Western-educated women became Islamic activists, for example, the well-known poet Tahereh Safarzadeh and professor and writer Zahra Rahanavard, as will be discussed later. Numerous women who had earlier exhibited secular tendencies in their social and personal relations, were now increasingly abandoning such Western attire as miniskirts and tight pants. Gradually they began to cover more and more of their bodies, hiding signs of sexuality in protest and solidarity but also as a new way of presenting themselves, their identities and signaling their allegiances. The *chador* or scarves worn with loose shirts and trousers, or other forms of the *hejab* or modesty, forcibly taken by Reza Shah Pahlavi were now becoming symbols of political resistance. Covering one's body was now a sign of discontent, even a language of protest, power, and politics.[89]

The final twenty years of Pahlavi rule persuasively illustrate the potent power of women as a political force in Iran. Despite twists and turns in Iran's tumultuous history, women's political participation has been pervasive. Yet the rise to power of Islamic activist women has paralleled the erosion of power of conformist and many nonconformist women. Many nonconformist women who had participated in the 1979 Revolution and had built a variety of feminist organizations with differing ideologies abandoned political activism or went into exile. With the creation of the new religious state, patriarchy and gender relations underwent significant changes again. Like the Pahlavis, the new Islamic regime drew on women as a source of legitimacy. The state also sought to support those women who represented its class and ideological make-up best. In turn, many Muslim women who cherished family values, gender difference, and strict

[88] MKO, Abrahamian, *The Iranian Mujahedin*, entire.

[89] Rahnavard, *Tolu'e Zan-e Mosalman* [The Dawn of Muslim Woman] as cited in Yeganeh and Keddie.

adherence to sexual codes welcomed the new state and took pleasure in seeing the *chador* and *hejab* returned to its place as the national couture, but maintained a more critical approach to the role of the husband and father, and patriarchal relations.

History has turned upside down: many of the formerly nonconformist women are now the newly proponent and privileged women; they are supporters and legitimizers of the revolutionary state. In this story, veiling became unveiling, and unveiling gave away to reveiling.

PART III

WOMEN IN THE ISLAMIC REPUBLIC OF IRAN

6

Women, the 1979 Revolution, and the Restructuring of Patriarchy

Holding their black *chadors* tightly under their chins with right hands and beating their chests with their left fists, hundreds of Muslim women organized and led by men marched in Tehran's streets to express support for their messianic revolutionary leader. They chanted: "Beloved Khomeini, Order Me to Shed Blood for You" (*Khomeini-ye Azizam Begu Barat Khoon Berizam*). While glorifying Islam and reviling the West, many revolutionary participants warned unveiled women: "Wear a Head Scarf or Get Your Head Knocked" (*Ya Rusari Ya Toosari*). They then threatened the uncloaked women with: "Death to Unveiling" (*Marg bar bi-Hejabi*). Other slogans linked unveiling to male impotence. One motto stressed, "Unveiling Stems From Men's Emasculation" (*Bi-Hejabi-ye Zan az bi-Qeyrati-ye Mard ast*) while another emphasized, "Death to the Unveiled Woman and her Cowardly Husband" (*Marg bar Zan-e bi-Hejab va Shohar-e bi-Qeyrat-e ou*). So powerful were messages that the *hejab* (cover or modesty) and reveiling became one of the most pervasive symbols of the revolution, standing for Islamism, anti-imperialism and anti-Westernism. The Islamic revolution was thus turning into a sexual counter-revolution, a struggle over women's sexuality.[1]

[1] "Beloved," "Wear," "Death," "Unveiling," and "Husband," communication from Haideh Sedghi, my sister, from Tehran to New York during late 1978 and early 1979. I also heard and recorded some of these slogans during my own research trips in early 1979, 1991, and 1997, but less so in 2002 and 2005. The last two slogans are still used today. *Hejab* literally means modesty; I use it here interchangeably with the veil or the *chador* or other forms of covers and clothings which include a combination of a headscarf, loose trousers and long coat, which continue to change in accordance with other styles, introduced on a daily basis.

Secular women, intensely politicized, participated with a plethora of ideologies.[2] Critical of cultural and economic trends in the subordination of women, they spoke against the recurring attempts at forced reveiling, although none linked it to the control of women's sexuality. Homa Nateq, a prominent and progressive historian, hailed Iranian women's heroic revolutionary activities, as she spoke to a large crowd at the University of Tehran in early 1979. Unaccustomed to covering her hair, she wore a hat – whether concealing her hair signified fear of zealots or political ambivalence is uncertain. She supported the revolution, while denouncing veiled women indirectly: "reactionary" women, like those mobilized by European and Latin American fascism, the Shah and the Women's Organization of Iran are instruments of the states' propaganda. She warned that women "must be alert" not to be used against "progressive men" by states who intend to neutralize their united opposition to despotism and oppression.[3] Writing more directly and angrily from exile, a few years later, Nateq expressed her astonishment at the "bewitched heroines" and their "religious fanaticism."[4]

The 1979 Revolution introduced a new chapter into women's history. It revered veiled women as powerful revolutionaries, and it devalued secular women as Westernized, monarchical (*Taquti*), and indecent. The symbolic meaning of reveiling became almost as potent as the loud voices of the participants who chanted "Death to the Shah and Imperialism" (*Marg bar Shah va Emperialism*). Communicated by wall grafitti, leaflets, word of

[2] Secular women, Comiteh-e-Ejad-e Jam'iyyat-e Bidari-ye Zanan, "Aqaz-e Bi-dari-ye Mellat," [The Beginning of People's Awakening]. Millett, *Going*, entire; UPI, "Iranian Women Rise Up," 4; Gregory, "Iran Women March," A1; Cummings, "Demonstration at Iran's Consulate," A8; and "15,000 Tehran Women Protest," A6. For an important study of the Islamic state and philosophy, see Enayat, entire. For general studies on the revolution and revolutionary thinking see, Abrahamian, *Iran*; Keddie, *The Roots*; Dabbashi; Amir Arjomand; Bakhash; M. Milani; and Moaddel, among others.

[3] "Reactionary" women, "Progressive men," and "alert," Nateq, "Movazeb bashim alayh-e Mardan" [We Must Be Careful Not to Be Used Against Men]. In that article, Nateq also criticized the WOI because its purpose was "to provoke women against men" and to passify them politically. In terms of her appearance at the university where she delivered that speech, an eyewitness account had observed Nateq with a hat covering her hair – personal discussions, February 20, 1996. In addition to being a respected historian, Nateq was a founder of the Marxist National Union of Women (NUW) and did not believe in separating women's organizations from men's. See Moghissi, *Populism*, 150 and 206, note 23.

[4] "Religious fanaticism," Nateq, "Women: the Demand of the Iranian Revolution," in Ridd and Callaway, eds., 47.

mouth, the media, and the new officials, an old Iranian cliche returned to the foreground: the "Woman Represents the Chastity of the Society" (*Zan Namous-e Jame'eh ast*). This message turned into a reality when Ayatollah Khomeini abolished the Family Protection Laws on February 26, 1979, and revoked women's rights to serve as judges on March 3, 1979. On March 29, 1979, he announced gender segregation of all beaches and sports activities, and three days later, he required all women to wear the Islamic *hejab* at work. Despite women's protests, reveiling became legally compulsory. It became a de facto national costume of Iranian women, when in 1983, the Parliament passed the Islamic Punishment Law (*Qesas*) that stipulated 74 lashes for violation of the *hejab*. In response to women's continued opposition to reveiling, in 1995, a note to Article 139 of the Islamic Criminal Code reaffirmed governmental penalty by mandating 10 to 60 days of imprisonment against those who publicly resisted the *hejab*. Thus concealing women's bodies, gender segregation and inequality became integral to state-building and its identity: Islamic, anti-imperialist, and anti-Westernist.[5]

Why was reveiling so significant that it became one of the fundamental policies of the Islamic state, and why did the new leaders, similar to Reza Shah, assign physical punishment for violation of veiling practices? The use of force to implement veiling observances reinforces the basic question that I raised earlier: what is the meaning of women's sexuality that its display or disguise assumes prominence for the state? From the early twentieth-century to the present, controlling women's sexuality remained at the core of the power struggle between rival groups in the political system and its religious contender, the clerical establishment. Heated debates addressed women's place in the society, and developmental projects incorporated women's labor while women's social image helped forge national and international identity.

Whether secular or religious or both combined, from the Pahlavis to the present regime, the state has played an instrumental role in modifying

[5] "Chastity," Goharol-Shari'eh Dast-e Qeyb, as cited in "Women in the Press," in *Zanan* (29 Tir, 75/ July 19, 1996), 11. Here, Qeyb was referring to society's image of women, presumably as it was formed in Iran after the 1979 Revolution. Abolished and revoked, see the following sections. *Qesas*, Paidar, *Women*, 339 and 342; and Gheytanchi, 439–452. In part, because of the negative portrayal of the IRI abroad for its treatment of women, during the late 1990s, the government introduced certain reforms, some of which reversed the earlier rulings of the revolution. Those reforms included the appointment of women to various high level governmental posts such as Shirin Ebadi's appointment as the first woman and the only female judge in 1996.

and restructuring gender relations and women's sexuality. In its attempt to "Islamicize" women's position, the Islamic Republic of Iran resorted to coercion, passed inegalitarian laws, and mobilized female morality squads or what I call the gender police, to enforce its codes of propriety. A divisive strategy that set working-class women against other women, the work of gender police contributed to state-building, despite challenges from defiant women. How the revolutionary state reconstructed women's sexuality and reveiled women, how it drew on women as a source of legitimacy, and how gender became inextricably linked to revolutionary ideals are the major foci of this chapter. Shifts in gender consciousness and women's responses will be considered later. Suffice to say that gender and reveiling integrated state and religion at the outset of the revolutionary upheavals. Women and unveiling challenged, if not threatened, that unity in subsequent years.

THE REVOLUTION AND ITS DISCONTENTS

Since the Iranian Revolution, the growing Islamic movements in the Middle East, North, West, and East Africa, and in South, West, and Central Asia as well as Eurasia have been the objects of critical inquiry. Samuel Huntington predicted the future of global tensions in terms of the "clash of civilizations" or frictions between political Islam and the West, or "the West vs. the rest."[6] But such narrow perspectives misinterpret Islam and Muslims, culture, and the dynamics of state behavior in different Muslim societies, assuming that they are homogenous and immutable. Given that the meaning of Islam changes historically and cross-culturally, state policies and political movements, at least in modern times, can also vary and be explained through their interactions with gender.

Nor do religious ideologies alone shape women's lives and gender relations in Islamic states. Women's position is historically specific and takes different forms in various cultures and societies, particularly those undergoing rapid transformation. Women's experiences are also shaped by their class, ethnicity, and nationality. Islam can be seen "as an ideological system" that provides "some unifying concepts that influence women's experiences of subordination," as Deniz Kandiyoti indicates. She suggests that "These are vested in the culturally defined modes of control of female sexuality, especially insofar as they influence subjective experiences of womanhood and femininity." Although religion and culture leave important

[6] "West vs. the rest," for example, see Huntington, entire.

imprints on women's lives, they must be understood within the broader historical, sociopolitical, and economic contexts as they may be shaped by trends in global political economy.[7]

Gender issues have been a dynamic component of the Iranian polity and culture, in particular from the 1979 Revolution to the present. At its inception, the revolution brought a temporary unity. It included solidarity among religious forces, classes, gender, and various political organizations. Immediately before and shortly after the revolution, both unveiled and veiled women joined together and demonstrated solidarity. Women's goals were inseparable from men's; almost all cooperated on the anti-Shah, nationalist, and anti-imperialist platforms. For the first time in the history of the modern Middle East, millions of Iranians – veiled and unveiled women, organized and unorganized, secular and religious, rich and poor, and old and young – participated in a revolution. Professionals and intellectuals, service workers and *bazaar* merchants, artists and nurses, students and teachers, and housewives and children joined to abolish the monarchy and its imperialist support. This initial phase of mass uprising brought an unprecedented degree of solidarity among different socioeconomic, religious, and gender groups. Religion was not yet a divisive force.[8]

Nor was women's clothing a subject of dissent. Depending on their cultural or class backgrounds, women dressed differently in public as they appeared with or without hats, scarves, or *chadors*, or wore jeans and jackets, shirts and skirts, and sandals or shoes. There hardly existed any signs of overdressing or heavy make-up as there was during the last few years of the Shah. French and Italian fashions almost disappeared from the streets. Many urban working-class and rural women continued to wear the *chador* or scarves, as was customary for such women under the Shah. A noticeable number of urban middle-class women who had joined various Islamic groups prior to the revolution became firm supporters of the new order and put on *chadors* or combined scarves with loose tunics and pants. On the other hand, urban women of the upper and middle-class and even some women from lower social echelons refrained from covering their hair. Women's choice of clothing came to an end as the thugs and some bystanders began publicly to threaten, attack, and

7 "Ideological system," "Unifying concepts," and "Modes of control," Kandiyoti, "Emancipated but Unliberated?" 309.

8 Revolution, see note 2 above; and to abolish, personal observations during the early phases of the revolution. See also Ashraf and Banuazizi, "The State, Classes and Modes," 3–40.

intimidate unveiled women. Several newspapers and leaflets criticized uncovered women as immoral, lax, or heretical. Women and sexuality were becoming increasingly contentious.

Like other revolutions, "the Spring of Freedom" (*Bahar-e Azadi*) led to the collapse of the brief coalition of class, gender, and religion, not long after the downfall of the old regime. Women's rights came under attack as new developments set the stage for forced reveiling. First, increasingly visible, veiled women appeared publicly in large numbers. At times, they outnumbered unveiled or unscarved women. Organized and led by male supporters of various Islamic groups, they wore their black *chadors* in demonstrations, street protests, rallies, and street gatherings. They also filled Tehran's *bazaars*, university campuses, boulevards and alleys, mosques, and seminaries. Second, pressure on unveiled women mounted as streetwalkers, armed guards, or individual male revolutionaries began to harass and physically abuse them in public. While participaing in a political debate outside the gates of the University of Tehran in May 1979, a bystander furiously informed me that a woman's place was not in the street to protest but at home to nurture her family and children.

The most alarming signal to reveiling came with the unanticipated Khomeini March 6, 1979 edict to impose the *hejab*. At first, both secular women and religious women who believed in women's right to choose demonstrated against the imposition of the *hejab*. Then, they wrote articles in various papers, held meetings at different universities, appealed to international women's organizations, and more importantly, they actively spoke and lectured in meetings, public institutions, and rallies. But women's opposition to the new dress code and the curtailment of their rights drew attention from various forces who actively broke into their demonstrations in order to silence their voice and discourage them from public appearance. Third, disillusioned with the revolutionary outcome and the violation of their rights, women intensified their underground political and publishing activities, and a few who feared for their lives left Iran and continued their struggle in exile. Thus, with the breakdown of unity came anarchy, with anarchy came repression, and with repression came coercion and the emergence of new forms of male dominance and violence against women.

Reveiling and backlash against unveling came from different currents and at different times. Of importance was the political strategy of the new religious leadership who placed anti-imperialism and anti-Westernism at the center of the revolutionary movement. Commmunicating to their supporters and actively mobilizing new recruits, they promoted *Shi'i* Islam as the basis of the new visionary social construct and popularized religious allegories to demonstrate the fallacies of the monarchy and the West. This strategy was successful. It appealed to active religious and secular groups including the left, intellectuals, nationalists, socialists, and other participants. It also served to bolster support and build alliances among the masses who advocated Islam and those who were alienated by the Shah's modernization, repression, Westernization, and secularization drives. Discussing the "revolutionary political culture," Farideh Farhi suggested that in part, the participants' "hyper-awareness of western 'eyes' had an effect on the way the drama unfolded in the prerevolutionary period." This drama eventually helped bring into focus the juxtaposition of sexuality with Western cultural influence or "cultural imperialism."[9] An anti-imperialism and anti-Westernism project actually overshadowed Islam, laying the groundwork for the victory of religion, and ultimately, the reconstruction of gender and sexuality.

Another crucial factor that contributed to the backlash against unveiled women was the strategic failure of progressive forces. Nationalism, anti-imperialism, and anti-monarchial tendencies, not gender equality, became the overriding concerns of the secular and democratic trends among the left. Considering national independence and anti-imperialism as the most pressing issues confronting the revolution after the Shah's overthrow, it became politically expedient to join the charismatic Khomeini against the Shah's supporters and his American allies. Although various groups formed different nationalist or socialist agendas on the meaning, the nature, and the future of the revolutionary regime, they failed to configure women's interests and the implications of coercive veiling in the new environment. Khomeini and his religious associates viewed unveiling and Western forms of women's emancipation as paradoxical to Islam. Embracing cultural and spiritual ties to Islamic precepts, Khomeini's followers and urban popular classes, including the rural-urban migrants and the *bazaaris*, had long rejected secularism and Western mores. During the revolution, many men intensified their assault on unveiled women by labeling them as "Western dolls" or "Western prostitutes" and victims of the "corrupt" West that had exploited Iran and allegedly influenced its women to become "loose" and "licentious." Secular forces failed to

9 "Revolutionary," "hyper-awareness," and "cultural imperialism," Farhi, "Sexuality," 11–12.

sustain the women's movement. Thus came the stage for Islamization of gender relations, and the consolidation of state power through reveiling.[10]

STATE-BUILDING, ISLAMIZATION, AND GENDER

The representation of women as "Islamic" and veiled proved central to the triumph of the revolutionary ethos. Unlike other major social upheavals, in Iran, actions that contained rather than confronted tradition encouraged the ensuing romanticization of the past and the purification of the present as well as patriarchal tendencies of the society. The significance of women for the success and legitimation of the revolution included the promotion of an Islamic and *Shi'i* heritage that would revive an identification of society's moral and ethical values with virtuous women as the bearers of cultural purity and authenticity. Second, through one of the very symbols, "woman," Iranian society expressed its anti-imperialist and anti-Western stance and reclaimed its old history of *Shi'ism* that had to be preserved in a pure state and society. Third, the "purification" of society (which later became one of the state's main objectives) through the control of women meant that women's movements and their labor for the nation, the revolution, and themselves would serve *not* women's *own* interest but the interest of patriarchy, as envisioned in this revolutionary period by male-dominated participants: the Islamists, the leftists, and the nationalists. The backlash against women continued as the veiled women became the most complete representation of "Islamic" rebirth and of everything that was associated with its antithesis: the monarchy, the West, and "Westoxication." Gender reconstruction accompanied consolidation of state power, state-building and the creation of new institutions.

Proclamations, laws, and policies curtailed women's rights and promoted the literal devaluation of women and gender inequality. Authorities introduced edicts, sometimes as *fatavin* (religious verdicts) and occasionally, through Friday Prayer Sermons. Some addressed specifically women's bodies and sexuality, for instance, the institutionalization of the *hejab* through the *chador*, the *rupush* (loose tunic), and the *rusari* (the

[10] Unveiling, see Moghissi, *Populism*; and Shaidian, "The Iranian Left," 223–247. Some male liberal intellectuals and secular progressive participants supported women's rights movements throughout the century, but as organizational members, they provided little support to women's activities and concerns during the 1979 Revolution. "Western," "corrupt," "loose," and "licentious," personal observation, 1979. Also some male demonstrators criticized and scolded me: "Westernized sister, go home."

scarf) or the *maqna'eh* (a tight scarf that covers all the hair, the neck, and shoulders). More drastically, proposed in 1980 and legislated in 1983, the *Qesas* (the Bill of Retribution) assigned 74 lashes to women who failed to observe reveiling rules and *lowered the official value of a woman to half that of a man* in adultery cases, cases involving death sentences. The *Qesas* weakened women's legal rights by stipulating that a woman's testimony would be equivalent to that of half of a man, or two women's testimony would be equivalent to one man's.[11]

Other edicts and laws reconstructed or maintained the existing gender inequality. Former President Ali Akbar Hashemi Rafsanjani legally sanctioned *Shi'i* temporary marriage and polygamy in a sermon in 1990, although some religious authorities had earlier encouraged it unofficially.[12] Another ruling lowered the age of marriage for girls from 18 to 9, and further upheld male superiority by reinstituting the pre-Pahlavi child custody laws that allowed men to retain their children after divorce. As this is written, the state has introduced changes in the child custody and divorce laws, both of which remain complex and inequitable. Although many divorces are initiated by women, children must use the surname of their father, not the mother's, even at parental request.[13]

Many other laws sanctioned gender segregation. Some injunctions required separation of public spaces by gender, such as swimming pools, beaches, sports, and offices. Most educational institutions and lecture halls became gender segregated, although some classes were mixed subsequently. Women using public transportation were assigned to the back of buses and fewer seats than men. Recently, public mini-buses and taxis have become gender mixed and both sexes sit or stand closely to each

[11] "Woman," for an analysis of the veil and its meaning during the revolution see, Yeganeh, "Women's Struggles." "Westoxication," the term Westoxication is from Al-e Ahmad, entire; and *Qesas*, Kar, "Jayegah-e Zan dar Qavanin-e" [Women's Position in the Iranian Penal Codes], *Zanan*, 16–26.

[12] Temporary marriage and polygamy, there were numerous teachings and different interpretations of Islam especially regarding women's sexuality. See Khomeini, *Resaleh-e*; Motahhari, *Mas'aleh-e*; and Shariati, *Fatima*. For a more recent journalistic account of women and sexuality see Sciolino, Elaine, "From the Back Seat in Iran, Murmurs of Unrest," A4; and Haeri.

[13] Divorces, Ebadi, "Vaz'e Huqugi-ye Zanan dar Iran," [The Legal Situation of Women in Iran], in *Jame'eh-e Salem*, 45; and Mahmoudi, A. *Nazariye'e Jadid* [New Perspectives]. On various interpretations of *Qesas*, see Saeed-Zadeh, "Khun baha-ye Zanan?" [Why Inequality in Qesas] and Kar, "Dad-Khast-e eslah-e Qavanin-e Keyfari-ye Iran." [A Request for Reforming], in *Zanan*. For a legal discussion of patriarchy in marriage, divorce, child custody, see Qa'ini, S., "Velayat-e Pedar," [Father's Rule, in *Zanan*. For an overall view of legal changes during the early period of the IRI, see Higgins, 1985.

other – the state somewhat disappears in taxis and mini-buses. Further, married women were forbidden to travel abroad unless they received written permission from their husbands, and until recently, single female students were prevented from pursuing graduate studies overseas.[14] In addition, employment directives (as will be discussed later) and recent legislation that endorsed gender segregation of medical facilities severely limited women's options and choices. Last, inheritance laws that are *Shari'eh* based continued to guarantee greater wealth for men as they stipulate exceedingly unequal property relations between mothers and sons and sisters and brothers.

Harsh sanctions accompanied frequently the implementation of gender-based regulations. During the early months of the revolution, the newly created forces of the *Hezbollah* (Party of God), often using revolutionary committees, enforced the rulings by intimidating, arresting, interrogating and sometimes imprisoning the defiant and unveiled or improperly-veiled women. Many adulterous women and prostitutes were flogged, stoned, or executed. Stoning continues today. Virgin female prisoners sentenced to execution were ordered to be tortured and raped because according to some religious interpretations virgins must be sexually fulfilled before death. Likewise, orders made homosexuality legally punishable, although gay men received more exemptions from punishment, perhaps because of higher regard for men's role in procreation. Sometimes their hair would be shaved unevenly in order to make them recognizable and shamed publicly; some were eventually stoned for what was considered illegitimate sexuality. Subsequently (as will be discussed), the gender police and other mobilized forces took charge of enforcing new mandates regarding sexuality, women's modesty, and gender relations.[15]

Postrevolutionary Iran, like many developing societies in the process of formation, provides a unique opportunity for the study of the centrality of gender and sexuality to politics. In replacing the Pahlavi regime,

[14] Married women, the Shah's government also required married women to obtain their husbands' written permission before traveling abroad. However, because women had greater freedom and more access to the bureaucracy, it was not very difficult to obtain such approvals. The Shah's state also encouraged single female students to travel abroad to pursue education, an opportunity that I took advantage of. Only recently, the current state has allowed single female students to go abroad alone.

[15] Stoning, Shadi, Sadr, "Payan-e Sangsar-e Zanan?" [The End of Women's Stoning?] in *Zanan*, Dey 1381/2002, 11–13. Raped, and illegitimate sexuality, Paidar, *Women*, 232; Afshar, *Islam and Feminism*, 17; and CBS, "Iran: A Revolution Betrayed," CBS TV Production, a documentary film that was produced possibly in late 1979 or early 1980; and gender police, Paidar, *Women*, Ch. 7.

the revolutionary state introduced new forms of gender relations, veiling practices, and gender segregation measures, paving the way for the building of an Islamic and *Shi'i* identity. Reveiling became one of the major objectives of revolutionary leaders. Despite their active participation in the social movement, women became a critical locus of the struggle for political power. Reversing and replacing many of the previous gender laws with stricter rules and curtailing decades of opportunities that had accompanied unveiling and gender policies for some women, the new clerical authorities sought to reshape the society according to their precepts. Women began to experience an upsurge of patriarchal norms in their private and public lives. Although the backlash and diminished possibilities could not send women back to the *andaruni* and their secluded lives at the turn of the century, reveiling became a new force in women's lives, symbolizing and fostering different meanings at different times.

REVEILING

During the revolution, wall grafitti, posters, the media, and stamps depicted vivid and colorful portrayals of the new veiled Islamic women. For the first time in Iranian history, a woman appeared on a stamp, costing 20 rials ($.03). At its center, the stamp had a sketch of a round-faced woman that was carved inside an oval-shaped empty shell.[16] She had no body, only a face cloaked in black, a face without wrinkles or lines, a face with a closed mouth and serious eyes looking into infinity. Except for a gun showing from behind her head, the background looked cold. There was no feeling, or passion. Only because her hair was covered, she could not be mistaken for a man. But this was the revolution's ideal woman: a pious Muslim and a militant fighter; more importantly, she was masculinized or perhaps, a de-sexualized woman. This reveiled woman whose sexuality was concealed became a centerpiece of the revolution and subsequently, the Islamic state.

Unlike Jamalzadeh's early twentieth-century women, the idealized revolutionary woman was more utilitarian and purposeful. Like ancient Persia's powerful Zoroastrian women, who guarded the sanctity of the temple by keeping and maintaining the fire, the new Muslim woman acquired new responsibilities: she became the guardian of religion, state, and society, all of which required veiling or the *hejab*, and she epitomized

[16] Stamp, Farhi also discusses the images of this stamp within the context of the male revolutionary culture – see her "Sexuality."

nationalism and anti-Western ethos. In a unique way, this new woman represented distinct images: as an embodiment of the illusion of an historical cultural authenticity based on Islamic and *Shi'i* history; as an alternative to the "immoral" West that had seized power from the East; and as an enforcer of social control over women through religious law, culture, and tradition. Thus, the Islamic Republic drew on reveiling to redefine women's sexuality as a kernel of the state and its legitimacy.

Iranian religious and feminist thoughts shed different light on women and sexuality. In their religious and political texts, major *Shi'i* scholars offer diverse views on gender relations, rules of sexual conduct, women's ascribed private and social behavior, and women's sexuality and its function for reproduction, family relations, and men's sexual desires. Exalting Fatemeh, the Prophet's daughter and the wife of his successor, Emam Ali, they glorify her as the role model of the real Muslim woman. In today's Iran, Fatemeh's birthday is celebrated as the Woman's Day. She is commemorated as the paragon of motherhood and wifely virtues, above all, a heroine who was an authentic and devout Muslim, devoid of anything impure, foreign, and alien to Islam.

Devoting particular attention to postrevolutionary developments and the backlash against women, Iranian feminist scholars see sexuality as an integral aspect of the state's ideology. Some consider the state's perception of women's sexuality in terms of continuity with the past: violent and culturally patriarchal as ingrained in the *Shi'i* and monarchical traditions of male domination and female submission. Others argue that the *Shi'i* jurisprudence has been ideologically ambivalent toward women and their sexuality, especially in marital relations, both permanent and temporary. Yet another critique of the revolutionary culture considers the rejection of women's sexuality and the hiding of women's bodies as the focus of politics derived from "the defense of revolutionary purity" and the uniqueness of *Shi'i* tradition, which eventually "rests on the shoulders of those women cloaked in pitch black veils."[17]

But reveiling is far greater than realized during the early stages of the revolution. In its various manifestations, it plays critical roles in politics and society. First, as a powerful political symbol, it legitimizes the Islamic state, almost as significant as the idea and practice of the nation itself, or the national anthem or even its flag. In their implementation

[17] *Shi'i* scholars, Khomeini; Motahhari; and Shari'ati; Fatemeh, Farhi, "Sexuality," 16–17; Some consider, Azari; and Moghissi; others argue, Haeri; and yet another critique, Farhi, "sexuality," 15–16; and Paidar, *Women*, entire.

of reveiling, clerical leaders condemned not only "unveiling" (*bi-hejabi)*, but also "improper-veiling" (*bad-hejabi*). Moreover, they assigned severe punishments to disobedient women. During the first few years of the revolution, state agents harassed, scorned, arrested, fined, and lashed many women for bad-veiling. In addition, the vigilantes, security forces, revolutionary committee members, members of the Party of God and the gender police (*zanan-e basiji*) scolded, interrogated, attacked, or intimidated women they considered improperly-veiled. By dismissing women's will or their desires to choose or not to choose the cloak, new pronouncements and coercive actions of the militia and state and non-state forces made reveiling obligatory and an important emblem of statehood[18] and its representation.

Second, reveiling fosters social order by regulating women's sexuality. From the outset, unveiled women became a social anathema but veiled women acquired revolutionary credentials. Extolling the concealed women, women's bodies were ordered to be disguised like "pearls protected inside a shell," as street murals conveyed and communicate today. Veiling guarded Islam, but significantly, it hid women's sexual power/energy from eliciting public disorder by distracting and arousing men sexually. Underscoring the necessity of the new dress code, in his February 1979 interview with Oriana Fallaci, Khomeini stated:

> The women who contributed to the revolution were, and are, women with the dress, not elegant women all made up like you, who go around all uncovered, dragging behind them a tail of men. The coquettes who put on make up and go into the street showing off their necks, their hair, their shapes, did not fight against the Shah. They never did anything good, not those. They do not know how to be useful, neither socially, nor politically, nor professionally. And this is so because, by uncovering themselves, they distract men, and upset them.[19]

On March 6, 1979, he declared the *hejab* edict, and devout women readily supported the measure.[20]

Most other religious leaders endorsed reveiling. Ayatollah Morteza Motahhari, a highly respected *Shi'i* scholar, defined the veiled Muslim

[18] "Unveiling" and "improper-veiling," Sciolino, "From the Back Seat," A4; and scolded, interrogated, attacked, and intimidated, "Andar Hekayat-e" [In Stories], 5–6; "Khatar-e Birun Budan-e Dast" [The Dangers of Not Covering], 13; "Rafsanjani: dar Barabar-e Hejab" [Rafsanjani: There is Resistance], *Ibid.*, 5; and "Ekhraj-e 'Bad-Hejab" [The Ousting of the Improperly-Veiled], 5.

[19] Fallaci, "An Interview With Khomeini," 31.

[20] Devout women, "Interview with Esmat Abad," in www.BadJens.com (May 13, 2000).

woman as one who "covers herself when associating with men, one who is not seductive and inviting." Similarly, the Islamic Republic's first President, Abolhasan Bani-Sadr, indicated in 1981 that "Research proved female hair had a kind of radiance" that required it to be fully covered. In 1986, Hashemi Rafsanjani, then Speaker of the Parliament and later the Iranian President, following an injunction from the *Qoran*, warned women to cloak themselves well: "Women can only keep uncovered their faces and hands," he said, "not their neck, their ears, bosoms, arms and legs." Then he cautioned women against the manner in which the feminine voice was sexually stimulating: "in their conversations, women should not speak in a tone that their voice and their tone would be arousing and seductive to men." The perceived danger in the power of women's sexuality and their body necessitated its concealment.[21]

Third, reveiling affirmed the requirement of modest and virtuous behavior expected of Muslim women.[22] The *hejab* is an institution with its own set of rules regarding women's conduct and their actions and interactions, in particular with men. This meaning of the *hejab* is not distinct and separate from its dress form, rather it is its adjunct. An observant woman is covered and restrained. She is chaste and obedient in private and public: at home, she is a subservient wife, a sexual servant and a nurturing mother, and if single, she is at fault socially and sanctimoniously; outside the home, she is diligent in how she walks, what she wears, how she talks, sits, and smiles, and how she moves her body and displays her ornaments. In a Friday Sermon, Hashemi Rafsanjani indicated that the *hejab* should "cover head, neck, breasts and especially the curves of the breasts definitely." Even if women cover themselves thoroughly, he ordered women should not wear

> ... tight clothing to visibly exhibit their bodies to the extent that they are eye-catching and attract men's attention; this is *bad-hejabi* (bad covering); ... Clothes must be so loose that they won't excite men. Nor should women speak in such a manner and such a tone of voice to excite and invite the opposite sex.[23]

[21] "Not seductive," Motahhari, *Masa'leh*, 79–83; "Research proved," Sciolino, "From the Back Seat." A4; and Rafsanjani, "Ra'ies-e Shoray-e Eslami Hodud-e Hejab" [The Speaker of *Majles* Announced], 5.

[22] Modesty, Mernissi's *Beyond* is one of the earliest books that showed that the sex-segregated institutions in the Muslim world intended to contain women's sexually induced behavior.

[23] "Tight clothing," "Ra'ies-e Majles-e Shoray-e Eslami [The Speaker of the Majles Announced], 5 and 12.

Despite Rafsanjani's warnings, the color, the form, and how much of the hair and the face the *hejab* could mask became the subject of great controversy.[24] *Zan-e Ruz*, a women's magazine, discussed bad-veiling or improper-veiling as:

> ... uncovered head, showing of hair, make-up, uncovered arms and legs, thin and see-through clothes and tights, tight clothes such as trousers without an overall over them, and clothes bearing foreign words, signs or pictures. The importers and traders of the latter type of clothes were also threatened with fines, imprisonment and flogging. The clothes women could wear in public [are] limited to the standard Islamic uniform of long, thick and loose overall, trousers, thick stockings and large headscarves folded in the front to cover every string of hair. These should be in small prints like the rest of the quote preferred colors [are] ... dark blue, black, gray and brown.[25]

In today's Iran, the black *chador* is a form of the *hejab* that is preferred by the stricter religious orders, and it is worn by high-level female officials or street demonstrators or some who participate in religious gatherings. Another form of the *hejab* combines a wide head scarf with loose and long tunics and loose trousers, usually in dark colors. In 2002, many young women in Tehran wore matching striped or colorful scarves and knee-high, light color, and tightly fit tunics over slim pants in public and private offices. In 2005, in larger cities, short and tight jackets substituted tunics, sometimes sandals were worn instead of shoes and more women wore make-up in public. Women working in international organizations appeared unveiled, but those in government facilities continue to dress up in dark *maqna'eh*, loose tunics, and trousers. Although substantial changes in the shapes and shades of the *hejab* are visible in today's Iran, modesty continues to depict and define devout Muslim women and thus the Muslim state itself.[26]

[24] *Hejab*, see some of the earlier works that were published both in Iran and the United States, including *Islamic Revolution*; *Mahjubah*; and *Message of Revolution*. Refer also to the American publication of *Women and Struggle in Iran*. For other works see Paidar, *Women*, and recent issues of *Zan-e Ruz* and *Zanan*.

[25] *Zan-e Ruz*, 60, 1988, cited by Paidar, *Women*, 344.

[26] Cloak, or the veil has never been a monolithic "Islamic" dress code for women or a symbolic representation of women. Historically and culturally specific, the veil's meaning has changed in different social and political environments subject to diverse women's views and their lifestyles. In Iran, literally denoting a "curtain" or one who sits behind a "curtain" (*pardeh neshin*), the *hejab* has commonly and traditionally come to refer to a piece of cloth by which a woman must protect her body from the men who are forbidden by religious authorities to glance at her. Prior to the 1979 Revolution urban women from all classes, in particular the middle-class and the wealthy abandoned the

SEXUALITY, MOBILIZATION, AND GENDER POLICE

States' mobilization of women for political support appears to be most prominent in postrevolutionary periods, when a new regime needs popular support for political legitimation. This was evident in the Bolshevik and Chinese revolutions. Within the Middle East and North African contexts, Turkey's nationalist movement and Algeria's anti-colonial forces recruited women and relied on them in the struggle for nation-building and political liberation. As states build alliances with different social classes and gender groups, women's mobilization can be a significant aspect of that connection. Little information about the mobilized women or the female gender police is available in Iranian women's studies despite their pivotal role in the implementation of reveiling and other gender policies. In their efforts to achieve political mobilization, both the monarchs and the *mullahs* have built alliances with different classes of women. But the experiences of the IRI, have been unique.[27]

One of the ways in which women were mobilized in the IRI was through Ayatollah Khomeini's call for the formation of the *basij* (mobilized) force in 1980, at the start of the Iran-Iraq War. He referred to the mobilized women as "typical symbols of devotion, self-sacrifice and love of God and Islam." During the war, Iranian women were incited by a call for *basij-e umumi* (public mobilization) to defend Islam in one of the bloodiest battles of modern history. The message enjoined women to marry those who had been wounded in the state's cause. Evoking "scenes of mothers,

cloak for Western style of attire. Those who continued to practice veiling, especially the poorer, middle-class, and older women, wore it for various reasons: some considered it as a religious obligation and cultural habit, others saw it as a form of modesty, and still a few used it to be more mobile or avoid dressing up, or avert public harassment. Postrevolutionary urban Iranian women became the major target of reveiling, although local habits formed the shape and extent of the cloak. Depending on their class background, their perception of modesty and trends in governmental policies, today's urban women wear different veiling fashions; and in rural and tribal areas, customs are entirely localized. Because they are the major target of the state's reveiling policy, urban women are my main focus. *Hejab*, for different meaning of the *hejab*, see Fernea, and Bezirgan, eds., *Middle Eastern Muslim*; Ahmed, *Women*; Kandiyoti, ed. *Women*; Haddad, and Findly, eds., *Women, Religion*; Badran and Cooke eds.; and Bamdad, *Zan-e* I and *Zan-e* II.

27 Mobilization of women, Molyneaux; Andors; Jayawardena; Massell; Kruks; Rapp and Young, eds.; Lapidus; and Andors; Turkey and Algeria, Jayawardena. *Feminism*; Alexander; Parker; Shahidian, "The Iranian Left"; Sedghi, "Third World Feminist;" and mobilized women, see references on Iranian women in Chapter 1.

wives and sisters who have lost their beloved [ones] in this war," the Ayatollah praised

> the marriage of a young girl [to] a . . . Guard who lost both of his arms . . . and [suffered injury to] both . . . eyes. . . . That brave girl . . . said, 'Since I could not go to the . . . front, let me offer my faith to this Revolution with this marriage.' The greatness of this act, its human value and the Divine blessings cannot be expressed. . . . [28]

Thus women were encouraged to bond with the state.

The bond between the state and gender led to the formation of other groups. First, women were recruited for war purposes. They were trained as guerrilla fighters or as regular soldiers, auxiliaries, nurses and cooks for the war zones. Women were also mobilized for non-combative activities in order to participate in "philanthropic" tasks in such areas as culture, education, sports, the arts, teaching and spirituality. Most importantly, women were recruited as morality squads. One official pamphlet referred to them as "guardians of orthodox Islamic culture," or female paramilitary force who would guard gender segregation, the *hejab* and modesty policies, including dress codes as enunciated by IRI authorities.[29] Because of their importance to the state and the politics of reveiling, I will highlight their activities, and refer to them as gender police. Serving the state, gender police became highly active during the early phases of the Islamic regime. They included female revolutionary guards, street patrols, and other paramilitary agents who police regulations pertaining to gender relations or offer assistance to the male police force to maintain social control. They generally represented families with lower incomes or poor backgrounds, usually from "south of Tehran," where many poverty-stricken and uneducated people live. Some Tehrani women refer to them as women with dirty mouths or *bad dahan* for their willingness to use obscene and vulgar language to embarrass and intimidate their targets. While a few are older, many of the gender police are between 16 and 30 years of age.[30]

[28] "Scenes of mothers," cited in *Women's Basiji*, n.p., possibly printed in 1995 in Tehran. See 24, as well as the back of the front cover page. I picked up this publication in Huairou, China in September 1995.

[29] "Guardians of Orthodox," *Ibid.*

[30] "Gender police," "south of Tehran," and *bad dahan*, my interviews, New York City, February 12, 1992. Here, the term "gender police" was suggested to me by Francine D'Amico. It refers to female police agents who enforce state policies, in this respect, gender public policies.

Not appearing in the Census Statistics, the gender police are visible in the streets of cities and towns. During the early years of the revolution, they walked in groups or individually and were sometimes followed by a van full of male revolutionary guards. For most of these women, this was perhaps their first activity in the labor force. Under Iran's poor economic conditions, especially the high inflation and unemployment, these women might receive salaries, or food and coupons for consumer goods, or welfare services, or a combination of these bonuses in exchange for their work. Little information is available on their numbers. In May 1996, one report indicated that 230,000 *basijis* were trained to provide "verbal advice" to those who fail "to observe Islamic dress code" during the "Week of Promoting Virtue and Prohibiting Vice." Whereas in 1991 and 1997 fear of gender police dominated large urban centers, in 2002 and 2005, I rarely encountered them in governmental offices and public spaces, perhaps because of the more liberal policies of the Khatami's rule.[31]

The most important activity of the gender police consists of enforcing modesty and dress codes. They follow the mandated rule of "enjoining the right and forbidding the wrong" and campaign "to eradicate depravity" and "anti-values."[32] They are recruited by various Islamic committees and associations and are organized into various groups. Some groups generally function in public spaces. They include such groups as the Mobile Security Women (*Zanan-e Sarallah*), *Women of the Party of God* (Zanan-e Hezbollah), and other Sister (*Khaharan*) organizations to intimidate, guide and oversee the behavior of other groups of women, and to install moral values in such public places as government offices, the post office, libraries and universities. Periodically the government increases pressure by assigning Search Committees (*Comite-he Gasht*), whereby a car full of men would be followed by a car full of women looking for offenders against Islamic mores. In patrolling the streets, they search for unmarried couples and those women who are improperly veiled or dressed immodestly in order to guide them to the right path.

Also prominent on the streets are female members of *Amr-e be Ma'ruf va Nahi az Monker* (The Promotion of Virtue and Prohibition of Vice). More frightening than others, these agents intimidate women, scold them,

[31] Census Statistics, there is no central office to coordinate the activities of all different groups of *basijies*, and it is difficult to obtain reliable information. Because of lack of scientific evidence, much of the information here is based on my own observation, as well as several individuals I interviewed for the study. "Advice," "dress code," and "Week," Reuters, "Basiji Islamic Code."

[32] "Enjoining," "forbidding," "eradicate," and "anti-values," *Basiji Women*, 9.

arrest them if necessary, and turn them over to the appropriate revolutionary committee for further investigation. In effect, the mobilized women have been inducted into a kind of corps of security agents, enforcing state law, while at the same time attempting to instill a new consciousness by "educating" nonconformist women on religious conduct and traditions. Thus the state has succeeded in setting mobilized women against those who are nonconformists.

The second major group of gender police consists of the *Harasat* guards or security officers at governmental offices. In order to ensure proper veiling and prevent women from wearing make-up or nail polish, the female guards check women as they enter buildings as employees or as customers. This is performed in a separate office from men, or if the space is too small, in a separate corner. Generally, every office has a search-room at the entrance. A "sister" may wish to check the identification card especially if the entering woman's scarf looks loose, and open the purse in search of make-up. If women are immodestly dressed, improperly behaved, or even if they carry cosmetics, they are given warnings, depending on the good heart of the guard. In 1991, a female guard gave me a large bobby-pin so that I could tie my scarf more securely under my chin when entering the Central Bank of Iran. One interviewee indicated that a woman was arrested and stopped from working for a few days, for "laughing."[33]

In contrast to other groups, the third group of mobilized women are gender auxiliaries who are organized for the state's various social and political projects. They participate in state-organized demonstrations and together with male zealots chant loud slogans against improper veiling, or accuse its violators of being "servants of the Shah," "prostitutes," "the Westernized," or "liberal" and "wealthy" women as they did during the early phases of the revolution. Socially and politically alienated by the Shah's regime, these women took pride in wearing the *chador* and in participating in state-organized demonstrations and Friday Prayers, thereby lending political support to the state. They included large numbers of slum-dwelling and poor women who have been "bought by the regular provision of rations and modest food supplies provided by the government." They also received food coupons, some medical expenses, and other subsidies (although due to rising economic problems, there has been a cutback in state subsidies). Such distribution policies perpetuate the victimization of poor women by their "integration" or their "marriage" to the state, in effect, ensuring economic and social dependency

[33] "Laughing," my interviews, New York City, February 12, 1992.

on the government.[34] By the end of Khatami's regime, these women were less visible as they were not needed by the state which had achieved consolidation, expressed a degree of law and order, and was experiencing economic difficulties.

In addition to their activities in the public space, the gender police are trained and ordered to intrude into the private lives of women suspected of improper conduct within the confines of their homes. Such encroachments on peoples' private lives often occur at parties or weddings of the middle-class and relatively well-to-do. Sometimes, the mobilized women, accompanied by members of the Revolutionary Committee, come to houses where parties are given, arresting unveiled women or those wearing heavy make-up, or arresting men and women if they are in mixed company. Sometimes, these forces arrest and fine violators. At other times, they accept bribes and then give advice on proper conduct.[35]

The mobilization of women under the Islamic regime is a complicated phenomenon. On the one hand, gender segregation policies require enforcement of those policies by women agents, thereby increasing their dependency on the state. On the other hand, it may endow some women with a sense of self that was repressed or non-existent under the secular state. The drive toward self-esteem was increasingly directed through identification with a state whose interest was defined not by the *Mostakfarin* (the privileged), or the *Taghout* (supporters of the Shah), but by the *Mosta'zafin* (the downtrodden and the poor). During the early periods of the postrevolutionary state, therefore, less privileged women achieved recognition, and the state, in return, received legitimation and consolidation from them. At the end of the Iran-Iraq War, the bond between the state and the poor began to wane. It was not until Mahmood Ahmadinejad's campaign for presidency in June 2005 that the alliance appeared to be reviving.

Overall, the revolutionary leaders praised and supported the newly mobilized women. Those women who were immobile or those whose husbands kept them at home joined the revolutionary forces and women's demonstrations. Symbolically, their "revolutionary" activities gained them their husbands' admiration. In turn, the revolutionary establishment

[34] "Servants," "prostitutes," "Westernized," "liberal," and "wealthy," for example, see Naderi's letter, "Andar Hekayat-e 'Tazahorat a'layh-e bad-Hajabi,' (In Stories 'Demonstrations Against Improper Veiling'") in *E'ttela't*, (1 Mehr 1364/ September 23, 1985), 6; "bought," Friedl, *Merip Reports*; and "marriage to the state," is borrowed from Ehrenreich, "Poverty in the American Dream," in her critique of AFDC for poor women.

[35] Bribes, Bahmanpour, "Hers."

praised these men not only as devotees of Islam and anti-imperialism, but also as martyrs, similar to those who shed their blood in the path of Islam. Thus the newly mobilized women became the status symbol of the revolutionary era, in contrast to the Westernized and unveiled women who had been the status symbol under the monarchical state. This may be the reason why the mobilized women continue their class war against their secular sisters. Yet, their new status, symbolic identity, and self-image are purchased at the price of greater subordination in both the private and the public domains.[36]

The mobilized women represent the changing state-gender alliance. While the Pahlavi state mainly responded to the interest of urban middle-class and well-to-do women, the Islamic state initially united itself with the urban poor and segments of lower middle-class, and later with some middle-class women and elite Islamic women. The *basiji* women have been unambiguously instrumental in the implementation of new gender relations in the IRI. This point sharply contradicts the thesis that middle-class women have been the primary engine of change in the "modernization" processes of Iran and the Middle East.[37]

Despite their contribution to the Islamic state and the implementation of reveiling and modesty rules, the gender police have been increasingly unable to prevent resistance, especially against the state's mandated rules relating to sexuality. Stories that are repeatedly told by Iranians and travelers from Iran allude to greater defiance of the public and in particular the youth. One observer stated that as teenage boys and girls were on the alert for the *basijis* in Tehran, they were flirting. The girls were:

> wearing baggy overcoats but showing liberal amounts of hair beneath their colorful head scarves – [the teens] circled coyly on the sidewalk, a few of them summoning the nerve actually to talk to one another. Asked whether he was having any success, a young man reached into his shirt pocket and triumphantly whisked out a scrap of paper. On it was written a phone number.[38]

A visitor from Tehran echoed a similar story. He said:

> While sitting at a park with my female university classmate, we were approached by the *basijis* and were asked what we were doing there. Because I was conservatively dressed and my friend was well-covered, we were not searched or arrested.

[36] Previously immobile women, personal communication, New York City, October 6, 1985; and subordination, Sedghi, "Women, the State."

[37] "Modernization," Moghadam, *Modernizing*.

[38] Baggy overcoats, Lancaster, "Iranian Crusade: Suspecting Liberal Tendencies in Schools, Clerics Launch 'Islamization' Crackdown," A31.

We were annoyed and there was no other place for us to go and not be harassed. But we found greater privacy in the confines of my apartment.[39]

Although substantiated data are missing which would fully explain the unintended consequences of the Islamic Revolution, in particular regarding modesty and gender relations, the state has been experiencing a backlash in its policies of sexuality, especially since the elections of the seventh *Majles* where democracy has suffered a setback.

From the beginning of the twentieth-century to the present, sexuality and veiling practices have been the two sides of the same coin in Iranian politics. Both Pahlavi and IRI leaders manipulated gender issues, through unveiling or reveiling policies, to promote their own political interests, build legitimacy for their own specific rules, and for state-building objectives. In 1936, the first Pahlavi monarch coerced women to *unveil* – in contrast to the Islamic state, which has forced women to *reveil*. The Shah used gender policies to promote secularization and Westernization; conversely, the IRI promoted Islamization and anti-Westernization by controling women's bodies and their sexuality as strategically vital to state consolidation of power.

But the current state is built on the ruins of the old state: reveiling and Islamization helped the clergy to reach its long-awaited dreams as they marked the end of centuries of drawn-out conflicts with adversarial governments to achieve religion's triumph, in particular over women. In defiance, women played important roles in changing, modifying and redefining the veil, reveiling, and gender discourse in different phases of the Islamic regime. With the presence of the gender police, sometimes visible, sometimes not, the Islamic regime has reconstructed women's sexuality, although in this process it has become more fluid as it has responded to some women's concerns, as will be discussed later. Yet in today's atmosphere of globalization and economic decline, reveiling has created unresolved contradictions for the Islamic regime, including the incorporation of women in the labor force and the ensuing shifts in the gender division of labor, both in production and reproduction spheres.

39 My interviews, New York City, Summer 1996.

7

The Gender Division of Labor

The Islamic regime views "women's work in the public sphere as incompatible with household responsibilities," wrote Jaleh Shadi-Talab, a Tehran University sociologist. Its policies, Shahla Jelodarzadeh, the Sixth *Majles* deputy noted, "give preference to men's employment" and "family management to women." Consistently criticized, Mitra Bagherian, a Plan and Budget economist indicated, "women are faulted for lack of compliance with the strict rules concerning head cover or overdress clothes, or even having a trace of cosmetics" and sometimes, are threatened with dismissal. This reflects governmental expectations on "the kind and the extent of the *hejab* at work which leave women contemptuous and cynical, if not rebellious."[1]

Despite earlier restrictions and harsh discriminatory policies that discouraged women's work outside the home, the post-war reconstruction policies and the introduction of economic liberalization induced more women to join the labor market. The number of women in private and public occupations grew, but the share of women in the labor force declined in comparison with the statistics of the late 1970s. Women also entered the educational system in large numbers, and by 2002, they constituted about 71 percent of university enrollments. Alarmed by this upward trend, some officials initiated in 2004, though unsuccessfully, a debate on a quota system to dissuade women from pursuing higher education. Although the Islamic regime preferred to keep women in the household,

[1] Household responsibilites, Shadi-Talab, Jaleh, "Pas az Bisto-Seh Sal," 18; "Family Management," as cited in S. Zar-Abadi, "Zanan Posht-e Divar," 15; "cosmetics" and "rebellious," Sedghi's interview with Mitra Bagherian, Tehran, 1997; enrollments, "Haftad-doyek dar sad-e Vorudiha-ye Daneshgah," 75.

and initially, underreported their labor force participation in the census statistics, with their presence in the economy and the educational system, women have begun to pose indirect challenges to those political and social taboos that uphold motherhood and wifehood as women's primary and only responsibility.

Women's participation in the labor force has been concurrent with an uneven economic development and the regime's integration into the global market. Like its predecessor, the state has relied on oil to interact with the world market and develop its economy. As OPEC's second largest oil producer, Iran holds 9 percent of the world's oil reserves and possesses its second largest natural gas reserves. Yet instability in the world oil market drastically affects its economic boom or bust cycles: oil revenues as a percent of Iran's annual exchange earnings have varied from 85 to 95 percent since 1979. During the 1990s, Iranian liberalization policies gave a modest boost to the economy, and later, brought growth and expansion. But liberalization did not curtail corruption, a high rate of population growth, inflation, pollution, and unemployment. How the Islamic state's integration into the world market reverberated into the economy and women's work, and how women subverted state actions to articulate their economic interests are the foci of this chapter. Shifts in the gender division of labor in the household, marketplace, and informal work sector suggest that despite the setbacks and gender bias, women are increasingly entering the workforce and more significantly, the educational system, thereby slowly transforming social and family relations.

INTERNATIONAL POLITICAL ECONOMY AND ECONOMIC CHANGES

The degree of a state's integration into the global economy depends on a complex web of economic and political relations affecting domestic development processes. In the Islamic Republic, these relations reflect the state's dependence on petroleum resources, its tumultuous interactions with the West, in particular the United States, and the continuous political squabbling among contending national forces. Together, they have generated problems for the economy and its ability to absorb women in the labor force. As a "rentier state," Iran's cumulative oil revenues reached about $100 billion in 1953–79. But shortly after the revolution and during the early period of the Iran-Iraq War in 1980–81, oil revenues descended to an average of about $11 billion. Later, in 1982–83 revenues rose to the $20 billion mark, but with the continuation of the war economy, oil exports plummeted to $6 billion in 1986. Subsequently, the 1990–91 Persian Gulf War improved Iran's oil revenues, which reached $18 billion in

1990, and averaged about 16 billion in subsequent years. In 1997, revenues increased to almost $21 billion, but in 1998–99, they decreased to $9.9 billion, only to ride on the upswing of $24.3 billion in 2000–01 and an estimated $22.9 billion in 2002–03. The unpredictable world oil markets generated unstable revenue for Iran's economy.[2]

During its first decade, the regime's foreign policy conduct also caused strains on its economy. Shortly after the revolution, students following Khomeini's teachings seized the American embassy, the "nest of spies," in Tehran. Although Washington failed in its helicopter rescue mission to free the hostages, it succeeded in freezing Iran's assets and organizing an international trade embargo against Iran. The "October Surprise" or the release of the hostages at President Ronald Reagan's election hardly improved relations between the two countries. Then, the 1980 Iraqi invasion of Iran, with its American support, ravaged Iran's economy further. Industrial output fell by 20 percent in 1980, imports and manufacturing activities dropped, deficits and international debt rose and many unemployed laborers joined the rank of petty commodity producers. Although higher oil prices helped the private sector to resume production and boost manufacturing in 1981–84, economic performance remained weak. The share of manufacturing and construction in non-oil GDP (Gross Domestic Products) decreased, that of the services was almost constant, and agriculture climbed. National income per capita plummeted by almost 50 percent and inflation remained rampant for most of the 1980s. These economic calamities, together with the accentuation of the war and vague economic plans contributed to an economic crisis.[3]

Unlike the Shah's vision of modernization, industrialization and integration within the global economy, the clerical state initially provided no clear economic plan. It declared that it was constructing an "Islamic" new order or an "Islamic" political economy chiefly self-sufficient and independent from the global market. It rejected Pahlavism, Westernism, and the United States or "the Great Satan," while promoting the slogan of "Neither East, nor West, but the Islamic Republic." It also curtailed freedom of speech and activities, fostered gender segregation and prevented women from the judiciary. While stressing private ownership, it also encouraged state intervention in the economy. Under Khomeini's leadership, the government confiscated "anti-revolutionaries'" wealth and assets,

[2] 16 billion, Behdad, "From Populism to Economic Liberalism," 674; 22.9 billion, International Monetary Fund, 28; and Salehi-Isfahani, 602–603.

[3] Industrial output, Behdad, "From Populism," 674; boost manufacturing, *Ibid.*, 4; agriculture climbed, Behdad and Nomani, "Workers, Peasants, and Peddlers," 675; and inflation remained, Behdad, "From Populism," 9.

nationalized banks, insurance companies, and other economic enterprises, and empowered entities such as the Foundation for the Oppressed (*Bonyad-e Mosta'zafin*). Finally, by pushing domestic capitalists out of the country, it actively disrupted production and accumulation. With capital and technology becoming less accessible, economic problems escalated.[4]

In an attempt to reform the ailing economy, the Islamic regime sought to introduce a liberalized path to development in the 1990s. After the U.S.S. Vincennes shot down an Iranian passenger airliner over the Persian Gulf, Iran accepted reluctantly the 1988 United Nations Resolution 598 to end the war hostilities. With Khomeini's death in 1989, Rafsanjani's government (1989–97) accelerated the liberalization of the economy. Indeed, both the World Bank and the International Monetary Fund approved the extension of $850 million in loans in 1994, but the United States blocked them. By 1995, Iran's foreign debt was $30 billion, which it continued to renegotiate. Subsequently the American policy of "dual containment" and its classification of Iran as a "rogue nation" and later, as "Axis of Evil" placed additional strains on its economy as it became increasingly difficult and costly to trade with other countries. But the return of higher oil prices and revenues boosted Iran's economy. The government cut its subsidies, reformed market institutions, and invited domestic and foreign capital to make investments. In 1986–96, gross national income in non-oil GDP grew and unemployment declined significantly. The highest rate of growth occurred in the industrial sector, with agriculture and services falling behind. Nevertheless, the economy continued to lag.[5]

Domestic obstacles to economic liberalization were numerous and diverse. First, the government "floated" the exchange rate from an officially fixed 70 rials to 1,750 rials per U.S. dollar in 1993, although in Tehran's black market, the exchange rate was higher. The government also decontrolled prices and increased the prices of goods. Consumer prices

[4] Global market, Behdad and Nomani, 673; the Foundation, Behdad, "From Populism," 3; and Behdad, "The Post-Revolutionary Economic Crisis," 99–103; economic problems, Razzaqi, and Bank Markazi Jomhuri-ye Eslam, *Bar-resi-ye Tahavvolat-e Eqtesadi-ye Keshvar Ba'daz Engelab*, 1361/1982.

[5] Rafsanjani's government, Behdad and Nomani, 672–676 and 683. Steps taken during his administration included market institutions reforms, resumption of Tehran stock activities, and governmental solicitation of some foreign capital. Oil revenues increased, reaching about $19 billion in 1996. In 1986–96, along with the rising of oil revenues, gross national income, and non-oil gross domestic products grew 3.5 percent and 3.6 percent, respectively. Liberalization also decontrolled prices slowly, decreased state subsidies, increased prices of goods and services that the government offered, relaxed some exchange restrictions and floated the rial in 1993. The United States blocked them, see Behdad, "From Populism," 11; renegotiate, Behdad, "Khatami and His 'Reformist' Economic (Non-)Agenda," entire.

soared by 359 percent in 1990–96 and popular dissatisfaction became a cause of concern. Third, Iran's reproductive policies induced mothers to have more babies during the Iran-Iraq War so that Iran's population growth became one of the highest in the world. In Tehran the 1979 population of almost 4 million swelled to 12 million by 1996; for the entire country, the population jumped from almost 38 million to 60 million in the period of 1976–96. Fourth, migrations to the cities from rural areas also burdened the economy. In 1976 more than half of the population lived in rural areas. By 1996, more than 60 percent were urban residents, despite the diminishing quality of life in urban areas, such as high air pollution, lack of housing and jobs, traffic jams, theft, drugs, prostitution, and crime. The population explosion and rural migration were compounded by a decline in wages, increasing poverty. In 2005, I witnessed children below the age of 10 laboring in shops and construction and as urban peddlers and beggars, sometimes late into the evening.[6]

But economic liberalization sparked some signs of improvement in the new millennium. First, rising oil prices favored Iran's economic growth, and the average growth rate of real GDP was 5.98 percent in 2000–04. Real GDP rose from 5.4 percent to 6.8 percent and remained almost constant at 6.5 percent in 2001–02, 2002–03, and 2003–04, respectively. Second, there was a modest change in the economic structure: agricultural contribution to the GDP was 17.2 percent in 1999–00, 16.6 percent in 2000–01, 16.4 percent in 2002–02, and estimated to be 16.6 percent in 2002–03. During the same period, the industrial sector improved slightly at the rate of 18.4 percent, 19.8 percent, 20.2 percent, 21.2 percent, and 22.5 percent respectively. The service sector declined little at the rate of 54.4 percent, 55.4 percent, 54.1 percent, 53.6 percent, and 51.9 percent, respectively. Thus, while reform created new wealth and power, in particular for domestic monopolies or the "political-financial mafia," the Islamic Republic's uneven integration into the global economy and its "zigzag" legacy of economic transition posed serious implications for changes in the gender division of labor.[7]

SHIFTS IN THE GENDER DIVISION OF LABOR

In the early days of the Islamic Republic and its backlash against the Shah's gender reforms, many women lost their jobs. Confined to their

[6] Consumer prices, Behdad and Nomani, 670–673; and prostitution and crime, *Ibid.*, 682–684; and Judah.

[7] Real GDP, IMF, 6 and 28; changes in economic structure, *Ibid.*, 9; and "political-financial mafia," Behdad, "Khatami."

homes, some women combined household production and reproduction with income-generating activities, thereby joining the growing ranks of the self-employed in the informal economy. Others retired from public life and devoted their time to wifehood and motherhood. Those women who stayed in the public sphere had to adjust to new market realities, policies, and cultural norms and expectations. Islamization projects, Haideh Moghissi noted, encouraged educational institutions and bureaucracy to inculcate *Shi'i* mores and foster occupations where women simultaneously predominated but were powerless. Because the regime viewed reproduction as a woman's primary obligation, there was justification for labor market discrimination, suggested Fatemeh Moghadam. Another perspective from Maryam Poya was that material conditions and women's responses exerted a greater impact on women's employment than did ideological factors. My own view is that the gender division of labor and specifically women's work underwent three shifts, during the early part of the revolution, the Iran-Iraq War, and the post-war reconstruction and liberalization periods.[8]

The early Islamization policies saw the first shift in the gender division of labor and the nature of women's work. Women's labor force participation decreased dramatically. Purification policies (*Paksazi*) resulted in many women losing their jobs, including those who either held high-level positions under the Shah or were suspected of being monarchists. They were told to stay home and develop "Islamic consciousness" and practice modesty. Other women took advantage of a law mandating part-time employment for women and a severance payment edict and returned home as full-time housewives and mothers. A large number of educated and professional women left the labor force voluntarily because of modesty rules, strict gender segregation measures, and workplace harassment. The revolutionaries' attitudes toward female members of religious minorities was mixed. Baha'i women were considered heretic and were dismissed. In contrast, Christian and Jewish women generally kept their positions because the Bible is respected as a holy book. But women who retained their employment – regardless of religious background – had to comply with *hejab* rules and were assigned to gender segregated tasks.[9]

[8] Informal economy, Behdad and Nomani; Islamization projects, among others see Bagherian, *Bar-resi Vizheh-giha-ye Eshteqal-e Zanan dar Iran 1355–1365*, 1, and her "*Eshteqal va Bikari-ye Zanan az Didgah-e Tose'eh*"; Moghissi, *Feminism and Islamic Fundamentalism*, 115; F. Moghadam, "Iran's New Islamic Home Economic"; and Poya, 17.

[9] Sedghi's interview with Mitra Bagherian, 1991. Bahai'es are considered outlaws and the system is intolerant of them.

Adhering to the Islamic tradition, the new leaders encouraged homemaking activities. Prophet Mohammad's declaration that "Heaven is Under Mother's Feet" echoed everywhere. Wall murals in Tehran repeated that a "Woman is the Educator of the Islamic Society" (*Zan Tarbiyat Konandeh-e Jame'-ye Eslami ast*). Relying on their interpretation of Islamic teachings, culture, and jurisprudence, the clerics argued that a woman's primary obligation was to the household not the labor market. They stressed the importance of women's biological and "natural" role in reproduction and required them to nourish their children and extend sexual services to their husbands. In return, they emphasized husbands' contractual and legal obligations to provide a bride price (*mehr*) and full financial support (*nafaqeh*) to wife/ves and their children. Thus came a new conceptualization for the construction of women's labor: the household, not the marketplace was the preferred place for women's work.[10]

The second shift in the gender division of labor came with the war economy during which time, women's labor force participation, in particular among the more devout supporters of the regime, increased slightly. The state's introduction of rationing pushed many women to stand in long waiting lines for food and gasoline. Islamic women of different classes volunteered their labor in the cause of *Shi'ism* against Iraqi secularism and socialism. Some served in the army and a few went to the war front. Others went to work in hospitals, rehabilitation, and charity centers. Many donated food and jewelry, and a few widows and unmarried women offered their services as wives to injured veterans. War casualties, economic dislocation, labor market rigidities, and the need for more women in the marketplace pressed upon the authorities the need to modify its ideological position on gender segregation. Slowly modifying his previous stance, Khomeini encouraged women to "participate in economic, political, and social affairs within the Islamic laws and regulation" and further, to join the war efforts as Mobilized Sisters (*Khaharan-e Basiji*). As demand grew, a few women entered teaching, medicine, and nursing professions and other services that resembled women's nurturing roles at home. The household continued to serve the needs of patriarchy and children.[11]

The third shift in the gender division of labor and women's work followed the post-war reconstruction. Liberalization improved the economy and women's employment opportunities slightly. But government policies

[10] *Nafaqeh*, F. Moghadam, "Iran's New."

[11] Islamic women, Sedghi, "Third World Feminism"; "Islamic law," *Ettela't* as cited in Poya, 80; and nurturing roles, Poya, ch. 4.

in response to the population explosion, had the unintended consequence of improving women's standing. In contrast to earlier pronouncements encouraging larger Islamic families, Khomeini's 1989 verdict (*fatva*) aimed at legitimizing the use of contraceptives and men's sterilization. Wall murals favored small families and aggressive family planning programs succeeded in curbing population problems. Although not legal, abortion became frequent, and the slow reversal of some past directives freed women from frequent pregnancies.[12]

In addition, the 1992 establishment of the Social and Culture Council of Women served as another mechanism to promote women's entry in the public space. More women began to enter the labor market, schools, and colleges. As science and education acquired prominence, and parliamentarians with university degrees debated in the halls of the *Majles* and other key political and economic establishments, educational institutions welcomed girls and women throughout the country. By the early 1990s, socioeconomic and political imperatives somewhat modified the rigid ideological/legal/religious interpretations of women's work and place in the society. This third shift slowly brought an increase in women's self-employment, their participation in the market, and educational attainment.[13]

WOMEN'S LABOR

Women's work in the Islamic state consists of three different types of interrelated labor: in the household, the workforce, and increasingly, the informal economy. Unlike the industrial West where demand for participation in paid production superseded household reproduction, Islamization projects gave precedence to reproductive labor and the strengthening of family values. From the outset, clerical leaders praised and exalted mothers and launched intensive campaigns to honor women's role in nurturing *Shi'i* children, reminiscent of Fatemeh's unfaltering devotion to her sons, in particular Emams Hussein and Hasan. New posters and murals publicized the importance of women as trainers of the Islamic community and state-supported communication networks promoted the role of motherhood and the image of pious and devout mothers. Biology became the prescribed destiny for all Iranian women. In the 1990s, this portrayal of

[12] Population policies are not gender neutral. Sometimes governments exploit women's sexuality to limit or expand their desired population level.

[13] 1990s, F. Moghadam, "Iran's New Islamic," entire.

women was challenged by economic realities as more women entered the labor market and the informal economy. But many women continued to remain responsible for work at home.[14]

The Household

With its active promotion of women's role in household production and reproduction, the new state altered the gender division of labor at home, intensifying women's work. The Iran-Iraq War, economic decline, the fall in incomes, and the growing scarcities and shortages of consumer goods created greater responsibilities for women as household chores exerted extra pressure on their time. Under the Shah, many families enjoyed the availability of modernized home technology, but during the first decade of the Islamic regime, they found it too costly either to refurbish their old household appliances or to replace them. Some women, who could hire maids or place their children in day care were unable to afford assistance in the Islamic state. Consequently, they spent their time on such tasks as shopping, cooking, sewing, and cleaning or even washing clothes by hand and ironing. Less-privileged women managed their family affairs as before, yet the soaring cost of transportation, food, and rents pushed many of them to work harder at whatever meager jobs they could land. While mothers and younger daughters cooperated with the raising of children and maintaining household subsistence, many women of all ages – especially the elderly – waited long hours in lines for food stuffs, kerosene, and oil. A few men assisted with shopping for groceries while working for a living or searching for employment. Nevertheless, the burden of household work remained on women's shoulders.[15]

In addition to the war, the ideological commitment of the young Islamic state to population growth added an extra burden to women's work in the household. In the 1980s, the state made contraceptives inaccessible and promoted the idea that when women cooperated with men to share their life-long responsibilities, they elevated Islamic moral values. These population policies accommodated official calls for legitimation of temporary marriage (*siqeh*). In 1990, President Rafsanjani stated in a sermon that "young people did not have enough money for a proper Persian wedding" and recommended that "it would not be un-Islamic for widows

[14] Work at home or household labor includes unpaid management work plus wifely and motherly activities. Here, work and labor are used interchangeably – paid or unpaid.

[15] Women's shoulders, this is based on my own observations and personal interviews during several field trips.

or divorced women to 'have a temporary relationship – temporary marriage – with someone else.'" Despite conflicting views within the government, one report indicated that "prostitution has made a comeback, and [Rafsanjani's] sermon gave impetus to an already growing call-girl business." Assailing male officials for bolstering *siqeh* marriage, one high-ranking woman scolded: "Only a backward looking think-tank would propagate imprisonment of women in homes and their status as temporary wives to rich men."[16]

Government policies succeeded. In 1976–86, the ratio of married to unmarried women rose from 47 percent to 57 percent. This rise accommodated a population growth rate of almost 4 percent per year. Consequently, the regime modified its previous pro-natalist stance and pledged to curb fertility rates in its First Five Year Development Plan (1989–93) and after. It set up a Fertility Regulation Council with the task of organizing educational programs for the public "to improve access to a wide range of contraceptive methods" free of charge and to conduct research studies on family planning methods. It distributed contraceptives, supported male and female sterilization, and called for smaller Islamic families. Relieved from the burden of reproduction and household work, some women began to rechannel their energies into studying, attending schools, or continuing their education at universities. But it was the economic requirements of the state, not Islam and Islamic interpretations, that shaped population policies directly, and exploited women's sexuality indirectly.[17]

On the domestic front, women made some small gains. Powerful establishment women have been especially active. As fervent supporters of the revolution, they claim a special privilege to hold the government responsible for its silence on women's subordination, lack of

[16] *Siqeh*, Sciolino, "From the Back Seat," A4; "Persian wedding," *Ibid.*; "call girl," *Ibid.*; and "rich men," Razai, 43–45. Using the system against its own restrictions, some divorced women rely on the *siqeh* system to justify their relationships to their traditional friends and relatives who would normally downgrade unmarried partnerships. Also, many secular women used the system during the revolution in order to avoid harassment while holding political meetings.

[17] 57 percent, "Davzdah Shart-e Estekhdam-e Khanevadeh," 1; 4 percent, Ashtiani, 13; family planning methods, UNFPA; and Nassehi, "The Islamic"; women's sexuality – note that in *siqeh* marital contracts, women negotiate a price for their sexual services for a specific designation of time, but in permanent marital contracts, the husband provides fianancial support or *nafaqeh* and the bride's price or *mehr*, and wifely duties consist of submitting to the husband's will and sexual demands, to bear his children, and perform household labor. Despite contractual agreements, both types of marriages provided little immunity for women, in particular at divorce.

compensation for their household activities and men's growing powers, especially at unilateral divorce. In a partial response to women's complaints and the rising divorces in 1984, the Islamic regime introduced new marital contracts with numerous provisions negotiable at divorce. Of interest is the "equal division" provision or the sharing of a man's wealth accumulated during marital life. It stipulated that a prenuptial agreement would legally entitle divorcing women to half of their husbands' earnings only if husbands agreed. A few elite women opted for a more effective reform by placing greater pressure on legislators to ratify the Labor Compensation Bill or the *Ojrat-ol Mesl* (wages in cash) Act. This was somewhat similar to the 1970s notion of wages for housework that American feminists introduced. A 1991 revised version of the divorce law stated that if the marriage contract failed to include the wealth sharing provision at a unilateral divorce, the husband must pay his wife "the wage equivalent" or wages for household work performed during marriage. Zahra Mostafavi, Khomeini's daughter, supported the bill in a nationally televised speech. Zahra Shoja'i, Khatami's Adviser on Women's Affairs, noted Islam hailed women's wages because "Islam does not require women to work at home for free. A woman deserves payment for housework." In 2002, upon further lobbying by female legislators, *Shoray-e Negahban* (the Guardian Council) modified the divorce measure. It authorized women to divorce their husbands, only if an Islamic judge endorsed their divorce applications on a case-by-case basis.[18]

Despite the decline in fertility, rise in marriage age, and marital reforms in recent years, most women would prefer to stay home than participate in the market. Educated, middle-class, and older women who were purged by purification policies felt too alienated to return to their profession, even if they were invited back. Those who were born after the revolution

[18] 1984, F. Moghadam; 1991, Ghazi, "Helping," A2 – this bill specified that a woman's claim for wages in cash is valid if the divorce is filed within three years after termination of the marriage. But skeptics argue that the legal system makes this difficult to apply. Not many women are familiar with the law, and many will not file a lawsuit. Moreover, because the law counts a woman's testimony as half of a man's, many women might find themselves unqualified. Furthermore, the high cost of litigation may discourage many women who cannot financially compete with men. If there were no difficulties for women to apply, it would still be nearly impossible for the man to generate enough payment to compensate for her many years of labor, especially for women of lesser means; Shoja'i, "Divorce Payment," A3; Council, "Iran Women Get More Divorce Rights," http://news.bbc.co.ny/2hi/middle_east/2534375.stm (December 12, 2002); and *Mir-Hosseini, Divorce*. Note that although divorce is on the rise, data are unavailable on lawsuits and women's success at receiving compensation for their household labor, which are costly and difficult to implement.

preferred to stay home because they could not land suitable employment or encountered gender bias at work. Although political and market conditions are becoming more hospitable to women's labor force participation, many women choose and follow the footsteps of their culture. Strong family ties persist in the Middle East and Iran, and many women draw their identity from being wives, mothers, and daughters, rather than as individuals or professionals.[19]

A sample survey of 250 educated married women, ages 20 to 50 conducted in Tehran in 2002 corroborated women's preference for the household than the marketplace. Twenty-two percent of these women were employed and the rest were housewives. The study asked: "if you and your husband had equal salary but one of you needed to quit your job to attend to family concerns at home, which one of you would resign?" Ninety-five percent of respondents favored that wives terminate their occupations, and only 3.3 percent wanted men to leave their posts to be househusbands. Even if women earned greater incomes, the survey found, 78 percent of respondents wanted the wives to leave their jobs while only 17 percent expected the husbands to stop working. Not surprised by her findings, Nahid Keshavarz concluded that most Iranian women identify themselves with the family as mothers and wives, not as market participants. Despite their disposition for home, more women welcomed the opportunity to join the public world of work when it opened its doors to them.[20]

The Marketplace

Depending on their political and economic projects, states often promote specific ideologies regarding labor requirements. The Islamic regime reinforced those cultural and religious precepts that assigned the public sphere of work to men and that of the private to women. While many women initially lost their jobs a few years into the revolution, the marketplace slowly began to open its doors to them with Rafsanjani's presidency. Census data do not support this, and the share of women in the active labor force remains lower than it was in 1979. But official compilation needs modification. For example, Census data do not enumerate rural women

[19] Decline in fertility, Salehi-Isfahani; and purification policies, Sedghi's interview with Fatemeh (Shahin) Erfan, former Deputy Mayor, 1997, 2002, and 2005.

[20] Nahid Keshavarz, 86–105. Of the total of women Keshavarz surveyed, 13 percent had higher education, 19 percent had college degrees, 25 percent had some university education, 39 percent had high school degrees, and 34 percent had less than high school diplomas. Their husbands' educational level was almost the same.

who perform unpaid labor or low wage family jobs. In addition, urban independent wage earners or professional women who work in the informal sector tend to underreport their labor activities. Other reasons for not disclosing income earning jobs to data collectors include tax evasion, resisting possible legal entanglement with authorities, or simply revealing little information (*kam goo'ie*). In contrast, the government excludes the income earnings of gender police's work from its data, as discussed earlier. Given this statistical quandary, it is possible that there is greater female participation in the labor market than officially stated.

The structure of the labor force and women's participation in it has undergone significant changes under the Islamic Republic. Nationwide, the labor force or active population (employed and unemployed) increased from 9.8 million to 12.8 million to 18 million in 1976, 1986, and 1996, respectively. Women's labor force participation decreased from 1.45 million in 1976 to 1.31 million in 1986, but rose to 2.0 million in 1996. Despite this rise in absolute number, in 1996 the percent share of women in the labor force was lower than in 1976. First, the percent share of active women in the total female population was 12.9 percent in 1976, 8.2 percent in 1986, and 9.1 percent in 1996. During the last days of the Shah, the share of active women was higher in Iran than in the entire Middle East, with the exception of Turkey and Israel. As the revolution progressed, a larger proportion of men entered the labor force, more women lost their jobs, and there was high enrollment of women in educational institutions, which together accounted for lower female participation in the labor market. Second, the percent share of active women in total labor force fell from 15 percent in 1976 to almost 10 percent in 1986, but rose to 12.53 percent in 1996. These data suggest that although the share of active women in the total labor force rose in 1996 in comparison to 1986, it was still lower than 1976. The increase between 1986 and 1996 occurred during the third shift in the gender division of labor, the period of liberalization, however, the percent share of active women in the labor force remained below that of the level of 1976.[21]

[21] Structure of labor, all figures here are based on the population of 10 years of age and older. Unless stated otherwise, all figures come from Statistical Center of Iran, *Iran Statistical Yearbook 1379*. International Labor Organization and the United Nations offer their own figures that are somewhat different. 2.0 million, *Ibid.*, 82–83; 1996 percent share (note that Bagherian's 1976 figures appear lower than previous Census's – possibly figures were lowered to hide the slow change). The share of Iranian women in 1976 labor force figures was high for the Middle East, but by 1986, this share was lower than all those countries. Whereas ideological factors, economic stagnation, and structural changes contributed to lower participation of women in Iran especially in agriculture

Political and economic reforms and ideological relaxation of the regime contributed to women's inducement to join the labor market. Nationwide, the total of employed women consisted of 1.2 million, 975,000, and 1.7 million in 1976, 1986, and 1996, respectively. In urban areas, women's employment increased: 460,000, 525,000, and 991,000 for the same years. As urbanization and migration to cities rose and educational opportunities increased in rural areas, employment of rural women declined from 752,000 in 1976 to 446,000 in 1986 but rose to 766,000 in 1996. By 1996, women's employment in both public and private occupations was greater than in 1976.

In 1996, urban women's employment was concentrated in the services. The distribution of women's employment in urban areas in 1996 was 21.2 percent in industry, 73.6 percent in services, and 2.1 percent in agriculture. But women's greater participation in the services reflect gender-typing occupations, a policy that the regime promoted along with its ideological predisposition.[22]

Gender-typing occupations have been more persistent in the state sector, particularly in education. The government has been the main employer of women, both in relative and absolute terms. Women's employment in the state sector grew from 30 percent to 42 percent to 60 percent in 1976, 1986, and 1996, respectively. The proportion of women with the rank of director or above has been constant for the past 40 years. Moreover, some women made it to the halls of the *Majles* as legislators and various ministries. Many female public servants entered health-related services and educational institutions. Promoting Islamic values and norms, the government invested in gender segregated schools, universities, and literacy classes specializing in reading the *Qoran*. The Ministry of Culture and Higher Education together with the Ministry of Education recruited

and manufacturing, women's percentage in education rose – see also F. Moghadam (her figures are based on ILO and *Salnameh*; mine are entirely based on *Salnameh*), and Bagherian; active, Statistical Center of Iran, *Socio-Economic Characteristics of Women in Iran 1986–96*, 1, 91, and 95.

[22] Women's employment, *Statistical 1379*, 82–83. The total population consisted of 23 million, 32.8 million, and 45.4 million in 1976, 1986, and 1996, respectively. Of the total, there were 11.2 million, 16 million, and 22.3 million women and 11.7 million, 16.8 million, and 23 million men during the same years. Men's participation in the total labor force continued to climb to 8.3 percent, 11.5 percent, and 13.9 percent during 1976, 1986, and 1996, respectively. In urban areas, labor force participation of women advanced from 489,000 to 741, 000 to 1.1 million in 1976, 1986, and 1996, respectively. Similar figures for men were 3.8 million, 6.3 million, and 8.5 million. For the same years, *Socioeconomic*, 195.

503,321 women, and the Ministry of Health and Medical Education employed 265,447 women in 1996. A 2002 governmental ruling also permitted women to serve as headmasters for boy's primary schools.[23]

These nationwide efforts to encourage learning opportunities created a valuable space for the growing youth population, and younger women took advantage of this option to nourish their minds. Some rural teenagers found *Qoran* reading classes preferable to staying at home and many welcomed the idea of interacting with a young male *mullah* as a teacher. In 1996, the nation's literacy rate among girls rose by 42.5 percent, and today, Iran is almost reaching total literacy. But with more girls and women in classrooms, labor force participation in rural areas dropped compared to urban areas, which offered greater job possibilities. The government's commitment to expand schooling and its increasing demand for female teachers came along with its commitment to gender segregation. Students who attended mixed schools under the previous regime had little choice but to change their schools at the outset of the revolution. Gender segregated schooling eventually became a norm, and traditional urban and rural families could send their daughters to schools for the first time, as all girls' schools were appealing to their cultural taste. The percentage of female students climbed from 14.85 percent to 16.58 percent to 26.6 percent in 1976, 1986, and 1996, respectively. This was a stark contrast to the early twentieth-century when only a few privileged girls had a limited opportunity for schooling and teaching.[24]

Women's educational progress has been unprecedented in the nation's history and unmatched in other Muslim countries. The conservative clerics and a few reformists continue to view women's work and their participation in professional fields threatening to their reproductive activities at home. From the outset of the revolution, the government deliberately included women in certain studies while it excluded them from many different fields. It provided access to traditional domestic fields such as hygiene, sewing, cooking, and homemaking. But after the war, it permitted the increasing number of women who had achieved high scores in their entrance examination at medical schools to enter obstetrics/gynecology, which was closed to men, pediatrics, dentistry, and family medicine. It also applied a quota system to female students and closed many fields of

[23] Absolute terms, Shadi-Talab; women's employment, F. Moghadam; Ministry, *Statistical 1379*, 109; and boy's primary schools, *Zanan* 87, 1381/2002, 68.

[24] Youth population, F. Moghadam; and *Qoran*, my 1997 interviews. Absence of teachers in some rural areas led religious men to take initiatives to teach; total literacy, *Socioeconomic*, 85; and percentage of female, *Ibid.*

study in technical and scientific areas and vocational schools. In 1994, it lifted the ban and permitted women to enter all fields of study. In 2002, 71 percent of entry level college students were women. Alarmed by the large number of women in education, some officials proposed a new quota system to limit the number of women who can enter medical schools and other areas of higher education. But women have made a space of their own, not so comfortably, but as professionals who study and practice as lawyers, doctors, journalists, deputies, corporate executives, professors, lobbyists, writers, film makers, and publishers.[25]

Women are eminently critical of their work environment. Their mobility and sexuality is constantly held in check on the grounds that they could seduce or arouse men's sexual passions. During the early revolutionary days, the sound of women's shoes, for example, was considered sexually stimulating. A female government employee expressed her dismay with the Dismissal Edict (*Hokm-e Ta'liq*) by saying that "every day when I come to work, the guards criticize my look, my overdress and my loose trousers. They make me tense and unhappy. I am always anxious at work." Although different offices practice various degrees of control, many organizations prefer the *chador* but accept the combination of the tunic and scarf provided that they are in navy, brown, gray, or black. All government offices have security patrols who check the appropriateness of the clothing and the *hejab* of employees or visitors. Sometimes in gender segregated booths, female guards conduct body and hand bag searches. In 1991, after a thorough search at Bank Markazi, a guard gave me a large safety pin to tighten my scarf under my neck. Another guard at the Bank-e Mellat checked a woman's purse and confiscated her perfume, make-up and hand lotion and recommended that the searched woman use oil and lemon juice on her hands. Other guards at the Ministry for the Promotion of Islam did not check employees' purses, perhaps assuming that women who work in that office observed the rules more carefully. Women are almost accustomed to irritating rules but many have learned to work with little incentives, I noticed in 2005.[26]

[25] Activities at home, Shadi-Talab, 18; family medicine, Moghissi, *Feminism*, 155–157; fields of studies, F. Moghadam, "Iran's New"; college level, *Zanan*, 95 1381/2002, 75; and university studies, Golnaz Esfandiar, "Number of Female University Students Rising Dramatically in Iran," http:www.payvand.com/news/03/nov/1133.html.

[26] "Anxious at work," personal interviews, Tehran, 1991; and perfume, and Ministry, *Ibid.* Note that security guards at government offices or airports became more relaxed under the Khatami regime; and they became more respectful to their visitors.

But perpetually criticized, searched, and watched, many women are losing their motivations. The Islamic state condemned the Pahlavis for promoting women as sexual commodities, yet it fails to value women's performance, and in many ways it trivializes their work. Some women complain about the lack of recognition in a male-dominated world of work. In my 1991 interviews, two highly educated women revealed their discontent because as professionals they "received little feedback or appreciation on [their] achievements and felt [their] contribution mattered scarcely." Discouraged and disappointed, they expressed little enthusiasm "to continue pursuing [their] interesting work." Another female official in a managerial position in one of the ministries indicated: "women run into all kinds of sexual discrimination in high level positions. We are systematically at war with male colleagues who will somehow try to humiliate us if they sense we are dedicated and ambitious." In 2002, another unhappy female official asked me about the possibility of moving to and living in New York. Many displeased female employees seek other work alternatives. They join rising educated and uneducated women who participate in the informal labor market and choose other channels of work by engaging in self-employment.[27]

The Informal Labor Market

The expansion of the informal labor market is one of the most distinct characteristics of the Islamic economy. It includes a substantial rise in petty-commodity production and self-employment. While some of these activities are reported, most stay outside the domain of governmental scrutiny. Official census provide data on the self-employed, those who seek work, the unemployed, and homemakers. Iranian labor studies view the urban self-employed as those who hold professional occupations or work in government administration, home industry, small workshops, grocery stores, family workers, street peddlers, and cab drivers. But women's participation in the informal sector has yet to be examined. Without substantiated data, this preliminary attempt can only highlight trends in women's self-employment and in turn, provide a comprehensive view of women's work in contemporary Iran. Some urban middle-class or educated

[27] "Interesting work," Sedghi's 1991 interviews, Tehran. In another field trip in 1997, I was unable to locate these two women at their jobs or home addresses; and "ambitious," Ghazi, "Helping Women," 2. New York, personal interviews, Tehran, 2002.

professional women manage various business ventures from home. There are also street vendors and *bazaar* peddlers in various cities. In 2002, I saw many Afghani refugees and Iranian women who begged or sold small items in *bazaars* of Bam, Kerman, Yazd, and Tehran, similar to their sisters in Qom and Ardebil that I witnessed in 2005. Runaway girls and prostitutes constitute another category of the urban self-employed. They remain outside the purview of official reports.[28]

The work of self-employed women is diverse. There are women who produce and exchange the products of their labor from their homes. Some run knitting and sewing businesses. An interviewee who had lost her government job after the revolution chose to take early retirement, and with her severance pay of 200,000 rials ($27,000), bought three knitting machines at the cost of 18,000 rials ($2,400) each to start her own home-based business. Another was a seamstress whose European fashion shop had been closed down; she started a boutique for her wealthy clients at her residence. Others began ballet, aerobics, yoga, meditation, and massage classes in their homes. Women have also opened up hair salons; some hired working-class women to provide services as waxers, threaders (*band-andaz*), or fortune tellers. Many women allocate a part of their living space to sell clothes or household items that belong to other women or their friends; they sometimes travel to neighboring countries to buy goods to sell. Part-time maids continue to work and assist the more privileged women with household chores. Those Iranian women who are English and French teachers or high school and college graduates provide private lessons in their homes to students preparing for university entrance examinations or in foreign language instruction. In order to avoid taxes and governmental interference, a small group of architects run home-based businesses. Overall, a lack of jobs, state restrictions, the need for an income, and the necessity to integrate professional with personal household work encourage many women to participate in the informal sector, which remains conveniently outside of governmental jurisdiction.[29]

[28] Government scrutiny, Behdad and Nomani, 678 and 682; and women's participation, Shadi-Talab, 2001 and 2003, 18–20. This section incorporates only that kind of work that may not be legally sanctioned or fail to appear in official statistics. Personal observation, interviews, and scattered studies reveal that home-based activities may take place outside the public sector, at home, or on the street.

[29] Home-based business, Sedghi's interviews, New York City, 1982 – exchange rate calculations are based on 1982 figures; fortune tellers, my various observations and interviews; and government jurisdiction, Sciolino, "From the Back," A 4; and Hedges, A4.

Difficult to acknowledge, but a different category of self-employed laborers consists of runaway girls, prostitutes (*fohasha* or *zanan-e khiabani*), and sex workers. Official reports do not discuss the activities of these women, although welfare authorities have noted with alarm the increasing numbers of women in these ranks. Unofficially there are an estimated 300,000 prostitutes in Iran, including 84,000 in Tehran. There are also an approximate two million homeless women, and one million who lack any kind of social benefits. Poverty, patriarchy, and drugs are major triggers in the lives of these women. As political, economic, and social conditions fail to meet the challenges of the poor and the underclass, many join the lives of these powerless women. Moreover, abusive fathers often push their children toward this dire destiny. While Iranian laws offer little empowerment to girls, they grant the ownership and possession of young daughters to fathers and authorize early marital contracts that entail the sale or exchange of daughters as sexual objects. Adult men involved in the drug trade have also been known to sell their daughters in exchange for cash or drugs. An addicted father forcibly sold his 15 year-old daughter several times in return for drugs or cash for the purchase of drugs.[30]

Many women are joining the rank of runaway girls and prostitutes. There are an estimated 2 to 6 million drug addicts in Iran, one-third of whom are women. Fifty percent come from families involved in the drug trade. There are an estimated 4,000 runaway girls. Many runaway girls leave their abusive parents in search of a more secure life. A few small town and country girls leave their parents' homes for larger cities only to discover a bleak future not better than the one they left behind. Young, high-priced call girls increasingly work as sex workers. In 2005, I witnessed exchanges between some of these well-spoken and chic women and their male accomplices in the luxurious Niavaran neighborhood of northern Tehran. Some need the cash income and some may engage in a form of social protest against taboos and alienation. In poorer sections of the capital, in its southern quarters, *chador*-clad women, some probably "heroine-addicted, sleep in certain parks and cluster near toilets for a quick wash or to shoot up." The growing concern with prostitution generated a heated debate on the establishment of "decency houses" to be drawn up

[30] Prostitutes, Tavakolli, *Fasl-e Zanan*, 67–73; and social benefits, Muir. Hopelessness and lack of social benefits contribute to this problem; and abusive fathers, Ebrahimi, 20–23 – see also Panahi's film, "The Circle." *Fasl-e Zanan* (1380/2001) devotes two sections to prostitution and street women. Purchase of drugs, Sadr, "Dokhtaran-e Irani," 12–14.

by the Interior Ministry's Deputy for Social Affairs. Some clerics opposed the plan, as it might be construed as a testimony to the regime's failure, or inconsistent with its Islamic principles. But the state has experienced other contradictions, in particular, regarding gender and women's work.[31]

CONTRADICTIONS

From the outset, the Islamic regime preferred to keep women at home and engaged with reproductive tasks to be consistent with its cultural heritage. Paradoxically, women's continued resistance called to question the state's preferences and its contradictory behavior. One of these contradictions involved Islam's interpretation of women's right to work and their participation in the labor market and the reality of preventing women from work under the new system. The religion sanctions women's economic activities and theoretically an Islamic state lacks religious authority or ideological arguments to prevent women from participating in the labor force. But the regime's gender segregated policies terminated many women's jobs, in particular those positions that required significant interaction with men. Inconsistencies between religious interpretations and state policies led to occupational discrimination to which elite Islamic women responded rigorously. Staunch advocates of the Islamic revolution, they claimed legitimacy to the state and demanded the elevation of their rights. They criticized the government for fostering patriarchal tendencies and accused it of failing to integrate women in the economy and high-level positions in politics.

In their attempt to amend the state's exclusionary gender policies, elite Islamic women challenged their own fathers, brothers, and husbands. They stressed the inherent tensions between Islamic precepts and regime practices. Fa'ezeh Hashemi Rafsanjani, a 1996 member of Parliament and the youngest daughter of former President Rafsanjani, argued that "Islam [is] liberating" and insisted that "wearing traditional clothing need not impede a woman's career." Shahla Habibi, a former special consultant to the President on Women's Affairs and a cohort of the Hashemi family, strongly advised senior officials to "put aside 'narrow-mindedness' and appoint women to high office." Maryam Behroozi, a former *Majles* deputy, criticized the government for "hypocricy" because Islam does not prevent women from top jobs; only backward men and an ignorant society

[31] 6 million, Tavakolli, "Ta'sir-e Amuzesh va Eshteqal," 1382/2003, 70; 50 percent, *Ibid.*, 71; 4, 000; *Ibid.*; taboos and alienation, Muir; and "shoot up," Judad, 44.

discriminate against women. Fatemeh Haqiqatjoo, another former *Majles* deputy noted that many men are assigned as "deputy ministers without having an hour of managerial experience. So why not give women these chances?"[32]

Prominent secular women also highlighted women's exclusion from public positions. Jaleh Shadi-Talab wrote that there are not theoretical impediments to women's participation in public space, but in practice, "gender has become the criterion for the selection of men to high-ranking positions" and "women to household management." Shirin Ebadi, the 2003 Nobel Laureate in Peace who was appointed in November 1996 as the first female assistant prosecutor, contended that regardless of their theological knowledge and their righteousness, women are categorically prevented from participating in major decision-making bodies. She noted that women are forbidden to serve as *Mojtaheds* (religious judges and interpreters), or lead Friday prayers because they are not superior to men. They are also prohibited by religious and civil laws to lead or serve as members of the *Faqih* (expert religious jurist). They are additionally banned from the *Shoray-e Khebregan* (the Experts Council) because it requires each member to be a *Mojtahed* prior to joining. Women are legally entitled to work with the *Shoray-e Negahban* (Guardian Council), but they are not appointed to this institution that oversees the state's political and theological interests. Last, women cannot be presidents. Thus, articulating their rights, elite Islamic women took the initiative to disclose the tensions between Islamic precepts and state practices, regarding women's work and gender bias.[33]

The second contradiction involved the tension between the "tradition" of women's labor force participation that had developed under the Pahlavi state and reversing it in the new society. The Islamic regime inherited an employment and educational environment that had been shaped considerably by women's integration into the workforce and their legitimate claim to earn a respectful living. Culturally and socially sanctioned, women's work acquired recognition and employed women obtained a degree of

[32] "Narrow-mindedness," and hypocricy, Behroozi; Ghazi, A11 and A2; and Haqiqatjoo, Bahari.

[33] "Gender has become," J. Shadi-Talab, "Zan dar Tose'eh," 8–9; Ebadi, *Tarikhcheh va Asnad-e Huquq-e Bashar*, 128. Article 115 of the constitution designates the president to be elected from among the high religious and political elites, but high religious authorities refuse to qualify women as elites to head the highest institution of the land. Despite legal barriers, a few women ran for president in the 1997 elections – Haeri, "Mrs. President: Women and Political Leadership in Iran," videotape, 2001.

financial independence as well as self-esteem and autonomy. Work also contributed to a relaxation of sexual mores and those cultural habits that reinforced segregation, limited public mobility, and regulated gender social relations. The Islamic regime's dissolution of these rights was perplexing to women who made a living under the previous state but became alienated and dismissed overnight. Purification and job dismissal policies that intended to address sexuality, women's work, and gender separation intimidated many employed and unemployed women who had long struggled for greater involvement in the labor market. Although the liberalization policies of the 1990s welcomed more women to join the occupational ladder, the repeal of the earlier policies left a permanent mark as it escalated the chasm between the state and gender.[34]

The third contradiction consisted of the state's need to develop gender-specific occupations while its overall plan was to restrict the labor force participation of women. During the first revolutionary decade, the regime's enforcement of gender segregation in the workforce intended to restrict women's opportunities and to prevent physical interactions between professional men and women. But these policies created a shortage of women in crucial positions such as teaching, medicine, and nursing. Given the Islamization mandates and the government's population increase programs, it was germane to encourage women to study, train, and work in those areas. Paradoxically, in order to resolve this contradiction, the state diminished educational standards of those professions. With little training or advanced education, a new labor force of semi-professional women in teaching, nursing, and medicine focused on women's needs and their healthcare. With economic reforms, this trend reversed itself somewhat as more women took advantage of availability of literacy and education classes, making their way to higher learning institutions and a more diversified labor market.

The fourth contradiction came with the reformist President Khatami who promised greater openness but failed to implement it fully. With Hojjatol Eslam (Sign of God) Seyyed Mohammad Khatami's election in 1997, the regime softened its foreign policy posture toward the United States, calling for "equal rights and dignity" of all nations, "civilizational dialogue," and the establishment of democracy, law and order, and civil society at home. Khatami promised, especially to women and youth, who were the backbone of his electoral victory, social and political participation, freedom of speech, openness, and democracy. He pledged to create

[34] Purification, Sciolino, "From the Back."

more jobs. But in the same year, the *Majles* passed two pieces of legislation that aimed at gender segregation in the workplace and further, the concealment of women's sexuality: it ruled to enforce gender segregation of all medical facilities and outlawed the publication of women's pictures on magazine covers and those writings that might elicit sexual tensions between men and women. Moreover, political squabbling between the supporters and opponents of reforms led to a crackdown on freedom of press, the banning of many publications, and arrest, imprisonment, disappearance, or execution of protesting newspaper editors, students, intellectuals, and activists. Thus, the promise of reform led to more perils for women.[35]

Overall, working women continue to fight an uphill battle, although economic growth has somewhat compensated for earlier layoffs and restrictions. Statistical reports indicate the recent share of women in the labor force has recently declined in comparison with the 1970s. But given the growth of the informal labor sector and under reporting, it is difficult to conclude with certainty if there really are relatively fewer women participating in the labor market now. Unemployment remains high for both women and men, but much higher for women, chiefly younger professionals. Significantly, more women are seeking higher education and the gap between male and female literacy, notably among the youths, is reducing sharply. Of paramount importance is the entry of educated and university female graduates in the workforce. Visibly present, professional women in the public space pose implicit challenges to those traditional norms and cultural taboos that uphold gender segregation and the primary importance of homemaking as women's identity.

Gender policies have been central to the state's development strategies and change in Iran. In its modernization and Westernization drives, the Pahlavi state attempted to integrate mostly urban women into the labor market and relaxed many of the traditional social and religious mores, especially those pertaining to sexuality. When the clergy regained power, it redefined the position of women as one of the *most* important political projects of the new state. It strove to regain control of women's sexuality and their paid work, while simultaneously sanctifying domesticity and women's role as reproducers. Concomitant with its Islamization programs, notably in the establishment of new sexual mores and

[35] "Civilizational dialogue," UNDP, *Human Development Report 2002*, 64. On the index of law and order, Iran receives −.39 in the UNDP study. Imprisonment, Abrahamian, "Iran" in Kesselman, et al.

gender segregation measures, the postrevolutionary state legislated new policies pertaining to women's work and men's control over their decisions. It restricted their employment opportunities, especially with the passage of a law mandating part-time employment for women and then, purification policies removed many women from the jobs. In this respect, as Poya suggests, "segregation has been successful in reconciling the needs of the economy with the ideological basis of the state" as women are placed in hierarchical work situations, excluded from mobility, and concentrated in low-status jobs. But turning the state's manipulative policies to their advantage, women pursued education and advanced to the rank of experts. In so doing, women exerted pressure upon the government to modify its stance by expanding women's employment and restraining its gender segregation policies at work. Although not always successful, women continue to resist the state and its authority.[36]

[36] Poya, 12.

8

Politics and Women's Resistance

Shirin Ebadi, the 2003 Nobel Laureate in Peace disclosed that "it is not easy to be a woman in Iran," because some laws "make it tough for women to be active." The civil rights advocate contends that the revolution made her "a fighter" like a "cacti in the desert" who stayed "strong to survive." Claiming that Islam is compatible with democracy, she asserts that the religion is misused by "male-dominated Muslim states" which justify gender inequality "when in fact this practice has its roots in patriarchal cultures prevailing in these societies." In her legal practice, she defends the rights of women, children, political prisoners and dissidents, although she spent twenty-five days in solitary confinement for having presented a witness in a political murder case. "Our lady of peace," chanted thousands of enthusiastic supporters at Tehran's airport as she returned home with her trophy. "This is not my award, it belongs to the people of Iran," she declared, with tears in her eyes. "This prize means freedom, development of peace and democracy." Today's Iranian women are "steel magnolias, not shrinking violets." They work, participate in politics, articulate their demands, and significantly, they seek entitlement to their rights, as women, and as equal members of the state and society. Rich or poor, secular or religious, young or old, women in the Islamic state find ways around or resist obstacles.[1]

[1] Ebadi, interview with *Le Monde*, 10–12; "fighter," Howard, 77; "male-dominated," as cited by O'Connor; "Our lady," "prize," and "democracy," *Le Monde*, *Ibid.*, 10; "magnolias," Sciolino, *Persian Mirrors*, 32; and household responsibilites, Shadi-Talab, "Pas az Bisto-Seh Sal," entire.

Women in the Islamic Republic are not passive. They are active and engage in the politics of resistance. They exert pressure on the system, pose important questions, express their concerns, and above all demand that they have rights as women and citizens. Not only do they seek responses to their interests, but they search for alternative ways to amend if not modify policies, thereby moving the wheels of incremental transformation. Active women are diverse and their activities intersect with their class background, ideology, the degree of their religious identity, and the geographical setting of their environment. More secular and middle-class, many urban opponent women redefine veiling practices and gender policies almost daily. They utilize innovative tactics and engage in unprecedented creative methods to challenge policies, and more slowly the parameters of the system itself. In contrast, the proponents, including urban elite and middle-class women, strive to promote women's rights within the confines of Islamic law. As discussed previously, there are also the less privileged gender police who bolster the state's legitimacy by inflicting mores on women's modesty and gender relationships. Not the focus of this book, the activities of small town and rural women warrant attention as well. While active women have overlapping interests and perspectives, in particular, in their critique of patriarchal tendencies, they differ on many issues, including veiling and reveiling, state-gender-religion relationships, and women's place in the Islamic society.

Governmental and religious leaders also have diverse views on veiling, women's position and gender relations. Although the *Majles* has enacted many laws on gender issues, the regime prefers not to promote public debate on the *hejab*, fearing that its "politicization" may intensify existing political divisions among contending political factions. How women with different views and political agendas attempt to subvert state actions to advance their interests and how they resist policies and state mandates and induce tangible and symbolic results are the foci of this last chapter. My purpose is to underline the politics of reveiling and its counterpart, the politics of resistance. It is my firm conviction that gender remains a core concern of politics as women continue to exert pressure on the state and its position of power. Gender is important to politics, and politics is important to gender.

WOMEN'S RESISTANCE

That many women have responded to the policies of the Islamic regime testifies to the strength of women's agency in Iran, unlike Afghanistan,

Kuwait, and Saudi Arabia. Women's growing awareness and resistance under the IRI have elicited more comprehensive scholarship than did prerevolutionary women. Writing from exile, some studies praised the accomplishments of "Islamic feminists" from "within an Islamic discourse." Haleh Afshar contended that the "Islamist elite feminists" are in the vanguard engaging the government and negotiating changes on behalf of women. She suggested that women have "bridged the gap that divided Islamists and secularists by fighting together for the cause of women." But arguing against the construct of "Islamic Feminism" as "oxymoron[ic]" and an intellectual creation in the West, Haideh Moghissi stated that women's activism and women's quest for gender equality and access to public life has been historically experienced in Islamic societies. Advocates of Islamic feminism, she maintained, virtually abandon "the secular democratic vision of feminism, sacrificing its hard-won achievements at the feet of an 'Islamic' vision of change." Presenting a different perception, writing from Iran, Nooshin Ahmadi Khorasani noted that active Islamic women refuse to call themselves feminists. Here, I explore the complex variations that exist among women's rights advocates in the Islamic Republic.[2]

Whether pro-regime or anti-establishment, urban or rural, well off or less privileged, religious or secular, active women are diverse and their experiences complex. They are opponents and proponents. As discussed in Chapter 5, categorizing women into groups allows the researcher to draw specific distinctions among them, although it can also obscure common interests that may bond them together. Primarily urban, middle-class or elite, active women increasingly include small town and some rural women. The latter, not the focus of this book, participate in electoral politics and local associations and frequently in non-governmental organizations or individually. The former work in private or government or state-related jobs, and they act as proponents or opponents of the state, its politics, and gender policies. Proponents refer to *Shi'i* women who believe in the unity of state and religion. They support the regime and its ideology, but differ among themselves on gender equality and veiling. This study considers proponent women to comprise two groups: devout Muslims and trespassers who have crossed the boundaries between religious and secular women with regard to women's positions and gender relations.

[2] "Islamic elite," Afshar, *Islam and Feminisms*, ch. 1 and Conclusion; Najmabadi, "(Un)Veiling Feminism," 29–45 and 30; Touhidi, "Gender and Islamic Fundamentalism," entire; Keddie, "Women in Iran Since 1979," 412–426; and Mayer, "Cultural Pluralism." Moghissi, *Feminism*, 134, 126, 137–144, and 145–6; and Khorasani, Ahmadi Khorasani, *Zanan Zir-e Sayeh*, 159.

Proponents are generally establishment and well-to-do women who draw political power from their male kin. They are parliamentarians, work in universities or other high governmental offices, or run non-state or religious organizations or publishing houses. Others serve the state including gender police as discussed before.[3]

In contrast, opponent women denote *Shi'i* and religious minority women who believe in the separation of state and religion. Despite their religious beliefs, they consider themselves secular as they regard religion as a private matter. They advocate gender symmetry and believe that women have a choice to veil or not to veil. They are primarily urban, mostly middle-class but some working-class as well. They comprise three groups – revolutionaries, rebels, and reformers. Revolutionaries contested coercive reveiling, rebels include the younger generation of women who defy modesty codes daily, and reformers, some of whom participated in the revolution, advocate women's rights, democratic rights, and freedom of expression. Opponent women tend not to hold political offices but instead are lawyers, filmmakers, novelists, students, teachers, journalists, publishers, and writers in addition to producers and directors of gender-sensitive films with international fame. They are in the vanguard of creating a new feminist movement.[4]

Although opponent and proponent women have ideological and political differences, at times, they cross each other's borderlines and form short-lived or long-term alliances. Occasionally, the concerns of proponents overlap with those of opponents, although their over-arching interests remain conflictual. Although the designation of boundaries is arbitrary, my intention is to highlight trends in women's political behavior and the dynamics of their political activism, not to focus on a fixed delineation of their activities. Today, women's quest for gender equality, women's rights, the elimination of patriarchy (*mard salari*), and legal and political reforms can be said to have invoked some change, modifying the state's actions. In my view, women's activism has pushed the Islamic regime to undergo an unanticipated challenge: opponent women

[3] Middle-class, because of their greater political participation, in this Chapter, I devote my attention to urban elite and middle-class women. It should be noted that during the last parliamentary elections, more rural and small town women participated than before; a thorough investigation of them will be done elsewhere. Nemazi, provided an analysis on February 20, 2004 at a Columbia University Middle East Seminar.

[4] The designation of categories of devout, trespassers, revolutionaries, rebels, and reformers is arbitrary. My intention is to distinguish different women activists and highlight their specific philosophies and actions rather than engage in generalized and definitional debates.

are resisting relentlessly, proponent women are trespassing the borderlines with secular women, and together, they are engraving an opening in the state system. Acting in their interest, women are threatening one of the most important pillars of the Islamic state – its control of women. In so doing, they participate in a new social movement with feminism at its core. Women's activism and awareness suggest that gender bias is strong in the Islamic Republic, despite the centrality of gender in politics and women's centrality as agents of social change.[5]

OPPONENT WOMEN

Secular and critical women who participated fervently in the 1979 Revolution to overcome tyranny are now joining the younger generation of women as opponents of the system. Revolutionary participants were mostly born after Reza Shah's abdication or during the early era of Mosaddeq's premiership to mothers who might have struggled against autocracy, patriarchy, and experienced forced unveiling. Some worked or studied or participated in various protest movements – their educated daughters currently follow their footsteps as rebels or join reformers. Opponents consist of religious and ethnic minorities as well as practicing *Shi'i* women who view religion as a private matter, not a state ideology and many do not regard biology as destiny. Primarily urban, middle-class and elite, these women consist of three groups: revolutionaries, rebels, and reformers who have broad common interests. As revolutionaries, many protested coercive reveiling and other setbacks related to women's position. As rebels, the younger generation of women are currently redefining modesty rules and participating in the reform movement. As reformers, many professional women stand for democratic change, freedom of expression, civil rights, and women's rights and condemn violations of human rights. Together, these three groups have been dynamic political participants since the revolution and continue to question gender inequalities and patriarchal tendencies. They respond to policy alterations and

[5] Prerevolutionary women, it is of paramount importance to explore the link between the active prerevolutionary and postrevolutionary women, a study that I hope to undertake in the future. Gender bias, Parsipoor, *Khaterat-e Zendan*; and Raha, *Haqiqat-e Sadeh*. Some oppositional women in exile have published their stories and their articles, and this study has incorporated those that are relevant to this work. Works of Mojahedin-e Khalq are excluded, as they are not a focus of this study. Overall, current activists differ from the prerevolutionary conformist and nonconformist women who participated in a different domestic and international context.

offer their own agenda as it is politically expedient. In so doing, they scrutinize the state and challenge its gender bias.[6]

This book has suggested that women's activities, their concerns, and their strategies to improve women's rights have changed throughout the twentieth and twenty-first centuries. When in 1979 masses of revolutionary women rose against dictatorship and patriarchy for the first time in Iran's history there was a violent backlash against their struggles. Women were dispersed, albeit temporarily. Many went into exile, so committed, that a few continued their activism by engaging in critical and feminist teachings and writings, or participated in international conferences or engaged in public debates. Some became alienated at home and others explored alternate paths to reestablish their assertiveness and their quest for equality. This section highlights the activities of revolutionaries, rebels who currently defy reveiling, and reformers, including attorneys Shirin Ebadi and Mehrangiz Kar. Together with the writer, student, and editor Nooshin Ahmadi Khorasani, sociologist Jaleh Shadi-Talab, publisher Shahla Lahiji, attorney Shadi Sadr, and other courageous feminists, they are challenging the system and bringing a new feminist movement into the fore.

Revolutionaries

During the anti-Shah movement and the revolution many women – some of whom returned as students from abroad – massively reacted to the reversal of unveiling, family laws, and the discriminatory tendencies of the new leadership. In response to Khomeini's edict that required all female government employees to wear the *hejab*, women from all walks of life waged vigorous campaigns and wrote pamphlets and articles in defense of their rights. Without support from male leftists and progressives or secular nationalist groups, thousands of unveiled women who had helped overthrow the ancien régime, organized sit-ins and came out to the streets to demonstrate fearlessly. They chanted: "Freedom for Women, Freedom for Society" (*Azadi-ye Zan, Azadi-ye Jame'eh*), "There is No Freedom at the Dawn of Freedom" (*Dar tolue' Azadi, Azadi Nist*), and "Freedom, Independence, Death to Dictatorship" (*Azadi, Esteqlal, Marq bar Estebdad*). Attempting to disperse the protesters, the mobs and the Revolutionary Guards fired into the air and verbally abused and harassed

6 Resisters, I observed their activities during several field trips to larger urban centers in Iran, in the north, north-west, north-east, and south-west provinces. Also see Satrapi.

them as "Western dolls" and "prostitutes." Determined to defend their rights, women continued their rallies, work stoppages, and strikes in hospitals, banks, schools, and the bureaucracy. This collision between the new leadership and women not only kept women at the center stage of politics, but it lent them temporary success. On March 9, 1979, the government announced that it endorsed "reasonable, not compulsory, *hejab*." In the summer of 1979, I continued to move around Tehran without a scarf or *rupush*, although fearing unsolicited intimidation, I kept a shawl in my bag.

But soon, reveiling and resistance became opposites: the more reveiling, the greater defiance. During its formation, the Islamic state in the process of formation required institutionalization of modesty. As a centrally significant policy and religious symbol, reveiled and veiled women would solicit greater legitimacy among the domestic supporters of the regime, and internationally, they would present the state with a distinct identity: Islamic and anti-Western. In June 1980, as part of Khomeini's decree, the *hejab* became mandatory for all working women in the public sector. Thousands of women reacted with determination: they engaged in street protests, lobbied, organized private and public meetings, handed out leaflets, and published newspapers. Their massive demonstrations and repeated protests compelled the first president of the Republic, Abdolhasan Bani-sadr, to reverse reveiling. Shortly after, thugs targeted women again. Despite their international support from various feminists and non-governmental groups, protesting women became increasingly vulnerable to the violence of the hoodlums, the newly formed *pasdaran* (Guardians of the Revolution), revolutionary committees, paramilitary security forces, armed members of *hezbollah*, and the gender police. Isolated and without much cooperation from men and progressive forces, fear of force and lack of security pushed women into retreat.

While the veil remained central to state-building, women's quest to defend their rights proved crucial to Iran's domestic politics and international affairs. During the early part of the revolution, domestic squabbling, the regime's crisis of legitimacy and Iran's international affairs prompted a greater need to control social forces. The new leadership aimed at containing the opposition, including secular and militant women. It also revered its supporters, including religious and veiled women as the symbol of revolutionary triumph and Islamic identity. The 1979 hostage crisis and the 1980–88 Iran-Iraq War helped to divert attention from national policies, and gender bias and violence against women lost their prominence in defense of national security. War damages were extensive and many Iranians and Iraqis died, and the national budgets of both countries were depleted. By 1981, the state succeeded in requiring all women to be veiled in public, a critical setback for women. In 1983, during the height of the war, the *Majles* passed the *Qesas*, which assigned 74 lashes to women who failed to observe reveiling. Thus, reveiling became mandatory not through consensus, but through coercion and fear of violent retaliation.[7]

Defiance is not fixed, rather it is a shifting behavior. With the growing of state pressure, women changed their tactics; they continued their opposition silently. In 1991, my interviews expressed their resentments. One woman asserted that reveiling "will not change women's public conduct because it is an action forced upon them." Another woman indicated that "sexual sins are committed under the guise of the *chador*; the veil will not protect women's chastity." A third contended: "regardless of the state's harsh measures, we will rebel in any way we can. Can authorities truly control women?" Yet another questioned: "can the government arrest and incarcerate all resisters?" And still another woman viewed the veil as a symbol of inferiority, "something that leaders want you to be." Other studies corroborated my interviews. A survey that intended to protect women from the assault of "prejudiced" people and propose recommendations to the government on "what determines the *hejab*," asked women's opinions on the kind, color, and style of veiling that was proper. A typical response was that of a college student who indicated her dismay with coercive veiling: "It is mandatory to wear *maqna'eh* at the university," but one can wear "a scarf" in the streets and "an overdress and trousers" to parties. Instead of focusing on veiling, she believed, "our priority must be to ensure that laws will not be based on the use of force." Another woman had a different response: "the *chador* is both my religious and national uniform; authorities must make it compulsory."[8]

Men became critical of reveiling too. One shopkeeper in a Tehran *bazaar* indicated to me: "the Prophet and the *Qoran* never specified what form of veil women should wear; national leaders cannot justify their actions in the name of religious instructions." Another shopkeeper stated: "nowhere did Islam declare that women should wear a similar kind of clothing as did Fatemeh, the Prophet's daughter." Some male intellectuals

[7] War, Hiro, 250–251 and 1–5.

[8] Sedghi's interviews in Tehran, 1991 and 1997, and interviews in New York City in 1992 and a survey, "Ch-e no' Hejab darid," 7–9 and 54–55.

saw reveiling as a sign of backwardness, and others viewed it in terms of state authoritarianism. One male commentator referred to the imposition of the veil as a "violation of liberty" for both men and women. Another male columnist suggested that instead of enforcing coercive veiling, "people should ignore unveiled" women. These views reveal the ongoing tension between the state and gender.[9]

Women's demonstrations and acts of protest and defiance during and after the revolution could not bring about a reversal of reveiling. Yet women's struggles continued, albeit in a different form. They began to challenge and redefine the state's mandates, not by street protests, but through quiet acts of rebellion.

Rebels

A new generation of women have begun to exert critical influence on the Islamic state. In need of exploration in Iranian studies, rebels consist of the young generation of women protesters and activists who are sometimes silent, sometimes not. Born immediately before or after the revolution, rebels, unlike their mothers, did not experience mass demonstrations or revolutionary upheavals and unveiling. Instead, they grew up in gender segregated, veiled, and legally, socially, and culturally restricted and discriminatory environments. Their subjective and objective contacts with the Islamic state, the 1990s liberalized atmosphere, and Iran's increasing integration into the globalized world, contributed to their awakening, search for a more meaningful life, and demand for the improvement of their condition and promotion of their rights. Many like the noted novelist Marjane Satrapi pursued education and became professionals and experts in various fields. The Internet, computers, and satellite dishes helped connect them to the outside world, including international women's conferences and debates on gender and justice, and most profoundly, to the lives of youth in other parts of the world.[10]

Rebels are active defiants of reveiling. Spontaneously and persistently, they have taken the task to define and redefine the shape, form and color of the *hejab*, a core concern of the Islamic regime and its founders. In larger urban centers, young women remodel the outfits they wear publicly – in private, they follow their own desired fashion liberally, despite fear of

[9] Shopkeepers and intellectuals, Sedghi's 1991 interviews in Tehran; and columnist, Kaviri, 3 and 71, "Mardom Bayad bi-Hejab-ha ra Tahvil Nagirand," 6–7.

[10] Satrapi, she portrays the life of a rebel who grew up in Iran and now lives in Paris.

retribution. They appear in black *chadors* or *maqna'eh* in state offices or in formal religious gatherings or universities where gender police and guards prevent their entry if they are improperly dressed. In northern Tehran, and some parts of cities like Kashan, Tabriz, and Kerman, instead of the mandatory veils and loose trousers, many wear short and tight jackets over demi-pants and tiny colorful scarves. They wear tiny shawls over their carefully made-up hair and show their bangs – often dyed. They hide their make-up under dark glasses, but occasionally, show their polished toes in sandals especially in Tehran. In addition, they disobey gender segregation of public transportation. They sit next to male strangers when the seats in the women's section of buses are full. In 1997, 2002 and 2005, I observed only one complaint from a male passenger. Depending on the political atmosphere of the day, state officials or vigilantes may be lax or strict, leaving rebels either free or arrested, fined, and sometimes jailed. Anticipating harassment, rebels continue to defy modesty codes. In so doing, they carve a limit to one of the salient features of the Islamic regime, its concealment of women's sexuality.

As new entrants in gender politics, the young rebels are making their presence felt. Together with other youth, they served as the backbone of Khatami's candidacy, who represented their desire for a more open society, law and order, freedom of expression, and freedom to choose. They campaigned for him by writing and designing leaflets, canvassing, and going door to door to encourage and mobilize voters. Most importantly, they cast their vote for him against the conservative candidate. As educated members of the labor market, these young rebels are slowly disrupting the basic social fabric of the patriarchal society by their active presence in important positions and professions everywhere. Rebels include young writers and editors such as Nooshin Ahmadi Khorasani who edited *The Second Sex* (*Jens-e Dovvom*), *Women's Chapter: A Collection of Feminist Writings* (*Fasl-e Zanan: Majmu'eh-e Ara' va Didgahhay-e Feministy*), and *Iranian Women Calendar* (*Salnamay-e Zanan*), Mahshid Fahsa, who constructs the Bad Sex (*Bad Jens*) web site, and attorney Shadi Sadr, among many others.

Politicized by the Islamic regime, and aware of their rights, a new generation of courageous opponent women are slowly re-emerging and re-defining reveiling. Through their activities, rebels are advancing the protests that their mothers started twenty-eight years ago against compulsory reveiling and discriminatory practices. Their actions along with those of the reformers continue to keep the state on guard.

Reformers

Formerly revolutionary participants, reformers dedicate their lives and careers to the promotion of women's rights. With the defeat of their struggles against reveiling and other predicaments, many revolutionary women went through a silent period of reflection and introspection, with a few conducting research on women. While some were detained, and a few received threats, others maintained their solace at home. But this was also a time to contemplate for shifting strategy – from being revolutionaries to becoming reformers. With Khatami's election to the presidency, several politicized and experienced women rechanelled their energy to advocate the rule of law, gender equality, and freedom. Their various activities included writing, teaching, and legal representation. They also formed non-governmental organizations that highlighted the abuse of women and children. Advocating democracy and rights, they generated new hope for Iranian women. Two such women are Shirin Ebadi and Mahrangiz Kar, who lives in the United States as of the writing of this book.

Shirin Ebadi, a judge, law professor, writer, and a former prisoner, is the first Iranian and Muslim woman nominated for the Noble Peace Prize, which she received without *hejab*. Born in Hamedan in 1947, she has two children and is married to an electrical engineer. A daughter of a commercial law professor, Ebadi grew up in a home that was spirited with legal tradition. She received her law degree from the University of Tehran in 1969. A top student among her contemporaries, she soon joined the judiciary, and in 1970, was one of the first Iranian women ever appointed as a judge. She presided over the Tehran City Court in 1975–79, but when the revolution occurred, she became a victim of purification policies. The revolutionary regime removed her from the bench and offered her a clerkship in the same court that she had headed, a position that she declined. Fighter and an optimistic Ebadi looked into the half-glass full and decided that "Instead of banging my head against a closed door, I'll become like water and run under the door." She devoted herself to the practice of law, defending the rights of women and children, and promoting human rights, all of which she pursues today.[11]

Ebadi is deeply concerned with women's rights. Her eleven books, practice as a defense attorney, and numerous international peace awards

[11] Ebadi, as cited in Howard, 77.

corroborate her contributions. Representing "Reformed Islam," she advocates a new interpretation of Islamic law that is compatible with human rights. She sees the "roots" of gender discriminatory practices in the Muslim world "in the patriarchal and male-dominated culture prevailing in these societies, not in Islam." In response to my query at the United Nations in June 2004, she stated that "I am not an Islamic feminist. This is wrong. I am a Muslim, and I believe in equality of all human beings." While she argues for a gender-neutral reading and interpretation of Islamic texts, she is vocal in her condemnation of Iranian laws because they "do not fit women's situation, especially educated women." She is particularly critical of those who sanction two men's testimony to be equivalent to one woman's, polygamy, and the laws of retribution.[12]

In her writing and actions, Ebadi promotes human rights, democracy, and freedom. Human rights, she suggests, must be promoted by each and every country, including her own motherland. While she believes in the separation of religion and state, she sees "no contradiction between Islam and human rights." In 2002, Ebadi and a few other lawyers founded the Center for the Defense of Human Rights in Iran to provide legal aid and assistance to the families of political dissidents. During the last parliamentary elections in Iran, she refused to cast her vote because she thought the progress of democracy had suffered a setback when the Guardians Council disqualified many candidates, including some incumbents, from running. Ebadi insists that "democracy is rule by people, it is not Western or Eastern, nor Islamic or un-Islamic." Furthermore, she asserts that it is "the corrupt regimes of Islamic countries that use Islam for their own illegal rule."[13]

An unrelenting supporter of children's rights, Ebadi has written extensively on the subject and defended children in court. In 1994, she established a non-governmental organization, the Association for the Support of Children's Rights in Iran that supports 600 homeless children. She also represented the Golshani case which received much international attention. In 1998, seven-year-old Arian Golshani was tortured and killed by her father (after divorcing her mother) and her step-brother. The court acquitted the father of murder and sentenced him to two years in prison

[12] "Patriarchal and male-dominated," Iranmania News, Iranmania.com December 11, 2003; "I am a Muslim," *Ibid.*; "educated women," *Ibid.*; and Ebadi's interview with Goodman, Democracy Now show, democracynow.org/, June 2004.

[13] Motherland, Iranmania.com; religion and state, *Le monde*; human rights, *Ibid.*; and Guardians Council, democracynow.org/; "democracy is," Ebadi's response to Sedghi's question that was posed to her at the United Nations, New York, June 2, 2004.

for "hurting" his daughter, despite the fact that he was a proven drug addict with a criminal record. It found the brother guilty and sentenced him to death by hanging unless his family paid a large sum of money for his blood. If a boy had been killed, Ebadi argued, the killer would have been hanged. The ruling cleric justified his decision saying that it was based upon the *Qoran* and could not be interfered with. Furious with the legal system, Ebadi vowed that "laws must be reformed." She did not "object to Islam," but she argued that the study of the *Qoran* and its interpretation cannot be reserved for clerics or men alone. Women are now educated and can do the same, she asserted.[14]

Although Ebadi is a high-profile and internationally recognized human rights advocate, her own rights were violated in Iran. She initially represented the family of the well-known liberals, Dariush and Parvaneh Foruhar, who were murdered in 1998 and 1999. She then served as an attorney for the family of a student, Ezzat Ebrahim-Nejad, who was killed during the 1999 student protests at Tehran University. Her investigations led her to find the links between "serial killings" of liberal activists and the regime's involvement in the crimes. Along with other attorneys, she was imprisoned for twenty-five days and placed in solitary confinement in 2000. All were prevented from practicing law for five years, and found guilty for slandering governmental officials. She also represented the prominent attorney, Mahrangiz Kar, and feminist publisher, Shah Lahiji, who were detained after they attended a conference in Berlin on reforms in Iran. Ebadi resigned after she was insulted by the court. Reports indicate that Ebadi has also escaped two assassination attempts.[15]

But Ebadi is receiving a global audience. *The New York Times* regularly prints her editorial contributions, for example her editorial article which criticized the World Bank for providing loans to dictators rather than the poor. Ironically, her 2004 tour of the United States earned her some criticism for participating in expensive fundraiser's activities with no audience participation, and her support of Islam. In Iran, she has received the admiration of the general public, although authorities refuse to acknowledge her global recognition because she defied the modesty codes outside the country and refused to cover her hair; vigilantes continue to disturb or suspend her speeches in Tehran – as they did to Sadigheh Doulatabadi and other active women of the 1920s and 1930s. Yet Ebadi's timing is

[14] "Laws must be," Amanpour, *60 Minutes*. Also see, Karimi-Majd, "Arian, Koodak-e bi-Panah: Chera B-e in Rooz Oftad," 9–16.

[15] "Serial killings," democracynow.org/; and assassination, de Bellaigue, 50–53.

different as she has won major domestic battles and acquired international respect and prominence. Ebadi has offered hope and restored confidence to Iranian women and men who insist on and uphold human rights and women's rights.[16]

An equally prominent attorney is Mehrangiz Kar. A civil rights and women's rights attorney, author of fourteen books, journalist and contributor to women's press, human rights advocate, professor and political prisoner, the intellectually renowned Kar lives a painful life. Born in Ahvaz in 1944, she moved to Tehran to study law and political science at the University of Tehran. After graduation, she worked at the Institute for Social Security. She was perhaps the only woman to publish over 100 articles on crucial social and political issues. Yet, similar to Ebadi, she lost her job after the revolution. Devoting herself to research, she co-authored with feminist publisher Shahla Lahiji, the history of women's identity in Iran. Another book compared Iranian laws with the Convention for the Elimination of Discrimination Against Women (CEADAW) and argued for change in Iranian laws and eradication of violence against women. In 1991–99, she collaborated with *Zanan* (*Women*) magazine, which she considered as a "very religious" but important publication with an "open-minded perspective." She contributed articles on women's legal and unequal status, almost monthly, although she maintained that addressing women's rights had "dangerous" risks. She also protested censorship of intellectuals by writing to former President Rafsanjani. In 2000, while she was serving her imprisonment term, she was diagnosed with cancer. Siamak Pourzand, her husband, also went missing and eventually was found jailed and tortured. She is currently undergoing treatment in the United States.[17]

Consistently using the law and her extensive knowledge of the legal system, Kar's own human rights were threatened. In 2000, along with a rare gathering of a few prominent secular and religious Iranian scholars, she participated in a conference on the faith of reform in Iran, organized by the

[16] "*The New York Times*," Ebadi and Attaran, "When Politics Corrupts Money," A21; and 2004 tour, one of the events took place in New York in June 2004, where Ebadi spoke at a gala dinner where dinners were sold for hundreds of dollars. Some complained about the high price and their inability to attend. While in New York, I could not obtain an appointment for an interview. Ebadi was also criticized by some feminists in exile for planning to attend another gala in Washington, DC with Iranian female supporters of the Bush administration, an invitation that Ebadi eventually refused. See pajoohesh@yahoogroups.com; and de Bellaigue, 50–53.

[17] Identity, Kar and Lahiji; and Kar, *Raf'e Tabi'z az Zanan*; and "religious" and "open-minded," *Bad Jens*, 4th edition, November 11, 2000.

prestigous Heinrich Böll Foundation in Berlin. Her presentation addressed barriers to the development of civil society in Iran. Criticizing the constitution, she predicted that "the 6th *Majles* will veto those reformist bills that expose the undemocratic institutions of the Islamic regime, including the Guardian Council and the Expediency Council." When this happens, Kar argued, "the reformist movement with its massive popular sentiment for reform will express formidable hostility towards these constitutional hurdles." During the conference, a couple of strippers from some exile opposition groups disrupted the proceedings; their actions had grave consequences for Kar, her colleagues, and the future of human rights in Iran.[18]

The regime responded to the Berlin conference fiercely. Upon their return home, eighteen conference participants were arrested and charged with violation of national security. The state-run television broadcasted and re-aired edited footage of the conference, including the participants' silence and inaction during the disruptions by strippers. "The state's intention," Kar maintained, "was to mobilize public sentiment against the conference speakers and to condemn the gathering of scholars from various political persuasions." Together with Shahla Lahiji, director of Roshangaran publishing house for women's books, Kar spent two months in the notorious Evin Prison, including one month in solitary confinement. There, she discovered that she had breast cancer. Kar and Lahiji "were the only defendants to undergo a closed-door trial, confirming suspicions of harsher standards applied to secular women activists." Both were sentenced to four years of detention. Feminists and Islamic advocates of women's rights, including Shahla Sherkat, the editor of *Zanan* publication refused to support her, as did the reformers. They possibly feared retaliation by the system or the loss of their jobs or even imprisonment. After being insulted by the court, Shirin Ebadi also withdrew her representation. With domestic and international pressure mounting, Kar was released on bail with a heavy fine. Despite pending charges, she was allowed to leave the country for medical reasons. Kar firmly believes that she received harsh treatment because authorities wanted to neutralize her "leadership" abilities (as that of others).[19]

[18] "6th *Majles*," "the reformist movement," and "hurdles," Kar's lecture at New School University, December 3, 2003.

[19] "State's intention," Kar's lecture at the New School; "closed door trial," *Bad Jens*, 2000; Sherkat and Ebadi, Sedghi's interview with Kar, New York, June 7, 2004; and "leadership," Sedghi's 2004 interview with Kar. Other female participants at the conference, Shahla Sherkat, and Khadijeh Haji-Moghaddam were both fined. Farideh Qeyrat, another feminist lawyer, defended Kar.

Kar stands for political openness and freedom of expression. In my 2004 interview with her, she rejected the idea of using new interpretations of the Islamic law to fit notions of democracy and human rights. "Even the powerful ones have not succeeded to implant these substructural changes," she suggested. "Religious law-making must contain equality for the rights of all people including non-religious people." But Kar maintained, "that doesn't make sense, unless religious structures are changed completely." It is possible to introduce some changes "within the system," knowing that there is "no room for equality," she asserted. These changes come in two ways. First, they can be outlined within the context of the nation's "national interest." For example, "advancing women's status through education is important for the interest of the system." Second, change can be addressed by substituting the membership of powerful organizations such as the Guardians Council with "those clerics whose ideas are in harmony with the international and internal social situation."[20]

Within the Iranian context, Kar sees herself as a secular woman who is also a feminist. She sees the root cause of gender discrimination in Iran in a patriarchy that has been historically strengthened by "power hungry religious men." Gender equality, she believes, must come in laws and culture, and there can be "no participation of religion in law." Despite her painful experiences at this moment, Kar is optimistic. Since the revolution, "Iranians, including religious scholars, have become more mature in their thinking and ideas. They will not be easily influenced [by demagogues]." Furthermore, "the regime cannot push women too hard, as social change has occurred." Women's education, the high rate of divorce, women's participation in city councils, electoral politics and the labor force, their modification of the veil, and their clashes with the gender police are all indications of their increasing awareness. Although progress has been made, women are "still too frightened of their husbands and the family to act collectively, for example, to sign a petition against child custody laws." With "international help and domestic support," Kar noted, Ebadi might bring some leadership to the women's movement. But because Kar

[20] This entire paragraph is based on my 2004 interview with Kar to whom I am grateful. She indicated that changing religious structures would entail a complete change of political power. As the Islamic regime's constitution stipulates that laws must not be contradictory to Islam and *fegh*, observing equality for all, including non-religious people cannot be upheld. Further, the notion of *feqh* itself is unclear. Because laws have not defined it, we do not know what it is, Kar indicated. It follows that whoever has more power, can provide a definition of *feqh*, on the basis of which, laws can be constructed and reformulated.

has been associated with "defeat," the women's rights activist believes "Kar cannot be a model of leadership at this time, during this political climate in Iran."[21]

Women's activism under the Islamic regime has been complex. Unlike the nonconformist women of the Pahlavi era and some revolutionary women, the more recent rebels and reformers do not involve themselves in clandestine guerrilla movements or write sexually liberating and politically inclined poetry. Because of the state's shifting policies, factionalism, and defeat of the rule of law, women are more cautious and crafty than their predecessors. By joining the female supporters of the regime, some find creative ways to "demand" their "rights." Some are prolific writers. Parinush Parsipur, a best-selling novelist and political prisoner, is now living in exile like Kar. Others present secular themes in their poetry, journals, legal activities, and film direction. Yet many women protest, as in December 1997, in defiance of gender segregation of sports events, where an estimated 5,000 women stormed the gates of Tehran's Azadi Stadium to attend a ceremony honoring the international victory of Iranian soccer players. Many more women, nationwide, protested the undemocratic parliamentary elections of February 2004, and many gathered in Tehran, in June 2006 to present their feminist demands, a demonstration which was broken up by guards and the gender police, which led to the arrest of a few. Continually participating in debates, actions, and activities, opponent women are representing their spirited presence in the Iranian polity and society. Along with opponent women, proponents are reasserting their place in Iranian women's history.[22]

PROPONENT WOMEN

Proponent women are somewhat new to Iran's history of political activism. During the last few years of the Shah's rule, an increasing number of women participated in various meetings that promoted *Shi'i* teachings and fomented opposition against the monarchy. Many were devout Muslims who interpreted and taught Islamic thoughts in private women's

[21] The entire paragraph is based on my 2004 interview with Kar.

[22] Secular themes, Rachlin; Ravanipoor; Parsipoor; and various issues of *Zanan*. Film direction – see Bani-E'temad's *Rakhshan, Narges, and Rusari-ye Abi*. Male filmmakers with secular themes related to women and gender include, Beizai's *Bashu, Qaribeh Kucheck*; and Kiarostami's *Zir-e Derakht-e Zaytoon*. Azadi, Mosavi, and *Zanan* 39 (1376/1998).

gatherings, and others slowly became dedicated Muslims and donned the *hejab*. They went to mosques and religious schools, sometimes in black *chadors* and sometimes not. Following their malefolk, they demonstrated in the streets and participated in Friday prayers. Subsequently, as the revolutionary processes unfolded and the Islamic regime came to power, proponent women supported the unity of state and religion and pledged to bolster the sanctity of the new order. Some acquired high-ranking positions in governmental and non-governmental organizations. In their alliance with the state, they were closely affiliated with powerful men in politics or the religious hierarchy. Winston Churchill is often quoted that, "behind every successful man, there is a powerful woman." The reverse is true in today's Iran: behind every successful woman, there may be a powerful man.

Although proponent women believe in promoting women's Islamic rights, there are differences among them. Primarily urban, they represent all classes but most prominently the elite, the middle-class, and many of the less privileged women. Here, I will consider two groups: the devouts and trespassers, each with its own variations. As devouts, some are conservatives and believe in complete gender segregation. Others believe in complementary gender roles, women's education, and equal political rights and are against discrimination. There are also some mild variations in their perception of modesty. In a 1986 seminar in Tehran, a female speaker, Robabeh Fiaz-Bakhsh, vehemently defended the veil. Its real intention is to protect women from "the dangers of sexual assault and sin," she noted. Moreover, she said that "women's clothing should be so loose that it must fall [away from] the body." In her view, the veil is a mechanism to combat the "world oppressor" [especially the United States], whose interests lie in its desire to unveil women, so that "it can intrigue and conquer women." Women's modesty or "*effat*," she maintained, is embodied in the *hejab*; if the "*hejab* is dismantled, women are dismantled too." But a 2001 presidential candidate, Moulud Shahidi Sales, in an interview, indicated that she wears the black *chador* because she has worn it since she was three years old; but it does not have to be black.[23]

Since the revolution, proponent women have grown to hold diverse views to the extent that a few may resonate secular perspectives. These trespassers are firm religious adherents but similar to opponent women, they strongly advocate women's rights. They believe in gender equality and the abolition of legal, political, and social discrimination against

[23] Fiaz-Bakhsh, 13; and Sales, Haeri, "Mrs. President."

women. They practice the *hejab* differently from the conservatives. The sixth *Majles* representative, Fatemeh Haqiqatjoo, goes to work in colorful, not black, shirts that are visible from underneath her *chador*. Editor Shahla Sherkat wears a *maqna'h*, not a cloak, in public. Yet some trespassers believe in gender difference. Fatemeh Hashemi Rafsanjani, the former president's daughter who headed the delegation to the First Organization of Islamic Countries' Symposium on Women's Role in Islamic Society held in Tehran in 1995, stated that her duty was to eliminate prejudice in order "to create an Islamic *umma* [community]" and "provide bases for the development of social justice and [e]qual rights for all the world's Muslim[s] and deprived women." But adhering to her religious perception of women as different from and implicitly inferior to men, as the Secretary General of the Women's Solidarity Association of Iran, she cautioned that "In view of their physical, emotional and physiological characteristics, women undertake appropriate responsibilities" in the society. She echoed the perspective of many proponent women who see biology as destiny: physical distinctions account for diverse tasks and responsibilities between women and men.[24]

Despite ideological and political differences among proponent women, they have induced notable changes in women's standing in the Islamic regime. These include increased attention to discriminatory penal and criminal codes, and gender bias and policies. They have also engaged in the interpretation of religious law pertaining to women, initiated legislative reforms on behalf of women, and supported women's education and women's studies curricula in some universities. Although they have experienced much defeat, their consistent attempts at questioning the government and the leadership remain illustrious. Once firm supporters of the Islamic state, though scrutinized, trespassers now express their grievance and ask variously for rights. In so doing, they join opponent women in challenging and at times, limiting the state's power. This section reflects on a few devouts and trespassers, but will not cover Mojahedin-e Khalq women.[25]

[24] Fatemeh, Hashemi Rafsanjani's statement appeared in *A Collection of Papers and Report*, and Women's Solidarity Association of Iran, *Paradise Under the Feet: Women in Iran*, 22.

[25] Devouts, this section highlights a few activists in order to provide a preliminary generalization. It is not intended as an analysis of women in Parliament or in governmental or all non-governmental positions. Mojahedin, Abrahamian, *The Iranian Mojahedin*, 230–235; and Sazeman-e Mojahedin-e Khalq-e Iran, *Women on the Way* I, and their *The Tale of a Great Determination*.

Devouts

Devout women are diverse, despite their strict adherence to *Shi'ism*. Some proponent women are remarkably religious and conservative. Others are religious but active in politics, and occasionally, they are highly critical of governmental actions, particularly regarding women's status and its gender policies. A few devout women have become religious interpreters or political activists, although the Islamic regime has not produced distinguished female Muslim scholars, theologians, or leaders. Khanum-e Amin, from the city of Isfahan, achieved the highest theological prestige among women. A *Mojtahid*, or religious teacher, author of nine books, scholar, and interpreter, Hajieh Khanum Seyyedeh Nosrat Beygom Amin, known as Khanum-e Amin, acquired recognition and rank among the clergy and made authoritative independent decisions on the interpretation of religious texts and law, including one on the *Qoran*. Yet because of her sex, she was forbidden to be a *Marja'e Taqlid* (source of imitation), or make decisions on interpretation of the *Shari'eh* that could be binding on *Shi'i* followers. Although her male colleagues discriminated against her on account of her sex, she had their respect for her theological and scholastic achievements. She was also considered an "inspiration" to women who studied religion. Powerful and visible among pious women, she was a leader who organized and mobilized women through her religious instructions, teachings, and activities, specifically through various committees and networks, charity works, and religious pilgrimages. She achieved praise and recognition during the first few years of the revolution, but her personal and professional life never became public.[26]

There are other female clerics who prefer to remain secluded and private. These devout women have little inclination to welcome outsiders into their lives or to allow new ideas in their thinking. In her study of *feqh* (Islamic jurisprudence) scholarship in the city of Qom, Ziba Mir-Hosseini talked with male clerics who produced the journal of *Payam-e Zan* (Woman's Message). The journal explored gender in light of Islam and defended gender inequalities in accordance with Islamic legal rules. Mir-Hosseini indicated that unlike the conversation she had with male clerics and contributors, she was unable to confer with the female clerics,

[26] Amin, Betteridge, 112–113, and 125–126. Amin was in her eighties when Betteridge interviewed her in 1976. We have no further information of Amin's age or the date of her death. However, Amin's religious knowledge and political power were widely known in Tehran and Isfahan. See also Ommol Benin, ed.

who were more conservative than their male colleagues. The female clerics objected to her association with the reformists who wanted change; they disapproved of her discussions with the male clerics of the journal – they also believed that the men had violated established rules by permitting a woman in their office.[27]

Unlike these female clerics, there are other devout women who are both vocal and active. Shahin Etezami Tabatabi, an outspoken devout woman, was one of the first religious women who wrote and lectured on behalf of the revolutionary government, gender difference and complementarity in Islam. She worked with the Women's Society of the Islamic Revolution and became a representative of the government at a 1979 Asian and Pacific conference on women, held in India. One of the earliest commentators on the position of the "new" Muslim woman, she criticized both the Western capitalist and Communist systems and offered Islam as a model. The West, she maintained, had turned women into sexual commodities, allowed women's abuse by their husbands and by multinational corporations, and made teenagers into alcoholics and drug addicts. In contrast, the Communists, in their attempts to free women from exploitation, had enslaved them as tools of production. The new Muslim woman should look neither to West nor East; she is "an independent individual rather than an appendage of her male counterpart." But she must conceal her "feminine attributes which emphasize her sexuality," so that men would perceive her as a "partner in the circle of humanity" not as a sexual object. Instead of competing with men, therefore, a woman "complete[s] and complement[s] them." Islam promotes "the difference between equality and similarity or sameness"; the objective should be "not similarity to men, but rather the higher goal of achieving harmony with nature and the universe."[28] The emphasis on complementarity of gender roles thus gained importance.

A'zam Taleqani, the daughter of the late Ayatollah Mahmood Taleqani, is another devout woman who became politically influential. Married at fourteen, she has four children. Before the revolution, she attended picnics outside of Tehran with other clerics who discussed revolutionary strategies. Imprisoned in 1975 and tortured, she demonstrated against the

[27] Qom, Mir-Hosseini's *Islam*; and male clerics, Mir-Hosseini's lecture at Columbia University, December 9, 1998.

[28] This paragraph is based on Etezadi, "Understanding Islam," in Tabari and Yeganeh, eds., 176–177 and her "The Changing Roles of Iranian Women," 14–16.

Shah and actively participated in the revolution. She won a seat in the first *Majles* and established a religious school where she taught Rafsanjani's daughters. She believes in advancing women's status and, in that light, she formed the Islamic Women's Association, which publishes *Hajar* (Pious Woman) newspaper. She also claims that Islam grants more financial rights to women than men: while women have the right to *mehr*, *nafaqeh*, *shirbaha*, and *ojratol-mesl*, men have greater inheritance rights. But the financial rights of single women remain unclear. I first met Taleqani at a United Nations session debating the Optional Protocols of the CEADAW in 1997. She was vocal and expressed interest in promoting women's education in Iran. At another U.N. meeting on the Commission on the Status of Women in 2002, she talked to me in a less crowded room while preparing to pray. But she was hesitant to discuss political issues – perhaps her 2000 political defeat had made her cautious.[29]

A vocal activist and interpreter of religion, Taleqani takes politics seriously, in particular women's participation. She ran for presidential elections in 2000 as she firmly believes Islam and the *Qoran* allow gender equality in political leadership. She claimed that her candidacy was a test for the openness of the Islamic Republic to women. She also declared her desire to clarify the constitution on who qualifies for presidential elections. But the Guardians Council disqualified her along with other devout women such as Dr. Fatemeh Fade'i Fath-Abadi, Leyla Taheri, and Molud Shahidi-Sales on the grounds that constitutionally, a woman was not considered a *rejal* or male elite, and therefore not fit as a presidential contestant. Arguing that *rejal* is a gender-neutral term in the Persian language and that she has the right to interpret laws, Taleqani unsuccessfully disputed the cleric's judgment. She has also criticized other laws, including the *Qesas* and the flogging of adulterous wives, and pledged to continue her battles against women's discrimination. Her current activities appear more focused on religious teachings than politics – as corroborated by her last remarks to me.[30] Despite variations among the devout women, it is the trespassers that have exerted significant pressure on the regime, and during that process, some of their own ideas have shifted slowly toward secular politics.

[29] Strategies, Howard, 137–138; and Sedghi's interview with Taleqani at the United Nations, New York, 2002; and inheritance, Shahreh-Kani, 6–7.

[30] Presidential contestant, Haeri, "Mrs. President" – note that secular women and trespassers were also disqualified.

Trespassers

Some proponent women are strong adherents of religion but they resonate, progressively, the gender concerns of secular opponent women. In need of further exploration and reflection, as a category, trespassers remain unfixed and changing. Their gender perspectives and activities are in a state of flux, as they have shifted over time and currently exhibit a greater attention to such issues as gender equality and the establishment of debates on various topics related to women's position. In my view, trespassers are many, including Shahla Sherkat, the editor of a powerful publication, *Zanan* (Women); Zahra Rahnavard, a Western-educated woman who is currently presiding over the all-women al-Zahra University in Tehran; Fatemeh Haqiqatjoo, the parliamentarian who rebukes the conservatives with her speeches; Fa'zeh Rafsanjani, a daughter of the former president and editor of the censured magazine, *Zan* (Woman); Zahra Eshraqi, Khomeini's granddaughter, who publicly condemns coercive reveiling; and Dr. Elah-e Kulai'e, a reformist representative to the sixth *Majles* and advocate of women's rights. More women qualify as trespassers but given their long-term activities, I will only reflect on Sherkat, whom I interviewed in 1997 and 2005, and Rahnavard.[31]

Zahra Rahnavard, a revolutionary supporter and promoter of women's rights, can be considered a trespasser. She is married to Iran's first post-revolutionary prime minister, Mir Hossein Mousavi. Educated in the United States, Dr. Rahnavard was seen as a secularist before the revolution. During the revolution, she began to reject Western feminism for seeing men as the main enemy of women and indicated that a "Muslim woman is a perfect woman, a multidimensional being." Under "true Islam," a woman realizes her maternal tasks: she will not send her infants to a nursery nor will she be a sex object; rather she relishes her reproductive tasks, cherishes her monogamous husband, and appreciates his financial support. But such a woman is also political: she develops political consciousness, participates in the liberation of her country, and partakes in the Islamic woman's movement, a movement of equal opportunity in which both women and men develop skills and potential. Rahnavard thus advocates greater political participation for women, and similar to other proponents, endorses family values. In her view, *hejab* is required but not

[31] I could not meet with Rahnavard in 2002. Her office required a long waiting time and a faxed request that would state specific questions for my interview. My stay in Tehram was too short for a long wait.

its black color – she herself appears in public with make-up under a black *chador*. After the revolution, she served as the editor of the well-known woman's magazine, *Ettela't-e Banovan* (Lady's Information) that went bankrupt, and then, she edited *Zan-e Ruz* (Woman of Today), another publication under the Shah. She became a professor and an architect at the University of Tehran and is currently the chancellor of al-Zahra University, which offers women's studies courses. She continues to be influential, and is often cited in various newspapers and magazines.[32]

Shahla Sherkat, is an editor with strong beliefs in Islam, feminism, and gender. A persistent trespasser and voice in highlighting the importance of women's issues throughout the life of the Islamic state, she has been instrumental in publicizing the intrinsic gender bias of the regime. Born in Isfahan to a religious civil servant father, she was raised as a modest girl. She wore the *hejab* at her father's insistence to school where she sat next to students with miniskirts. Her mother encouraged her to attend the University of Tehran and the family moved to the capital. Pursuing a career in journalism, she played a prominent role in "the Islamization of the women's press" during the early revolutionary days, and as a dedicated Muslim, she associated herself with feminism. In 1982, she joined *Zan-e Ruz* of the Keyhan Publishing Institute as an editor, and Mohammad Khatami's colleague. Eventually she became critical of the magazine's portrayal of women as homemakers under the shadow of their husbands and the lack of freedom of press. Frustrated, Sherkat resigned in 1991. A few months later in 1992 she founded *Zanan*, which continues to be published today as a major feminist magazine with the longest history in the Islamic state.[33]

Sherkat's stance in *Zanan* is intriguing, if not quietly subversive. She is Muslim but critical. She is a feminist but not contrite. She covers a wide range of theoretical, personal, journalistic, and scholarly accounts by academicians, feminists and anti-feminists, and secular and religious women and men. Introducing debates on feminism in Iran and the West, for the first time in Iran, *Zanan* has moved forward discussions on women's rights and gender parity. One of the contenders in a feminist dialogue, in *Zanan*, turned out to be a young male cleric who wrote legal arguments on gender and Islam. Recognizing gender inequalities in Iran, Sherkat continues to

[32] Rahnavard, many of my interviewees in Iran during several trips made this comment, which was also echoed by Kar in my interview; influential, Rahnavard's assistant required that I fax the objective of my interview in advance. Because of my short stay, and other commitments, I could not meet with her.

[33] Feminism, Mir-Hosseini, *Islam*, xv; and press, Howard, 144.

argue for all forms of gender equality. She takes "issue with the very premises on which the official *Shi'i* discourse on the position of women is based, and laying bare their inherent gender bias." She has also printed articles on the nature of women's oppression, men's violence and abuse, patriarchy, drugs and addiction, sex tourism, stoning, prostitution, runaway girls, unequal laws, gender discrimination in the job market and political offices, feminist theories, and women's movements. She persists in promoting gender awareness, as it was clear in her meeting with me in 1997, when she articulated her interests in receiving book reviews and articles from the United States on sexuality and feminism.[34]

Sherkat stands for reform in Iranian politics and freedom of expression. Planning to mobilize women to participate in electoral politics, she served as the only woman among Khatami's advisory group to run for the presidency. In an effort to educate women on the presidential election, she participated in Khatami's campaign by devoting a large section of a *Zanan* issue to candidates and critics of the electoral system. In April 1997, she published interviews with Khatami in which he stated that "laws pertaining to gender equality will benefit civil society" and acknowledged "the culture of patriarchy as one of the most important impediments to women in Iran." In contrast, Ali Akbar Nateq Nuri, a conservative contender refused an interview. With his permission, however, Sherkat published her questions to him which included: "What is your understanding of feminism?... Do you call your wife by your eldest son's name in the company of strangers?... Have you ever punished your wife?... How?"[35]

But Khatami's election could not guarantee Sherkat's freedom of expression. She was imprisoned in 2000 upon returning from the Berlin Conference. The Revolutionary Court finally fined and released her. One of the most active and prominent feminist contributors to *Zanan*, Mehrangiz Kar, discontinued her contributions to the magazine. Kar indicated to me in 2004 that Sherkat refused to support her while she was detained or thereafter, allegedly because "the magazine was more important" than Kar. Subsequently, Sherkat became disenchanted with the Guardians Council's disqualification of women from presidential elections. She noted that "elections are germane to freedom, but men decide who is free and what entails freedom. Men choose women's educational fields and whether or not women can run in elections. This is wrong. Freedom and

[34] Islam, Mir-Hosseini, *Ibid.*, xv; the male cleric is Seyyed Mohsen Saeed-Zadeh; and bias, Mir-Hosseini, xv.

[35] Presidency, Howard, 124; and How, *Zanan*, 34, 2–5.

the right to be free must be respected. You cannot disqualify candidates because they are women." But Sherkat has made her mark: she has proven affirmatively that the revolution has failed women. Despite changes in the character of *Zanan* as a result of restriction of freedoms, Sherkat's influence remains potent.[36]

Many proponent women hold gender issues as a focus of their activism, despite being devout or stepping over the boundaries of secular women as trespassers do. They are not "Islamic feminists." This book rejects that notion. Supporting state-religion integration, some proponent women participate in politics and legislative change within the framework of the state's philosophy of gender and its codes of reveiling and gender-segregation, although in many ways and forms, an increasing few are challenging the system, its laws, and patriarchal structures and norms, pushing it to respond to women's rights and gender equality. Both opponent and proponent women have mobilized themselves against the establishment and its arbitrary rules. They have done this in different ways and to different degrees. Occasionally the two groups have united to address specific issues regarding gender relations and women's position, but frequently they have lacked the same common ideology, goal, and strategy. Consequently, their alliance has been short and illusive. Although they endeavor to introduce reforms or pressure policy-makers to respond to women's welfare and their unequal status, their concerns as individuals, members of various public institutions or journalists, writers and educators, or as lawyers or members of women's organizations are chiefly within the state's paradigm. In short, they want to reform the system.[37]

Whatever the debate among women, gender inequality, arbitrary rules, undemocratic norms, gender abuse, compulsory reveiling, or obstruction of freedoms are within the order of the day. Despite the differences between opponents and proponents, women's defiance continues and more women express criticism and participate in bringing political change. Although postrevolutionary power struggles and "radical political culture," suggested Paidar, defined the concept of gender relations, gender policies remains contradictory "in purpose and effect."[38] Given the inconsistent policies and the turbulent factionalism among leaders, this observation is plausible. But it is important to recall that consistent "Islamization" policies remain the essence of how women and gender

[36] Disqualify, Haeri, "Mrs. President."

[37] "Islamic, feminists," see the beginning of this chapter and Introduction.

[38] Paidar, *Women*, 353.

relations are conceptualized in Iran's politics. During the past twenty-eight years, women have continually articulated their interests. At this time, it is not what happens to gender issues; rather, it is how the system will respond to increasing channels of women's resistance. Women's activism has cracked the veil, if not the very legitimacy of the Islamic state.

Iran has entered the new millennium with a history of the state's manipulation of gender and sexuality. Since the rise of Pahlavism, both the secular and religious states regulated women's lives and mobilized them in different ways and for different ends. Over many decades, state–clergy strife over gender continued. It is interesting that the secular state attempted to undermine the power of the clergy by depriving them of control over women. And that the clergy, when it regained power, redefined the position of women as the centerpiece of its Islamization program. The clerical state was born in the ruins of the monarchical establishment. Since its inception, the persistent political contest between the regime and gender has prolonged: reveiling, discrimination, and gender bias have politicized women, and women have politicized reveiling and Islamization policies. Clearly, the "power" of disempowered and modest women is potent. Iran has marched into this century with women as a powerful catalyst of political change.

Conclusion

When a women's suffrage bill was introduced in the 1906 parliamentary debates, cleric deputy Sheikh Asadollah reacted with dismay: "never in a life of misfortune had his ears [been] assailed by such an impious utterance." Women lack "souls" and "rights," he argued: "God has not given them the capacity" to participate in "politics and elect the representatives" of the country; nor have women "the same power of judgment as men have." Should "the weaker sex" be enfranchised, he asserted passionately, the entire system would crumble and that "would mean the downfall of Islam." It nearly took ninety-one years to realize Asadollah's fear: the politicization of women who would thus exert power to upset the status quo.[1]

Whether opponents or proponents, employed or unemployed, urban or rural, veiled or unveiled, Iranian women today are visibly contesting the system of gender asymmetry. In an event unprecedented in Iran or any other Muslim country, in May 1997, the large electorate of dissident women defeated the presidential candidacy of the conservative cleric Nateq-Nouri. Women were crucial to the landslide victory of the reformist cleric Seyyed Hojjatol-Eslam Mohammad Khatami who had pledged equal opportunity and high governmental positions for women, not because of their gender but because of their merit. Speaking for the reformist coalition in 2005, Dr. Elahe Kulai'e became the first Iranian spokeswoman to represent a presidential candidate in the history of the Islamic regime, although Dr. Mahmood Ahmadinejad won the seat of

[1] "Judgment," and "sex," see Ch. 1, where women in the constitutional era is discussed, and appropriate quotations are provided.

presidency for 2005–2009. Almost a century after Asadollah's remarks, the observer is compelled to ask: how can the spontaneous subversive vote of masses of women and their political actions be explained during the 1997 and 2005 elections? What does women's overwhelming participation and their leadership in electoral politics suggest for the relationship of women to politics and more specifically, veiling, unveiling, and reveiling? Does not women's political behavior abate the myth of orientalists who view women as secluded, or that of Western governments who partially justify their invasion of the Middle East to liberate women, or that of much Middle Eastern scholarship that ignores gender as a crucial category for understanding politics and development?[2]

Re-visiting the themes of veiling, unveiling, and reveiling within the historical and cultural contexts of Iran's development is critical to the understanding of the specific circumstances of women's lives, gender dynamics, and gender politics. During most of the twentieth and twenty-first centuries, Iran witnessed shifting alliances and realignments among different groups, classes and factions, and a continuing power struggle between secular and religious forces, especially over the state's domination. Control over women's sexuality constituted one of the most persistent themes in this contest between secular and religious forces. Although Iranian *Shi'i* philosophy and practice regarding female and male sexuality varied, women's sexuality occupied a prominent place at their core. This concern was tightly interwoven with every political, economic, social, legal, cultural, and religious norm and policy of every political administration in modern Iran. Underlining the importance of women's sexuality and labor to politics and developmental processes, I have argued that states manipulate gender for purposes of legitimacy and consolidation of their powers, and for their foreign policy pursuits. But women's drive to articulate their own interests constrains and modifies the state's behavior and gender policies. Thus, the state can modify gender and patriarchal relations, however, women's resistance and more generally women's political participation can itself constrain and subvert the state's actions. In this book, I suggest that veiling, unveiling, and reveiling represents the dynamic relationship between women and politics. This relationship must be seen not only within the context of Iran's development but the emergence of women as potent agents of political and social change.

2 "Khatami," Reuters – Khatami's message was also electronically disseminated through IRNA, April 7, 1997. For a coverage of presidential candidates' views on women, see the special issue of *Zanan* (Women) no. 34 (Ordibehest 1376/April 1997).

A salient feature of Iran's development consists of changes in the gender division of labor and the emergence of women as important influences in the economy. At the turn of the twentieth-century, under the Qajar dynasty (1796–1925), there existed what I call a "Qoranic gender division of labor," corresponding to work roles as spelled out in the *Qoran*. With the exception of carpet weavers, vendors, domestic laborers, and seamstresses, the majority of women, particularly in urban areas, participated in household production. If they were wealthy, they spent largely idle lives in the private world of polygamous families, children, eunuchs, and servants. Together, the gender division of labor, a subsistence economy, and a weak state allowed the household to remain the focal point of patriarchal control over women's sexuality and labor. Women remained veiled.

Centralization, modernization, secularization, and Westernization of the state under the Peacock Throne of the Pahlavi dynasty (1925–79), reinforced by commercialization of the economy due to rising oil revenues and Iran's rapid integration into the global market economy, modified the traditional gender division of labor and women's labor. Assuming partial patriarchal power, the Pahlavi state gradually manipulated and redefined some gender policies including those related to women's work. Economic development and public policies encouraged women's gradual integration into newly created jobs and previously gender segregated occupations, especially in health, education, and the growing industrial and service sectors. Women were unveiled forcibly.

While responsible for household work, educated working women who were increasingly embracing secularism found themselves at a perplexing crossroad. On the one hand, with improved employment and educational opportunities, working women experienced subordination by new hierarchies based on market forces, class, and gender relations. On the other hand, with their gradual but small financial and social autonomy, for the first time, these women could make independent decisions and life choices. Living, studying, and working was an uphill battle, but women born in the late 1940s claimed a distinct place in the 1960s and 1970s. Pioneers in Iranian history, a new and small group of professionals began to mark the society with their distinct feminist consciousness and yearning to bring about social change. Women welcomed the prospect of being their own sovereign, myself included, determining their own destiny. Some became political as "conformists" or "nonconformists." Others chose careers and engaged in the highest educational endeavors at Iranian or Western universities. While many continued their activities in Iran, part of the Iranian brain drain was comprised of women and scholars who currently live in exile. Despite its twists and turns, the rapidly growing Iran of the 1960s and 1970s offered a boost to the lives of employed and educated women who became increasingly visible in public.

The revolution and the formation of the Islamic Republic of Iran (1979–) brought a shift in the gender division of labor, and women's work intersected with women's sexuality. At the outset, economic decline and the tighter alliance of politics and religion contributed to the alteration of women's work and their educational attainment. Establishing the preeminence of religion over the secular and Westernizing order of the ancient regime, one of the earliest policies of the IRI included the disempowerment of women. Losing the little ownership they had over their own bodies and lives, women found their sexuality and domestic labor increasingly under men's will and whim, and their marketability restrained. Women were reveiled forcibly.

In its attempt to consolidate its powers, the Islamic state embarked upon a purification policy, which every revolution deems necessary. At first, it instituted gender segregation regulations at work and in the public. Harassed, alienated, and excluded, many women abandoned their jobs or were dismissed. Severe economic calamities that came with the Iran-Iraq War also undercut women's employment, except in urgently needed gender segregated teaching and nursing occupations and the newly created jobs, as the gender police. So volatile was the new environment that it discouraged educated and professional women from pursuing their objectives. But with the increase in oil revenues, Iran's uneven integration into the global economy, and the "zigzag" legacy of economic transition, there came another shift in the gender division of labor in the 1990s. While "Heaven" remained under "mothers' feet," as the cultural cliche suggests, women's labor force participation improved slightly, and many women began to engage actively in the market. A significant feature of today's economy includes the expansion of the informal sector that draws for the first time a sizable number of runaway girls, prostitutes, and sex workers. Of paramount importance has been the entry of women to universities who constitute 71 percent of the student body and who may have the potential to alter the gender asymmetry and the existing family relations. It is my argument that this economic change over a century led to the creation of a force of women that significantly took initiatives to transform slowly gender and social relations.

A second feature of Iran's development consists of the dynamic interaction between the state and gender. Each of Iran's gendered states of the Qajars, the Pahlavis, and the Islamic Republic had a distinct political system with its own specific domestic and foreign policies. Patriarchy, classes, and gender relations also assumed forms unique to each state, as did women's activism and their feminist expressions and movements. Depending on its national or international objectives, although curtailing freedoms, the state remained flexible to modify policies and respond to some constituent demands, including those related to gender interests. State studies, therefore, benefit by incorporating a gender lens.

Whether in its postulation of laws or legislation, edicts, sermons or Friday prayers, state policies may encourage or discourage women's choices. With the downfall of the weak Qajar state, Reza Shah's state altered family statutes. It modified the terms of marriage contracts and the age of consent for marriage, while it also retained certain cultural practices such as the Islamic injunction regarding multiple marriage, divorce, child custody, property relations, adultery, and criminal punishment. In addition, it introduced feminism from above or "state feminism" and outlawed independent women's organizations. Conscious or unconscious of its consequences, it seized some patriarchal power from the clergy, fathers, and sons, thus *transforming* its nature. Reza Shah's abdication in 1941 and the almost disappearance of the state in 1941–53 fostered the rise of democratic women's organizations. I suggest that women's autonomy grew in an atmosphere of almost statelessness, or failed states.

The twin pillars of modernization and repression strengthened the gendered state after the 1953 CIA coup, although ironically, some aspects of public policies embodied emancipatory tendencies. The Shah's White Revolution and his Land Reform curtailed some of the clerical powers and their wealth, despite the clergy's vehement protests. Women's suffrage also undermined the power of the religious establishment who challenged it fiercely. Ashraf Pahlavi played a particularly pivotal role as she supported the promulgation and implementation of the Family Protection Laws and the Women's Organization of Iran. Thus, state policies that addressed women's enfranchisement, in effect, reduced some of the powers of patriarchy and religious authorities. But the state-clergy contest for power was short-lived. The Islamic regime established its hegemony over the civil society first and foremost by exploiting gender issues. Gender became one of the most crucial concerns of the Islamic state.

The Islamic state built itself on the ruins of the old regime, that it inherited. It neutralized the opposition, curtailed liberties, and promoted new forms of gender relations, paving the way for an "Islamization" of the private and public spheres. Its Islamization project meant instituting the *hejab*, encouraging the *sigheh* (temporary marriage) and polygamy, lowering marital age, enacting the *Qesas* (the Bill of Retribution), and upholding unequal inheritance laws among many other measures. By so doing, the new state used gender as an agenda to recover social legitimacy that the clergy had lost under the Pahlavis, and more broadly, under thirteen centuries of monarchical rule in Iran. Since the rise of the Pahlavis, I suggest one continuing pattern in Iran's history has been the state's manipulation of women's sexuality and labor for purposes of consolidation and legitimation. For the state and politics, gender matters.

A third feature of Iran's development consists of the state's symbolic use of gender to bolster national identity and buttress legitimacy in global relations. Domestic politics and policies are often linked to the international stage, and world politics is often, if not always, gendered. Representing the state's ideology, gender and women's bodies communicate powerful messages to the nation and beyond, especially to the Western Hemisphere and hegemonic powers. The depiction of women's bodies as uncovered or masked, exposed or concealed, and their designation as "Western" or "Islamic" contribute to a specific form of national identity. Unveiling can be construed as a sign of emulation of the West and integration in the globalized and modern universe, whereas reveiling can be interpreted as the rejection of the West and the construction of authentic and Islamic history. Both forms of representations are distortions. Both confront women with the dilemma of what I earlier called the "double-edged sword" of "national and international patriarchy."[3]

Iran's international relations, like other modern states, are gendered. Reza Shah's attempts at modernization and Westernization were largely copies of Turkey's Westernization campaign by Attatürk in defiance of Islam and in support of European capitalism. In actual fact, Reza Shah and his Court allies used women to counter clerical power and enhance the Westernization and modernization images of the new secular and centralized state. It unveiled women, altered family laws, and slowly integrated women into the public space. It also modified the social and political landscape of the country, which women had come to represent to the world. But symbols may not be true reflections of the reality: unveiling failed to connote gender equality or modernization to many observers.

The Shah's use of gender imagery was far more extensive than his father's. Perhaps not in Oriana Fallaci's perceptions, but women's emancipation and Westernization were intended to negate traditional mores.

[3] "Gendered," Tickner; *Gender*, Enloe, *Bananas*; and Peterson and Runyan, *Global*; and "international patriarchy," Sedghi, "Third World."

They accompanied the rhetoric of the state's integration into the orbit of the market economy and its collaboration with the West. Indeed, his majestic and lavish plans as well as his modernizing measures were so well publicized abroad that the monarch received support from many Western authorities and the media, especially from such American presidents as Eisenhower, Kennedy, Nixon, and Carter, and such senators and their wives as Mr. and Mrs. Jacob Javitts. Even some American feminists such as Betty Friedan praised the Shah's reforms and gender policies.[4]

Iranian women, in particular elite women, also entered into alliance with the state in order to boost and publicize the Shah's international image. Through her endeavors abroad and her self-proclaimed "global responsibilities," Ashraf Pahlavi actively participated in international women's meetings and symposia. Eminently elegant in their Parisian high-fashion and ancient Persian jewels, the Shah's three official wives also provided glamour and prestige to the glories of monarchy and the Peacock Throne in the Western world. Undoubtedly, the symbolic representation of women and gender contributed to the enhancement of the state's image abroad. On the other hand, such uses of women's bodies and sexual politics delegitimated the state in the hearts and minds of the domestic opposition and the 1979 revolutionaries.

Naturally, the Islamic state fostered a *Shi'i* identity. It symbolized women as the guardians of religion, state, and society. It portrayed them as bearers of tradition and cultural authenticity and hailed them as paragons of motherhood reminiscent of the role of the Prophet's daughter, Fatemeh. It presented the daughters and wives of the martyrs and the gender police as warriors against the "immoral" West. The depiction of reveiled women in black *chadors* created powerful images of the Islamic regime to its citizens, neighbors, and the world during the early phases of the revolution. Wall graffiti and slogans condemned "modestly-veiled" or "badly-veiled" women as "Western dolls" or "prostitutes," along with other mottos that expressed "anti-imperialism" or "death to America." Women's attempts to question adverse policies invited hostile objections or their outright rejection as the representation of the West's "corrupting cultural onslaught." Alternatively, the use of "Islamic" gender imagery underlined the assertion of clerical and patriarchal power, in particular over women's sexuality. For the state's national identity, women's bodies matter.

[4] Fallaci, "A Shah's." See also Chs. 4 and 5 of this book.

The Islamic state's use of gender imagery reverberated negatively in the West. Veiled women wrapped in black *chadors* helped form perceptions of Iran in the Western press, which referred to them as "ships under sail" and increasingly subordinated to men. During the 1997 presidential election, most Western coverage of Iran presented at least one picture of a woman in a black veil. This semiotics reached its height in a *New York Times Magazine* article about elite Islamic women and their role in the promotion of Islamism. Both the Pahlvais and the Islamic regime exploited gender and its symbolic representation to communicate their political philosophy and legacy. Whereas the Pahlavis presented Westernized women as a symbol of secularization and modernization, the IRI portrayed Islamized women as a symbol of *Shi'ism* and de-Westernization. Thus, states draw upon gender to define and re-define their domestic and global objectives.[5]

The fourth significant feature of Iran's development elucidates the birth of feminists, feminism, and women as active agents of political and social change. Women's activism is not new to Iran, but feminism as a concept is. It highlights the articulation of subjective and objective experiences of inequality and discrimination, as well as the drive to contest and confront them in various small or large groups. Iranian women have made important contributions to the advancement of women's position as they have revealed their determination to reform the male-dominant culture, polity, and society. What has inspired women historically to cross the strict confines of their households is complex. Feminist movements have typically encompassed ideas about women's past and immediate oppression and exploitation, and they have proposed actions to amend these injustices. As women experience a gendered system first hand, those who seek to redress the situation develop specific goals and strategies suited to their own life circumstances. Hence, feminism and feminist movements *change* over time. The roots of feminism have spread in Iran. The direction of feminism remains uncertain.[6]

Throughout the twentieth and the first few years of the twenty-first centuries, Iranian women's interests and activities were diverse. As individuals or members of organizations of various persuasions, they participated openly or secretly and undertook a wide range of political and cultural tasks. They wrote feminist and emancipatory poetry, stories, novels, pamphlets, biographies, and books, and they created feminist art and feminist legal theories. They also built schools and founded women's journals,

[5] "Ships," Lerner; and New York, Sciolino, "The Chanel."

[6] Feminist movements, Sedghi, "Feminist."

periodicals, and newspapers, as well as producing feminist films and defending women's rights as attorneys, academicians, teachers, or students. In their endeavors, under the most arduous circumstances, in Iran or in exile, women have begun to write their own history.

Feminism, or women's aspirations to promote their interests and gender equality, intersected with women's multi-layered experiences, and varied historically in different Iranian states. Class, ideological dispositions, and religious affiliations influenced women's agency. Naturally geography had its own role. While my focus has been on urban women, rural or tribal women have largely different lives. Religious minorities such as Christians, Zoroastrians, Jews, and Baha'is encounter different challenges than *Shi'i* women who are the main axis of this study. Educational and professional identifications as well as political persuasions have also influenced forms of feminism and how they contributed to women's movements. Although in some ways women's differences transcended their individual life stories, they link together as women striving for social change.

Feminist consciousness and women's activities have been dynamic, being transformed and transforming as women attempted to improve their lives and redress obstacles imposed by the family, the state and society. During the late nineteenth-century, a few women who voiced public opposition succeeded in influencing the course of the tobacco uprisings. It was during the Constitutional Revolution that more women articulated their interests and even formed organizations that included a few liberal male thinkers and politicians. Some of the women of this era carved their own space among the early Iranian feminists, despite the obstacles they experienced in the family and society. Bibi Khanum Astarabadi and Taj ol-Saltaneh sharply criticized corrupt monarchy, widespread poverty, and patriarchal practices while advocating their desires for independent life-styles. Often articulating their dismay with religious fervor, especially when they enunciated their concern to liberate Iran from despotism and European imperialism, these and other women mobilized against the veil and polygamy, while also demanding better lives for children, education, and women's enfranchisement. As I have shown, the organizational efforts and journalism of Mohtaram Eskandari, Sadigheh Doulatabadi, and a few exemplary women exemplified this outspokenness on behalf of their sex.

Iran's modern history demonstrates the power struggle between the state and clergy over women's sexuality, with the veil at the center of this political contest. Whereas the 1920s witnessed the growth of women's consciousness and activities under a weak state, the 1930s saw the growth of an all-pervasive state hegemony, as the state-sponsored women's organizations replaced a nascent independent women's movement. The first Pahlavi state suspended women's claims to reform the male-dominated society and its autocratic rule. Its modernization drives coopted or suppressed any opposition, and the clergy's power – including their control over women's sexuality and labor – was formidable. Although possibly not Reza Shah's intent, his edict to unveil sharpened the definitive nature of state-gender-clergy relations in the decades to come. The "emancipation" of women became a potent weapon that the state used in its efforts to weaken the clergy.

But with the return of a weak state or a failed state, women's activities bloomed. Reza Shah's abdication in 1941 created a political vacuum and a degree of openness. Women who were born in the 1940s, as discussed earlier, occupied a unique intellectual and professional position during the subsequent decades. A few who had been active earlier began to participate in the Democratic Society of Women, an affiliate of the Tudeh Party. The society became one of the most dynamic and politically vital organizations and drew upon such noted women as Maryam Firuz, Badr-Monir Alavi, and Dr. Khadijeh Keshavarz for leadership. Linking issues of class and gender, oppression and exploitation, the Society lobbied and challenged the government to enfranchise women in 1944, and later, during Premier Mohammad Mosaddeq's leadership in 1951 and 1952. Despite their intense efforts, the power rivalry between the secular and religious forces continued to block women's right to vote.

Not discussed from a gender perspective, 1953 and the establishment of U.S. hegemony became critical in Iranian women's history. Without the CIA's overthrow of Mosaddeq's government, in cooperation with Ashraf Pahlavi, the twin sister of Mohammad Reza Shah, the 1979 Revolution would have been highly unlikely. Once the Peacock Throne was restored, Ashraf Pahlavi became the champion of women's rights at home and abroad. Amalgamating all women's groups in what was subsequently developed into a state-sponsored organization or the Women's Organization of Iran (WOI), she began to launch her activities in gender politics. Instrumental in women's suffrage as one of the pillars of the White Revolution, Ashraf Pahlavi helped the secular state triumph over religion and its authority over women. The White Revolution stripped the clergy of its economic and patriarchal power. It also created new allies and enemies among women.

Women articulated different interests under the Shah's state. Women of the 1960s and 1970s remained active, but they did so in different ways, to different degrees, and followed different political persuasions. Although there is not yet a definitive study of these women, this book has identified two loosely-defined categories. "Conformist" women consisted of elite women, the WOI members, and a few others who supported the state and entered the public arena by participating in political and social institutions. "Nonconformist" women attempted to challenge the state, but were denied participation. Many of these women joined organizations with diverse socialist ideologies; others chose Muslim organizations. For the first time in Iranian history, women in large numbers cooperated with organized men, but only a few reached leadership ranks. By contrast, independent secular women, some of whom believed in a mixture of socialism and feminism, produced symbolic and abstract writing or poetry, as did the celebrated Furuq Farrokhzad. Yet a chasm existed between these two categories of women. Women's varied interests led to divisions among those organizations. Despite ideological and partisan differences, common concerns pertaining to women overlapped among some active women.

Women's activities took a dramatic twist during the 1979 Revolution. The pre-conditions for the emergence of a women's movement seemed imminent as secular and religious, veiled and unveiled women of various backgrounds, classes and age groups demonstrated solidarity based on nationalism, anti-imperialism, and opposition to the Shah. Women's concerns were, however, pushed aside by all groups. But the coalition of revolutionary participants collapsed as soon as religion came to the fore, laying the groundwork for the ultimate supremacy of the Islamic state. It is interesting that the monarchical state attempted to undermine the power of the clergy by depriving it of control over women. When the clergy gained state power, it redefined the position of women as one of the main centerpieces of its Islamization program.

With the formation of the Islamic state, women shifted their interests and intensified their militancy. During the early phases of the revolution, in cooperation with other oppositional groups, many women of divergent ideological persuasions engaged in feminist and political activities. But the imposition of state restrictions and the growing patriarchal power pushed many women to redefine their objectives. Acting on their own interests, women went to political polls in massive numbers. They organized in universities and, as lawyers, began to defend women's rights violations. They wrote and many pursued education at different levels. As of the writing of this book, women constitute the largest pool of university entrants. With new awareness, many women joined hands to struggle for their rights.

Active women continue to "demand their rights," and do so despite their varying gender philosophies.

Postrevolutionary active women consist of "proponent" and "opponent" women. Both have their own specific political and religious stances, although at times, their gender interests overlap. Proponent women uphold Islamic notions of gender and gender difference. I classify them as devout, trespassers, and gender police. Many of them engage in legislative and bureaucratic politics in and outside of the *Majles*. Similar to Pahlavi women, some of these women participate in international women's meetings as governmental representatives or members of non-governmental organizations (NGOs), promoting the state's Islamic identity to the global community. A few devout women engage in theological studies and interpretation of religious doctrine. Similarly, trespassers who comprise journalists, and university and state officials foster women's interests with different degrees and understanding of women's rights. With the 2005 election of Dr. Mahmood Ahmadinejad, some of these women began to cross their paths, turning to secularism, as my interviewees revealed in 2005. But acting against women's interest are gender police, whose visibility had become less sporadic and intrusive than during the first fifteen years of the revolution, especially during the Khatami regime. Under the present state, they are increasingly returning to the public space. Inaccurately called Islamic feminists, proponent women continue to legitimize the state's raison d'être as I discussed earlier. A few trespassers are the exception to this norm, although their activities must be studied over the long term.[7]

Opponent women believe in the separation of state and religion and in gender parity. I distinguish them as revolutionaries, rebels, and reformers. They include philosophers, doctors, writers, teachers, students,

7 "Islamic feminists," Najmabadi; and "Islamic Feminisms," Touhidi, "Modernity"; and Fernea. Originally a term used among Arab feminist writers, "Islamic feminism" is a fallacious concept. Despite different perspectives, as a concept, feminism generally stands for women's choice and gender equality. However, the so-called Islamic feminists advocate women's choice within the confines of religion and refrain from endorsing gender equality. Because they view biology as destiny due to physical differences, women and men play different roles in an Islamic society. In this light, they cannot qualify as feminists. In Iran, many active Muslim women preceive freedom of choice and gender equality within the context of religious precepts and doctrine. As this book has shown, there are conflicting demands between the prerogatives of religion and women's interests. Even if active Muslim women attempted to promote women's interests, as many have done, their "feminist" vision continues to be blurred in various ways, in particular regarding the physiological gender difference and its implication for the gender division of labor and the women's unequal place in the family and polity.

researchers, filmmakers, publishers, lawyers, poets, and painters in Iran and in exile. The 1979 revolutionaries have given birth to rebels and a few are reformers today. Depending on the type of their activities, they may be punished or praised by the state and its agents. When they challenge veiling, they risk arrest and harassment, just as when they wear head scarves that barely cover their hair. With their massive political participation in the 1997 presidential elections, they acted as a pressure group and President Khatami cordially acknowledged their contributions and promised their inclusion in his administration. Women's political and social presence went beyond the national boundaries and the world celebrated Iranian women's struggles as the 2003 Nobel Peace Laureate was awarded to Shirin Ebadi. The United States also celebrated the Iranian best-selling novelist, Azar Nafisi, who is widely criticized by Iranians in exile.[8]

Unprecedented in Iranian and Middle Eastern societies, today's Iranian women are pushing forward their own feminist struggles, making their presence known. Appearing in their "Islamic" *hejab*, both Shahla Sherkat and Shirin Ebadi may portray the image of state supporters, although their work and ideas can qualify them as secular feminists. In contrast, attorney Mehrangiz Kar left the country leaving behind her incarcerated husband. Zahra Kazemi, an Iranian-Canadian journalist died from a beating while taking photographs during an anti-regime demonstration in 2004. With disappointing reforms and increasing trends toward a more controlled political climate, the future remains unknown. Ahmadinejad's short term in office leaves little room for a substantiated and balanced discussion – briefly one year into his presidency, in June 2006, a women's gathering was disrupted by state agents, including the gender police and a few were taken into custody.[9] But what is certain is that the feminist movement that began during early twentieth-century Iran has now given birth to women who are divided, but at times hold complementary values. Despite differences, women have ventured into the new millennium with painful yet powerful memories of the struggles of their sisters. The present activities of a younger generation of women such as Nooshin Ahmadi Khorasini, Shadi Sadr, and Fatemeh Kulai'e, and others, attest to the presence of untiring feminists and active women who will march forward in support of women's interests in Iran.

What implications does this study of Iranian women's experiences suggest to political scientists interested in the developing world? In this age of

[8] Nafisi, Byrne, A12.

[9] June 2006, *Zanan*, (Tir 1385 / July 2006), entire.

globalism dominated by models of economic privatization and political liberalization, Iranian women's political behavior poses questions with profound challenges to dominant developmental paradigms. An offshoot of Western liberal democratic thought, secularism offers a promise for political change by separating politics from religion. But the failed secular state of the Pahlavis with its secular tendencies produced neither a strong participatory electorate, nor a political culture conducive to pluralism and greater feminist voice. At best, it produced a political environment with some opportunities for some women. It is probable that Iran's experiences with secularism were too short to suggest a more critical effect.

Yet secularism proved vulnerable to the culture of *Shi'ism*, repressive states, and the revolutionary forces it spawned. Currently, a residue of secularism persists, and it coexists with *Shi'ism* and *Shi'i* popular and political cultures. The 1997 voter turnout – and especially the massive votes of women and youth – brought a reformist to the Iranian presidential palace whose beliefs sparked greater ideological discord among the ruling circles. In Iran, secularism could not elicit the development of electoral politics, but the women's vote did. Women's power is potent; the implications are indispensible to the analysis of political development and democratic politics.

A single case study of gender in Iran cannot provide a basis for positing universalizing tendencies for Islamic and Middle Eastern societies. Islamic revivalism in Iran has its own unique history and culture that are not repeated in other social contexts and other Islamic societies. Iran's *Shi'ism* and its *Shi'i* history have been distinct, so also have been its different and varied philosophy of gender and sexuality. Moreover, development processes, state formation, and its interaction with social forces have been specific in Iran. Although some Muslim women began to formulate their own "Islamic" concepts of sexuality, in particular after the 1979 Revolution, gender ideas of male theologians and politicians remained most dominant during the twentieth-century. Omitting considerations of concrete historical evidence would lead to false generalizations about Islam, gender, and sexuality. Similar to many societies, the state's active interference in regulating women's lives continues in Iran. But continuing women's dynamic responses that put the state on hold despite shifts in governmental administration and philosophy, which constitute what is specific, or intrinsic to Iran.

Possibilities for future studies are vast. Iranian women's history is old. But Iranian women's studies is young. Little has been published, especially as pertains to the Pahlavis, when women were often portrayed as victims explicitly or implicitly, and if women were active agents, the state often discredited their cause or retaliated against them. By contrast, the new research suggests that the growth of feminism, feminist consciousness, and women's rights groups have posed definite challenges to the state, limiting its gender policies and legislation. One obstacle to the state's power has been the unintended consequences of women's political participation and women's respective demands upon the government for greater improvement in their lives, greater access to political power and economic resources, and greater equality with men. An in-depth study of women's voting behavior as an aspect of their political and social agency to subvert the system is in order. More expeditiously, as the reformist era came to an end with disappointments over Khatami's powerlessness and factional conflicts, it would be interesting to investigate the potential seeds of more militant forms of activism among women.

Other concerns remain unexplored. Will there be possibilities of further divisions among women of different class backgrounds and religious persuasions, or will differences among women lead to greater and complimentary interests than they did during the 1953 oil protests, the 1979 Revolution, and the 1997 presidential election? Will economic development, if the American sanction is lifted and Iran's sovereignty maintained, provide a greater openness to women's labor force participation? And if so, would a larger force of employed women introduce a greater challenge to the dominant culture of gender inequality, or how would they respond to the state? Or will popular demands for political openness take precedence over economic development and gender equality? What would be the promises of Ahmadinejad's government to women and freedom of expression and actions?

The clock cannot be stopped or turned back. Veiling, unveiling, and reveiling has spawned women's defiance. However deplorable to enforce coercive reveiling, the *hejab* has fulfilled its political function: it has legitimized the Islamic regime and its political and symbolic representation. Khatami's reformism did not address reveiling. Although it is too soon to generalize about Ahmadinejad's gender politics, it is highly improbable that he will challenge the politics of reveiling. But pluralism and participatory democracy negate the compulsory politics of reveiling. Instead, a responsible and responsive alternative is a *choice* to veil or not to veil. If the state dismisses its own constituency and the civil society, where will the impetus for political and social change come from? Perhaps the diverse perspectives and activities of women and open-minded men can exert greater pressure on the state to promote gender equality if Iran is to meet the requirements of the twenty-first century. Perhaps women can succeed in defining their own interests and their human rights, and be the *sole* owners of their own mind and body. But achieving these goals, in part, would mean denying the state the ability to exploit women symbolically and tangibly as totems of sexuality and modesty. The challenge comes not from the top but from women and men who continue their defiance and resistance in order to build a just and equalitarian future.

Glossary

Adl Justice.

Akhund Low-ranking clergyman/woman or *Molla*. Former is dominant.

Amr-e be Ma'ruf va Nahi aza Monker The Promotion of Virtue and Prohibition of Vice.

Andaruni The Persian equivalent of a small *haram* where wives, children, servants, and eunuchs lived.

Anjomans Societies.

Asir Captive. It is the title of one of Furug Farrokhzad's works.

Azadi, Esteqlal, Marq bar Estebdad "Freedom, Independence, Death to Dictatorship." A slogan frequently heard during the 1979 Revolution.

Azadi-ye Zan, Azadi-ye Jame'eh "Freedom for Women, Freedom for Society." One of women's slogans during the 1979 Revolution.

Bad dahan Those with dirty mouths.

Bad-hejabi Improper-veiling.

Bahar-e Azadi "The Spring of Freedom" or the birth of the 1979 Revolution.

Band-andazes Women threaders who visit homes or those who mostly work in beauty parlors today.

Banovan Ladies.

Basij-e umumi Public mobilization.

Bi-hejabi Unveiling.

Chador A long veil that covers women from head to toe.

Chaqchur Loose trousers.

Dallaks Women or men who wash bodies in public baths but sometimes visit homes to assist with bathing and massaging.

Dar al-Fonun The first secular high school for wealthy male students.

Dar al-Mo'allemat Teachers' school.

Dar tolue' Azadi, Azadi Nist "There is No Freedom at the Dawn of Freedom," women's slogan during the 1979 Revolution.

Danesh (Knowledge) is the first Iranian women's journal edited by a woman.

Divar (Wall). It is the title of one of Furug Farrokhzad's works.

Effat Modesty. Usually reserved for women, not men.

Faqih Expert religious jurist.

Farah Pahlavi University. Iran's first women's institution of higher learning.

Fatavin Religious verdicts, or plural for *Fatva*.

Feqh Islamic jurisprudence.

Fohasha Prostitutes.

Harasat Security guards on duty at governmental offices or streets.

Havades Accidents.

Hejab A curtain in its literal meaning. In Iran, it refers to women's clothing that covers their entire body, protecting them from the strangers' eyes. Women have reinterpreted the form of *hejab* differently. Today, some wear it as *chador*, others in some combination of tunics, pants, and scarves. The term also refers to women's modesty and their chastity.

Hezb-e Zanan-e Iran The Women's Party of Iran.

Hezb-e Rastakhiz The Resurgent Party.

Hezbollah The Party of God.

Hojjatol Eslam The sign of God. A title given to recognized *Ulama* such as Mohammad Khatami.

Hokm-e Ta'liq Dismissal edict.

Jahan-e Zanan *Women's World*. One of the earlier women's journals.

Jam'iyyat-e Nesvan-e Vatankhah The Patriotic Women's Society. One of the earlier active women's organizations.

Jam'iyyat-e Zanan The Women's Society, an earlier women's organization.

Jame'y-e Democrat-e Zanan The Democratic Union of Women, an earlier militant feminist organization.

Kafan-e siah Pejorative reference to the black veil, especially prior to 1936.

Khaharan-e Basiji Mobilized sisters who act as gender police or morality guards.

Kanun-e Banovan Women's Center for the gathering of the Court and related women.

Khoms Religious alms giving.

Mabi' Object for sale, or a term referring to women's sexuality.
Majles The National Consultative Assembly.
Maktab khaneh Religious literacy schools that taught the *Qoran*, most dominant before Reza Shah's secular educational reforms.
Manzel The home, or a term referring to women.
Maqna'eh A tight scarf that covers all the hair, neck, and shoulders.
Mard-salari Male-domination.
Marja'e Taqlid Source of imitation in Shi'ism.
Mehr Brideprice.
Mohtaram Eskandari A socialist, feminist, and the founder of an important women's organization that had the longest history of any such organization.
Mosta'zafin The downtrodden and the poor.
Mostakfarin The privileged, wealthy, and at times, monarchists.
Mote'h A custom that allowed men to have sexual access to multiple women.
Moti'eh Those, primarily women, obedient to men's will.
Mojtahed Islamic scholars.
Mulla or *Molla* or *Mullah* A low-ranking clergyperson.
Nafaqeh Islamically required financial support by a husband to his wife.
Nang Social disgrace.
Nekah Marriage.
Namous Personal, public, and social honor, a term used by men in reference to their womenfolk.
NIRT The National Iranian Radio and Television under the Shah.
Osian (Rebellion) Title of one of Furug Farrokhzad's works.
Paksazi Purification policies.
Pardeh-neshin One who sat inside behind the curtained windows, or a veiled woman.
Pasdaran Guardians of the revolution.
Ojrat-ol Mesl Wages in Cash Act.
Qesas The Law of Retribution enacted under the Islamic Republic. A victim or victim's family receives retribution/blood money from the those who committed a crime against them.
Qavanin-e Jaza'ie The Penal Code.
Qavanin-e Madani The Civil Code.
Qoran-khani Gatherings to read the holy Muslim book.
Rakhtshoors Laundresses who wash clothes by hand.
Rejal A controversial term referring to male elite or female elite. The IRI abides by the former, but active women by the latter.

Rooz-e Azadi-ye Zan Women's Emancipation Day.

Rouzeh-khani Gatherings to commemorate religious rituals and history.

Rubandeh A short scarf that maskes the entire woman's face.

Rupush Loose tunic that became fashionable under the IRI.

Rusari Scarf.

Sadaq Nuptial gift.

Salnamay-e Zanan Iranian Women Calendar.

Saman (Price) A reference to the price of woman's sexuality.

Saman-e boz' The price for a woman's sexual organ.

Sazeman-e Zanan-e Tarafdar-e E'lamiyy-eh-e Huquq-e Bashar The Women's Organization in Support of the Declaration of Human Rights.

Sazeman-e Radio va Television-e Melli-ye Iran The National Iranian Radio and Television (NIRT).

Sena Senate.

Shi'i Islam A sect of Islam, the followers of Imam Ali, the Prophet's son-in-law.

Shoray-e Khebregan The Experts Council in IRI.

Shoray-e Negahban The Guardians Council, a powerful organ of the IRI.

Shora-ye A'li-ye Jam'iyyatha-ye Zanan The High Council of Women's Organizations.

Shora-ye Zanan-e Iran Women's Association of Iran.

Shari'eh or the *Shariah* Islamic law.

Shora-ye Zanan-e Iran Women's Association of Iran.

Shoukufeh (Blossom) was the first journal both edited and published by a woman.

Siqehs or *Mot'eh* Temporary marriage. It is a *Shi'i* doctrine that allows both sexes to contractually marry for a designated price and time from one hour to ninety-nine years. Most practioners are, however, men.

Sufreh Religious feasts and commemorations. In recent years, it is mainly practiced by the wealthy who provide lavish food and gatherings.

Sunnis Majority sect of Islam.

Sureh A *Qoranic* chapter.

Tavallodi Digar (Another Birth) A work by Furug Farrokhzad.

Torshideh Aged as a pickle. A term refered to unmarried women, even as early as twenty-five years old or younger.

Toubi Azmoudeh The first Iranian Muslim woman to establish a school, *Namous*, in Tehran, 1906.

Ulama Religious scholars.

Vaqf Resources of financial, land, and water resources available to the clergy.

Zai'feh Weakened, a term used in reference to women.

Zaban-e Zanan *Women's Tongue*, the first publication to use the word *zan* (woman) in its title.

Zan Tarbiyat Konandeh-e Jame'ye Shar'ieh Ast "Women is the Educator of the Islamic Society," a wall grafitti slogan under the IRI.

Zanan-e basiji Mobilized women by the Islamic state an organ of which is the gender police or morality squads.

Zanan-e Hezbollah Women of the Party of God.

Zanan-e Sarallah Mobilized women or Mobile Security Women.

Zaqeh-neshin Dweller of Tehran's worst shantytowns.

Zina or *Zena* Fornication, sexual union of unmarried couples. In the IRI, this is a crime with punishments such as killing, flogging, stoning, and long-term imprisonment.

Zinat Pasha A woman from the city of Tabriz, who is described as "passionate, brave, and enlightened," led a group of armed and veiled women in the *bazaar* against the tobacco concession.

Selected Bibliography

Interviews

Open-ended interviews were conducted with female and male officials, employers, and employees of various public and private organizations in Iran, in 1974, 1975, 1977, 1979, 1991, 1997, 2002, and 2005. Due to their request for anonymity the names and titles of these individuals will not be given. Interviews were conducted as follows: Cultural and Social Council for Women, Department of Manpower Statistics; Economic Statistics Department; Bank Markazi Iran; Iranian National Radio and Television and its various subsidiary units; Ministry of Information; Ministry of Justice; Ministry of Labor; The Plan and Budget Organization; Women's Organization of Iran; State Organization for Employment and Administrative Affairs; Statistical Center of Iran; the Senate; university members; peasant women; various factories; feminist organizations; households; and political activists of various organizations. Other interviews were conducted with housewives, scholars, feminists, and activists in the United States in 1980–2004.

Documents, Books, and Articles

A Collection of Papers and Report. Tehran: The First OIC Symposium on Women's Role in Islamic Society, April 19, 1995.

Abdullaev, Z. Z. "Promyshlennost i Zarozdenie rabochego klassa Irana V Knotse XIX VV [Iranian Bourgeoisie and Working Class in 1900s]. In *The Economic History of Iran*. Edited by Charles Issawi. Chicago: University of Chicago Press, 1971.

Abrahamian, Ervand. *Iran Between Two Revolutions*. Princeton: Princeton University Press, 1982.

———. *Khomeinism: Essays on the Islamic Republic*. Berkeley: University of California Press, 1993.

———. "Shariati: The Iranian Revolution." *Merip Reports* 102 (January 1982).

———. "The Guerrilla Movement in Iran, 1963–1977." *Merip Reports* 86 (April 1980).

______. *The Iranian Mojahedin*. New Haven: Yale University Press, 1989.

Abu-Lughod, Lila, *Veiled Sentiments: Honor and Poetry in a Bedouin Society*. Berkeley: University of California Press, 1986 and 1999.

Afari, Janet. "On the Origins of Feminism in Early 20th-Century Iran." *Journal of Women's History* (Fall 1989).

______. *The Iranian Constitutional Revolution, 1906–1911; Grassroots Democracy, Social Democracy, and the Origins of Feminism*. New York: Columbia University Press, 1996.

______. "[Feminist Movements] In the Late Qajar Period." In *Encyclopaedia Iranica*. Edited by Ehsan Yarshater. New York: Bibliotheca Press, 1999.

Afkhami, Gholam Reza, and Seyyed Vali Reza Nasr, eds. *The Oral History Collection of the Foundation For Iranian Studies*. Bethesda: The Foundation For Iranian Studies, 1991.

Afkhami, Manhnaz. "Women in Post-Revolutionary Iran: A Feminist Perspective." In *In the Eye of the Storm: Women in Post-Revolutionary Iran*. Edited by Mahanaz Afkhami and Erika Friedl. Syracuse: Syracuse University Press, 1994.

Afshar, Haleh. "Behind the Veil: the Public and Private Faces of Khomeini's Policies on Iranian Women." In *Women in the Middle East*. Edited by Salman Magida. London: Atlantic Highlands, 1983.

______. *Islam and Feminisms: An Iranian Case-Study*. New York: St. Martin's Press, 1998.

______. *Salanmeh-e Pars* [Persian Yearbook]. Tehran: A. Jahid, 1311/1932.

Ahmadi Khorasani, Nooshin. *Zanan Zir-e Sayeh-e Pedar Khandeh-ha*. Tehran: Tose'eh, 3rd printing, 1380/2001.

______, ed. *Fasl-e Zanan: Majmo'eh-e Ara Va Didgah-e Feministi* [Women's Chapter: The Collection of Feminist Ideas]. Tehran, 1380/2001.

Ahmed, Leila. *Women and Gender in Islam*. New Haven: Yale University Press, 1992.

Akhavi, Shahrokh. "Shi'ism, Corporatism, and Rentierism in the Iranian Revolution." In *Comparing Muslim Societies: Knowledge and the State in a World Civilization*. Edited by Juan Cole. Ann Arbor: University of Michigan Press, 1992.

______. *Religion and Politics in Contemporary Iran: Clergy-State Relations in the Pahlavi Period*. Albany: State University of New York Press, 1980.

Alam, Asadollah. *The Shah and I: The Confidential Diary of Iran's Royal Court, 1969–1977*. Translated by A. Alikhani and N. Vincent. New York: St. Martin's Press, 1992.

Al-e Ahmad, Jalal. *Qarb Zadegi* [Westoxication]. Tehran: Mo'tarezeh, 1343/1974.

Algar, Hamid. "The Oppositional Role of the *Ulama* in Twentieth Century Iran." In *Scholars, Saints, and Sufis*. Edited by Nikki Keddie. Berkeley: University of California Press, 1971.

Algar, Hamid. *The Roots of the Islamic Revolution*. London: I.B. Torus, 1983.

Amanat, Abbass, ed. *Taj Al-Saltana: Growing Anguish: Memoirs of a Persian Princess From the Harem to Modernity 1884–1914*. Translated by A. Vanzan and A. Neshat. Washington, DC: Mage Publishers, 1993.

Amini, Fatemeh. *Hamse-ye Yek Payedari-ye Bozorg: Sharh-e Mokhtasar-e Zendegi-ye Enqelabi* [The Story of a Great Power: A Brief Description of Revolutionary Life]. Long Beach: The Islamic Students Association, n.d.

Amir Arjamand, Saeed. *The Shadow of the God and the Hidden Imam: Religion, Political Order, and Societal Change in Shi'ite Iran from the Beginning to 1890.* Chicago: University of Chicago Press, 1987.

Amuzegar, Habib-allah. *Maqam-e Zan dar Afarinesh* [Women's Status in the World]. Tehran: Eqbal, 1344/1961.

Amuzegar, J., and M.A. Fekrat *Iran: Economic Development Under Dualistic Conditions.* Chicago: University of Chicago Press, 1971.

Andors, Phyllis. *The Unfinished Liberation of Chinese Women: 1949–1980.* Bloomington: Indiana University Press, 1983.

Ardalan, Zafar-Dokht. "Barresi va Tahlil-e Madh-e Dahom-e E'lamiyeh-e Jahani Raf'-e Tabi'z az Zan" [*An Investigation and Analysis of Article Ten of the World Declaration for the Prevention of Discrimination Against Women*]. Tehran: WOI, 1354/1975.

Ashraf, Ahmad. "Historical Obstacles to the Development of a Bourgeoisie in Iran." In *Studies in the Economic History of the Middle East: From the Rise of Islam to the Present Day.* Edited by M.A. Cook. New York: Oxford University Press, 1970.

______, and Ali Banuazizi. "The State, Classes and Modes of Mobilization in the Iranian Revolution." *State, Culture and Society* 3 (Spring 1985).

______, and Ali Banuazizi. "Classes in the Pahlavi Period." In *Encyclopaedia Iranica.* Edited by E. Yar-Shater. New York: Center for Iranian Studies, Columbia University, 1992.

Ashtiani, Mehrangiz Changizi. "Country Profile on Women [:] Islamic Republic of Iran." Tehran: n.p., probably 1995.

Azari, Farah, ed. *Women of Iran: The Conflict With Fundamentalist Islam.* London: Ithaca, 1983.

______. "Islam's Appeal to Women in Iran: Illusions and Reality." In *Women of Iran: The Conflict with Fundamentalist Islam,* London: Ithaca, 1983.

Bagely, R.C. "The Iranian Family Protection Law of 1967, A Milestone in the Advance of Women's Rights." In *Iran and Islam.* Edited C. E. Bosworth. Edinburgh: Edinburgh University Press, 1971.

Bagherian, Mitra. *Barresi-ye Vizheh-giha-ye Esqal-e Zanan dar Iran 1355–65* [An Investigation of Specifics of Women's Employment in Iran 1976–86]. Tehran: The Plan and Budget Organization of Iran, 1369/1990.

Bahrampour, Tara. *To See and See Again: A Life in Iran and America.* New York: Farrar Straus & Giroux, 1999.

Bakhash, Shaoul. *The Reign of the Ayatollahs.* New York: Basic Books, 1979.

Bamdad, Badrol Moluk. *Zan-e Irani as Enqelab-e Mashrutiyyat ta Enqelab-e Sefid* [Iranian Women from the Constitutional Revolution to the White Revolution] I and II. Tehran: Ebbn-e Sina, 1347/1968.

Banani, Amin. *The Modernization of Iran, 1921–1941.* Stanford: Stanford University Press, 1984.

Bank Markazi Iran. *Bulletin* no. 17. Tehran: Bank Markazi, 1937.

Bank Markazi Iran. *Gozaresh-e Salaneh va Taraz-Nameh-e Bank-e Markazi-ye Iran* [Annual Report and Balance Sheet of the Central Bank of Iran]. Tehran: Bank Markazi Iran, 1353/1974; and 2434/1975.

Bank Markazi Iran. *Natayej-e Barresiy-ye Budjeh-e Khanevarha-ye Shahri-ye Iran sar Sal-e Bist-o-panj Sio-seh.* [The Results of the Investigation of the Family Budget in Urban Iran in 1974], Sec II. Tehran: Bank Markazi Iran, Economic Statistics Department, 2533/1974.

Bank Markazi Jomhuri Islami Iran. *Annual Review 1373, 1994–95*. Tehran: Bank Markazi, n.p.

Bank Markazi Jomhuri-ye Eslam. *Bar-resi-ye Tahavvolat-e Eqtesadi-ye Keshvar Ba'daz Engelab* [Investigation of Changes in Country's Economy After the Revolution]. Tehran: Iran, 1361/1982.

Bank Markazi. *Consumer Price Index in Urban Areas of Iran, Ordibehesht 2536.* Tehran: Economic and Statistics Department, 1977.

Bargozideh-e Asar-e Furuq Farrokhzad [Selections of Furuq Farrokhzad Poetry]. Tehran: Morvarid, 1356/1977.

Basu, Amrita, ed. *The Challenge of Local Feminisms: Women's Movements in Global Perspectives*. Boulder: Westview Press, 1995.

Bauer, Janet. "Conversations Among Iranian Political Exiles on Women's Rights: Implications for the Community-Self Debate in Feminism." *Critique* (Spring 1994).

Bayat-Phillip, Mangol. "Women and Revolution in Iran, 1905–11." In *Women in the Muslim World.* Edited by Lois Beck and Nikki Keddie. Cambridge: Harvard University Press, 1978.

Beck, Lois. "The Religious Lives of Muslim Women." In *Women in Contemporary Muslim Societies*. Edited by Jane Smith. Lewisburg: Bucknell University, 1983.

Behdad, Sohrab. "From Populism to Economic Liberalism: The Iranian Predicament." In *Iran's Economy: Dilemma of an Islamic State.* Edited by Parvin Alizadeh. London: I.B. Tauris, 2001.

______. "The Post-Revolutionary Economic Crisis." In *Iran After the Revolution.* Edited by Rahnema Saeed and Sohrab Behdad. London: I.B. Tauris, 1995.

______, and Farhad, Nomani. "Workers, Peasants, and Peddlers: A Study of Labor Stratification in the Post-Revolutionary Iran." *International Journal of Middle East Studies* 34 (2002).

Behrangi, Samad. *Kend-o Kav Dar Masa'el-e Tarbiyati-ye Iran* [Delving Into the Educational Problems of Iran]. Tehran: Bamdad, n.d.

Beneria, Lourdes. "Reproduction, Production and the Sexual Division of Labor." *Cambridge History of Economics III*, 3 (1979).

______, and Shelly Feldman, eds. *Unequal Burden: Economic Crises. Persistent Poverty, and Women's Work*. Boulder: Westview Press, 1992.

______, and Gita Sen. "Accumulation, Reproduction, and Women's Role in Economic Development: Boserup Revisited." *Signs* 7 (2) (1981).

Betteridge, Ann. "To Veil or not to Veil: A Matter of Protest or Policy." In *Women and Revolution in Iran*. Edited by Nashat Guity. Boulder: Westview Press, 1983.

Bill, James Alban. *The Politics of Iran: Groups, Classes and Modernization.* Columbus: Charles E. Merrill Publishing Co., 1972.

Boris, Eileen, and Elizabeth, Prugl, eds. *Homeworkers in Global Perspective: Invisible No More.* New York: Routledge, 1996.

Boserup, Ester. *Women's Role in Economic Development.* New York: St. Martin's Press, 1970.

Browne, Edward Granville. *A Year Amongst the Persians: Impression as to the Life, Character and Thought of the People of Persia, Received During Twelve Months' Residence in that Country in the Year 1887–1888.* London: Adam and Charles Black, 1984, reprint, 1950, 1893.

______. *The Persian Revolution of 1905–1909.* Cambridge: Cambridge University Press, 1910.

Buci-Gluckmann, C. *Gramsci and the State.* London: Laurence and Wishart, 1980.

Bulleton-e Haftegi-ye Sazeman-e Zanan-e Iran [The Weekly Bulletin of WOI] 386 (1354/1976).

Bulleton-e Haftegi-ye Sazeman-e Zanan-e Iran [The Weekly Bulletin of WOI] 454 and 455. (2535/1976).

Bulleton-e Haftegi-ye Sazeman-e Zanan-e Iran [The Weekly Bulletin of WOI] 456 (2535/1976).

Butler, Judith, and Joan, Scott, eds. *Feminists Theorize the Political.* New York: Routledge, 1992.

Center for Women's Participation. *Women's Participation and Seventh Government.* [In Persian] Tehran: The Center for Women's Participation, 1380/2001.

Charrad, Mounira. *States and Women's Rights: A Comparison of Tunisia, Algeria and Morocco.* Berkeley: University of California Press, 1993.

Chehabi, Houchang. "Staging the Emperor's New Clothes: Dress Codes and Nation Building Under Reza Shah." *Iranian Studies* 26 (3/4) (Summer/Fall 1994).

Contrell, Alvin and Hanks, Robert. "The Future Role of Iran." In *The U.S. Role in a Changing World Political Economy: Major Issues for the 96th Congress.* Washington, D.C.: U.S. Government Printing Office, 1979.

Dabashi, Hamid. *Theology of Discontent: The Ideological Foundation of the Islamic Revolution in Iran.* New York: New York University Press, 1993 and New Jersey: Transaction Publishers, 2006.

Dehghani, Ashraf. *Hamase-ye Moqavemat* [The Epic of Resistance]. Tehran: The Organization of the Iranian Fedai'e Guerrillas, 1357/1978; or *Hamase-ye Moqavemat* [The Epic of Resistance]. U.S.: The Organization of the Middle East National Front, 1354/1974; or *Torture and Resistance in Iran: Memories of the Woman Guerrilla A. Dehghani, Member of the O.I.P.F.G.* Translated by Peggy Huff. London: The Iran Committee, n.d. Translation and printing, possibly 1977.

Department of Commerce. *U.S. International Commerce Overseas Business Reports.* Washington, D.C.: Department of Commerce, October 1977; December 1977; September 1978; and October 1978.

Department of Defense. *Security Assistance Agency, Foreign Military Sales and Military Assistance Facts.* Washington, D.C.: Data Management Division, DSAA, December 1980.

Department of Defense. *U.S. Overseas Loans and Grants and Assistance From International Organizations*. Washington, D.C.: AID, July 1945–September 1977.

Ebadi, Shirin. *Tarikhcheh va Asnad-e Huquq-e Bahari* (as barabari) *dar Iran*. [History and Documents of Human Rights in Iran]. Tehran: Roshangaran Publishers, 1373/1994.

Elwell-Sutton, L.P. *Elementary Persian Grammar*. Cambridge: Cambridge University Press, 1972.

Enayat, Hamid. *Modern Islamic Political Thought*. Austin: University of Texas Press, 1982.

Engels, Frederick. *The Condition of the Working Class in England*. Stanford: Stanford University Press, 1968.

Enloe, Cynthia. *Bananas, Beaches and Bases: Making Feminist Sense of International Politics*. Berkeley: University of California Press, 1990.

Esfandiari, Haleh. "Iran: Women and Parliaments Under Monarchy and Islamic Republic." In *Princeton Papers in Near Eastern Studies* 2 (1993).

______. *Reconstructed Lives: Women and Iran's Islamic Revolution*. Baltimore: The Johns Hopkins University Press, 1997.

Etezami, Shahin. "Understanding Islam." In *In the Shadow of Islam: The Women's Movement in Iran*. Edited by Azar Tabari and Nahid Yeganeh. London: Zed Books, 1982.

Ettehadieh, Mansureh, and Cyrus Sa'dunian, eds. *Khaterat-e Taj os-Saltaneh* [The Memories of Taj al-Saltaneh] Tehran: Naqsh-e Jahan, 1362/1983.

Fakhr Sadat, Amin. "Zan va Amuzesh" [Women and Education]. In *Naghsh-e Zan dar Barnameh-e Omrani-ye Sheshom-e Keshvar* [Women's Role in the National Sixth Plan]. Edited by Women's Organization of Iran. Tehran: WOI, 2535/1976.

Falk, Richard. "Iran and American Geopolitics in the Gulf." *Race and Class* 21 (1) (Summer 1979).

Fallaci, Oriana. "A Shah's View of the World," *New York Post* (December 29, 1973).

______. "An Interview with Khomeini." *The New York Times Magazine* (October 7, 1979).

Fanon, Frantz. *A Dying Colonialism*. Translated by Haakon Chevalier. New York: Grove Press, 1967.

Farhi, Farideh. "Sexuality and the Politics of Revolution in Iran." In *Women and Revolution in Africa, Asia, and the New World*. Edited by M.A. Tetrault. Columbia: University of South Carolina Press, 1994. Also presented at the Annual American Political Science Association Conference. San Francisco, 1990.

Farmaian, Farman Sattareh (with Dona Munker). *Daughter of Persian: A Women's Journey From Her Father's Harem Through the Islamic Revolution*. New York: Anchor Books, Doubleday, 1992.

Farmayan, Hafez. "Politics During Sixties: A Historical Analysis." In *Iran Faces Seventies*. Edited by Ehsan Yar-Shater. New York: Praeger, 1971.

"Farmayeshat-e Shahansah Aryamehr." [The Shah's Proclamations]. In *Kongereh-e Bozorgdasht-e Chehelomin Salruz-e Azadi-ye Ejtemai-ye Zanan* [The

Congress of Celebrating the Fortieth Day of Social Emancipation of Women]. Tehran: Oft, n.d.

Farrokhzad, Pooran. *Karname-ye Zanan-e Kara-ye Iran: az diruz ta Emruz* [Encyclopedia of Famous Women of Iran: From Yesterday to Today]. Tehran: Nashr-e Qatareh, 1381/2002.

Ferdows, Adel. "Women and the Islamic Revolution." *International Journal of Middle East Studies* 5 (1983).

Fernea, Elizabeth, Warnock. *In Search of Islamic Feminism: One Woman's Global Journey*. New York: Doubleday, 1998.

Fernea, Elizabeth, and Q. B. Bezirgan, eds. *Middle Eastern Muslim Women Speak*. Austin: University of Texas Press, 1977.

Filmer, Henry. *The Pagent of Persia*. Indianapolis and New York: Bobbs-Merrill, 1936.

Friedl, Erika. *Women of Deh Koh: Lives in an Iranian Village*. 2nd ed. New York: Penguin, 1991.

Frye, Richard. *Persia*. New York: Schocken Books, 1969.

Furuq Farrokhzad: Bargozideh-e Asar, 1 [Furuq Farrokhzad: Selected Works]. Tehran: Morvarid Publications, 1343/1964 and 1350/1971.

Gasiorowski, Mark J. "The 1953 Coup D'Etat In Iran." *International Journal of Middle East Studies* 19 (3) (August 1987).

General Department of Civil Regulation. The Plan and Budget Organization. *Selected Statistics*. Tehran: The Plan and Budget Organization and Statistics Center of Iran, 1972/1973.

Ghani, Cyrus. *Iran and the Rise of Reza Shah: From Qajar Collapse to Pahlavi Power*. London and New York: I.B. Tauris, 1998.

Ghavimi (Khashayar Vaziri), Fakhri. *Karnameh-e Zanan-e Mashhur-e Iran* [The Record of Famous Iranian Women]. Tehran: Vezarat-e Amoozesh va Parvaresh, 1352/1973.

Gheytanchi, Elham. "Appendix: Chronology of Events Regarding Women in Iran since the Revolution of 1979." In *Social Research, Iran Since the Revolution* 67 (Summer 2000).

Ghiasi, Mohammad. "Bar-resiy-e Vaz'e Ejtemai'y-e Manateq-e Roostai'e" [An Investigation of Social Situation of Rural Areas]. Tehran: Plan and Budget Organization, 1351/1972. Unpublished paper.

Ghoussoub, Mai. "A Reply to Hammami and Rieker." *New Left Review* 170 (1988).

______. "Feminism – or the eternal Masculine – in the Arab World." *New Left Review* 161 (January-February 1987).

Gilsenan, Michael. *Recognizing Islam: Religion and Society in the Modern Arab World*. New York: Pantheon, 1983.

Goharol-Shari'eh Dast-e Qeyb, as cited in "Women in the Press." In *Zanan* (Women) (29 Tir, 75/ 19 July 1996).

Gole, Nilufer. *The Forbidden Modern: Civilization and Veiling (Critical Perspectives on Women and Gender)*. Ann Arbor: University of Michigan Press: 1996.

Gozaresh-e Fa'liatha-ye Sazeman-e Zanan-e Iran: *Az Panj-e Azar Mah Ta Payan-e Esfand Mah-e Hezaro-Sisado-Panjah-o Yek* [Activities Report of the WOI, November 1971–March 1972]. Tehran: Sazeman-e Zanan-e Iran, n.d.

Graham, Robert. *Iran: The Illusion of Power*. rev. ed. London: Croom Helm, 1979.

Gramsci, Antonio. *Selections From the Prison Notebooks*. Edited and translated by G. Hoare and G. N. Smith. London: Lawrence and Wishart, 1971.

Haddad, Yvone and John, Esposito, eds. *Islam, Gender and Social Change*. New York and London: Oxford University Press, 1998.

Haddad, Yvonne Yazbeck, and Ellison B., Findly, eds. *Women, Religion, and Social Change*. New York: State University of New York Press, 1985.

Haeri, Shahla. *Law of Desire: Temporary Marriage in Shi'i Iran*. Syracuse: Syracuse University Press, 1989.

Hajibashi, Jaleh. "Feminism or Ventriloquism: Western Presentations of Middle Eastern Women." *Middle East Report* 172 (1991).

Halliday, Fred. *Iran: Dictatorship and Development*. New York: Penguin, 1979.

Hammami, Rema, and Martin Reiker. *Feminist Orientalism and Orientalist Marxism*." *New Left Review* 20 (1988).

Hartman, Heidi. "Capitalism, Patriarchy and Job Segregation by Sex." In *Capitalist Patriarchy: The Case of Socialist-Feminist*. Edited by Zillah Eisenstein. New York: Monthly Review Press, 1979.

Hatem, Mervat. "Discourses on the 'War on Terrorism' in the U.S. and its Views of the Arab Muslim and Gendered 'other.'" In *Journal of Middle East Studies*. 11 (2) (2004).

Hegland, Mary. "Political Roles of Aliabad Women: The Public-Private Dichotomy." In *Women in Middle Eastern History: Shifting Boundaries in Sex and Gender*. Edited by Nikki Keddie and Beth Barren. New Haven: Yale University Press, 1991.

Higgins, Patricia. "Women in the Islamic Republic of Iran: Legal, Social, and Ideological Changes." *Signs* 3 (10) (1985).

Hillman, Michael, ed. *Forugh Farrokhzad: A Quarter-Century Later*. Austin: Literature East and West, 1988.

______. *A Lonely Woman: Forugh Farrokhzad and Her Poetry*. Washington, D.C.: Three Continental Press and Mage Publishers, 1987.

Hiro, Dilip. *The Longest War: The Iran-Iraq Military Conflict*. New York: Routledge, 1991.

Hoodfar, Homa. "Bargaining With Fundamentalists: Women and the Politics of Population Control in Iran." *Reproductive Health Matters* 8 (November 1996).

______. "Devices and Desires: Population Policy in the Islamic Republic of Iran." *Middle East Report* (October 1994).

Horney, Karen. *Neurosis and Human Growth: The Struggle Toward Self-Realization*. New York: W. W. Norton, 1950 and 1970.

Howard, Jane. *Inside Iran: Women's Lives*. Washington, D.C.: Mage, 2002.

Hudson, Michael. "Democratization and the Problem of Legitimacy in Middle East Politics." *Middle East Studies Association Bulletin* 22 (2) (December 1988).

Huntington, Samuel P. *The Clash of Civilizations and the Remaking of World Order*. New York: Simon and Schuster, 1996 and 1997.

Hurewitz, J.C. "The Persian Gulf: After Iran's Revolution" *Headline Series* 244 (April 1979).

Hussain, Farida, and K. Radwan. "The Islamic Revolution and Women: Quest for the Quranic Model." In *Muslim Women*. Edited by Farida Hussain. London: Croom Helm, 1984.

International Labor Organization. *Employment and Income Policies for Iran*. Geneva: International Labor Office, 1973.

International Monetary Fund. *Islamic Republic of Iran: 2003*. 11RNEA0012003 (2003).

Iran Who's Who 1976. 3rd ed. Tehran: Echo of Iran, 1979.

Islamic Revolution: Dimensions of the Movement in Iran 1 (1 and 9) (April and December 1979).

Issawi, Charles. "The Economy: An Assessment of Performance." In *Iran Faces Seventies*. Edited by Ehsan Yar-Shater. New York: Praeger, 1971.

Ivonof. *Tarikh-e Novin-e Iran* [The Contemporary History of Iran]. Translated by H. Tizani. n.p., n.d.

Jalali, B. *Parliamentary Proceedings* (January 4, 1953).

Jamalzadeh, Seyyed Mohammad. *Yeki Bud Yeki Nabud* [Once Upon a Time], 5th printing. Tehran: n.p., 1333/1954.

Javadi, Hasan, Manijeh Marashi, and Simin Shekarloo, eds. *Ro'ya Rui'e-ye Zan va Mard dar A'sr-e Qajar, Do Resaleh: Ta'dib al-nesvan va Ma'ayeb al-rejal*. [Two Essays of the Qajar Period: Disciplining of Women and Vices of Men]. Chicago: The Historical Society of Iranian Women, 1992.

Jayawardena, Kumari. *Feminism and Nationalism in the Third World*. London: Zed Books, 1986.

Jazani, Bijan. *Iran: The Socioeconomic Analysis of a Dependent Capitalist State*. London: The Iran Committee, 1973.

Johnson, Chalmers. "Preconception vs. Observation." In *Comparative Politics: Notes and Readings*. 9th ed. Edited by B. Brown. Orlando: Harcourt, Inc., 2000.

"Jonbesh-e Zan dar Iran" [The Women's Movement in Iran]. *Nimeye Digar* [The Other Half] 2 (2) (Autumn, 1363/1984).

Joseph, Suad. "Women and Politics in the Middle East." *Middle East Report* 16 (1) (1986).

Kamankar, Ahmad. *Qanun-e Asasi, Gavanin-e Jaza'i* [Constitutional Law, Criminal Codes]. Tehran: Javadian, 1354/1975.

Kandiyoti, Deniz. "Emancipated but Unliberated? Reflections on the Turkish Case." *Feminist Studies* 13 (2) (Summer 1987).

______. "Identity and Its Discontents: Women and the Nation." *Millennium: Journal of International Studies* 20 (3) (1991).

______, ed. *Women, Islam and the State*. Philadelphia: Temple University Press, 1991.

Kar, Mehrangiz. Paper presented at New School University. New York, December 3, 2003.

______. *Huquq-e Siasi-ye Zanan-e Iran* [Women's Political Rights in Iran]. Tehran: Entesharat-e Roshangaran va Motale'at-e Zanan, 1376/1997.

______. Raf'a Tab'eiz as Zanaz [Abolishing Gender Discrimination]. Iran-Tehran: Parvin Publication, 1377/1998.

Kar Mehrangiz and Shahla Lahiji. *Shenakht-e Hoveyat-e Zan-e Irani dar Gostarah-e Pishtarikh va Tarikh [The Quest for Identity: The Image of Iranian Women in Prehistory and History.* Tehran: Roshangaran, 1372, 1993.

Karsavi, Ahmad. *Tarikh-e Mashrooteh-e Iran* [The History of the Iranian Constitutional Movement]. Tehran: Amir Kabir Press, 1940/1961.

Katouzian, Homa. *The Political Economy of Modern Iran: Despotism and Pseudo-Modernism, 1926–1979*, New York: New York University Press, 1981.

Kawar, Amal. *Daughters of Palestine: Leading Women of the Palestinian Movement.* Albany: State University of New York Press, 1996.

Keddie, Nikki. "Oil, Economic Policy and Social Conflict in Iran." *Race and Class* 30 (1) (Summer 1979).

______. *Roots of Revolution: An Interpretative History of Modern Iran.* New Haven: Yale University Press, 1980 and 2003.

______. "Stratification, Social Control and Capitalism in Iranian Villages: Before and After Reform." In *Rural Politics and Social Change in the Middle East.* Edited by Robert Antoun and I. Harik. Bloomington: Indiana University Press, 1972.

______. "The Economic History of Iran, 1900–1914, Its Political Impact: An Overview." *Iranian Studies* (Spring-Summer 1992).

______. "Women in Iran Since 1979." In *Social Research: An International Quarterly of the Social Science.* Special Issue. *Iran Since the Revolution* 2 (Summer 2000).

______, and Lois, Beck, eds. *Women in the Muslim World.* Cambridge: Harvard University Press, 1978.

Kesselman, Mark, Joel, Krieger, and William A., Joseph. *Introduction to Comparative Politics.* New York: Houghton Mifflin, 2004.

Keshavarz, Nahid. "Kar-e Khanegi-ye Zanan: Moshkeli keh Tamami Nadarad" [Women's Household Labor: A Problem Without End]. *Fasl-e Zanan: Majmoo'ye Ara va Didgah-e Feministy* [Women's Chapter], 3 (1382/2003).

Ketab-e Salnamey-e Keyhan. 0301007, (1964/1343) as cited in Farmayan, Hafez. "Politics During Sixties: A Historical Analysis." In *Iran Faces Seventies.* Edited by Ehsan Yar-Shater. New York: Praeger, 1971.

Keyhan Research Associates. *The Employment of Women in the Higher Echelons of the Public and Private Sectors.* Tehran: Women's Organization of Iran, 1975.

Khamsi, Farhad. "Land Reform in Iran." *Monthly Review* 41 (2) (June 1969).

Khomeini, Ruhollah Musavi. *Resaleh Towziholmasael* [The Thesis of Explaining Problems]. Tehran: Eslamiyyeh Books, n.d.

______. *Mas'aleh-e Hejab* [The Hejab Problem]. Tehran: Sadra, 1365/1386.

Kian-Thébaut, Azadeh. *Les Femmes Iraniennes Entre Islam, État et Famille* [The Iranian Women in Islam and the Family]. Paris: Maisonneuve and Larose, 2002.

Lambton, Ann. *Landlord and Peasant in Persia.* London: Oxford University Press, 1953.

______. *The Persian Land Reform: 1962–1966.* Oxford: Clarendon Press, 1969.

______. "Persia Today." *The World Today* 17 (2) (February 1961).

______. "Some Reflections on the Questions of Rural Development: Land Reform in Iran." *Economic Research* 3 (9 and 10) (August 1965).

Langer, Frederic, and editors. "Iran: Oil Money and the ambitions of a Nation." *International Herald Tribune.* (March 1979).

Lasswell, Harold. *Who Gets What, When, and How.* New York: Meridian Books, 1958.

Lazrek, Marnia, *The Eloquence of Silence: Algerian Women in Question.* New York: Routledge, 1994.

Lerner, Daniel. *The Passing of the Traditional Society: Modernizing the Middle East.* Glencoe: Free Press, 1958.

Looney, Robert. *A Developmental Strategy for Iran Through the 1980's.* New York: Praeger, 1977.

______. *Income Distribution Policies and Economic Growth in Semi-Industrialized Countries: A Comparative Study of Iran, Mexico, Brazil, and South Korea.* New York: Praeger, 1975.

______. *The Economic Development of Iran: A Recent Survey With Projections to 1981.* New York: Praeger, 1973.

MacKinnon, Katherine. "Feminism, Marxism, Method and the State." *Signs* 10 (1) (1984).

Mahdi, Akbar Ali. *Teen Life in the Middle East.* Westport: Greenwood Press, 2003.

Mahmood, Saba. *Politics of Piety: The Islamic Revival and the Feminist Subject.* Princeton, Princeton University Press, 2004.

Mahmoudi, A. *Nazariye'e Jadid Dar Bareh-e Barabari-ye Zan Va Mard Dar Qesas* [New Perspectives on Gender Equality in Qesas]. Tehran: 1365/1987.

Malekzadeh, Mehdi. *Tarikh-e Inqelab-e Mashrutiyat* [The History of the Constitutional Revolution], Vol. III. Tehran, 1328/1949.

Manji, Irshad. *The Trouble with Islam: A Muslim's Call for Reform in Her Faith.* Canada: Random House Canada, 2004.

Manoochehran, Mehrangiz. *Enteqad-e Qavanin-e Asasi va Madani va Kayfari-ye Iran as Nazar-e Huquq-e Zan* [A Critique of the Constitutional, Civil, and Criminal Codes Pertaining to Women's Rights]. Tehran: Khoushes, 1342/1963.

Marbo, Judith. *Veiled Half Truths: Western Travellers' Perceptions of Middle Eastern Women.* New York: St. Martin's Press, 1991.

Massell, Gregory. *The Surrogate Proletariat.* Princeton: Princeton University Press, 1974.

Maud, Constance Elizabeth. "The First Iranian Feminist." *The Fortnighty Review.* (June 1913).

Mayer, Ann Elizabeth. "Cultural Pluralism as a Bar to Women's Rights: Reflections on the Middle Eastern Experience." In *Women's Rights, Human Rights: International Feminist Perspectives.* Edited by Julie Peters and Andrea Wolper. New York: Routledge, 1996.

Mazlooman, Reza. "Zan Koshi dar Lavay-e Qanun" [The Murdering of Women Under the Law]. Tehran: Women's Organization of Iran, 1353/1974.

Mernissi, Fatima. *Beyond the Veil: Male-Female Dynamics in a Modern Muslim Society.* Bloomington and Indianapolis: Indiana University Press, 1987.

Mies, Maria. *Patriarchy and Accumulation on a World Scale.* London: Zed Books, 1999.

Mihan-e Ma [Our Nation]. Special Issue. Tehran: Danshkadeh-e Ulum-e Ertebatat-e Ejtemani, n.d.

Milani, Farzaneh. "Revitalization: Some Reflections on the Work of Saffar-Zadeh." In *Women and Revolution in Iran.* Edited by Nashat Guity. Boulder: Westview Press, 1983.

———. *Veils and Words: The Emerging Voices of Iranian Women Writers.* Syracuse: Syracuse University Press, 1992.

Milani, Mohson. *The Making of Iran's Islamic Revolution: From Monarchy to Islamic Republic.* Boulder: Westview Press, 1994.

Millett, K., Ann Roberts, David Weissbordt, and Alan Silver. Transcript of press conference, November 22, 1974, 1:00 PM, by the delegation in Washington D.C. as distributed by the Committee for Intellectual and Artistic Freedom in Iran. New York, possibly 1974.

Millspaugh, Arthur Chester. *The Financial and Economic Situation of Persia, 1926.* New York: Imperial Persian Government, 1926.

Minces, Juliette. *The House of Obedience: Women in Arab Society.* Translated by M. Pallis. London: Zed Books, 1982.

Ministry of Interior. *Sar Shomari-ye Amari-ye 1335* [Census Statistics 1956]. Tehran: Ministry of Interior, 1341/1962.

Ministry of Justice. *Bar-resi-ye Amari-ye Ezdevaj* [A Statistical Investigation of Marriage]. Tehran: The Ministry of Justice, 2533/1974.

———. *Barresi-ye Amari-ye Ezdevaj va Talaq dar Tehran-e Bozorg* [A Statistical Investigation of Marriage and Divorce in Greater Tehran]. Tehran: Ministry of Justice, Statistical Center of Iran, 2536/1977.

Ministry of Labor. *Qavanin-e Moqarrarat-e Kar va Ta'min-e Ejtema'i* [The Labor Laws and Social Welfare]. Tehran: Mo'sesse-e Kar va Ta'min-e Ejtema'i, 1352/1973.

Mir-Hosseini, Ziba. Paper presented at Columbia University. New York, December 9, 1998.

———. *Islam and Gender: The Religious Debate in Contemporary Iran.* Princeton: Princeton University Press, 1999.

Mo'ini Araqi, Mahmood. *Bar-resi va Tahlil-e Madh-e Sheshom-e E'lamieh-e Jahani-ye Raf'e Tab'iz az Zan va Moqayesat-e on ba Moqararat-e Qanuni-ye Iran* [An Investigation and Analysis of the Sixth Article of International Declaration Abolishing Discrimination Against Women and its Comparison with Iranian Laws]. Tehran: WOI, 1353/1974.

Mo'tazed, Khosro. *Fowziyeh: Hekayat-e Talkh-kami-ye Qesseh-e Joda'ie* [Fowziyeh: Bitter Stories of Separation], II. Tehran: Alborz, 1373/1994.

Moaddel, Mansoor. *Class, Politics, and Ideology in the Iranian Revolution.* New York: Columbia University Press, 1993.

Moghadam, Fatemeh. "Commoditization of Sexuality and Female Labor Force Participation in Islam: Implications for Iran, 1960–1990." In *In the Eye of the Storm: Women in Post-Revolutionary Iran.* Edited by Mahnaz Afkhami and Erika Friedl. New York: Syracuse University Press, 1994.

———. *From Land Reform to Revolution: The Political Economy and Agricultural Development in Iran.* New York: Tauris, 1996.

———. "Iran's New Islamic Home Economic: An Exploratory Attempt to Conceptualize Women's Work in the Islamic Republic." In *Research in Middle East Economics*. Edited by Cinar Mine. Special issue. *The Economics of Women and Work in Middle East and North Africa*. Amsterdam: JAI Press, 2001.

Moghadam, Valentine. *Modernizing Women: Gender and Social Change in the Middle East*. Boulder: Lynne Rienner Publishers, 1993 and 2003.

Moghissi, Haideh. *Feminism and Islamic Fundamentalism Limits of Postmodern Analysis*. London: Zed Books, 1999.

———. "Women, Modernization, and Revolution in Iran." *Review of Radical Political Economics* 23 (3 and 4) (1991).

Mosaheb, Qolam-Hossein. *Da'erat al-Ma'ref-e Farsi* [the Encyclopedia of Persian]. I, Tehran: Frankline, 1345/1966.

Molyneux, Maxine. "Mobilization Without Emancipation? Women's Interests, State and Revolution." In *Transition and Development: Problems of Third World Socialism*. Edited by Richard R. Fagen, Carmen Diana Deere, and Jose Louis Coraggio. New York: Monthly Review Press, 1986.

Monira, Charrad and M. Deitch. "Gender and State Power: A Theoretical Investigation." Paper presented at the ASA Meeting, 1986.

Moser-Khalili, Moira. *Urban Design and Women's Lives* Tehran: Women's Organization of Iran, 1975.

Mossavar-Rahmani, L. Yasmin. "Family Planning in Post-Revolutionary Iran." In *Women*. Edited by G. Nashat. *Women and Revolution in Iran*, ed. by G. Nashat. Boulder: Westview Press, 1983.

Motahhari, Morteza. *Nezam-e Huquq-e Zan dar Islam* [The System of Women's Rights in Islam]. Tehran: Ziba, 1353/1974.

———. *Mas'aleh-e Hejab* [The Hejab Problem]. Tehran: Sadra, 1365/1986.

Najmabadi, Afsaneh. "Hazards of Modernity and Morality: Women, State and Ideology in Contemporary Iran." In *Women, Islam, and the State*. Edited by D. Kandiyoti. Philadelphia: Temple University Press, 1991.

———. "Feminisms in an Islamic Republic." In *Transitions, Environments and Translations: International Feminism in Contemporary Parties*. Edited by Joan Scott, C. Kaplan, and P. Keates. New York: Routledge, 1997.

———. "(Un)Veiling Feminism." *Social Text* 18 (3) (2000).

———, ed. *Women's Autobiography in Contemporary Iran*. Cambridge: Center for Middle Eastern Studies of Harvard University, Harvard University Press, 1990.

Naqd-e Feministi, Mohagerat dar Asar-e Zanan-e Dastan Nevis-e Irani [Feminist Talks, Exile's Impact on Iranian Women Novelists]. Los Angeles: M & M, 1997.

Narimian and Safa'i. *Parliamentary Proceedings* (December 30, 1952).

Nashat, Guity, ed. *Women and Revolution in Iran*. Boulder: Westview Press, 1982.

Nateq, Homa. "Negahi b-e Barkhi Nevisande-ha va Mobarazat-e Zanan dar Douran-e Mashrutiayyat" [A Look at Some Writers and Women's Struggles During the Constitutional Revolution]. *Keta-e Jom'eh* (1358/1979).

———. "Women: the Demand of the Iranian Revolution." In *Women and Political Conflict: Portraits of Struggle in Times of Crisis*. Edited by Rosemary Ridd and Helen Callaway. New York: New York University Press, 1987.

National Radio and Television. *Bayagani-ye Karmandan* [Personnel Files]. Tehran: National Radio and Television, Office of Administrative Affairs and Records, 2536/1977.

Nelson, Barbara J., and Najma Chowdhury, eds. *Women and Politics Worldwide.* New Haven: Yale University Press, 1994.

Nemazi, Siamak. Paper presented at Columbia University. New York, February 20, 2004.

NIRT (Sazeman-e Radio va Television-e Iran). *Gozaresh-e Salanmeh-e Sazeman-e Radio Television-e Melli-ye Iran dar Sal-e 1353* [The NIRT Annual Report, 1974]. Tehran: Sazeman-e Radio va Television-e Iran, n.d.

Nirumand, Bahman. *Iran: Imperialism in Action.* New York: Monthly Review Press, 1969.

Nooshin, Ahmadi Khorasani. *Zanan Zir-e Sayeh-e Pedar Khandeh-ha.* Tehran: Tose'eh, 3rd printing, 1380/2001.

"Notq-e Vala Hazrat Shahdokht Ashraf Pahlavi" [The Speech of Her Majesty Princess Ashraf Pahlavi]. In *Kongereh-e Bozorgdasht-e Chehellomin Salrouz-e Azadi-ye Ejtemi-Ye Zanan* [The Congress of Celebration of the 40th Day of Social Emancipation of Women]. Tehran: Women's Organization of Iran, n.d.

Office of Women's Studies and Research. "Bar-resi-ye Ejmali-ye Sharayet-e Kargar-e Zanan-e Irani" [The Investigation of the Conditions of Female Workers]. n.p., 1348/1969.

Ommol, Benin, ed. *Sal Nameh-e Zana-e Daneshgahi-ye Iran 1381* [Iranian University Women Calendar 2000]. Tehran: Al-Zahra University Press, 2002.

Opie, Anne. "Qualitative Research, Appropriation of the 'Other' and Empowerment." *Feminist Review* 3 (1991).

Pahlavi, Farah. *An Enduring Love: My Life with the Shah – A Memoir.* New York: Simon and Schuster, Inc., 2004.

Pahlavi, Mohammad Reza. *Answer to History.* Briar Cliff Manor: Stein and Day, 1980.

______. *B-e su-ye Tamaddon-e Bozorg* [Towards the Great Civilization]. Tehran: Pahlavi Library Publication, 1357/1978.

______. *Mission for My Country.* New York: McGraw Hill, 1962.

______. *Twelve Speeches by His Imperial Majesty Mohammad Reza Pahlavi Aryamehr, Shahanshah of Iran, on Ideological Basis of Iran's National and International Policy.* Tehran: Pahlavi Library, 1974.

Pahlavi, Princess Ashraf. *Faces In A Mirror: Memoirs From Exile.* New Jersey: Prentice-Hall, 1980.

Paidar, Parvin. *Women and the Political Process in Twentieth-Century Iran.* London: Cambridge University Press, 1995.

Pakizegi, Behnaz. "Legal and Social Positions of Iranian Women." In *Women in the Muslim World.* Edited by Lois Beck and Nikki Keddie. Cambridge: Harvard University Press, 1978.

Papaneck, Hanna. "The Ideal Woman and the Ideal Society: Control and Autonomy in the Construction of Identity." In *Identity Politics & Women: Cultural Reassertions and Feminisms in International Perspective.* Edited by Valentine Moghadam. Boulder: Westview Press, 1994.

Parliamentary Proceedings. (December 1906).

Parliamentary Proceedings. (August 1944).

Parsipour, Shahrnoosh. *Khaterat-e Zendan* [Prison Memoir]. Stockholm: Baran, 1996.

______. *Sag va Zemestan-e Boland* [The Dog and Long Winters]. Tehran: Pars, 1369/1990, 1st printing, 1355/1976.

Patai, Ralph. "The Dynamics of Westernization in the Middle East." *The Middle East Journal* 9 (1) (Winter 1955).

Pateman, Carole. *The Sexual Contract*. Stanford: Stanford University Press, 1988.

Peace Review. Special issue on Women and War (3). (September 1996).

Pedrazzani, Jean M. *L'imperatrice d'Iran: le Mythe et la Realité*. Paris: n.p., n.d.

Peteet, Julie. *Gender in Crisis: Women and the Palestinian Resistance Movement*. New York: Columbia University Press, 1991.

Peters, Julie, and Andrea Wolper, eds. *Women's Rights, Human Rights: International Feminist Perspectives*. New York: Routledge, 1996.

Peterson, V. Spike, and Ann Sisson Runyan. *Global Gender Issues*. Boulder: Westview Press, 1993 and 1999.

Pirnia, Mansureh. *Salar-e Zanan-e Iran* [Great Women of Iran]. Maryland: Mehr Iran, 1374/1995.

______. *Safarnameh-e Shahbanoc Farah Pahlavi* [The Travels of Empress Fareh Pahlavi]. Maryland: Mehran Iran, 1371/1992.

______. *Gozaresh-e Eqtesadi-ye Sal-e 1368* [The Economic Report of 1989]. Tehran: The Plan and Budget Organization of Iran, 1369/1990.

Poya, Maryam. *Women, Work, and Islamism*. New York: St. Martin's Press, 1999.

Public Relations Office of the Parliament. *An Introduction of Parliamentary Members of of the Sixth Majles* [in Persian]. Tehran: Publicity and Publications Office, 1379/2000.

Rachlin, Nahid. *Foreigner*. New York: W. W. Norton & Company, Inc., 1978.

Raha, M. *Haqiqat-e Sadeh: Khaterat az Zendanha-ye Jomhuri-ye Eslami-ye Iran* [Simple Facts: Memories of Women's Prisons in the Islamic Republic of Iran]. I. Hanover, 1371/1992.

Rahnavard, Zahra. *Tolu'e Zan-e Mosalman* [The Dawn of Muslim Women]. In *In the Shadow of Islam: The Women's Movement in Iran*. Edited by Azar Tabari and Nahid Yeganeh. London: Zed Books, 1982.

Ramazani, Nesta. "Women in Iran: The Revolutionary Ebb and Flow." *Middle East Journal* 47 (1993).

Rastakhiz-e Kargaran [Workers' Resurgence], 17th Azar, 1354/1975 as cited in *Artesh-e Azim-e Zanan b-e Mayda Miad* [The Great Army of Women is Coming to the Front] Tehran: n.p., n.d.

Rastegar, Ezzatollah. "*Sokhanrani.*" Paper presented at the National Labor Conference. Tehran: The Ministry of Labor and Social Welfare. 1354/1975.

______. "Tose'-ye Eshteqal-e Zanan" [Development of Female Employment]. Tehran: The Ministry of Labor and Social Affairs, n.d., possibly, 1354/1976.

Ravanipoor, Monir. *Del-e Fulad* [Steel Heart]. Tehran: Shiva, 1369/1990.

Ravasani, Schapour. *Iran*. Stuttgart: Alektor-Verland, 1978.

Razzaqi, Ebrahim. *Eqtesad-e Iran* [Iran's Economics]. Tehran: Nashani, 1367/1988.

Rice, Collier C. *Persian Women and Their Ways*. London: Seeley, Service and Company, Limited, 1923.

Rodinson, Maxime. *Islam and Capitalism*. New York: Pantheon Books, 1973 and 1974.

Roosevelt, Kermit. *Countercoup: The Struggle for the Control of Iran*. New York: McGraw Hill, 1979 and 1980.

Rooznameh-e Iran [Iran's Newspaper], 1301/1922 as cited in Sheikholseslami, *Zanan-e* [The Iranian Female Journalists and Intellectuals]. Tehran: Mazgrafic, 1351/1972.

Rouleau, Eric. "The Shah's Dreams of Glory." In *Iran Erupts*. Edited by Alireza Nobari. Stanford: Iran Documentation Group, Stanford University, 1978.

Rowbotham, Sheila. *Women, Resistance, and Revolution*. New York: Vintage Books, 1974.

Royanian, Simin. "A History of Iranian Women's Struggles." *The Review of Iranian Political Economy and History* 3 (1) (Spring 1979).

Rustow, Dankwart, and John Mugno. *OPEC Success and Prospect*. New York: New York University Press, 1976.

Saadawi, Nawal. *The Hidden Face of Eve*. Boston: Beacon Press, 1980.

Sackville-West. *Passenger to Tehran*. London: Hogart Press, 1926.

Sadeghipoor, Reza. *Majmu'at-e Sokhanrinha-ye* [The Collection of Speeches of the Late Majesty Reza Shah the Great]. Tehran: 1343/1964.

Sadr, Hasan. *Huquq-e Zan dar Islam va Orupa* [Women's Rights in Islam and Europe]. Tehran: Mousavi, 1347/1968.

Sadr-Hashemi, Mohammad. *Tarikh-e Jarayed va Majallat-e Iran* [The History of Iranian Newspapers and Journals], I-III. Isfahan, n.d., 1327/1948.

Safar Nameh-e Shahbanoo Farah Pahlvai [The Travels of Empress Farah Pahlavi]. Maryland: Mehr Iran, 1371/1992.

Saikal, Amin. *The Rise and Fall of the Shah*. Princeton: Princeton University Press, 1980.

Salehi-Isfahani, Djavad. "Demographic Factors in Iran's Economic Development." *Social Research, Iran Since the Revolution*. Special issue 67 (2000).

Salman, Magida, et al. *Women in the Middle East*. London: Zed Books, 1987.

Salnameh-e Zanan-e Iran [The Yearbook of Iranian Women]. Tehran: Sazeman-e Zanan-e Iran, 1345/1966.

Sanasarian, Eliz. *The Women's Rights Movements in Iran: Mutiny, Appeasement, and Repression From 1900 to Khomeini*. New York: Praeger, 1982.

Sanghvi, Ramesh, Clifford German, and David Missen, eds. *The Revolution of the Shah and the People*. London: Transorient, 1967.

Satines, G., C. Tavris, and T. Jayarante. "The Queen Bee Syndrome," *Psychology Today* (January 1974).

Satrapi, Marjane. *Persepolis: The Story of a Childhood*. New York: Pantheon Books, 2003.

———. *Chicken With Plums*. New York: Pantheon Books, 2006.

Sayigh, Rosemary. "Roles and Functions of Arab Women: A Reprisal of Orientalism and Arab Women." *Arab Studies Quarterly* 3 (3) (1981), 258–74.

Sazeman-e Radio va Television. *Masa'el-e zanan-e Karmand-e Doulat*. Tehran: National Radio and Television of Iran, n.d.

Sazeman-e Radio Va Television-e Iran. *Gozaresh-e Salnameh-e Sazeman-e Radio Television-e Melli-ye Iran dar sal-e 1353* [NIRT Report, 1974]. Tehran: Sazeman-e Radio va Television-e Iran, n.d.

Sazeman-e Mojahedin-e Khalq-e Iran. *Women On the Way of Liberation* [in Persian] I, Long Beach, 1359/1980.

______. *The Tale of a Great Determinism: A Brief Account of the Revolutionary Martyr Mojahed-Amin* [in Persian]. Long Beach, 1359/1980.

Schizarizi, Asghar. *The Constitution of Iran: Politics and the State in the Islamic Republic*. London and New York: I.B. Tauris, 1998.

Sciolino, Elaine. *Persian Mirrors: The Elusive Face of Iran*. New York: Touchstone, Simon and Schuster, 2000.

______. "The Chanel Under the Chador." *The New York Times Magazine* (May 4, 1997).

Scott, Catherine. *Gender and Development: Rethinking Modernization and Dependency Theory*. Boulder: Lynne Rienner Publishers, 1995.

Sedghi, Hamideh. "Global Feminism, Local Agendas and Actions." In *Socialism and Democracy* 19 (2) (2005).

______. "Muslims in the West's Imagination: Myth or Reality." In *Socialism and Democracy* 16 (1) (2002).

______. "[Feminist Movements] in the Pahlavi Period." In *Encyclopaedia Iranica*. Edited by Ehsan Yarshater. New York: Bibliotheca Press, 1999.

______. "gender and aeging: problems, perceptions, and policies." Report prepared for the Secretary General. United Nations Econonic and Social Council. E.N. 6/1999/3. New York, 1999.

______. "The State, Women, and Development: A Comparative Appraisal of Secular and Religious Politics in Iran." In *The Gendered New World Order: Militarism, Development, and the Environment*. New York: Routledge, 1996.

______. "Third World Women's Perspectives on World Politics." In *Women, Gender and World Politics*. Edited by P.R. Beckman and F. D'Amico. Westport: Bergin and Garvey, 1994.

______. "The State and the Sexual Division of Labor in Iran." Paper presented at the Annual Meeting of British Society of Middle East Studies. London, 1986.

______. "Women and Class in Iran, 1900–1978." Ph.D. dissertation, City University of New York, 1982.

______. "A Critique of Works on Twentieth Century Iran and Iranian Women." *New Directions in Middle Eastern Studies Newsletter* 1 (2) (1980).

______. "An Assessment of Works in Farsi and English on Iran and Iranian Women: 1900–1977." *The Review of Radical Political Economics* 12 (2) (1980).

______. "Women in Iran." In *Women in the World: A Cross-Comparative Study*. Edited by L. Igalitzin and R. Ross. Santa Barbara: ABC-Clio Press, 1976.

______, and Ashraf Ahmad. "The Condition of Women in Iran." In *Iran: Past, Present, and Future*. Edited by J. Jacqz. Aspen: Aspen Institute for Humanistic Studies, 1976.

Shaidian, Hamed. "The Iranian Left and the 'Woman Question' in the Revolution of 1978–79." *International Journal of Middle East Studies* 26 (1994): 223–247.

Shari'ati, Ali. *Fatima is Fatima*. Tehran Foundation: The Shariati Foundation, n.d. Translated by Bakhtiar, Laleh, 1980.

———. *Zan-e Mosalman* [Muslim Women]. Tehran Foundation: The Shariati Foundation, n.d. Translated by Bakhtiar, Laleh, 1979.

Sheend, Vincent. *The New Persia*. New York: the Century Co., 1927.

Sheikhoeslami, Pari. *Zanan-e Rouznameh Negar va Andishmand-e Iran* [The Iranian Female Journalists and Intellectuals]. Tehran: Mazgrafic, 1351/1972.

Shievers, Lynne. "Inside the Iranian Revolution." In *Tell the American People: Perspectives on the Iranian Revolution*. Edited by David Albert. Philadelphia: Movement for a New Society, 1980.

Shuster, Morgan. *The Strangling of Persia: Story of European Diplomacy and Oriental Intrigue that Resulted in the Denationalization of Twelve Million Mohammedans: A Personal Narrative*. New York: The Century Company, 1912.

Sick, Gary. *All Fall Down: America's Tragic Encounter with Iran*. New York: Penguin Books, 1986.

Skocpol, Theda. "Rentier State and Shi'a Islam in the Iranian Revolution." *Theory and Society* 11 (May 1982).

———. *States and Social Revolutions: A Comparative Analyses of France, Russia, and China*. Cambridge: Cambridge University Press, 1979.

Soltani, Amir Hosein. "*Bar-resi-ye* Amuzesh va Eshteghal-e Zana-e Kargar dar Iran" [An Investigation of Female Workers' Education and Employment in Iran]. Tehran: Sazeman-e Radio of Television, 2536/1977.

Statistical Center of Iran. *Iran Statistical Yearbook 1379*. Tehran, 2001.

———. *Socioeconomic Characteristics of Women in Iran 1986–96*. Tehran: 2001.

———. *Salnameh-e Amari-ye Keshvar* [Annual National Statistics, 1972]. Tehran: Statistical Center of Iran, 1352/1973.

———. *Sar Shomari-ye Omumi-ye Nofus va Maskan* [National Census of Population and Housing]. Tehran: Statistical Center of Iran, 2535/1976.

Stockholm International Peace Research Institute. "U.S. Military Sales to Iran." *Yearbook of World Armaments and Disarmaments 1976–1977*. New York: Humanities Press, 1977.

Storke, Joe. *Middle East Oil and the Energy Crisis*. New York: Monthly Review Press, 1975.

Sultanzadeh. "Moqeiyyat-e Zan-e Irani" [The Status of Iranian Women] in his *Asnad-e Rarikhi: Jonbesh-e Karqari, Soshel Demokrasi va Komonisti-ye* [Historical Documents: The Worker, Social Democratic, and Communist Movements of Iran], vol. IV. Italy: Mazdak, 1975. Translated from the 1922 German version.

Sykes, Ella. "Persia." In *Women of all Nations* IV. Edited by Joyce T.A. New York: Funk and Wagnalls, 1915.

Tabari, Azar, and Nahid Yeganeh, eds. *In the Shadow of Islam: The Women's Movement in Iran*. London: Zed Books, 1982.

Tabari, Ehsan. "Reaction and Social Thought in the Contemporary Middle East." In *Political and Social Thought in Contemporary Middle East*. Edited by Kemal Karpat. New York: Praeger, 1968.

Taj (Langarudi), Mohammad Mehdi. *Dastan-e Zanan* [The Story of Women]. Tehran: Zohreh, 1350/1971.

Tamizi, Bakri. *Naqd-e Feministi, Mohagerat dar Asar-e Zanan-e Dastan Nevis-e Irani* [Feminist Talks, Exile's Impact on Iranian Women Novelists]. Los Angeles: M & M, 1997.

Targhi-Tavakoli, Mohammad. "Imagining Western Women: Occidentalism and Euro-Eroticism." *Radical America* 24 (July–September 1993).

Targhi-Tavakkoli Mohamad, and Afsaneh, Najmabadi, eds. *Bibi Khanum Astarabadi's Ma'ayeb al-rejal* [Bibi Khanum Astarabadi's Vices of Men]. New York: 1992.

Tarikh-cheh va Fa'liyyatha-ye Sazeman-e Zanan-e Iran [History and Activities of the Women's Organization of Iran]. *Mihan-e Ma* [Our Nation]. Special issue. Tehran: Daneshkadeh-e Ulum-e Ertebatat-e Ejtemai,' n.d.

"Ta'sir-e Amuzesh va Eshteqal dar Kahesh-e Asib-ha-ye Ejtema'i dar Mian-e Zanan" [The Impact of Education and Work on Reducing Social Abuse Among Women]. *Fasl-e Zanan* 3, 1382/2003.

Tavaf-Chian, Shokuh, and Yasemin Vafa. *Dar Bareh-e Masa'leh-e Zan* [About the Women's Problem]. Tehran: 1357/1978.

The Autobiography of H.I.H. Princess Soraya. Translated from German by C. Fitzerald. London: Arthur Barker Limited, 1963.

The Center for Women's Participation. *Women's Participation and Seventh Government* [in Persian]. Tehran: The Center for Women's Participation, 1380/2001.

The Constitution of the Women's Organization of Iran. Tehran: n.p., n.d.

"The Guerrilla Movement in Iran, 1963–1977." *Merip Reports* 86 (March/April 1980).

The Iranian Mojahedin. New Haven: Yale University Press, 1989.

The Office of Women's Studies Research. "Bar-resi-ye Ejmali-ye Sharayet-e Kargare-e Zanan-e Irani" [The Investigation of the Conditions of Female Workers]. n.p., 1348/1969.

The Plan and Budget Organization of Iran. *Degarguniha-ye Ejtema'i va Eqtesadi-ye Zanan-e Iran* [Social and Economic Changes in the Position of Iranian Women]. Tehran: Plan and Budget Organization of Iran, Statistical Center of Iran, 1352/1973.

Thompson, E.P. *The Making of the English Working Class*. London: Alfred A. Knopf, Inc. and Random House, Inc., 1968.

Tickner, J. Ann. *Gender in International Relations*. New York: Columbia University Press, 1992.

Tilly, Louise A., and Joan W. Scott. *Women, Work, and Family*. New York: Rinehart and Winston, 1978.

Touba, Jacqueline Rudolph. "The Relationship Between Urbanization and the Changing Status of Women in Iran, 1956–1966." *Iranian Studies* 5 (1) (Winter 1973).

Touhidi, Nayereh. "Gender and Islamic Fundamentalism: Feminist Politics in Iran." In *Third World Women and the Politics of Feminism*. Edited by Chandra Mohanty. Bloomington: Indiana University Press, 1991.

Tucker, Judith. *Women in Nineteenth Century Egypt*. New York: Cambridge University Press, 1985.

UNDP. *Human Development Report 1995*. New York and Oxford: Oxford University Press, 1995.

UNDP. *Human Development Report 2002 Deepening Democracy in a Fragmented World*. New York and Oxford: Oxford University Press, 2002.

UNFPA. "Reproductive Health/Family Planing Activities in the Islamic Republic of Iran." New York: UNFPA, 1997.

U.S. Military Sales to Iran. *Yearbook of World Armaments and Disarmaments 1976–1977*. New York: Humanities Press, 1977.

Vaz'e Zanan-e Ruspigar [The Condition of Female Prostitutes], as cited in *Setam Keshidegi-ye Zan dar Iran* [Women's Oppression in Iran]. New York: Fanus, 1351/1972.

Vezarat-e E'tela't va Jahangardi. *Fehrest-e Nam va Onvan-e Maqamat-e Mamlekati* [List of Names and Titles of Iranian Officials]. Tehran: Markaz-e Madarek va Asnad, 1354/1975–1355/1976.

Warriner, Doreen. *Land Reform in Principle and Practice*. Oxford: Clarendon Press, 1969.

Willber, Donald. *Riza Shah Pahlavi: The Resurrection and Reconstruction of Iran, 1878–1944*. New York: Exposition Press, 1975.

Wise, David, and Thomas B. Ross. *The Invisible Government*. New York: Vintage Books, 1974 and 1969.

Women's Organization of Iran. *Bar-resi-ye Masa'l va Moshkelat-e Khanevadeh* [An Investigation of Family Problems and Issues]. Tehran: WOI, 1343/1974.

Women's Organization of Iran. *Naghsh-e Zan dar Barnameh-e Omrani-ye Sheshom-e Keshvar*, 2535/1976.

Women's Solidarity Association of Iran. *Paradise Under the Feet: Women in Iran*. Tehran: The Islamic Republic of Iran, n.d.

Woodsmall, Ruth. *Moslem Women Enter a New World*. New York: Round Table Press Inc., 1936.

______. *Women and the Near East*. Washington, D.C.: The Middle East Institute, 1960.

World Bank Annual Reports. Washington, D.C.: The World Bank, March 1973.

Yamani, Mai, ed. *Feminism and Islam: Legal and Literary Perspectives*. New York: New York University Press, 1997.

Yeganeh, Nahid. "Jonbesh-e Zan dar Iran" [The Women's Movement in Iran]. *Nimeye Digar* [The Other Half] 2 (2) (Autumn, 1363/1984).

______. "Women's Struggles in the Islamic Republic of Iran." In *In the Shadow of Islam: The Women's Movement in Iran*. Edited by Tabari Azar and Nahid Yeganeh. London: Zed Books, 1982.

______, and Nikki Keddie . "Sexuality and Shi'i Social Protest in Iran." Cole and Nikki Keddie. Edited by Juan. In *Shi'ism and Social Protest*. New Haven: Yale University Press, 1986.

Yousef, Nadia. *Women and Work in Developing Societies*. Westport: Greenwood Press, 1976.

Yuval-Davis, Nira, and Anthias Floya, eds. *Woman, Nation, State*. London: Macmillan, 1989.

Zamani, Mostafa. *Payman-e Zanashu'i* [Matrimonial Treaty]. Qom: Payman, 1350/1971.

Zendegi-nameh-e Emam Khomeini [The Biography of Imam Khomeini] I. (Panz-dah-e Khordad Publishers), n.d.

Zonis, Marvin. *Political Elites in Iran*. Princeton: Princeton University Press, 1971.

Newspaper and Magazine Articles

A Survey. "Ch-e No' Hejab Darid" [What Kind of *Hejab* Do you Have?]. *Zan-e Ruz* (4 Mordad 1365/July 25, 1986).

Azadi. "Women Defy Authorities." *Irish Times* (December 3, 1997).

Bagherian, Mitra. "Eshteghal va Bikari-ye Zanan az Didgah-e Tose'eh" [Women's Employment and Unemployment from the Development View]. *Zanan* (1371/1992).

Bahari, Mazian. Newsweek. (August 21, 2002). Online at wsiayg://79/http: www.msnbc.com/news/605146.asp.

Bidari-ye Zan [Women's Awakening]. *Tir* (1357/July 1978).

Boyle, Kay. "Sisters of the Princess." *The Nation* (March 6, 1976).

Branigin, Walter. "Pahlavi Fortune: A Staggering Sum." *Washington Post* (January 17, 1979).

Brooks, Geraldine. "Teen-Age Infidels Hanging Out In High Tops and Jeans, Iranian Youths Are Quietly Tara Bahrampour." Her "Under Wraps." *The New York Times Magazine* (July 10, 1994).

Byrne, Richard, "A Collision of Prose and Politics." *The Chronicle of Higher Education* (October 13, 2006).

"Ch-e No' Hejab Darid" [What Kind of *Hejab* Do you Have?]. *Zan-e Ruz* (4 Mordad 1365/July 25, 1986).

Chittenden, A. "Bankers Say Shah's Fortune Is Well above a Billion." *The New York Times* (January 10, 1979).

Cooley, John K. "U.S. Faces Sticky Question of Backing the Shah of Iran." *Christian Science Monitor* (November 1978).

Comiteh-e Ejad-e Jam'iyyat-e Bidari-ye Zanan. "Aqaz-e Bi-dari-ye Mellat, Aqaz-e Bi-dari-ye Zanan" [The Beginning of People's Awakening, the Beginning of Women's Awakening]. *Ayandegan* (12 Bahman 1357/February 3, 1978), 12.

Committee for Artistic and Intellectual Freedom in Iran. "Defend Women Political Prisoners in Iran." New York: possibly 1975.

Committee for Artistic and Intellectual Freedom in Iran. "Women in the Shah's Prison: The Case of Vida Hadjebi Tabrizi." New York: possibly 1974.

"Control-e Hejab" [Control the Hejab]. *Iran Times* (1 Farvar din 1365/March 21, 1986).

Cummings, Judith. "Demonstration at Iran's Consulate Backs Women's Rights Movement." *The New York Times* (March 16, 1979).

______. "15,000 Tehran Women Protest For Fifth Day Over Dress Code." *The New York Times* (March 13, 1979).

Dagens Nyheter (August 31, 1973) as cited in The Committee for Artistic and Intellectual Freedom in Iran.

Daniszewski, John. "Iran Loosens Up." *Los Angeles Times* (December 23, 1997).

"Davzdah Shart-e Estehkam-e Khanevadh" [Twelve Rules for Family Stability]. *Iran Times* (June 13, 1986).

de Bellaigue, Christopher. "Stalled in Iran." *The New York Review of Books* (June 2004).

Dopoulos, Philip. *The New York Times* (Supplementary material from The New York Times News Service and the Associated Press). (October 7, 1978).

Ebadi, Shirin and Amir, Aharan. "When Politics Corrupts Money."*The New York Times*. Op-Ed (June 16, 2004).

Ebadi, Shirin in interview with *Le Monde* as cited in *Tehran Post* 9 (98) (Aban 1392/November 2003).

______. "Bound but Gagged." *The New York Times*. Op-ed (November 16, 2004).

______. Interviewed by Amy Goodman. *Democracy Now Show* (June 9, 2004).

Ebrahimi, Zahra. "Yek Mah ba Zanan dar Majles" [One Month in the Parliament With Women]. *Zanan* 94 (1381/2002).

E Hela' at-e Salnameh (1342/1963) Sec I, 50. Cited in Farmaian.

"Empress Farah Talks of Shah and Women's Rights in Iran." *Christian Science Monitor* (February 8, 1978).

Esmat, Abad. Interviewed by www.Badjens.com (May 3, 2000).

Etezadi, Shahin. "The Changing Roles of Iranian Women." *Islamic Revolution* (December 1979).

Ettela' at. 11 Sharivar 1331/1952 as cited by Akhavi, Shrokh. *Religion and Politics in Contemporary Iran: Clergy-State Relations in the Pahlavi Period*. Albany: State University of New York Press, 1980.

Ettela'at. 13945 (1351/1972), as cited in Mazlooman, Reza. "Zan Koshi dar Lavay-e Qanun" [The Murdering of Women Under the Law]. Tehran: Women's Organization of Iran, 1353/1974.

Ettela'at 14275 (1352/1972), as cited by Mazlooman, Reza. "Zan Koshi dar Lavay-e Qanun" [The Murdering of Women Under the Law]. Tehran: Women's Organization of Iran, 1353/1974.

Ettela'at. 14039 (1351/1972), as cited by Mazlooman, Reza. "Zan Koshi dar Lavay-e Qanun" [The Murdering of Women Under the Law]. Tehran: Women's Organization of Iran, 1353/1974.

Ettela'at 14230 (1352/1973), as cited in Mazlooman, Reza. "Zan Koshi dar Lavay-e Qanun" [The Murdering of Women Under the Law]. Tehran: Women's Organization of Iran, 1353/1974.

Ettela'at-e Banovan. Tehran, 1977.

"Farah: The Working Empress." *Time* (November 4, 1974).

Fiaz-Bakhsh. "Khatar-e Birun Budan-e Dast va Surat-e Zan az Hejab" [The Dangers of Showing Women's Face and Hands Uncovered]. *Iran Times* (March 28, 1986).

Friedan, Betty. "Coming Out of the Veil." *Ladies Home Journal* (June 1975).

Gorgin, Ira. Interviewed by Furus Farrokhzad. *She'ir-e Emruz* [Today's Poetry]. Tehran, 1964.

Gregory, Jaynes. "Iran Women March Against Restraints on Dress and Rights." *The New York Times* (March 11, 1979).

"Haftad-do-yek dar sad-e Vorudiha-ye Daneshgaha Dokhtar Hastand" [71% of University Entrants Are Girls]. *Zanan* 95 (1381/2002) 75.

Hedges, Chris. "Darakeh Journal: With Mullah's Eluded, Hijinks in the Hills." *The New York Times* (August 8, 1994).

Huquq-e Zanan. Various issues, Tehran, Iran.

Huguq va Ejtema'. Various issues, Tehran, Iran.

Ghazi, Katayon. "Iran Offers an Islamic Way to Improve the Lot of Women." *The New York Times* (December 21, 1994).

"Iran Hoveyyat-e Tarikhi" [Iran: Historical Identity]. *Keyhan* (1978).

"Iran: 'No Worse in Human Rights'." *CAIFI Newsletter* 2 (1) (March 1976).

"Iran Parliament Is Back In Session." *The New York Times* (October 7, 1963)

"Iran-Time for Protest." *The Guardian* (January 31, 1976).

"Iran Women Get More Divorce Rights." Online at http://news.bbc.co.uk.ny/2hi/middle_east/2534375.stm (December 12, 2002).

Jaynes, Gregory. "Iran Women March Against Restraints on Dress and Rights." *The New York Times* (March 11, 1979).

John, K. "U.S. Faces Sticky Question of Backing the Shah of Iran." *Christian Science Monitor* (November 1978).

Judad, Tim. "The Sullen Majority." *The New York Times Magazine* (September 1, 2002).

Kar, Mehrangiz. "Jayegah-e Zan dar Qavanin-e Keyfari-ye Iran" [Women's Position in the Iranian Penal Codes]. *Zanan* (Khordad/Tir 1372, June/July 1993).

Kashani. "A Message," *Tehran Mosavver*, April 4, 1952 as cited in Abrahamian, *Iran*. Princeton: Princeton University Press, 1982.

Kaviri, Mohammad. "Zan, Ya Mard, Ya Azadi?" ["Woman or Man or Liberty?"]. *Zan-e Ruz* (8 Ordibehesht 1358/April 28, 1979).

Keyhan 8522 (1350/1971).

Keyhan International. (January 5, 1975).

Keyhan. (21 Mehr, 1354/October 13, 1975).

Keyhan-e Havai'i. "Hoveyda: Azadi-ye Zan Biganeh Kardan-e OO Az Khanevadeh Nist" [Hoveyda: Woman's Emancipation Does Not Mean Her Estrangement From Her Family]. *Kehan-e Havai'i* (January 7, 1976).

"Khatar-e Biran Budan-e Dast Va Surat-e Zan Az Hejab" [The Dangers of Not Covering Hands and Face]. *Iran Times* (March 28, 1986).

Lancaster John. "Iranian Crusade: Suspending Liberal Tendencies in Schools, Clerics Launch 'Islamization' Crackdown." *Washington Post* (December 15, 1996).

Longinotto, Kim and Ziba, Mir-Hoseini. "Divorce: Iranian Style, A Documentary Video," 2003.

Mahjuubah: The Magazine for Muslim Women. Tehran: Islamic Republic of Iran. (June/July 1982).

Maknoon, Sorayya. "Hijab and Women's Political Participation in the Society." *Tehran Times: Special Issue on Women's Week* 18 (178) (November 5, 1966).

"Mardom Bayad Bi-Hejab Ha Ra Tahvil Nagirand" ["People Should Ignore the Unveiled"]. *Zan-e Ruz* (6 Mordad 1363/July 28, 1984).

Mohammad. "Zan, Ya Mard, Ya Azadi?" [Woman or Man or Liberty?]. *Zan-e Ruz* (8 Ordibehesht 1358/April 28, 1979).

Mosavi, Shahron. "Behind the Scarves: Iran Second Sex Seethes." *Business Week* (February 23, 1998).

Naderi. "Andar Hekayat-e 'Tazahorat A'Lay-he Bad Hejabi" [In Stories: Demonstrations Against Bad-Veiling]. In *Ettela'at* (1 mehr, 1364/September 23, 1985).

Nassehi, Guity. "Islamic Republic of Iran, Women: A Situation Analysis." A revised paper for UNDP, June 1996.

Nateq, Homa. "Movazeb bashim àlayh-e Mardan be-kar Keshideh Nashavim" [We Must Be Careful Not to Be Used Against Men]. *Ayandegan* (Baham 16, 1357/February 5, 1978).

Negah-e Zanan. Various issues, 1979 Tehran.

Nimeyeh Digar. Various issues, 1982–1993, London and New York.

Nur al-Elm [The Light of Knowledge]. Tehran, n.d.

Pahlavi, F. "Hameh-e Rah-ha-ye Fa'liat Beru-ye Zana-e Iran Goshudeh Ast" [All Activity Roads are Open to Iranian Women]. *Keyhan* 19 Tir (2536/July 3, 1977).

Pahlavi, Ashraf. Op. Ed. "And thus Passeth International Women's Year." *New York Times* (January 5, 1976).

Payam-e Hajar. Various issues. Tehran.

Payam-e Zan. North York, Canada, 1996.

Pesara va Dokhtaran. Various issues. Tehran.

Pirouz. *Sefid va Siah* [White and black]. Tehran.

"Princess Pahlavi: Friend of Women or Ally of Repression," Committee for Intellectual Artistic Freedom in Iran. New York, 1978.

Qa'ini, S. "Velayat-e Pedar [,] Mafhum Va Damaneh." [Father's Rule [,] Meaning and Extent]. *Zanan* (Women) 36 (1376/1997).

"Queen of Iran Accepts Divorce as a 'Sacrifice'." *The New York Times* (March 15, 1958).

"Rafsanjani: Dar Barabar-e Hejab Moqavemant Vujud Darad" [Rafsanjani: There Is Resistance Against Veiling]. *Iran Times* (1986).

Raha, M. *Haqiqat-e Sadeh: Khaterat az Zendanha-ye Jomhuri-ye Eslami-ye Iran* [Simple Facts: Memories of Women's Prisons in the Islamic Republic of Iran]. I. Hanover (1371/1992).

"Ra'ies-e Shoray-e Eslami Hodud-e Hejab Zanan Ra E'lam Kard" [The Speaker of *Majles* announced the limits of *Hejab*]. *Iran Times* (September 12, 1986).

Razai, Behjat. "Out of the Frying Pan into Fire." *The Middle East* (May 1991).

Razavi, Yaseen. "Empress Reveals Women's Role in Iran." *Tehran Journal* 22 (6342) (July 30, 1975).

Reuters. "Basiji Islamic Code." (Tehran: May 21, 1996).

______. "Iran Vote Should Prompt U.S. Rethink." Online, (May 27, 1997).

Roya, Karimi-Majd. "Arian, Koodak-e bi Pana: Chera Beh in Rooz Oftad" [Arian, Why Did this Helpless Child Have Such a Destiny?!] *Zanan* 37 (1376/1999).

Sadr, Shadi. "Dokhtaran-e Irani and Bardeh Bardari-ye Modern" [Iranian Girls and Modern Slavery]. *Zanan* 92 (1381/2002).

______. "Payan-e Sangsar-e Zanan, How?" [The End of Women's Stoning?] *Zanan* 95 (1381/2002).

Saeed-Zadeh, M. "Khun Baha-ye Zanan, Chhera Na-Barabar?" [Why Inequality in Qesas?]. Zanan 37 (91376/1997).

Sanat-Carr F. "Khomeynism." *Nazm-e Novin* [The New Order] 7 (Spring 1364/1985).

Sazeman-e Mojahedin-e Khalq-e Iran. *Women on the way of Liberation* [in Persian] I. Long Beach (1359/1980).

Sciolino, Elaine. "From the Back Seat in Iran, Murmurs of Unrest." *The New York Times* (April 23, 1992).

Shadi-Talab, Jaleh. "Pas az Bisto-Seh Sal Ma'ulan Negarn-e Tanaqoz-e Mian-e Eshteqal-e va Khaneh-dari-ye zanan [After Twenty-Three Years, Authorities Worry about Incompatibility between Women's Work and their Household Labor]. *Zanan* 77 (1380/2001).

Shadi-Talab, Jaleh "Zan dar Tose'eh" [Women in Development]. *Zanan* (1372/2003).

"Shah Enough." *Women's Wear Daily* (February 3, 1978).

Shahreh-Kani, N. "I want to Clarify the Term 'Rajal!'" *Zanan* 34 (1376/1997).

Shojai Zahra as cited in "Iran Panel Backs Divorce Payments." *Special to the New York Times* (December 17, 1992).

"Stalled in Iran." *The New York Review of Books* (June 2004).

Subverting Their Parents' Revolution." *The New York Times Magazine* (April 30, 1995).

Taubman, Philip. "The Courageous Women of Iran." *The New York Times* (December 26, 1997).

Taubman, Philip. "The Profane and Defiant World of the Iranians." *The New York Times Editorial Observer* (November 24, 1997).

Tavakolli, Nayereh. "Ta'sir-e Amuzesh va Eshteqal dar Kahesh-e Asib-ha-ye Ejtema'i dar Mian-e Zanan" [The Impact of Education and Work on Reducing Social Abuse Among Women. *Fasl-e Zanan* 3 (1382/2003).

The Associated Press, "IOC Urged to help Muslim women." Online, October 15, 1996).

The Tale of a Great Determination: A Brief Account of the Revolutionary Life of Martyr Mojah-e Amin [in Persian]. Long Beach (1359/1980).

The *Times of London*. (August 22, 1911 and August 28, 1911).

Thurgood, Liz. "Iranian Police Tighten Screws." *Manchester Guardian Weekly* (January 9, 1977).

UPI. "Iranian Women Rise Up in Revolt." *New York Post* (March 8, 1979).

Women and Struggle in Iran (Spring 1985).

Zanan. Various issues 1992–2007, Tehran.

Zanan. 33 (Tir 1385/July 2006).

"Zanan dar Daneshgah-e Farah Pahlavi Naqsh-e Mohemmi Khahand Dasht" [Women Will Have an Important Role at Farah Pahlavi University]. *Kayhan Hava'ie* (January 5, 1975).

"Zanan Moharezeh Mikonand" [Women in Struggle]. North California: The Committee of the Iranian Women Association (n.d., probably mid-1970s).

Films, Videos, Radio Reports, and Web Sites

Amanpour, Christian. *60 Minutes*. May 10, 1999.

www.Badjens.com. 4 November 21, 2000, and May 13, 2000.

Bahari, Maziar. "Give Women a Chance," News Week in Arabic (August 21, 2001) wysiwyg://79/http:www.msnbc.com/news/605146.asp.

Bani-Etemad, Rakhshan. *Rousari-ye Abi* [The Blue Scarf] A film produced in Tehran, 1995.

______. *Narges*. A film produced in Tehran, 1991.

______, Bashu, *Gharibeh Koucheh*. [Bashu, The Little Stranger]. 1986.

Behdad, Sohrab. "Khatami and His 'Reformist' Economic (Non-)Agenda." *Middle East Report Online* (2001).

Branigin, Walter. "Pahlavi Fortune: A Staggering Sum." *Washington Post* (January 17, 1979).

Dariush, Mehrjooyi's. *Dayereh-e Mina*. Produced in Iran during the 1970s but was banned.

Ebadi, Shirin. *Iranmenia News* (December 11, 2003).

Ebadi, Shirin. "Vaz'e Huqugi-ye Zanan dar Iran" [The Legal Situation of Women in Iran]. *Jame'eh-e Salem* (Mordad 1357/July 1996).

Ebadi's interview with Amy Goodman. *Democracy Now* (June 9, 2004).

Esfandiyari, Golnaz. "Number of Female University Students Rising Dramatically in Iran." http://www.payvand.com/news/03/nov/1133.html.

Gogin Iraj interview with Furuq Farrokhzad. "She'ir-e Emruz" [Today's Poetry]. Tehran (1964).

Haeri, Shahla's. "Mrs. President: Women Political Leadership in Iran." (2001).

Haghighatjoo, Bahari Maziar. *Newsweek* (August 21, 2002).

http://news.bbc.co.uy/2hi/middle_east/2534375.stm (December 12, 2002).

Interview with Pooran Farrokhzad. Conducted and translated by *M.S.* for *Bad Jens*. (11 Mordad 1379/August 1, 2000).

Islamic Revolution: Dimensions of the Movement in Iran (Jamada 1399/April 1979 and Mohrram 1400/December 1979).

Kiarostami, Abbas. *Zir-e Derakht-e Zeytun* [Under the Olive Tree]. A film produced in Tehran, 1993.

Lydens, Jackie. "Report of Presidential Elections" [in Iran]. *National Public Radio*. New York (May 21, 1997).

Moshavi, Shahron. "Behind the Scarves: Iran Second Sex Seethes." *Business Week* (February 23, 1998) and *Zanan* 39 (1376/1998).

Nuir Jim. "Iran 'Brothel Plan' Rejected." *BBC News* (September 1, 2002).

pajoohesh@yahoogroups.com, especially a letter by Zohre Nayeri (May 26, 2004).

Panahi, Jafar. *The Circle*. A film produced in Tehran, 2000.

Slavi, Barbara. "A Lifting of Veils as Iranians Try to Soften Image." *USA Today*. Online. (November 7, 1996).

Walters, Barbara. "Empress Farah Talks of Shah and Women's Rights in Iran." *Christian Science Monitor* (February 8, 1978).

Women and Struggle in Iran 4 (1985). Published in the United States.

United Press International. "Iranian Women Trawl the Job Market." (March 29, 1996) as it appeared in Lexis Nexis (TM) Academic, November 16, 2006.

Index